Human Geography: a Welfare Approach

for Margaret with love

Human Geography

A Welfare Approach

David M. Smith

St. Martin's Press   New York

Contents

Preface

This book offers a restructuring of human geography around the theme of *welfare*. Since the end of the 1960s the condition of mankind has emerged as a major concern of the geographer, with a growing emphasis on economic and social problems, relevance in research, and influence on public policy. Considerations of equity or social justice are supplementing those of efficiency previously adopted in passing judgements on the spatial arrangement of human activity. While the so-called quantitative revolution and the discovery of models has brought more sophistication in research methods, it has tended to produce a mechanistic geography somewhat removed from reality. To respond adequately to the problems of the modern world, human geography must be firmly rooted in human life, calling on the new methods to illuminate human problems rather than being largely moulded to techniques. The theme of human welfare provides an integrating focus for a more "relevant" human geography.

A welfare approach involves judgements among alternative structures or states of society. In geography, the judgements are between alternative *spatial* arrangements. Few people would question the legitimacy of an applied aspect to human geography, yet any attempt to recommend or advocate a particular course of action inevitably involves value judgements that can easily conflict with the ethics of scholarly objectivity and political neutrality still widely held in academic life. Thus the application of human geography in such normative fields as urban and regional planning requires a more-than-usual dose of intellectual discipline. That it also requires sound understanding of the way in which human life is actually organized in space, and the capacity for skilled scientific analysis of problems, should go without saying. This applies no less to the social activist lacking inhibitions about advocacy than to the more detached scholar seeking solutions without involvement. Social activism prompted by deep concern for one's fellow beings is highly laudable, but it is of limited effect without a sound body of positive knowledge. To "change the system" is obviously facilitated by knowledge of how the system works.

The welfare approach to human geography attempts to provide both positive knowledge and guidance in the normative realm of evaluation and policy formulation. This is a formidable task, for the fields of inquiry outside geography from which assistance may be derived extend from certain environmental sciences right through the social or behavioural sciences and into the study of ethics and philosophy. No single scholar can be well enough versed in all these fields to provide a comprehensive and balanced view: keeping up with literature in human geography itself is hard enough today, with the proliferation of textbooks, periodicals and discussion papers. The approach in this book leans most heavily on economics, and on the recent literature concerned with "social indicators" or the monitoring of social progress. This is in part an outcome of my own interests and expertise. It also reflects the belief that the major tasks facing mankind have to do with getting the best we can from limited resources—assuming that there is some kind of solution to the broader problem of people learning to live together in a cooperative spirit of mutual assistance instead of in aggressive competition. Economics deals with resource allocation and with how production and distribution are organized. Social indicators help us to identify the outcomes and to judge what is better or best. The heavy reliance on the work of other social sciences reflects the view that a broad multi-disciplinary perspective is essential in modern human geography.

Breadth of scope and limitation of space means that many important issues raised in this book can be treated only briefly. What is attempted is the construction of a skeletal framework for a welfare-oriented geography, complete enough to indicate general form without being specific on some of the detail. If the approach carries any conviction, others may be led to add the necessary flesh, or some changes in form based on different disciplinary perspectives.

As will be shown later, certain well developed bodies of knowledge in existing sub-fields of human geography fit logically into the framework offered in this book. Some of the flesh exists in advance of the skeleton. Examples include location theory in economic geography and work on human spatial interaction. In these cases integration with the welfare theme is achieved more by reference to the literature than by extensive repetition of existing knowledge. Most space is devoted to exploration of less familiar territory.

Discussion of the new techniques and models introduced into human geography in recent years has been largely omitted. Apart from space considerations, this is justified to some extent by the fact that many of these devices, while of technical interest, have as yet little revealed capacity to shed light on the type of problems raised by the welfare approach. In any event, familiarity with conventional statistical methods and techniques for the analysis of spatial patterns of location and movement should now be assumed in the student of human geography. There is an ample choice of other works covering this material. If the present book is used as a basic text in human geography prior to or parallel with quantitative training, my *Patterns in human geography: an introduction to numerical methods* (David & Charles, 1975; Penguin, 1976) would be an appropriate companion volume, demonstrating the application of a wide range of techniques in social problem situations. Placing emphasis in the present book on the problems instead of the techniques is an overt statement of current professional priority.

If light on numerical techniques, the book may appear to the impatient activist to be rather heavy on theory. There are lengthy and, at times, quite intricate discussions of various aspects of spatial welfare theory, to provide the necessary background for more applied research. Simple graphic models and imaginary cases are used extensively, to assist exposition. Neither these nor the algebraic formulations should cause undue mental discomfort for the undergraduate reader. A knowledge of elementary economic theory will help, but this is not assumed.

Value judgements are involved in the structure and content of any human geography text. It therefore seems wise at the outset to make explicit those of particular importance in guiding the present volume. The first is that the development of *useful knowledge* is a superior academic ethic to the development of knowledge for its own sake. What kind of knowledge is useful, and for whom, is itself a contentious matter, as we shall discover in some subsequent discussions. This leads to the second value judgement underpinning the book—that the focal point of human geography should be *the quality of human life*. How quality of life is defined is, of course, subject to many further value judgements, as will be explained in the exposition of the welfare approach. It is sufficient here to say that it concerns efficiency in the use of resources and equity or fairness in distribution of the benefits and penalties of life. Useful knowledge promotes the creation of a just world society in which the satisfaction of human needs has first priority.

Value judgements are also implicit in the particular approach adopted, based as it is on the belief that certain forms of intellectual activity are likely to be effective means of enhancing human life. To contemplate the application of scientific measurement and analysis to something as abstract and personal as the quality of life is itself a product of a particular intellectual climate, influenced by Western logic, positivist scientific philosophy, and belief in rational problem-solving. To advocate a particular academic approach is to some extent an act of faith. Experience alone is the final arbiter between the more or less effective bodies of knowledge.

The approach adopted here attempts to suggest ways in which the geographer may address the question of what *should be*, along with the traditional concern with what *is*. It is the neglect of the normative issues and associated value judgements that marks the weakness of existing textbooks in human geography. Their vain striving for objectivity and political neutrality distracts attention from the basic problem of equity in distribution. Spatial inequality of human life chances is a focus of this book, but its purpose is to trace the origins of inequality rather than to condemn injustice. The analysis will inevitably reveal certain fundamental weaknesses of the contemporary capitalist-competitive-materialistic society, but the temptation to offer a more radical critique of existing structures has been resisted, in favour of an approach that builds on the discipline's established intellectual tradition. At the risk of appearing ambivalent, the exposition deliberately juxtaposes alternative perspectives on both theoretical and practical problems, so that what makes most sense of reality can emerge in a comparative framework. Again at the risk of ambivalence, an attempt has been made to provide the basis for an applied geography relevant both to liberal intervention and radical structural reform, for to concentrate on the latter overlooks the fact that most social change is incremental rather than revolutionary.

After an introductory chapter outlining the welfare approach, the book is divided into four parts. Part One offers a theoretical foundation, necessary before empirical problems can be properly formulated and explanations or solutions sought. Part Two provides a bridge from theory to reality, covering the problems of evaluation of spatial distributions and the application of a welfare approach to the planning of change. Part Three presents selected case studies designed to demonstrate the practical use of the knowledge of Parts One and Two to real-world situations. Part Four offers brief thoughts on desirable forms of human spatial and societal reorganization, followed by some conclusions on the nature of inquiry in human geography.

Copyright Acknowledgements

The author and publishers gratefully acknowledge permission to reproduce or modify material from copyright works from:

Antipode and R. Morrill for Fig. 7.11;[1] the Association of American Geographers and S. Bederman for Fig. 11.5; P. S. Hattingh for Fig. 9.1; Manchester University Press for Figs. 11.14 and 11.15; Mouton et Cie, The Hague, and Jan Drewnowski for Fig. 7.13; Oxford University Press, Nairobi, R. Jolly and M. King for Figs. 11.6 and 11.7; The Pergamon Press for Fig. 9.3; *Professional Geographer* and G. Shannon for Fig. 11.8; Regional Science Research Institute, Philadelphia, J. B. Schneider and J. G. Symon for Figs. 7.8 and 7.10; *Southeastern Geographer* and S. Bederman for Figs. 10.8 and 10.9; Witwatersrand University Press for Fig. 9.4. Acknowledgement is also due to William Heinemann Ltd, Laurence Pollinger Ltd, the Viking Press Inc., and the Estate of Mrs Frieda Lawrence, for permission to quote from the writings of D. H. Lawrence.

[1] Numbers refer to figures in this book.

Author's Acknowledgements

This book began life in 1973, as Occasional Paper No. 11 in the *Environmental Studies* series of the Department of Geography and Environmental Studies, University of the Witwatersrand—written during the tenure of a visiting lectureship. I am grateful to the University for the opportunity to explore what I then saw as a new systematic specialization in geography, now offered as an alternative approach to human geography as a whole. Readers familiar with the original monograph will find in the present work an almost complete rewriting and expansion, with some major shifts of emphasis in the theoretical perspectives.

Grateful acknowledgement for various kind of assistance is due to the following: Ronald Beazley (Southern Illinois University), for initial guidance on reading in welfare economics and for a critical review of the theoretical sections of the original monograph; Sanford Bederman (Georgia State University), for providing data on Atlanta; Denis Fair (University of the Witwatersrand) and Bruce Young (Wilfred Laurier University), for helping to clarify some of the content of Chapter 9; Michael Chisholm (Cambridge University), for a most constructive review of the draft manuscript; Roger Lee (Queen Mary College, University of London), for a helpful critique of the theoretical chapters; Eric Rawstron (Queen Mary College), for many years of encouragement and for protecting me from some of the less fruitful distractions of university life while this book was written; Linda Agombar, for producing an immaculate typescript to a demanding schedule; Fiona Rees, for help with references and proofs.

As always, the deepest debt is to my family, without whose support (and endurance) no book could be completed. Michael helped with some calculations. Tracey behaved herself, most of the time. To thank Margaret adequately leaves me unusually lost for words, except those of my dedication.

David M. Smith
Loughton, Essex
March 1976

I

Introduction: Geography and Human Welfare

There was a time when meadow, grove, and stream,
The earth, and every common sight,
    To me did seem
    Apparelled in celestial light,
The glory and the freshness of a dream.
It is not now as it hath been of yore;—
    Turn whereso'er I may,
    By night or day,
The things which I have seen I now can see no more.

William Wordsworth, *Intimations of Immortality from Recollections of Early Childhood*, 1807

There was a time when geographers accepted the world very much as they found it. While not necessarily seeing the divine hand behind the spatial arrangement of man's works, they were at least tempted to think in terms of Adam Smith's "invisible hand" of the market, guiding human affairs towards some universally beneficial outcome. But the hands laid on the landscapes which inspired Wordsworth are those of a species whose actions show clearly that the pursuit of individual self-interest is not destined to produce the best of all worlds. As likely as not, the meadow is now built-on or smothered in DDT, the grove cut down and the stream flowing with effluents, while to see many of the common sights of the contemporary city in a favourable light requires more than the imagination of a poet. The state of the modern world is a matter of extreme concern—particularly to the geographer who understands something both of human frailty and of the delicacy of man's earthly environment. Increasingly, human geographers and other social scientists are reluctant to leave the fate of mankind to politicians and planners, far less to hidden hands. They now seek a much more active role in the promotion of human welfare.

1.1 Revolution in human geography

The problem of defining human geography is sometimes resolved by recourse to the axiom that geography is what geographers do. As a recognition that human geography has few really distinctive academic features, to define the subject by the type of investigation conducted has much to commend it. While such expressions as "the study of spatial organization", "areal differentiation", "location analysis" and "spatial behaviour" may help to capture the general concerns of scholars who call themselves (human) geographers, these are not the sole preserve of a single discipline. With the emergence of regional science in the 1960s and the growing spatial awareness of economists and other social scientists interested in urban and regional analysis, there is now very little that the human geographer can claim as his or her exclusive domain.

So why have a field of inquiry called human geography? Why help to perpetuate part of a rather arbitrary and often unhelpful disintegration of the study of human existence? The only convincing argument is that the geographer still has some distinctive point of view. We may have lost our monopoly on spatial wisdom, or the capacity to understand how human life is organized on the surface of the earth, but we remain the only scholars who put space and location first. Geography still has a capacity to offer a broad, synoptic view of spatial relationships in human affairs, transcending the conventional subdivision of phenomena into "economic", "social", "political", and so on. The only other discipline that could make this claim with any legitimacy is regional science, as represented in the ambitious general theory of Isard *et al.* (1969). But even here human geography has something to differentiate it. While regional science is strongly characterized by the abstract theoretical approach of the economist, human geography is traditionally an empirical subject deeply rooted in the reality of experience.

The empirical spatial perspective may be the geographer's major theme, but human geography as what human geographers actually do is subject to perpetual variation. The past two decades have seen some particularly important changes, in subject matter, methodology and philosophy (Chisholm, 1975). Such has been their impact that they are commonly described as revolutions.

Until the middle of the 1950s human geography was more art than science. Facts were often established by casual observation in the field rather than by careful measurement; causal relationships came from intuitive judgement rather than from formal hypothesis testing; and the grand regional synthesis towards which the geographer worked was more of a literary masterpiece on a specific territory than something from which generalizations might emerge. The only theory to which observed location patterns could be referred was environmental determinism and its later variants such as "possibilism", relics of which still remain in some regional geography textbooks. Applied human geography was confined to vague connections with town planning, conservation and resource inventory.

All human geography of this era was not worthless, of course. The very flimsy establishment of cause and effect, particularly when guided by determinism, certainly produced some erroneous findings. But many of the human geographers of the first half of this century combined acute skills in fieldwork with a feel for the reality of man–land relationships which perhaps enabled them to get closer to real life than most practitioners of today's more sophisticated approaches. The old regional mono-graphs may well be "the tombstones of European geography" (Gould, 1973, 257), but at least they make a more decorative cemetery than some of today's computer-generated research. Nevertheless, human geography in the middle of the 1950s remained largely oblivious of the scientific methods in common use in other fields such as economics and sociology.

Then came the "quantitative revolution". The efforts of a few pioneers who began experimenting with statistics in geography (e.g. McCarty *et al.*, 1956) soon built up into a popular new approach to measurement and the establishment of empirical associations. This was assisted by the growing ease of access to computers, which enabled geographers to pro-cess much larger volumes of numerical data. The first book on statistical methods for geographers appeared (Gregory, 1963), to be followed by others (Cole and King, 1968; Yeates, 1968; King, 1969), by the first readers in quantitative geography (Garrison and Marble, 1967; Berry and Marble, 1968), and then by further texts at different levels (Tidswell and Barker, 1971; Theakstone and Harrison, 1970; Hammond and McCullagh, 1974; Yeates, 1974; Smith, 1975c). Within a decade the quantitative revolution had substantially changed the conduct of inquiry in human geography.

But to describe the "new" geography of the 1960s simply as quantita-tive or statistical is an oversimplification. Closely associated with the geo-grapher's emerging numeracy was the discovery of models (Chorley and Haggett, 1967a). Model building is itself related to the development of spatial theory, for mathematical models are generally specific or opera-tional versions of some theoretical structure. The contemporary geo-graphical interest in theory dates from roughly the same time as the be-ginning of the quantitative revolution. Three influential works in spatial economic theory appeared (Lösch, 1954; Greenhut, 1956; Isard, 1956), a seminal text in regional science soon followed (Isard, 1960) and, together with the classic work of Christaller (1933) on central places, these provided a foundation for a new theoretical approach to economic geo-graphy. Growing interest in the conduct of inquiry and the philosophy of science culminated in Harvey's *Explanation in Geography* (1969), which raised the "nature and purpose" debate previously focused on the work of Hartshorne (1939; 1959) to new intellectual heights.

The human geography of the 1960s was thus characterized as much by its growing maturity and diversity as by the label "quantitative". The mainstream of quantitative analysis proceeded to a substantial extent in-dependent of the theoretical thrust, the main inspiration for which was spatial economics rather than statistics or mathematics. The development and testing of models provided some connection, but much quantitative analysis was pure empiricism with little guidance from or contribution to theory. Only in the study of settlements as "central places" did loca-tion theory and statistical methods blend closely together.

Much of the energy of the quantitative revolution was expended on the development of research techniques. But by the middle of the 1960s the preoccupation with statistics, models and theories was beginning to generate a new integrated approach to the substantive content of the subject. The first book-length attempts to pull quantitative methods and theory together in geography were by Bunge (1962) and Haggett (1965), who led the subject further towards the numerical analysis of location patterns in the context of human spatial organization. Subsequent general textbooks developing this theme include those by Morrill (1970), Adams, Abler and Gould (1971) and Cox (1972), while Haggett (1972) and Kolars and Nystuen (1974) have attempted even broader views incorporating the physical environment. These general approaches built on work of the quantitative—model building—theoretical type in systematic subfields such as transportation, population geography, industrial location and urban geography, where modern textbooks began to appear at the beginning of the 1970s.

During the quantitative revolution the focus of attention in human geography was on methods rather than subject matter. Topics which received particular attention, such as diffusion of innovation, social ecology of cities and multivariate regionalization, owed their popularity as much to the availability of convenient techniques or computer programs as to the intrinsic interest of the subjects themselves. Applied human geography in regional planning and urban development was often merely an opportunity for the application of some favoured technique, which may have been quite ill-suited to the problem at hand. The *avant-garde* of the quantitative movement was not generally among the most conspicuous participants in the resurgence of interest in public policy issues during the latter part of the 1960s.

Human geography's second revolution has been characterized alternatively as "radical" (Smith, 1971b) or concerned with "social relevance" (Prince, 1971). The quantitative revolution had never been accepted by a substantial old guard on both sides of the Atlantic, but at the end of the 1960s the younger generation of American geographers also began to express disquiet. Concern at the impersonal, mechanical approaches of the new geography was, in fact, part of a more general feeling that the discipline was failing to respond to major contemporary social issues. Particular targets were pollution, poverty, hunger, racial discrimination, social inequality or injustice, and the exploitation of colonial territories by the governments and businesses of capitalist nations.

Although the radical/relevance revolution, as a major shift in professional direction, occurred at the end of the 1960s, research on social issues had been building up steadily throughout the decade. Problems of regional economic distress attracted much attention in Western Europe and North America, and some of the new techniques of multivariate areal classification found outlets in the measurement of "economic health" following the work of Thompson *et al.* (1962). The study of physical health, in the form of medical geography, was developing strength (Stamp, 1964; Howe, 1972; McGlashen, 1972). And basic research on economic development continued to occupy geographers working in underdeveloped areas of Africa, Asia and Latin America (Dickinson and Clark, 1972). Other attempts to broaden the scope of the human geographer's concerns included the suggestion that a level-of-living index might be used in regional delimitation (Lewis, 1968) and the efforts of Gould (1969) to relate space preference to a "welfare indicator".

From the beginning of the 1970s the literature on social problems and what may loosely be termed welfare issues expanded rapidly. Poverty formed the subject matter of two issues of *Antipode*, a new radical journal (Peet, 1970; 1972), and of the first book in a "problems" series in geography (Morrill and Wohlenberg, 1971). Texts on the black ghetto (Rose, 1971), the geography of crime (Harries, 1974) and health care (Shannon and Dever, 1974) followed. The first collection of papers on the geography of social problems was published (Albaum, 1972). Calls for a "geography of social well-being" have been made (Smith, 1972a; 1973a; Knox, 1975). Chisholm (1971a) has suggested welfare economics as a possible alternative to conventional microeconomics as a point of departure for location theory, and the possibility of welfare as a focal point in human geography has already been tentatively explored (Smith, 1973c; 1974d). And Harvey (1972a; 1973) has drawn attention to the question of social justice in a spatial context.

That this growing interest in welfare matters should have taken place when it did was no accident. Like other scholars, human geographers are creatures of their times, reacting to the intellectual, social and political climate in which they live. Just as in the United States the era of the quantitative revolution was one of societal preoccupation with technological gymnastics (as exemplified by space exploration) and with a rational managerial approach to human affairs, so the late 1960s which spawned the relevance movement was one of radicalism among the young (and some not-so-young) prompted by the disillusionment with the war in Viet Nam and with the apparent insensitivity of government to various manifestations of social injustice. Radical geography is the geography of the years of the "pollution crises" and of "crisis in the cities". It is also the geography of the end of the post-war era of continuous growth in the real standard of living, in which distributional issues are taking on a new urgency.

The relevance movement, like the quantitative revolution, has taken a number of different forms. The question of just what it means to be "relevant" has been debated at length, for example in a series of papers in *Area* (Chisholm, 1971b; Eyles, 1971; Berry, 1972; Dickinson and Clark, 1972; Blowers, 1972, 1974; Smith, 1973b). The inevitable division between liberals and radicals has occurred, the former working for incremental change within "the system" while the latter hold that nothing short of revolutionary socialism can create a just society out of the inhumanity of the modern capitalist-corporate state. Some of the former have attained influential positions in policy-making, consultancy and officially sponsored research. The latter, inspired mainly by Marx, attempt to restructure geography to the needs of a new kind of society.

For human geography to be relevant to the needs of a society, whatever its form, it must focus directly on the type of problem faced by people in their everyday lives. The quantitative revolution and its aftermath gave something of the intellectual rigour essential for the tough analysis required in any public policy context. The relevance revolution directed attention back to real human problems. To bring together the diverse threads of two decades of development in human geography as a social science truly relevant to this day and age needs an integrating theme. The concept of welfare provides such a theme.

1.2 The welfare theme

Welfare economics is the only field of inquiry in which welfare matters have received rigorous attention. For an opening definition of our welfare theme, "geography" or "geographical" may be substitutes in definitions of welfare economics. Following Henderson and Quandt (1958, 201):

> The objective of welfare *geography* is the evaluation of the social desirability of alternative *geographical* states.

Following Mishan (1964, 5–6):

> Theoretical welfare *geography* is, then, that branch of study which endeavours to formulate propositions by which we may rank, on the scale of better or worse, alternative *geographical* situations open to society.

Following Nath (1973, 11):

> Welfare *geography* is that part of *geography* where we study the possible effects of various *geographical* policies on the welfare of society.

These statements might suggest a new systematic branch of human geography dealing with "welfare", just as economic geography deals with economic phenomena, social geography with social phenomena, and so on. However, the position to be developed here is that welfare issues pervade the whole of human geography and that the welfare theme thus defines a new human geography.

A geographical "state" or "situation", in the sense used above, may refer to any aspect of the spatial arrangement of human existence. It may relate to the spatial allocation of resources, income, or any other source of human well-being. It may concern the spatial incidence of poverty or any other social problem. These expressions may also be used to describe industrial location patterns, the distribution of population, the location of social service facilities, transportation networks, patterns of movement of people or goods, and indeed any spatial arrangement which has a bearing on the quality of life as a geographically variable condition. And beneath them all, of course, is the type of society—the economic, social and political structures that generate the patterns.

But if any and all geographical patterns are subject to a welfare interpretation, confusion may arise. This is because some patterns will be far more important than others in spatially differentiating human life chances. For the welfare theme to focus human geography on what really matters to man, a specific recognition of the *primary* concern of the subject is required. The cue comes from two quite well-known definitions of other social sciences. Lasswell (1958) has defined political science as the study of "who gets what when, how". Samuelson (1973) sees economics as concerned with "what, how, and for whom". Human geography may be defined as the study of "who gets what *where*, and how" (Smith, 1974d). This is what the welfare theme means in a spatial context.

Defining human geography as *the study of who gets what where, and how*, provides a frame of reference for the restructuring of the field in a manner which facilitates the analysis of all human geographical patterns in terms relevant to human life chances.

Defining human geography as the study of who gets what where, and how, focuses immediate attention on fundamental questions of subject matter. Each of the words "who", "what", "where" and "how" poses its own set of problems. Asking "who?" requires us to consider relevant ways in which the population of whatever territory is under investigation may be aggregated, on the basis of such common characteristics as social class, economic status, race and so on (assuming that studying the life experience of every individual is impracticable). Asking "what?" raised the question of what it is that gives human beings satisfaction, happiness, or a high (or low) life quality—including the "bads" as well as the "goods". Asking "where?" raises the basic geographical question of the most sensible subdivision of territory for the purpose of investigation— a particularly important problem in welfare research, for a distribution (e.g. of income) which is highly unequal at one level of areal aggregation may appear equal at another. Asking "how?" requires the identification and understanding of the structure, process or causal mechanisms at work within a society, leading to a particular pattern of who gets what where.

The questions of who, what and where define the dimensions of a specific version of the geographical data matrix or information table popularized in recent years (Berry, 1964; Chorley and Haggett, 1967b; Yeates, 1974). In this three-dimensional box-like structure (Figure 1.1) each small square or cell potentially contains a fact or observation in numerical form (e.g. X_{ij}). The horizontal axis identifies the various attributes $(1, 2, \ldots, i, \ldots, m)$ from which human beings derive their satisfaction or dissatisfaction. The vertical axis identifies the areal subdivision (e.g. nations, regions, neighbourhoods) or locations $(1, 2, \ldots, j, \ldots, n)$ for which observations are required. The third axis permits the disaggregation of the population into relevant groups $(1, 2, \ldots, k)$. Each axis involves an important problem of classification. Putting sensible and accurate numbers in the matrix is the problem of measurement. The form of this spatial welfare data matrix in any specific investigation arises from the research objective and the broader context in which it rests.

Some clarification of the meaning of the term welfare is required at this point, for differences in current usage are confusing (Smith, 1975a). The word welfare is sometimes applied to a form of social security payments, and "social welfare" to a set of social policy measures; neither of these uses are adopted in this book. A distinction is sometimes made between *economic* welfare and *general* or social welfare, the former usually referring to what people get from the consumption of goods and services purchased by money or available as a public provision, while the latter

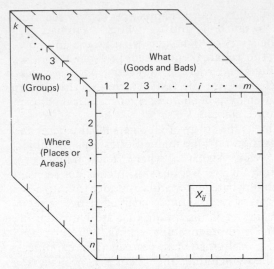

Figure 1.1 The geographical welfare data matrix.

embraces all things contributing to the quality of human existence; the broader sense is the one adopted in this book. Our spatial concept of welfare incorporates everything differentiating one state of society from another. It includes all things from which human satisfaction (positive or negative) is derived, and also the way in which they are distributed within society. Welfare is not thought of as a directly observable condition, like the weather, but we can judge whether it has increased or decreased with a change in society, from time to time or place to place, if appropriate assumptions are made and rules followed.

Using the term welfare in a geographical context raises special difficulties. It is occasionally employed to refer to the local or territorial level of something which has to do with the standard of living, i.e., "welfare" as a spatially variable condition. However, the *geographical* distribution of things from which people derive satisfaction, like the interpersonal distribution, is itself a part of welfare—the state of society at large. So when the interest is specifically in the distribution of some aggregate of goods in the broadest sense, an alternative term such as gross product or real income is preferred to welfare. At various points in this book expressions such as "well-being", "level of living" and even "quality of life" are used to describe the state of the population as it varies among a set of territories. Exactly what this phenomenon is called is not particularly important, for, like higher abstractions such as fulfilment or happiness, it derives its meaning from the conditions contributing to that state as people view it, not from the name itself. It is important that "welfare" should not be used in this context however, for welfare concerns not only the *what* but also *who* gets it *where*.

1.3 The scope of human geography as spatial welfare analysis

The welfare theme helps to clarify four basic tasks which have defined the scope of human geography for some time. These are descriptions, explanation, evaluation and prescription. To these might be added a fifth—implementation.

Description involves, first and foremost, the empirical identification of territorial levels of human well-being, or whatever we care to term the human condition. This is a major and immediate research task, on which surprisingly little work has yet been done. In Britain, for example, the mapping of regional income levels is a recent innovation, and spatial variations in many other conditions contributing to human well-being had received little attention until the work of Coates and Rawstron (1971). The economic, demographic and social patterns with which geographers are traditionally more familiar properly belong to a second level of significance—objects of legitimate curiosity but relevant to the welfare theme only in so far as they help to differentiate human life chances geographically. To date, most of the descriptive research on spatial variations in human well-being has been undertaken in the United States (e.g. Smith, 1973a). But a start has now been made elsewhere, for example the work of Knox (1974a; 1975) in Britain.

Explanation covers the *how* of our earlier definition. It involves identifying the cause-and-effect links among the various activities undertaken in society, as they contribute to determining who gets what where. This is where the analysis of the kind of economic, demographic and social patterns mentioned above logically fits into the welfare structure. For example, the location of an industry might be regarded as an independent variable (cause) in an explanatory model, with areal variations in human well-being, suitably defined, as the dependent variable (effect). The spatial patterns of private productive capacity, public service facilities, expenditure on social programmes, movement of people to work, can all be viewed in the same way. We need to know far more about the origin of these individual patterns if we are really to understand how they contribute to human well-being as a spatially variable condition. As has been the case in human geography for some time, explanation takes us well beyond spatial patterns and into the other social sciences. It should take us right to the core of a society.

Evaluation involves making judgements on the desirability of alternative geographical states, and the societal structures from which they arise. To say that one spatial pattern of human well-being is preferable to another is to say that a higher level of welfare is attached to it. Such judgements must be made with reference to equity, as well as to the efficiency criteria with which the geographer is more familiar. With suitable rules, any spatial pattern of production or distribution can be judged against criteria relating to social justice, or whether the residents of the territories in question get their just deserts in the light of prevailing (or alternative) societal values. Geographical patterns of all kinds can be judged with respect to their contribution to human well-being, with the objective function of welfare maximization substituted for the more conventional but less satisfactory optimizing criteria of profit maximization, cost minimization, or economy in the coverage of distance. The difficulty of making such judgements, if not immediately apparent, will be revealed during the course of this book. But however daunting, judgements among alternatives must be made, and with extreme skill, if the general welfare is to be improved. As one writer on social policy succinctly puts it, "to do better, we must have a way of distinguishing better from worse" (Rivlin, 1971, 144).

Prescription requires the specification of alternative geographical states, and alternative societal structures designed to produce them. This is the process of planning the spatial organization of human activity, i.e. spatial *reorganization*. Prescription involves answering the ethical question of who *should* get what where.

Implementation is the final process of replacing a state deemed undesirable by something superior. It concerns the question of *how*, once it has been decided who should get what where. Just what role should be adopted by the geographer *qua* geographer in changing the world is a matter of some contention, which will be considered towards the end of this book. All that need be said here is that practically everything a scholar does has some potential impact on society and its individual members; the line between analysis and advocacy is often arbitrary. Even to do nothing may not be neutral, if supportive of the *status quo*.

The scope of human geography, as outlined here, may be summarized in a simple diagram (Figure 1.2). The territorial levels of well-being can be thought of as represented by a set of magnitudes of some indicator S^o_j (observed well-being); $j = 1, 2, \ldots, n$. These arise as outputs of some set of operations, converting certain resources or inputs into things which enhance human well-being. The space economy and other relevant spheres of human activity such as the provision of education and health care belong in the Operation box. Understanding how this system works is the explanatory stage of inquiry. Ideally, there is a specification of who should get what where—a desired state represented by the indicator S^*_j, and the observed state can be evaluated with reference to this. The attainment of the objectives implied by S^*_j is achieved by a control mechanism which seeks to improve operational efficiency and distributional equity, and by feedbacks from evaluation to alter the inputs or change the way in which the system works. This is the implementation stage. The evaluation of the spatial distribution represented by S^* as superior to S^o implies that the level of welfare attached to the former (W^*) is higher than that of the latter (W^o).

The development of *territorial social indicators* occupies an important place in this welfare view of geography, particularly at the descriptive stage. Of the numerous discussions of different types of indicators (see Smith, 1973a, ch. 6), that by Culyer, Lavers and Williams (1972) is as helpful as any in the present context. They propose three kinds of indicators, relating respectively to outputs, needs, and possibilities for increas-

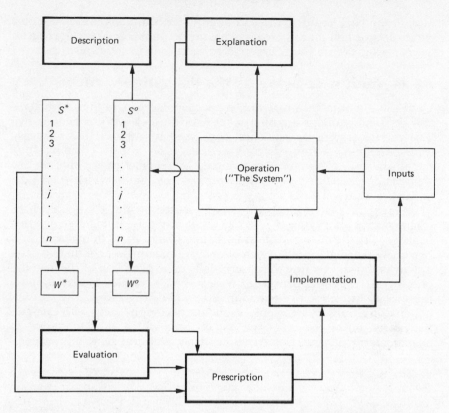

Figure 1.2 The scope of applied human geography based on the welfare theme.

ing outputs to meet needs. In a geographical context the output measures (S^o) establish the actual territorial level of well-being, or levels if more than one indicator is required (e.g. the columns in Figure 1.1). The measures of need identify the local differences between S^o and S^*, a prior condition of which is, of course, the setting of the desired or target levels. The third measure relates to the effectiveness of alternative ways of meeting need, and can take the form of social production functions or cost-benefit ratios, which may vary with locality. Such indicators provide the building blocks from which spatial social policy can be constructed so as more effectively to satisfy human needs.

By no means everyone would relish existence in such a carefully managed society. In any event, this view is nearer an idealist's dream than a statement of attainable research objectives. Human well-being, whatever it may be, is presently incapable of measurement in a generally accepted way, and probably always will be. The system generating it can never be specified exactly, or even approximately in the near future; in any event it is in a constant state of change. And public intervention is seldom if ever as rational as the above discussion might imply, if only because of conflict over priorities. However, it does no harm to keep an ideal in the back of our minds, as a reminder of the inadequacy of our efforts and of how much progress has to be made, or as a warning of where "progress" in the policy-related social sciences logically leads.

1.4 Human well-being as the disciplinary focus

Until the quantitative revolution made regional geography unfashionable, regional synthesis was often taken to be the focal point of geography. The various systematic branches, supported by their related sciences, were sometimes portrayed diagrammatically as feeding their findings into the central core of the subject, occupied by regional geography. In the welfare approach this view may be replaced by one in which the study of human well-being becomes the core.

In Figure 1.3 the focal point is represented by the who-gets-what-where matrix of Figure 1.1, p. 8. This is where human geography begins—with the distribution and consumption of those things on which human well-being depends. Each of the various sub-fields of human geography is shown as aiding the description and explanation of the content of this matrix. Each is concerned with specific variables contributing to the spatial distribution of the sources of well-being among the various population groups. For example, economic geography deals with the spatial expression of the economic mechanisms which allocate resources among alternative ends in alternative places. Political geography is con-

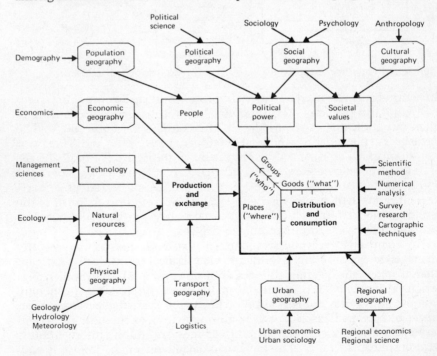

Figure 1.3 Geography and related disciplines, focused on the study of human welfare.

cerned with power in space, as different groups occupying different areas exercise differential claims on what is produced. Social and cultural geography help to interpret the value basis of how preferred group life-styles vary geographically, and with them the criteria of human well-being or the good life. And so on. Further out are the systematic sciences supporting human geography's sub-fields, by providing most of the theory and concepts which we apply in the space dimension. In addition to the various social sciences, the diagram shows what may be termed the management sciences, contributing operational research methods, theories of administration, logistics and so on, to the analyses of more technical aspects of spatial organization. Physical geography finds a place through its capacity to help us understand the role of physical resources and environmental constraints. By no means all possible inter-disciplinary connections are shown in Figure 1.3, which is merely representative of what the welfare focus means. Also omitted are flows from geographical knowledge into other fields.

Urban and regional geography appear in the bottom right-hand corner of the diagram. Far from eclipsing regional geography, the welfare theme reveals it in a new light. Now, regional geography becomes the analysis of who gets what where in a specific territorial context. Its traditional role of synthesis is revived, with the basic subject matter or criteria of areal differentiation defined by reference to the welfare data matrix. Regional geography is thus very much alive, though most existing texts written under this rubric are not, and will have only slight relevance to the welfare approach.

Urban geography is, in a sense, regional geography at the urban scale. The welfare data matrix defines those criteria of city classification or internal differentiation which are most relevant to the human condition. Just as regional geography now receives the support of the theory and methods of regional science, so urban geography benefits from urban economics, urban sociology and other branches of knowledge which have emerged in recent years to facilitate the study of cities and the formation of urban planning policy.

As well as contributing to the sub-fields of human geography, each of the disciplines identified in Figure 1.3 will have its own perspective on the central problem of the quality of human life, brought to bear in human geography via its sub-fields. There is the environmental perspective, rooted in the physical and biological sciences, and concerned with the balance and harmony between man and nature as expressed in the pollution problem, for example. The economic perspective covers efficiency in resource allocation and also equity in distribution. Demography concerns the number and characteristics of people, and is likely to stress the problem of population growth and pressure on scarce resources. Political science emphasizes conflict, government institutional arrangements and the exercise of power. The sociological perspective provides guidance on human groupings (e.g. class, ethnicity and race) and on societal values. Psychology addresses fundamental human needs and the individual behavioural response, while the cultural perspective provided by anthropology sheds light on alternative ways of living in different places. An historical approach is implicit in each of these views. As well as the varied perspectives different modes of inquiry will be represented, from the economist's predilection for abstract theory and mathematical models, to the psychologist's emphasis on the direct monitoring of human experience through survey research, and the participatory observation favoured by some anthropologists.

With the combined wisdom of these diverse disciplinary perspectives, not to mention the deliberations of philosophers, it is pertinent to ask what special contribution can be expected from the geographer. This brings our discussion full circle, back to the question of a disciplinary definition at the start of this chapter. To claim to be the great synthesizer, in the sense of pulling together the knowledge of other disciplines, was a favoured position in geography not long ago. There was a hint of this in the argument made at the outset that geography has a capacity to offer a broad synoptic view transcending disciplinary subdivisions of phenomena. But geographers are now more circumspect in making claims to the level of understanding that this role would require. It is on the spatial perspective that the geographer must make the case for a place in the "welfare sciences". The basic contribution of the geographer lies in the recognition that location in space is very much relevant to the individual's life chances; different peoples occupy different territories, and different territories attract or repel different sources of human well-being or ill-being. It is in giving substance to this observation and its welfare implications that geography has a distinctive contribution to make.

1.5 Positive and normative approaches

The scope of human geography structured around the welfare theme includes both normative and positive elements. The difference between the two is important; a writer on the economics of social policy has summarized it as follows (Culyer, 1973, 3):

> In the first [normative], value-judgements about what in general ought to be done in society are made and inferences are drawn from these basic ethical assumptions for specific, recommended, courses of action. The second [positive] is value-free in the assumptions of the analysis and positive economics is intended to be entirely predictive of observable social events. Positive economics, however, requires value-judgements concerning the method to be adopted. For example, a value-judgement about what constitutes a refutation of someone's theory, or a value-judgement about what is a "good" theory. These value-judgements belong, however, to a different level of discourse from those required in recommending public policy. Indeed, positive economics cannot recommend any policy. It can only point out the observable consequences of this or that policy.

This distinction has become somewhat blurred in geography's relevance revolution, as well as in economics. On the positive side, a particular body of theory may not be quite so ideologically neutral as the quotation above might imply. Much supposed positive theory in economics reflects a particular view of life, stressing for example the competitive individualism and private ownership of resources on which capitalism depends. Geographers are becoming sensitive to the possibility of adopting unsuspected value judgements (Buttimer, 1974), and those who care to look for them will doubtless find some ideological predispositions in this volume. The reliance placed on neo-classical economics as a point of departure for spatial welfare theory makes this almost inevitable, though some care has been taken in deciding what to accept and develop from this body of knowledge. Whether the result is "good" theory must be judged by where it leads—by the light it sheds on the reality of life and by whatever improvements may come to pass as a result. Some readers will doubtless find "counter-revolutionary" or "status-quo" tendencies (Harvey, 1972b). Others may more easily appreciate the implications of particular applications of conventional theory, for example in the spatial allocation of resources so as to implement specific (e.g. egalitarian) distributional objectives.

Economists have for a long time held that there is no obligation to do anything other than positive work. This conforms to a quite widespread value judgement in favour of ethical or political neutrality in academic life. The line sometimes drawn between the positive or "scientific" problem of *economic* welfare and the normative problem of *social* welfare is relevant here: "The former is concerned with the *quantity* of satisfactions and the efficiency with which the provisionally given wants are satisfied; the latter is concerned with the *quality* of wants and with the question of how far the individual succeeds in living the good life. We need not pass from the former to the latter unless we wish to do so" (Myint, 1948, 215). We decidedly wish to do so, and substantial sections of this book are concerned with the normative problem of the quality of human life as a spatially variable condition.

Returning to the five sequential tasks defining the scope of human geography in section 1.3, description and explanation are usually considered positive activities in the sense explained in the first quotation above. The transition to clearly normative work comes with evaluation, for *any* attempt to pronounce alternative spatial arrangements of things as "better" or "worse" involves value judgements. Prescription is also a normative activity, for it requires the recommendation of a particular state or course of action. Any statement of what *should* be is a value position, the validity of which depends on moral or ethical postulates and not on empirical verification.

It is in questions of distribution that the problems of normative analysis become particularly difficult. And as human geography is very much concerned with distribution in space, i.e. among groups of people identified by area of residence, it is hard to imagine an entirely positive human geography. Even if it is strictly descriptive and explanatory, its choice of phenomena to examine is already a value judgement, because some criteria of significance or relevance must be used in the process of selection. In evaluation and prescription, it is easy to overlook the fact that advocating such policies as urban renewal or the improvement of transportation systems involves important distributive judgements, for some people in some localities will gain or lose more than others as a consequence. Who *should* get what where is a normative question, subject to positive analysis only when the ethical assumptions have been made clear—and these may be governed by the type of society in which we live.

The normative nature of so much of the welfare approach to human geography does not provide licence for unrestrained value judgements, however. The more values impinge on scholastic activity, the more discipline is needed. A major task is thus to develop intellectual structures to guide the evaluation of alternative spatial arrangements of human affairs in such a way that the arbitrary value content of any policy recommendations is minimized, or that what is proposed follows logically from stated goals. The purpose is to ensure that judgements among alternative geographical states are made on the basis of reasoned analysis. While it would be most unwise to dismiss an intuitive feel for the needs of one's fellow beings as a basis for action to improve the lot of mankind, good intentions alone are not enough. The job of the human geographer, like any other scientist, is to provide means whereby the full power of human intellect may be applied to the solution of problems.

1.6 Welfare problems in human geography

The best way to explain the welfare approach more specifically is to indicate the kind of real-world problems that it is designed to tackle. This section briefly considers some welfare issues at different spatial scales, the purpose at this stage being simply to introduce the problems. In order to analyse them and possibly come up with some solutions, we require a body of theory and devices suitable for evaluation and planning. Developing this is the task of Parts One and Two. Part Three will show how this knowledge can be applied to the type of situation outlined here.

By almost universal consent, one of the major problems facing the modern world is the difference among national levels of development. We have become accustomed to seeing the world divided into nations labelled "developed" and "underdeveloped" or "less developed", with perhaps an intermediate level between them. The European nations, the USSR and the United States dominate the "highly developed" group. The "intermediate" group includes the poorer parts of Europe and the better-off Latin American countries. The "less developed" category covers almost all Africa and Asia and substantial parts of South America.

But just what is meant by "development"? Samuelson (1973, 765) offers the definition that, "A less developed country is simply one with real per capita income that is low relative to the present-day per capita incomes of such nations as Canada, the United States, Great Britain and Western Europe generally." What this means in practice is that annual per capita income in the less developed countries (LDCs) averages barely $(US) 100 compared with $5,000 in North America. Roughly two-thirds of the world's people live in the LDCs, with only about an eighth of the world's income; the 20 per cent of total population in highly de-

Table 1.1 Population and Gross National Product in major world regions, 1972

Region	Population		Gross National Product	
	millions	per cent	$ millions	per cent
Asia	2,003	53·9	572,000	14·3
Western Europe	397	10·7	1,057,000	26·5
Eastern Europe	352	9·5	748,000	18·7
Africa	322	8·7	78,000	2·0
Latin America	294	7·9	181,000	4·5
North America	231	6·2	1,259,000	31·5
Middle East	101	2·7	48,000	1·2
Oceania	16	0·4	52,000	1·3
Total	3,716	100·0	3,995,000	100·0

Source: *Business International*, 4 Dec. 1973. GNP is virtually the same as national income.

veloped nations share about 60 per cent of world income—half of it going to the USA. Table 1.1 summarizes the distribution of population and output by major world regions. Almost a third of all gross product is accounted for by North America, with only just over 6 per cent of the world's population. Western and Eastern Europe (including the USSR) together contribute 45·2 per cent of production with only a fifth of total population. Asia, with over half the world's people, accounts for only 14·3 per cent of production, while Africa and Latin America together have 16·6 per cent of the total population but produce only 6·5 per cent of all GNP.

Development is not solely a matter of income and production, of course. Other figures can be cited to show the disadvantaged position of the LDCs with respect to nutrition, health, eduction and various other social criteria of well-being. Recent statistics from the United Nations (Harrison, 1975) reveal: per capita food production in the developed countries up 20 per cent between the early 1960s and 1973 compared with only 1 per cent in developing countries; almost full enrolment in primary education in the developed countries compared with only 59 per cent in Asia and 48 per cent in Africa, reflected in illiteracy rates of 47 per cent in Asia and 74 per cent in Africa in 1970; 23·78 doctors per 1,000 population in Russia and 14·85 in Europe compared with 2·84 in Asia and 1·36 in Africa. And in the poorer nations, up to an annual per capita income of $300, economic "development" has tended to increase the share of income going to the richest one-fifth of the population. Development is thus a multi-faceted phenomenon, in both its nature and its impact. Clarifying its meaning is a major task in contemporary social science, including human geography (see Chapter 8).

The gap between rich and poor nations is wide, and apparently getting wider (Donaldson, 1973, 9–17). Narrowing the gap is a frequently espoused goal. Samuelson continues his definition of the LDCs cited above by saying, "Optimistically, a less developed country is one regarded as capable of substantial improvements in its income level."

What is the basis for such optimism, if any? For some time national development programmes in the LDCs have operated on the assumption that industrialization is the panacea for their ills: economic progress is seen to lead necessarily to social progress. The results have not been very convincing, however. The more fortunate LDCs may be achieving fairly rapid economic growth, but even if this can be sustained it would take many decades and in some cases centuries to catch up with the highly developed nations. And economic growth is certainly not proving a predictable route to social justice, in the sense of a more equal sharing of the national product. Indeed, it would be rather surprising if industrial or agricultural development programmes implemented without basic economic-structural reforms did not have the effect of strengthening the power of the existing political and land-owning elite, as has happened in parts of Latin America and South East Asia. Those LDCs whose development is largely dependent on external sources of technical assistance, finance and enterprise are now seeing the consequent economic and political dependency as a mixed blessing. And the same is true of the cultural impact of western-style development.

Perhaps rapid economic growth is not the most effective means of achieving general social progress. The coincidence of the two is being increasingly questioned today, as the less desirable side-effects of industrialization in the LDCs become more apparent and as the rising affluence in some of the most highly developed nations is seen to be accompanied by social ills of new and frightening forms. The rewards of economic growth are no longer as clear as they once appeared.

An important task for human geography is to build up more sophisticated knowledge of the process of development and underdevelopment. This involves disentangling complex networks of economic, social and cultural relationships, and also the ecological relationships in a balance so easily disturbed by ill-conceived "development" projects. Whether the objective is development in its broadest sense or progress towards specific goals such as improving education and reducing infant mortality, any proposals made by geographers must be based on sound knowledge of how the existing system works and of the likely impact of change.

One of the greatest dangers in the present situation of development inequality is its potential for human conflict. This applies to inequality within nations as well as among them. A high degree of internal inequality is a common characteristic of intermediate and less developed countries, in many of which the wealth and political power is still largely in the hands of a small urban elite or capitalist-landowner class. This is true of most Latin American nations, of some in South East Asia, and also of poorer European nations. It is particularly true of those parts of the world where remnants of former colonial régimes survive, the most obvious example being southern Africa.

Southern Africa provides a particularly interesting case for the examination of inequality in level of development viewed from a welfare perspective. The map of southern Africa has been portrayed as one of islands of advanced economic activity within a sea of backward territory where subsistence is still dominant (Green and Fair, 1962). Most economic activity is concentrated in metropolitan cores, to which the less advanced areas are tributary in a spatial sense (Fair, 1971, 330–31). During the colonial era the cores acted as centres of power for the white elite. They were also intermediate stores for the wealth or surplus value extracted by the commercial agricultural sector in the rural periphery, on its way back to Britain, Portugal, or wherever the source of investment capital happened to be. Since independence, the racial distinction between core elite and peripheral counter-elite has been largely removed, but the basic geography of economic dependency remains. As Davidson (1975) argues, the colonial structures geared to external economic exploitation have not altered in most African countries despite independence. The space-economy may still operate more in the interests of European demands for primary goods than as a means of satisfying African needs.

The core–periphery structure of the space-economy is shown with particular clarity in the Republic of South Africa. Figure 1.4 illustrates a three-dimensional representation of the "surface" of Gross Domestic Product per square mile, plotted from data for about fifty areal subdivisions. The Witwatersrand conurbation centred on Johannesburg stands out as the major peak, where more than three-quarters of national wealth is generated. Lesser peaks correspond with the coastal cities of Cape Town and Durban. Between these metropolitan cores are largely agricultural areas, where the generally low level of GDP is interrupted only by minor local elevations corresponding with the secondary industrial centres. Most of the whites live in the cities. Much of the poor and economically backward periphery is occupied by the so-called Homelands or Bantustans, set up for the African population under the policy of *apartheid* or "separate development". As less than a fifth of the total population, the whites get over two thirds of the national income; as two-thirds of the population, the Africans get less than a fifth of the income. Contemporary South Africa provides an interesting laboratory within which to apply the welfare approach to human geography. *Apartheid* has been soundly condemned by almost every nation in the world, including the inhabitants of some rather fragile glass-houses. The transparent injustices of racial discrimination seem to make moral judgements easy, yet the reality is not quite as readily grasped as either opponents or proponents of *apartheid* would have us believe (see Chapter 9).

Even the richest nations have spatial variations in levels of human well-being. The core-periphery dichotomy in southern Africa finds expression in most other nations of the world, with peaks of affluence corresponding with the major metropolitan centres of industry and commerce, surrounded by troughs representing the rural areas in which people are often not so well off. Broad regional differences can also be found, and extreme inequality often occurs in individual cities.

The United States is a case in point. General material standards of living are higher than anywhere else in the world. Yet millions of Americans live in poverty and social deprivation in city slums, and in parts of the rural south people can be found living in conditions as bad as

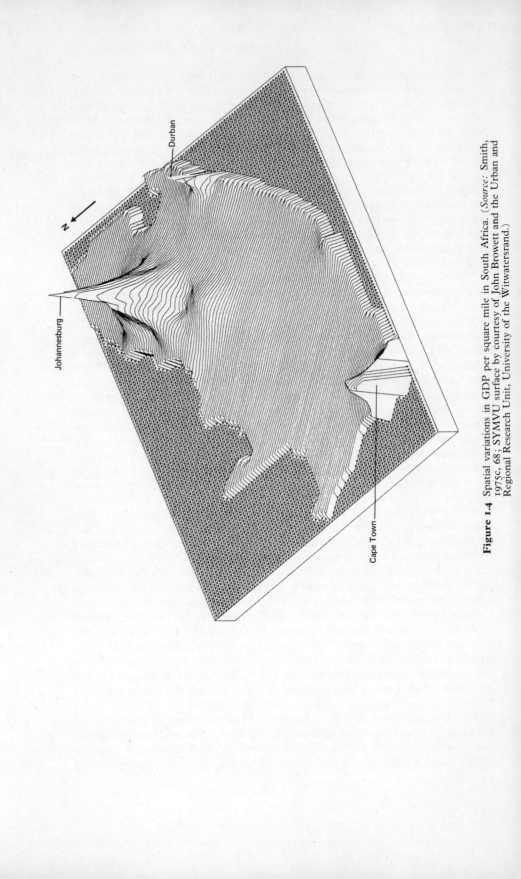

Figure 1.4 Spatial variations in GDP per square mile in South Africa. (*Source*: Smith, 1975c, 68; SYMVU surface by courtesy of John Browett and the Urban and Regional Research Unit, University of the Witwatersrand.)

anywhere in Europe. The persistence of widespread poverty accompanied by other social problems such as crime and drug addiction in the most affluent nation in the world is a contradiction which underlines the failure of economic growth under a capitalist system to uplift the lives of all people to current standards of decency. Substantial geographical inequalities in human well-being appear to be an inevitable consequence of such a system. Inter-state variations in per capita annual income range from $5,340 in Connecticut down to only a little over $3,000 in Mississippi. Twelve per cent of Americans have incomes below the officially recognized poverty level—a total of over 6 million families or about 26 million people in all, according to US Census Bureau estimates for 1976.

As at the international level, income alone is unlikely to be a satisfactory general measure of human well-being. Indeed, the higher the level of affluence, the more people may look to non-material sources of satisfaction. In the United States the geographical patterns of such conditions as housing quality, education and health tend to follow income quite closely. But others, such as crime, adopt different forms; some of the most affluent states (e.g. New York and California) have the worst figures for crime, delinquency, drug addiction and other symptoms of social disorder. We will return to this in Chapter 10, where the United States provides a case study of how the abstract concept of human well-being may be subject to measurement.

It is in the cities that the inequalities of American society are most obvious. It is here that tall glass-and-concrete office blocks rise beside the slums, as a visual indication of the juxtaposition of commercial affluence and personal poverty before recourse to statistics. It is here that the records of the health department can reveal local levels of infant mortality ranging from less than 10 per 1,000 live births in the rich suburbs up to 60 or more in the heart of the ghetto. The highest infant mortality figures are comparable with those of intermediate nations and even some of the LDCs (Bunge, 1974, 52). It is in the American city that we find such clear evidence of the inability of the allocative and distributive mechanisms of the capitalist system to bring basic services to all people.

Something of the range in personal circumstances in a fairly typical American city is illustrated in Figure 1.5a. The histogram shows median family income in Atlanta, Georgia, by census tracts—small areas of relatively homogeneous socio-economic character. Although the city average is $7,700, eighteen of the 112 tracts have figures of less than $5,000 and one falls just below $2,000. But seven tracts have median family incomes of over $15,000 a year and in one it is as high as $30,000. The median family in the richest part of the city has fifteen times the income of the equivalent family in the poorest part. The geographical grouping of low-income families is mapped in Figure 1.5b. A concentration of tracts with more than a quarter of families below the official poverty level exists around the central business district (CBD), with a secondary concentration to the north-west. One tract has 70 per cent of families in poverty. In the northern suburbs less than 3 per cent of families are below the

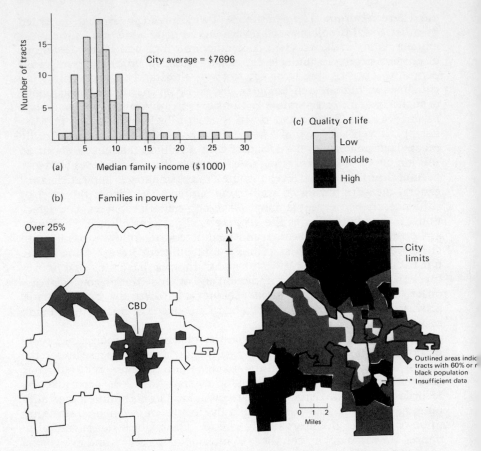

Figure 1.5 Income levels and the "quality of life" in Atlanta, Georgia. (*Source:* Bederman, 1974; Adams and Bederman, 1974; data on median income from US *Census* 1970.)

poverty line. Figure 1.5c maps "quality of life" by tracts, based on a composite indicator incorporating measures of health, public order, housing quality, socio-economic structure and density, developed by Bederman (1974). The correspondence between the two maps is clear—within the city low incomes tend to correspond with low performance on other social conditions.

Another quite obvious correspondence is between low levels of well-being and the racial composition of the population. In Figure 1.5b all the tracts with over 25 per cent of families with incomes below the poverty level have black populations comprising over 60 per cent of the total. All but one of the predominantly black tracts fall into the medium or low levels on the quality of life index, while all but two of the other tracts are in the high or medium categories. Racial differentiation is by no means confined to South Africa.

Recognition of the kind of problems observed in a city such as Atlanta raised the question of planning. Surely, problems of localized poverty in an affluent society can easily be solved by public action and so-called "welfare" programmes. Slums can be cleared, hospitals and clinics built, jobs provided, schools refurbished, and so on. The continuing world-wide expansion of cities has proceeded largely on the belief that planning would somehow sort things out. But what is commonly termed the urban crisis in the United States and elsewhere seems to suggest that urbanization is proceeding somewhat ahead of our capacity to control or manage the process without some alarming social consequences. New York may be the richest city in the world, but its public finances are in chaos and it is popularly believed to be ungovernable. In the so-called Third World of developing nations the unconstrained dynamic of urbanization has led Berry (1973, xv) to remark that "public powers have been swamped by the scale and pace of change in spite of highly centralised and increasingly authoritarian governmental forms".

Part of the problem is that building and running modern millionaire cities requires sophisticated technological and managerial skills of a kind which may have been achieved in space exploration but not yet in our earthly pursuits. But more fundamental is a failure of the planning pro-cess to meet some of its objectives in circumstances where the problems seem well within our control. The primary function of the city under capitalism—that of generating profits and concentrating wealth—seems inconsistent with the provision of what the mass of the people require to satisfy basic needs, including hospitals, good schools, recreational facilities, cheap public transport and an environment conducive to full personal development. The ethics of the marketplace and reverence for technology pervade city government and planning. Social problems have often been subjected to purely physical solutions, on the assumption that in the "right" physical environment human behaviour will take on desired forms. Some benefits certainly come from urban renewal and expressway construction, for example, but they do not necessarily flow in the direction of residents whose needs might be considered greatest.

There is a growing awareness in contemporary planning that all physi-cal development has a potential income-redistributive impact. Defining income in broad real terms as total command over society's resources, every development proposal has the capacity to benefit some people in some places more than others. Indeed, it would be very difficult if not impossible to construct anything anywhere which would be of equal benefit to every citizen. Geographical distance and accessibility alone mean that some will be (literally) better placed to enjoy the advantages or disadvantages, whether the structure is a hospital, concert hall, motor-way, factory or sewage works. Location decisions and plans for the spatial allocation of resources must be made with great care, if the benefits and penalties are to be apportioned among the population in a predictable and equitable manner.

Applied human geographers sometimes take inspiration from the advice of Lösch (1954, iv) that "The real duty ... is not to explain our sorry reality, but to improve it. The question of the best location is far more dignified than determination of the actual one." How we decide what is best is a welfare issue, requiring judgements as to who *should* reap the benefits or pay the price of access or proximity to a specific facility. Location/allocation problems bring the spatial planner face to face with the hard reality that every location decision involves implicit or explicit ethical judgements. Two basic questions thus arise: how decisions are made as to the "proper" distribution of gains and losses in the process of development, and how particular projects or resource allocations can be tested for their distributional impact measured in terms of costs and benefits.

The range of practical decisions in which these problems arise is enormous. They include identification of priority areas, planning the routes of motorways, the location of factories or other sources of employment, the spatial arrangement of facilities providing medical care, the distribution of council or public housing projects, the allocation of special funds for neighbourhood renewal projects and so on, the disposition of policeman or patrol cars, the location of airports, the siting of noxious facilities, and many others. Each of these decisions can be made in many different ways. Each can have a different impact, with respect to stated policy goals and general distributive effects. In Chapter 11 a selection of case studies of actual location and allocation problems are examined, to show how some of the concepts and techniques explained in Parts One and Two may be applied in practice. This is where human geography begins to come to grips with real welfare problems, the solution of which can have a critical bearing on who gets what where.

Part One

Theoretical Perspectives

Wherever something new is being created, and thus in settlement and spatial planning also, the laws revealed through theory are the sole economic guide to what *should* take place.

August Lösch, *The Economics of Location*, 1954

There can be no ideal goal for human life. Any ideal goal means mechanization, materialism and nullity. There is no pulling open the buds to see what the blossom will be. Leaves must unroll, buds swell and open, and *then* the blossom. And even after that, when the flower dies and the leaves fall, *still* we shall not know. There will be more leaves, more buds, more blossom: and again, a blossom is as an unfolding of the creative unknown. Impossible, utterly impossible to preconceive the uncreated blossom. You cannot forestall it from the last blossom. We know the flower of to-day, but the flower of to-morrow is beyond us all. Only in the material-mechanical world can man foresee, foreknow, calculate and establish laws.

D. H. Lawrence, "Democracy", 1936

The development of theory is an attempt to impose intellectual order on reality. Two purposes are served: theory assists us to understand the world as we observe it, and also provides guidance on how we may improve life. Understanding the world of man involves the capacity to predict the outcome in given circumstances: to make the unexpected expected, or at least less of a surprise. Improving the world involves prediction also, for it is folly to implement a change without some confidence that the outcome will be as desired.

The strength of sound theory lies in its capacity to explain by reference to processes that are understood, rather than simply to observed associations. At present, theory in human geography is rather primitive, with very few laws that provide invariant links between cause and effect. As a practical guide to what should take place, existing spatial social-economic-political theory is of limited assistance, the only integrated view thus far presented (Isard *et al.*, 1969) being at a high level of abstraction. But we must make what we can of the theory at our disposal, for once the value judgements implicit in the setting of planning goals have been made, theory is our sole guide to spatial policy. That we should not expect too much from theory is implicit in the recognition of its present inadequacy. We must also be wary of assuming that anything so intangible as the quality of life is subject to effective mechanical manipulation based on scientific inquiry.

The theory offered in the chapters that follow is an outline approach to spatial welfare problems, not a rigorous integrated body of knowledge. Some explanation of the order of the material is required, so that the logic of the exposition is clear from the outset. We begin with a brief discussion of human needs and wants (Chapter 2), to explore something of the scope of what really matters to man. Then we consider consumption theory, looking critically at the conventional economic formulations of the satisfaction of needs and wants (Chapter 3). The process of production as the creation of value (Chapter 4) is central to who gets what where, through the moulding of societal and spatial structures. Finally, Chapter 5 directly addresses the issue of spatial distribution, as an outcome of the prevailing mode of production, institutions and allocation of power. While "consumption", "production" and "distribution" appear in separate chapter headings, the presentation stresses their inter-dependence.

Although perspectives from a number of different disciplines appear, the content leans most heavily on economics. As others have pointed out (e.g. Harvey, 1967; 1969) theory in geography is largely derivative, concerned with playing out in a spatial context concepts from elsewhere. Economics provides the only rigorous body of knowledge dealing specifically with the concept of welfare, but using economic theory as a point of departure does have some dangers. It is now recognized that neo-classical theory (i.e. the content of most textbooks on economic theory) is seriously deficient with respect to its accuracy as a description of how the economy actually works and its interpretation of the welfare outcome of a market system. Economics provides an "image of economic society" (Galbraith, 1975, 21) which, if false, creates a false consciousness or failure to understand whose interests are served by the existing system. Marxian economics offers different perspectives that avoid the ideological bias of conventional theory, with its stress on individualistic competitive ethics. While Marx does not offer an *explicit* theory of welfare (Mishra, 1975, 287) much of importance is implicit in his writing on capitalism and the socialist alternative. The question of who gets what where is highly relevant under socialism, for experience suggests that a planned economy cannot dispense with discussion of "welfare criteria" (Dobb, 1969, 4). The chapters that follow thus attempt to provide a perspective with some relevance to a socialist society as well as exploring the economic basis of the problem of spatial inequality under contemporary capitalism.

Ultimately, a body of theory must stand or fall by its use—by its capacity to shed light on reality and to assist with the implementation of improvements. Part Three of this book will attempt to establish that the theory set out below and extended into more practical knowledge in Part Two is useful, as a guide to the way things are and to how they ought to be.

2

Human Being: Needs and Wants

What is it to be human? What is human *being*? These may seem philosophical questions quite beyond the traditional realm of geography, but if human geography is to be truly concerned with individual or group well-being, then the nature of human being is a necessary starting point. Theory in human geography must be rooted in the reality of human existence.

2.1 Needs and wants

Being human requires the satisfaction of needs or wants. This is the origin or motivation for human actions, from buying a beer to planning a city. Satisfying needs or wants involves cooperation with other people, for no-one is completely self-contained. It can also lead to competition. The regulation of human behaviour in the pursuit of needs and wants is the prime source of social relationships, political institutions and modes of production. It is the source of our codes of morality, of the laws derived from them, and of the various other ways in which we try to resolve conflict. The individual human being will presumably view his or her life quality in terms of the extent to which perceived needs and wants are satisfied.

The distinction between needs and wants provides an entrée to the question of what human satisfaction depends on. The term need implies an imperative—something really necessary to an individual, rather than merely the source of acquisitive desire. Need implies reference to some standard, such as specific medical treatment or a minimum calorific intake *needed* to ensure bodily survival. Needing access to a kidney machine is an example; "needing" (i.e. wanting) a beer is not.

But not everyone with severe kidney disease receives renal dialysis or a transplant. There are not enough machines or spare kidneys to go round. That an individual has a clinical need for some means of survival is not an imperative to the extent that society will actually satisfy the need. And the patient will not necessarily "want" the treatment and all it entails. To decide that a need exists can be a purely technical matter, but to decide which needs are to be satisfied and for whom involves ethical questions. The definition of needs itself becomes highly value-loaded as soon as we get away from minimum survival standards scientifically established. Specifying educational needs, for example, is meaningless outside a given societal context. Although the difference between needs and wants is that the former carries connotations of approbation with respect to some standards external to the desires of the individual, this begs the question of how such standards originate. The answer is to be found in the nature of a society as well as in the nature of human being.

The most "basic" human needs are those relating to physical survival. The preservation of individual human life is not an absolute value transcending all others, however; some societies execute people and all accept deaths on the road as part of the price of personal mobility. Survival needs stem from our biological being; as Fletcher (1965, 19) puts it:

> Like all other creatures, you and I, and all men [*sic*], inherit—with the nature and function of our bodies—a number of impulses which drive us to seek appropriate satisfactions. For example, we need to breathe, to maintain a certain body temperature, to eat and drink, to rest and sleep, to exercise ourselves in work and play, to evacuate waste materials from our bodies. And all these impulses are necessary for our survival, our health and contentment. Most of these needs require objects for their satisfaction—food, drink, clothing, shelter, and the like and we have to work, fight, compete or cooperate, in order to secure them.

Satisfying biological needs has an emotional element as well as ensuring survival. Closely related to the basic impulses we have certain broader desires; Fletcher (1965, 19) goes on:

> we tend to fear all that is unfamiliar, unknown, all that threatens the secure satisfaction of our needs, and the security of all the people, things, places we have learned to love. We try to avoid pain, frustration, thwarting, and instead we look for fulfilment, pleasure, and happiness.

Human needs are thus mental or psychological as well as physical.

Other writers offer slightly different perspectives. For example, Lasswell and Kaplan (1950) have recognized in human needs two important sets of values, relating respectively to "welfare" and "deference". *Welfare* values include the well-being of the individual in terms of health, safety, wealth, skill and enlightenment (knowledge, etc.); *deference* values include the respect, rectitude and affection derived from relationships with other people. Dahl and Lindblom (1963) suggest that the prime goals in Western societies "include existence or survival, psychological gratification (through food, sex, sleep and comfort), love and affection, respect, self respect, power and control, skill, enlightenment, prestige, aesthetic satisfaction, excitement and novelty" (quoted in Chadwick, 1971, 148).

One of the most influential attempts to categorize human needs is the hierarchical arrangement proposed by Maslow (1954). His argument was that "higher" needs emerge successively as "lower" ones are satisfied. The first or lowest level is *survival*, involving the struggle to sustain life by acquiring food, clothing, shelter and so on—the most primitive and "prepotent" of all needs. The second is *security*—involving the safety of the environment and protection from physical danger or catastrophe. The third is *belongingness and love*—the need for affection, fulfilling interpersonal relationships, conformity to group norms and so on. Fourth is *esteem*, or the need for recognition, prestige, status and dominance.

Finally, at the highest level, *self-actualization* or the desire for self-fulfilment—living up to one's full potential and becoming everything that one is capable of becoming. Similar views have been put forward by other psychologists and sociologists.

The position of any individual or group with respect to their hierarchy of needs can vary in time and space. Societies at early stages of development will be preoccupied with survival and security. In advanced societies people will be more concerned with self-actualization or personal fulfilment. But the progression is not a simple one, coincident with national or regional level of economic development. The most economically advanced nations may be the most concerned with survival and security, judging by the size of their armed forces and defence budgets. In American cities there is the continuing paradox of physical insecurity on the streets of the affluent society, with young people often finding needs for belonging and love fulfilled in social causes and communes instead of through participation in conventional work or family life. The individual status and esteem found in performing a particular role in a "primitive" society may have to be acquired through symbols such as expensive cars in the "advanced" nations.

While recognizing certain basic needs "which do not seem to have changed since the beginnings of *homo sapiens*" (Mandel, 1962, 660), Marxian analysis stresses an historically and culturally relative concept of need. Need arises from a specific social and economic situation, which can vary from place to place, and in which spatial organization can play an important part. Thus the urban American family may "need" at least one reliable automobile simply to get the husband to work, the wife to the shops and the children to school, such is the spatial form of the modern city and the inadequacy of public transport. The means of satisfying basic needs are now largely assured in the advanced capitalist world, but they have been replaced by new wants. Far from being more satisfied, the mass of the people are trapped in a competitive, dehumanizing struggle to acquire more and more things, creating feelings of powerlessness or alienation and threatening relationships of cooperation and group solidarity.

Failures of need satisfaction in the modern world are often attributed to a "revolution of rising expectations". This has been fostered by almost a quarter of a century of continuous economic growth in the advanced industrial nations, providing an ever-increasing range of goods and services to satisfy needs or wants successfully created or titivated by advertising, fashion and the desire to emulate others. "As affluence increases, goods become increasingly dispensable or even frivolous" (Galbraith, 1975, 174), yet continued economic growth depends on people wanting and buying them. Means and ends have thus become confused. Also part of the process is the tendency of governments to stimulate expectations through social policy, as exemplified by the so-called War on Poverty of the 1960s in the United States. This is another aspect of the relative nature of need satisfaction. As Campbell (1972, 442) puts it: "Satisfactions and frustrations depend jointly on objective reality on one side and aspirations and expectations on the other. Concern over the quality of life must include a hope for personal development beyond the individual's present limits of vision. Upgrading the quality of life implies progressive liberation from the constricting limits of modest aspiration levels and increasing fulfilment of the human potential." But unless a system generating rising expectation has the capacity to "deliver the goods", people end up worse off in a real sense. Then they may move from aspiration to frustration and aggression, expressed in revolution or other forms of social violence (Stagner, 1970, 65–6). The truly happy individual may well be the one with aspirations realistically adjusted to personal circumstances within his or her control. But in some circumstances revolution may be the only way for an oppressed class to realize their legitimate aspirations to become what they can become.

Thus human being is essentially a relative state. Feelings of well-being are a subjective experience, perhaps reflecting the difference between expectation and reality (Smith, 1973a, 74–5). Expectation may be generated by observation of the condition of some reference group within society, perhaps leading to a sense of what Runciman (1966) terms *relative deprivation*. This is related to knowledge of others, which in its turn may be a function of position in geographical space. Marx expressed the situation in an apt analogy (Tucker, 1972, 180):

> A house may be large or small; as long as the surrounding houses are equally small it satisfies all social demands for a dwelling. But let a palace arise beside the little house, and it shrinks from a little house to a hut. The little house shows now that its owner has only slight or no demands to make; and however high it may shoot up in the course of civilization, if the neighbouring palace grows to an equal or even greater extent, the occupant of the relatively small house will feel more and more uncomfortable, dissatisfied and cramped within its four walls.

As communications between peoples become more effective and as knowledge of the world of others grows, so those in the huts see the palaces more clearly. Thus the people in the underdeveloped world as well as the poor in advanced nations see that they are still struggling to meet the most basic needs, while others enjoy undreamed-of affluence.

While the steady progression of human beings up a ladder of need satisfaction is too simple a concept to fit the complexities of modern society, it does offer a first step towards the empirical investigation of levels of well-being. As is recognized in one of the research papers (US Office of Education, 1969, 18–19) prepared in connection with the first American attempt at a national social report:

> Such a categorization of needs provides a basis for describing an individual's overall welfare, or, in broad terms, the quality of his life. To the extent that individuals can afford to be concerned with their higher needs and are little constrained by their lower needs, they are free to actualize themselves in whatever way is most natural to them. The more they are able to do this, the higher the quality of their lives.

Opportunity for personal fulfilment expands with choices available—with the freedom to exercise and realize personal preferences. While the nature of the good life is ultimately an individual matter, the extent to which human beings have common needs suggests some consensus as to quality of life criteria. It is to this question that the discussion now turns.

2.2 "Quality of life" criteria

Any attempt to identify levels of human well-being as a spatially variable condition requires specific criteria capable of measurement. The idea of trying to measure an abstraction like the quality of life is anathema to many people, even perhaps an assault on the individual (as in the case of the researcher asking a survey respondent what he valued most in life, to be told only "my privacy"). According to some, it is "inextricably linked with a traditional Western logic system that is being replaced by a new approach stressing the symbiotic rather than the competitive"; hence "any attempt to classify and quantify QOL fa :tors merely serves to prolong an outdated system, and hence should not be undertaken" (Marugama, cited in Environmental Protection Agency, 1972, I-37). There is also the quite plausible view that such data can be abused, for example by a city or national government representing a small elite for whom any information simply enhances their capacity to repress the mass of the people. The position here is that rational planning for superior spatial arrangements of society requires some information on how things are. Who uses it and in whose interests is a relevant issue, but not one that generally justifies ignorance rather than knowledge.

There are two obvious ways of determining criteria of human well-being or life quality. The first is to derive them from theory in psychology or sociology, of the kind outlined in the previous section. The problem here is that, despite certain similarities in the views expressed, there is no generally accepted social theory setting out the precise conditions un-ambiguously defining human well-being, along with their relative weights. This problem has been recognized frequently in the literature on social indicators (Smith, 1973a, 58–61). The second method is to ask people how they view their own state of well-being, satisfaction or happiness, attempting to discover by direct inquiry what this state is de-pendent on. There has been considerable interest in the direct monitoring of the quality of life via survey research in recent years (e.g. Krieger, 1969; Stagner, 1970; Abrams, 1973) but this has not yet reached the stage at which it could form a basis for definitive lists of criteria except for restricted populations.

An example combining survey research with social-psychological theory is provided by a recent comparative study of the Scandinavian countries (Allardt, 1973; 1975). This recognized three dimensions of overall individual need satisfaction: having, loving and being. *Having* in-cludes some of Maslow's more basic needs relating to survival, and largely corresponds to what is generally referred to as standard of living; it is measured by data on housing and income. *Loving* refers to such condi-tions as companionship, affection, belonging and solidarity realized in reciprocal personal relations. *Being* refers to a dimension with alienation at one extreme and self-actualization at the other; like loving, its measurement requires survey research. Research into individual attainment levels on these criteria shows Finland consistently performing worse than Denmark, Norway and Sweden. Despite the possibilities of this approach, it is as yet experimental and expensive to undertake given the sample sizes needed to reveal spatial trends.

A third approach containing elements of both those outlined above is to refer to "expert opinion", or the judgement of scientists and representatives of public views. A danger here is that these people may not truly represent the concerns of the populace at large. There is a possibility that experts will express elitist views, arising as much from their own personal predispositions and class affiliation as from accurate scientific knowledge of the way ordinary people think and feel. But despite these problems, the informed judgement of students of society, augmented by positive knowledge of actual social concerns, seems the most likely route to the specification of criteria of human well-being at present.

Some recent research by Dalkey and Rourke (1973; Environmental Protection Agency, 1973, I-46–51) provides an example. They have applied a procedure known as "Delphi" (consulting the oracle) to identify group value judgements with respect to what determines the quality of life. A sample of college students were asked to list items they considered most important to their sense of well-being, satisfaction or dissatisfaction with life, or happiness. Similar items were grouped into general components, which were then weighted by the participants. The most important component included "loving, caring, affection" and so on, the second stressed self-respect, while the third encompassed peace of mind and emotional stability. Fourth came sex. The results thus emphasize strongly the subjective, psychological, individualistic and emotional aspects of life. They are culturally and historically specific, reflecting a society in which more basic needs for food, shelter and so on are largely assured. A problem with a list of this kind, like some of the psychological criteria mentioned in the previous section, is that the items are difficult to define in operational terms. Thus the extent to which these kind of needs are actually satisfied is extremely difficult to identify empirically.

Another application of the Delphi technique is reported by Koelle (1974). The purpose was to arrive at an operational definition of the quality of life by generating a list of weighted goals. A chief goal was set ("improvement of the quality of life"), with four primary goals relating respectively to material, physical, mental and spiritual improvements. There are also sixteen interim goals and almost a hundred sub-goals. The primary and interim goals are as in Table 2.1. Participants in the experiment were required to give weights to these goals, in accordance with their individual preferences. They also had to do this with respect to what they would like to see achieved in Western Europe and the developing countries, and what they see as prevailing in Eastern Europe. The collective weights on individual preference are shown in Table 2.1. When these are compared with the other preferences (Koelle, 1974, 3), material goals are viewed as much more important for the developing world than the weights in the table show, with spiritual goals much less important. Eastern Europe is seen as more preoccupied with material goals than Western Europe, but not substantially different on mental goals.

As mentioned above, a difficulty with this kind of analysis is that the preferences expressed may be unrepresentative. Participating in the Koelle study were predominantly highly educated males working in science, engineering and other technical fields. The most popular item in Table 2.1 is preservation of the natural environment, which has more than twice the weight of restoring health, improvement of housing quality and improvement of family or group harmony (the three with the lowest weights). These value judgements would not be shared by everyone, even in affluent Germany where the study was undertaken. Preoccupation with environmental quality is more a concern of the relatively well-to-do than people struggling to make a living. The sudden interest in this issue at the end of the 1960s was very much a middle-class phenomenon; the limited evidence available suggests less concern on the part of low-income groups (Wood *et al.*, 1974, 127–8). For group value judgements to have more than narrow academic interest, they must incorporate a wide range of human experience.

Table 2.1 "Quality of life" goals used by the Berlin Centre for Futures Research

	Primary and interim goals	Weights
A	*Improvement of the material quality of life*	185
	1. Improvement of housing quality	47
	2. Better general supplies in quantity and quality	49
	3. Better use of natural resources	48
	4. Reduced destruction of useful material goods	41
B	*Improvement of the physical quality of life*	269
	1. Preservation and improvement of the state of health	68
	2. Reduced violence against people	44
	3. Restoration of health in case of sickness	48
	4. Preservation of the natural environment	109
C	*Improvement of the mental quality of life*	288
	1. Improvement of educational facilities and equal educational opportunities	71
	2. Better utilization of available knowledge	80
	3. Improvement of mental qualities and general knowledge	85
	4. Improvement of cultural environment	52
D	*Improvement of the spiritual quality of life*	258
	1. Better utilization of individual talents and capabilities	74
	2. Improvement of the harmony within family or social groups	43
	3. Greater involvement in large social groups and social affairs	70
	4. Improvement of the moral and ethical standards and state	71
		1000

Source: Koelle (1974).

As another example of possible criteria of human well-being, Table 2.2 lists "social concerns" considered common to most member countries of the Organization for Economic Co-operation and Development. This has been compiled by a working party of specialists, as a preliminary to the development of social indicators. A social concern is "an identifiable and definable aspiration or concern of fundamental and direct importance to human well-being" (OECD, 1973, 8). Emphasis is on ends rather than means of achieving them, in the belief that economic growth is not an end in itself but an instrument for creating better conditions of life and that "increased attention must be given to the qualitative aspects of growth, and to the formulation of policies with respect to the broad eco-

Table 2.2 List of social concerns common to most OECD countries

A   *Health*
   1. Probability of a healthy life through all stages of the life cycle
   2. Impact of health impairment on individuals

B   *Individual development through learning*
   1. Acquisition by children of the basic knowledge, skills and values necessary for their individual development and their successful functioning as citizens in their society
   2. Availability of opportunities for continuing self-development and the propensity of individuals to use them
   3. Maintenance and development by individuals of the knowledge, skills and flexibility required to fulfil their economic potential and to enable them to integrate themselves in the economic process if they wish to do so
   4. Individual satisfaction with the process of individual development through learning while he is in the process
   5. Maintenance and development of the cultural heritage relative to its positive contribution to the well-being of the members of various social groups

C   *Employment and quality of working life*
   1. Availability of gainful employment for those who desire it
   2. Quality of working life
   3. Individual satisfaction with the experience of working life

D   *Time and leisure*
   1. Availability of effective choices for the use of time

E   *Command over goods and services*
   1. Personal command over goods and services
   2. Number of individuals experiencing material deprivation
   3. Extent of equity in the distribution of command over goods and services
   4. Quality, range of choice and accessibility of private and public goods and services
   5. Protection of individuals and families against economic hazards

F   *Physical environment*
   1. Housing conditions
   2. Population exposure to harmful and/or unpleasant pollutants
   3. Benefits derived by the population from the use and management of the environment

G   *Personal safety and administration of justice*
   1. Violence, victimization and harassment suffered by individuals
   2. Fairness and humanity of the administration of justice
   3. Extent of confidence in the administration of justice

H   *Social opportunity and participation*
   1. Degree of social inequality
   2. Extent of opportunity for participation in community life, institutions and decision-making

Source: OECD (1973).

nomic and social choices involved in the allocation of growing resources" (Ministerial statement, OECD Council meeting, May 1970, quoted in OECD, 1973, 3).

The criteria are much more specific than those derived from a psychological perspective. They are intended to form a basis for the compilation of data, to be used eventually in policy design and evaluation at the national and sub-national level. However evocative such terms as alienation or self-actualization may be in expressing deep human needs, they have to be given a more concrete identity if deliberate planning for the improvement of human well-being is to be undertaken.

2.3 Level of living and state of well-being

In the study of human needs and the quality of human life it is easy to confuse means and ends. Perhaps some abstraction such as happiness, satisfaction or fulfilment is the only end that could legitimately be identified for human being, in which case practically everything we do becomes a means. But a distinction can be made between the *state* of human being at any point in time and the *level* or *flow* of the sources of well-being on which the state depends. This is the basis of a particularly helpful approach suggested by Drewnowski (1974), as a synthesis of work on levels of living previously undertaken at the UN Research Institute for Social Development. An outline of this approach provides a link between the general discussion of human being and the elements of theory to be presented in the next few chapters. It also offers a reminder of the essential unity of the process of human need satisfaction.

Drewnowski's approach rests on a distinction between the *state of well-being* and the *level of living*. The state of well-being is seen as a stock analogous to product or income. At any time, the state is the result of past flows of goods and services consumed by the population in the

Table 2.3 Composition of Drewnowski's state of well-being index*

---

1 *Somatic status* (physical development level)
   a. Nutritional status
   b. Health status
   c. Life expectancy
   d. Physical fitness

2 *Educational status* (mental development)
   a. Literacy
   b. Educational attainment
   c. Congruence of education with manpower requirements
   d. Employment

3 *Social status* (social integration and participation)
   a. Integration
   b. Participation

Source: Drewnowski (1974).
*Note: well-being is substituted for the original term "welfare", for reasons explained in Chapter 1.

satisfaction of their needs. Increases in human well-being result from the level of flows during the time period in question. The production of goods and services is thus viewed as the generation of inputs into need satisfaction; the state of well-being is the output.

Drewnowski proposes that the state of well-being could be measured by an index, the composition of which is shown in Table 2.3. Three major components are recognized, reflecting respectively the physical, mental and social status of the people. Individual indicators are suggested to measure each of these, with respect to both average aggregate levels and distribution among the population.

Level of living is defined by reference to the content of another pro-

Table 2.4 Composition of Drewnowski's level-of-living index

1   *Nutrition* (food intake)
   a. Calories intake
   b. Protein intake
   c. Per cent of non-starchy calories

2   *Clothing* (use of clothes)
   a. Cloth consumption
   b. Footwear consumption
   c. Quality of clothing

3   *Shelter* (occupancy of dwellings)
   a. Services of dwellings
   b. Density of occupation
   c. Independent use of dwellings

4   *Health* (health services received)
   a. Access to medical care
   b. Prevention of infection and parasitic disease
   c. Proportional mortality ratio

5   *Education* (education received)
   a. School enrolment ratio
   b. School output ratio
   c. Teacher/pupil ratio

6   *Leisure* (protection from overwork)
   a. Leisure time

7   *Security* (security assured)
   a. Security of the person
   b. Security of the way of life

8   *Social environment* (social contacts and recreation)
   a. Labour relations
   b. Conditions for social and economic activity
   c. Information and communication
   d. Recreation: cultural activities
   e. Recreation: travel
   f. Recreation: sport and physical exercise

9   *Physical environment*
   a. Cleanness and quietness
   b. Public amenities in the neighbourhood
   c. Beauty of the environment

Source: Drewnowski (1974).

posed index (Table 2.4). Nine components are recognized, each with their individual indicators. The resemblance to the OECD social concerns (Table 2.2) and to some other recent definitions of human well-being or life quality makes it a particularly useful list of the conditions towards which description of geographical variations in levels of living might be directed.

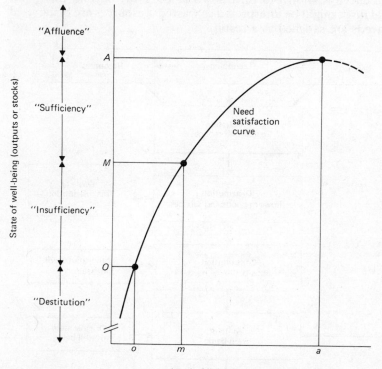

Figure 2.1 The need satisfaction curve, set in the conceptual framework of Drewnowski (1974).

Each element of the level of living feeds into part of the state of well-being. Taking some liberties with Drewnowski's formulation, a *need satisfaction curve* may be identified, relating stocks to flows or output to input in any facet of human life (Figure 2.1). Any single indicator of well-being will have critical points, which Drewnowski (1974, 83) suggests might be the "rock-bottom level" (O), decent conditions (M) and affluence (A). These might be established by scientific inquiry or expert opinion. The maintenance of a state of well-being at any level is dependent on a specific level of flows, determined by the relevant technical relationships. In Figure 2.1, the inputs or flows o, m and a correspond with what is required to maintain people at the critical points on the well-being scale. The form of the curve as drawn indicates decreasing marginal satisfaction, i.e. as flows increase, the impact on level of well-being is less than proportional.

This condition can expect to hold in a wide range of human activities; for example, once hunger is satisfied or comprehensive health care provided, further flows of food or medicine are unlikely to improve our physical status very much. Drewnowski proposes that beyond the point of affluence a situation of "over-abundance" may be reached. We can have too much food and medicine, resulting in a decrease in satisfaction. Thus the curve is shown to turn down at the end; beyond this point additional flows might be interpreted as wasted: resources are being used but no needs are satisfied as a result.

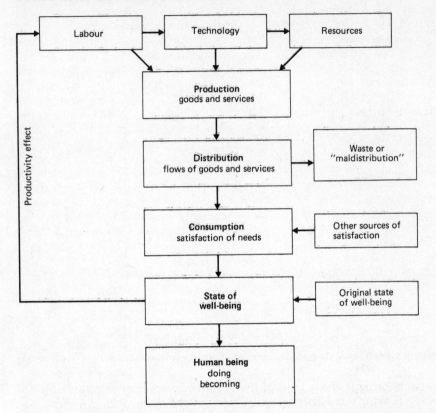

Figure 2.2 The derivation of human well-being, as suggested by Drewnowski (1974).

Piecing together the different elements of human need-satisfaction relationships is a major challenge to research. Drewnowski's attempts at guidance in this direction, in the form of an outline mathematical model, will be discussed at the end of Chapter 7. Drewnowski's overall view is summarized in Figure 2.2, which provides a convenient framework from which to embark on more detailed discussion of how needs are satisfied. We begin with labour and resources, which, when coupled with a technology, enable goods and services to be produced. Labour produces capital and develops technology, which in its turn creates resources out of the natural environment. The process of distribution among people and territories controls the flow of goods and services into consumption, or the satisfaction of needs. Some (perhaps much) production is wasted, by virtue of "maldistribution" allocating it to the over-endowed rather than the more needy. "Other" sources of satisfaction are shown, in recognition of the fact that the flows from production are not the only contribution to needs. Consumption leads to the state of well-being. This has a feedback loop to labour in the form of a productivity effect; a better educated and healthier workforce may produce more goods and services, or enjoy more leisure at the same level of output, than one that is ignorant and unhealthy.

Although the state of well-being might be regarded as the legitimate end to this process, it is necessary to extend it one step further. Drewnowski recognizes two sides to the level of well-being—passive and active. As what a population *receives*, the flow of well-being has a passive character, while a more active view might be in terms of what people can *give* in consequence of their present state. Drewnowski (1974, 80) suggests that, "By stressing the active aspect of the state of welfare [i.e. well-being], we extend the concept of welfare beyond the purely 'consumption' approach. We are thus open to the fact that welfare does not depend only on what one gets but also on what one is able to contribute to the good of society." As we now move into a discussion of consumption, and eventually into the identification of territorial levels of human well-being measured by what people get, it would be as well to recall these sentiments occasionally. Human being does not end with receiving. It may indeed be "better" to give than to receive. Perhaps, in the final analysis, this is the essence of human being. But before who *gets* what where can be abandoned for a more elevated view of life, people have to be freed from the tyranny of the need to get so as to survive, or so as to self-actualize in the affluent society where materialistic fulfilment can never be completely fulfilling.

3

The Consumption Approach:
Utility and Welfare

We seek a basis for understanding the fundamental welfare question of who gets what where, and how. A convenient starting point is the conventional (neo-classical) economic analysis of consumption. Two major purposes are served by this approach. First, it provides certain concepts and analytical techniques which are helpful in the study of spatial welfare problems. Secondly, we can expose some of the weaknesses of a body of theory which, while making claims to objectivity and ethical neutrality, is in important respects ideological. In particular, the association of welfare maximization with an economic system driven by individualistic self-interest and competition is increasingly being seen to operate to the advantage of "capital" or big business, and to the detriment of the general quality of life. The problem in this chapter is to sort the helpful notions from the obfuscation.

Before proceeding, it is important to point out that much of what follows here and in the next two chapters is of necessity the barest outline of knowledge set down at greater length and with more rigour in economics textbooks. For the sake of brevity some assumptions are left unstated and the exposition is confined largely to what can be accomplished through geometric models and the simplest symbolic statements. Further guidance on conventional economic theory can be found in standard texts such as Samuelson (1973) and in dictionaries of economic terms (e.g. Bannock, Baxter and Rees, 1972). A helpful critique from the radical perspective alongside neo-classical analyses is provided by Hunt and Sherman (1972). Brief introductions to welfare economics include Nath (1973) and various writings of Mishan (e.g. 1964; 1969a); more formal treatments can be found in such texts as Graaff (1957), Henderson and Quandt (1958), Nath (1969) and Winch (1971). The basics of Marxian economics are set down in Mandel (1962) and, more briefly, in Mandel (1973) and Desai (1974) for example.

3.1 Demand and supply

Demand is the desire for goods or services. Implicit in this is the ability and willingness to pay a price, which is sometimes termed *effective demand* to distinguish it from desire not backed up by purchasing power. Every act of consumption entails a price of some kind, though not necessarily in money; picking an apple from a neighbour's tree involves effort (and risk of prosecution) and even the utilization of a supposedly free good like medical care under the National Health Service exacts a price in waiting time. The alternatives forgone in the consumption of a particular thing are the *opportunity cost*, e.g. monetary price if this is a correct measure of the sacrifice involved. The price a consumer is prepared to pay for something thus provides a possible measure of its worth, or *value*.

The relationship between demand and price is conventionally described by the *demand function* $Q=f(P)$, where Q is the quantity consumed, P is price and f means "some function of". The precise form of this relationship in any actual case is found from observation. As an example, suppose that the number of loaves of bread consumed over a given period of time at different prices was as shown by the *demand curve* in Figure 3.1, which could relate to a single customer or to the collective

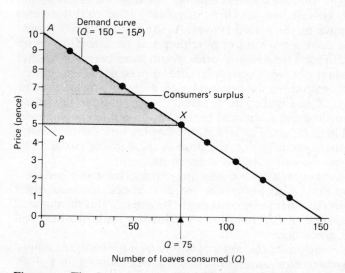

Figure 3.1 The demand curve, price, level of consumption and consumers' surplus.

consumption of a community. At zero price 150 loaves are consumed, this being the limit to eating capacity; at the other extreme of 10p, the price is just high enough to prevent the consumption of any bread. The "curve" is in this case a straight line because of the values chosen. The downward slope of the demand curve reflects the widespread tendency for people to consume more of a good or service when it is cheap than when it is expensive—the so-called *law of demand*. To find how much bread would actually be consumed in Figure 3.1, all that is needed is a specific price. Suppose that this is set at 5p, as the profit-maximizing price of a private monopoly capitalist or the "socially just" price arrived at by some central planner. The level of consumption would be 75 loaves.

Two important concepts relating to demand may now be introduced. The first is that of *utility*. This is something invented by economists to assist with the analysis of how people supposedly make choices in consumption and other spheres of human activity. Utility was originally conceived of as a measure of the subjective feeling of individual satisfaction, which might be capable of empirical identification. Now it is more commonly interpreted simply as that which individuals try to maximize. Thus in choosing to purchase 75 loaves in the case above, the consumer(s) would be viewed as revealing a specific preference, the fulfilment of which would maximize utility. To consume more, or less, would conflict with the preferences expressed in demand and thus reduce utility.

A second concept, which will be found useful in subsequent analyses, is that of the *consumers' surplus*. This can be explained by returning to Figure 3.1, and interpreting the prices as the maximum the consumer would be prepared to pay for that particular quantity of bread. For example, the consumer would pay a very high price for the first loaf, because the need or want for it is very intense; the most he or she would pay for each subsequent loaf (i.e. the "marginal valuation") decreases in the manner shown by the demand curve. As the price actually charged is 5p, consumers make some kind of psychic profit on consumption up to the seventy-fifth loaf, for a higher price would have been paid rather than going without the bread. These differences represent the consumers' surplus. Their magnitude in the case under consideration is the volume of the triangle APX in Figure 3.1. It can be interpreted as the utility derived from consumption additional to that accounted for by expenditure on the good in question. The size of this surplus varies with demand *elasticity*, or sensitivity to price (i.e. the slope of the demand curve). The larger the surplus, the better off the consumers.

Price is not the only consideration affecting demand for goods and their level of consumption. Also important are consumers' incomes, their tastes, and the price of other things that might be bought. But the demand curve can be regarded as incorporating all influences on how much will be purchased at given prices.

It is now time to introduce the concept of *supply*. This concerns ability or willingness to provide, or the quantity that will be produced for a given return. In a competitive, market-regulated economy, the usual assumption is that the quantity will increase as price increases. As price is to some extent an outcome of what consumers are willing to sacrifice for the product, level of output involves the interaction of supply and demand. The conventional analysis of a market is shown in Figure 3.2, where the baker *supply curve* is superimposed on the consumer demand curve from Figure 3.1. This reveals a point of intersection (X) where supply and demand correspond. At this *equilibrium* position 60 loaves are supplied and purchased, at a price of 6p each. Anywhere to the left of X there will be excess demand over quantity supplied, which will tend to push up price and thus increase supply; anywhere to the right there is excess supply, which will tend to reduce price and increase demand.

In neo-classical economic theory, markets working perfectly will automatically find the equilibrium price and quantity, automatically adjusting to changes in supply and demand. For example, a general drop in demand

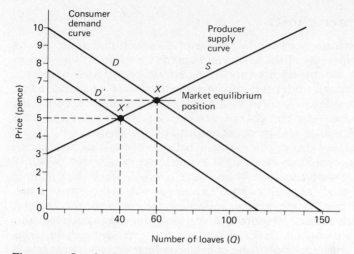

Figure 3.2 Supply, demand, and market equilibrium.

reflected in the new demand curve D' brings a new equilibrium at X' where 40 loaves are sold at 5p each. In practice, however, supply is often fixed by the producer, giving a horizontal supply "curve". For example the motor manufacturer in a capitalist economy may decide how many cars to produce next year without much recourse to direct expressions of consumer preference, relying on vigorous sales and advertising campaigns to stimulate demand or desire on the part of a public already predisposed to prefer cars to many other goods. As Mandel (1962, 375) puts it:

> It was not, after all, the "need to have a car" that created the motor industry; it was this industry that created the need to have a car. It is the investment of enormous amounts of capital in new sectors of industry (and, to a subsidiary extent, publicity for their products) that changes the taste of consumers, and not the changing taste of consumers that brings about the flow of enormous amounts of capital into certain sectors, or, even less, technical innovations.

The conventional view of supply and demand in the market is criticized by radical economists. Some see it as conflicting with Marxian theory of prices, in which the value of goods derives from human labour (see Chapter 4) without regard to the subjective utility perceptions of individual consumers. However, the two theories are compatible, at least to the extent of consumer desires influencing level of demand and output if not price (Johansen, 1963; Sherman, 1972). The more serious objection to the neo-classical view is that it takes the incomes and tastes of the consumer as given, instead of tracing them back into the economy and society. This problem will become more apparent as we broaden our view of consumption.

3.2 **Consumer choice**

Satisfying individual needs and wants involves selection among various possible combinations of the goods and services available. This has to be done within the constraints imposed by limited resources (i.e. income or goods for barter), under the influence of the prevailing social milieu of custom or fashion. Choice is also constrained and influenced by the production system—by the general process of resource allocation that determines the nature and prices of what might be chosen.

The neo-classical theory of consumer behaviour explains how an individual or household may be thought to maximize satisfaction or utility by selecting among alternative "bundles of goods". These can include such "social" goods as health and education as well as the more usual kind of "economic" commodities. Indeed, to be complete the analysis should implicitly include all sources of satisfaction among which the consumer makes a conscious choice. However, this excludes certain items of *unintended* consumption (to be considered later in this chapter) on which the individual may not be able to exercise choice, thus greatly limiting the usefulness of what follows as a general theory of consumption. The theory of consumer behaviour as set down here rests on the important ethical premise that the individual is the best judge of his or her own well-being—the assumption of *consumer sovereignty*. What is chosen necessarily maximizes utility.

The conventional analysis is shown in Figure 3.3. There are two goods X and Y, with respective unit prices of 2 and 5 ($\$$, £, etc). The consumer has 100 to spend; the *budget constraint* shows the combinations of commodities obtainable with this, e.g. $20Y$ and no X, $50X$ and no Y, and so on. The slope of the line is the ratio of the two prices. The tastes of the consumer are expressed in *indifference curves*, which show combinations of goods providing the same level of utility or staisfaction. Indifference curves are convex to the origin, because it is assumed that as

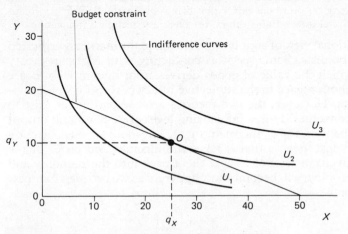

Figure 3.3 The conventional analysis of consumer choice.

the consumer gets more of one good he or she will be more willing to give up an additional unit in order to obtain more of the other; the slope of the curve measures the rate of substitution between the two goods. Moving away from the origin, each indifference curve indicates a higher level of satisfaction. The set of curves is the individual's "utility map" in "commodity space" (i.e. a diagram with goods or commodities along the axes), indicating how he or she would choose if given a choice. Utility is maximized where an indifference curve is tangent to the budget line, i.e. at O in Figure 3.3. This shows the optimum combination q_X, q_Y. Any move away from O along the budget line will take the consumer on to a lower level of utility; any move towards a higher curve will violate the budget constraint.

Generalizing to a case with any number of goods, the consumer has a personal *utility function*, which may be expressed:

$$U = U(q_1, q_2, \ldots, q_m)^1 \qquad [3.1]$$

This says that overall utility is some function of the utility derived from the various quantities of m goods. If we knew all that there is to know about the individual concerned, or if we observed his or her true preferences as revealed in consumption, then we could specify exactly what combination of things should be included for utility to be maximized. The solution is analogous to that in Figure 3.3, except that it is in m-dimensional commodity space. It identifies the position at which any substitution among goods will reduce utility.

The theory of consumer choice outlined here has serious shortcomings. The budget constraint and the preferences expressed in the indifference curves are strongly influenced by the society in which the individual lives. Income reflects position in the economic, social and political structure, and perhaps position in geographical space. It also depends on the prevailing mode of production and its arrangements for distributing rewards. Poor people may not be able to express demand effectively in the marketplace, thus limiting opportunity for satisfaction; some patterns of consumption are recognized as unattainable—they are *repressed preferences* (Eyles, 1971; Hodder and Lee, 1974, 54). The distinction is similar to that between consummation and desire; as Marx (1844; Tucker, 1972, 82) put it, "The difference between effective demand based on money and ineffective demand based on my need, my passion, my wish, etc., is the difference between *being* and *thinking*."

Consumer tastes are the subject of all manner of external influences, including advertising. The capacity to realize satisfaction from disposal of income, however large or small, is also restricted by limitations of knowledge that may constrain real freedom of choice. There is also the possibility of too much choice; Mishan (1967, 158) cites the case of the

---

[1] This is an undefined function which can be used to derive the formal conditions for utility maximization. As elsewhere in this and subsequent chapters, the notation follows general convention in economics. Thus instead of having f in the utility function we have U, and in the social welfare function (see below) it is W. Both U and W may be read as "is a function of" or simply "depends on".

man perfectly happy with the only shirt on the market but perpetually anxious about making the right choice when many types are available. Thus to judge the actual outcome of consumer choice as socially desirable, or even in the best interests of the individual, is far more difficult than the analysis above might suggest. As Hunt and Sherman (1972, 201) remind us, "the pattern of consumer demand is forced into a particular form by many things other than the actual pleasure or satisfaction derived directly from consumption of each commodity".

We are now in a position to see the fundamental objection to the neoclassical model of consumer market behaviour. The approach is essentially individualistic: "The individual is treated as the primary atom, and his wants or preferences as the ultimate data of the [welfare] problem; individuals being regarded as independent units with respect to the influences affecting demand" (Dobb, 1969, 5). Attention is thus diverted from the broader structure of the society and economy, which so influences and constrains "choice" that the term choice and its implication of freedom of action seems singularly inappropriate. It is plainly absurd to see what is "chosen" by the consumer in the modern capitalist–corporation state as necessarily maximizing individual satisfaction. While correctly identifying tastes, prices and the income constraint as the immediate determinants of consumption patterns, the model in Figure 3.3 tells us nothing about how these conditions originate. This takes us on to the broader question of how resources are allocated among alternative collective consumption possibilities.

3.3　Collective choice and resource allocation

If it were somehow possible to aggregate all real consumer preferences into a single function, we could apply this to the community income or resource constraint in an analysis of collective choice analogous to the simple model of individual consumer choice explained above. However unrealistic this may appear, it does allow us to approach the complex question of collective choice, i.e. how a community might maximize collective utility or welfare. It also enables us to introduce some production considerations vital to consumption, in a model that has broad applications in problems of resource allocation.

The basic analysis can be explained by an imaginary illustration. Suppose that a community (i.e. any group of individuals or households) has to allocate a fixed sum of £10M to the provision of two goods: health and education. What would be the optimum investment strategy? The first step is to determine what the resource constraint means in terms of the possible levels of health and education that can be attained. Given the most efficient ways of using the money in each sector, it would be possible to specify relationships between volume of inputs measured in monetary units (C) and the volume of outputs (Q) measured by some indicator of health or education level. In Figure 3.4a graphs depict imaginary expenditure–output relationships. These are specific versions of the need satisfaction curve introduced in the previous chapter (Figure 2.1).

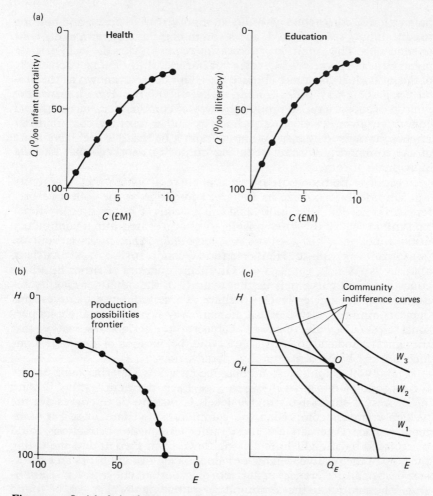

Figure 3.4 Social choice between two goods, illustrating the welfare-maximizing consumption levels.

Level of health is measured by infant mortality and education by illiteracy; the points from which the curves are plotted show rising levels of infant survival and literacy with successive increments of £1·0M of input. The curves represent *production functions* of the form $Q=f(C)$. The fact that these functions are non-linear indicates the condition of decreasing returns to scale; as relatively high levels of health or education are attained, a given increase in expenditure will have less output than at a lower level. At the extreme, a complete elimination of infant mortality or illiteracy would imply zero benefits from any further expenditure.

From these two production functions it is possible to find the various combinations of health and education outputs corresponding with different resource allocations. This is illustrated in Figure 3.4b. The ten points plotted correspond with allocations of £10M to health and nothing to education, £9M and £1M, and so on to nothing on health and £10M on education. The condition of decreasing returns makes the locus of these points concave to the origin, instead of linear as in the budget constraint of the individual consumer (Figure 3.3). This curve is known as the *production possibilities frontier* or *social production frontier*. Here it shows the limits to what society can produce by way of combinations of health and education, given its existing technology and a resource constraint. It implies that a fixed quantity of inputs cannot be made to yield any more of one commodity without reducing output of another—just like the individual's income.

In order to find the position on this curve at which the community will supposedly maximize its welfare, knowledge of the collective preferences is needed. Each individual will have his or her own utility function and in theory they are considered as aggregated into a community utility function. Thus a set of *community indifference curves* is built up (see Graaff, 1957, 48–52; Henderson and Quandt, 1958, 219–21; Mishan, 1964, 42–5; Winch, 1971, 51–5). Given any quantity of either health or education, each curve tells us the quantity of the other commodity required to attain a given level of welfare. These indifference curves thus depict community tastes, in just the same way as private ones depict personal tastes. They are, of course, subject to the serious reservation that they imply a societal consensus and avoid the question of how value conflicts are resolved—a matter considered below.

A family of community indifference curves is superimposed on the social production frontier in Figure 3.4c. Each of the curves W_1, W_2 and W_3 represent successively higher levels of welfare. The curves are the welfare contours comprising the community "welfare map" in commodity space. Alternatively, these rather unrealistic abstractions could be replaced by straight lines sloping down from the left and indicating the ratio of the relative weights or values of the two goods, as an expression of societal preferences in the form of a constant substitution relationship. The solution to the community's optimizing problem can be found in a manner analogous to that for the individual consumer. Welfare is maximized where the social production frontier just touches the highest indifference curve, i.e. at O in Figure 3.4c. Any shift from O will either reduce welfare or violate the resource constraint. At this position the imaginary community will set its expenditures at £6M on health and £4M on education. Its level of health will be Q_H (4·3 per cent infant mortality) and its level of education will be Q_E (5·0 per cent illiteracy). If there were m goods the nature of the solution would be the same, but in m-dimensional space instead of the two illustrated here.

In arriving at a particular allocation of investment and combination of goods, the form of the community indifference curves is obviously very important. Conventionally, they measure levels of welfare on an *ordinal* scale,[2] just as do individual indifference curves. The actual shape of the curves in a diagram like Figure 3.4, with cardinal output indicators along the axes, implies specific trade-off conditions. The rate at which improvements in health and education might be substituted is an ethical matter, in that it requires comparison between the value of saving the lives of infants and making people literate. Once the various combinations of goods on the social production frontier have been established, the particular welfare-maximizing combination is entirely a matter for value judgements. Whether the outcome is arrived at by the deliberate, conscious choice of the people, by a central planner or by some hidden hand depends on the nature of the society concerned.

The condition of community preferences is accommodated in welfare economics by postulating a *social welfare function* (SWF). Henderson and Quandt (1958, 217) provide the following definition:

> A social welfare function is an ordinal index of society's welfare and is a function of the utility levels of all individuals. It is not unique, and its form depends upon the value judgements of the person for whom it is a desirable welfare function. In certain cases it may be impossible to decide upon an acceptable form for the social welfare function by common consensus; it may then have to be imposed in dictatorial fashion. Whatever the case may be, its form depends on the value judgements of its promulgators.

Alternatively, it is a preference ranking placed by a society on a set of alternative situations (Bannock, Baxter and Rees, 1972, 379). There are various shorthand expressions for a social welfare function (Smith, 1975a). In the present context we are concerned with a *commodity* SWF which expresses welfare as some function of the total quantities (Q) of the various goods available (1, 2, ..., m), i.e.

$$W = W(Q_1, Q_2, ..., Q_m) \qquad [3.2]$$

The SWF is maximized by choosing the "best" combination of goods, subject to the resources available and prevailing production techniques or the constraint represented by the social production frontier. In the case described by Figure 3.4, the commodity SWF is:

$$W = W(Q_H, Q_E),$$

which is maximized subject to the individual health and education production functions and the total investment.

The analysis may now be extended into geographical space. Assume that the situation in Figure 3.4 refers to a community located at L and that there are numerous other communities one of which is L'. The richer the resource base and the higher the level of technology at any locality, the more health or education it will be able to produce. This might enable the social production frontier at L' to be pushed beyond its position in L. Similarly, local preferences can lead to a different set of commodity indifference curves. Suppose that we set the production frontiers and indifference curves of the two localities at a certain distance from each other,

---

[2] *Ordinal* measurability implies that only the direction or sign of a change in welfare can be ascertained. Thus alternative situations can be ranked and any ordered set of numbers can be given to them. *Cardinal* measurability is anything above ordinal, i.e. welfare measured on an interval or ratio scale. Economists prefer the assumption of ordinal preferences because this reduces the value judgements implied.

in a three-dimensional diagram with linear geographical space (distance) added to the two dimensions of commodity space (Figure 3.5). Given the constraints on production and the preferences expressed in the indifference curves, and assuming welfare optimizing behaviour, the communities are at O and O' respectively. Now consider the line Q_H to Q'_H. This joins the two points representing the output levels of health, and can be regarded as a gradient of spatial changes in health as measured by the chosen indicator. It increases from L to L' as infant mortality declines. Similarly $Q_E Q'_E$ in relation to the base line LL' is the education gradient, falling slightly from L to L' as illiteracy rises.

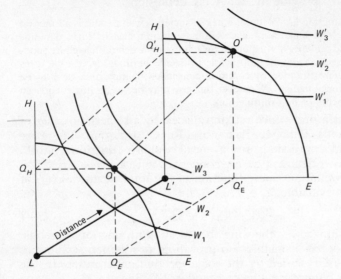

Figure 3.5 The community consumption levels of two goods at two locations, within a framework of local welfare maximization.

In a spatial extension of neo-classical theory, then, the local mix of goods and services through which people seek to satisfy needs and wants will be determined by the interplay of resources and technology on the one hand and values or preferences on the other. As these conditions vary geographically, so will the "what" in our who-gets-what-where formulation. Local efficiency in resource transformation is a technical problem, full discussion of which is reserved for the next chapter. The technology available for the production of any goods and services, from beer to health care, can vary from place to place. Adoption of optimal technology is in part a cultural matter. Among other things, this is related to how far a community is open to the spread of ideas, which in its turn can be a result of location in space relative to centres of technological innovation. Also relevant on the production side is the local resource endowment—traditionally the first consideration to a geographer. Preferences can vary spatially with differences in economic and social conditions. A rich community may have different tastes from a poor one because of different life style and the greater range of choice made possible by higher disposable income. The composition of the population will affect preferences: the services required to satisfy the needs of a retirement community are quite different from those for people at earlier stages in the life cycle. There are also important cultural predispositions influencing local tastes. There has been little systematic empirical research on the geography of tastes, a major exception being the work of Elliston-Allen (1968) in Britain.

3.4 Conflict and freedom in consumption

While the analysis in Figures 3.4 and 3.5 may appear credible with respect to deliberate community allocation of resources between two public services, it is much more difficult to see it as a model of collective choice in the marketplace. If there are reasons to question the concepts of the utility function and revealed preference as relevant to the explanation of what *individual* consumers actually get, then any aggregation of these artifacts will be no less fallacious. But the neo-classical analysis does help to raise important issues. Paramount among these are how the preferences that actually determine the allocation of scarce resources among alternative ends comes into play—whose real preferences they are, and whose interests are served by the outcome. In the usual competitive model community preferences will reflect "money votes" in the marketplace, so the existing distribution of income, however unequal, will have a major bearing on what is produced and the price at which it is sold. As Dobb (1969, 23–4) explains, "a given distribution of *money* income between persons or classes will have a different welfare-significance—will yield a different pattern of distribution of *real* income—for every different structure of relative prices". In short, the outcome will reflect the preferences of those with most money.

A major deficiency of the conventional analysis is the implication of community consensus implicit in the welfare contours and the SWF. In reality, there are likely to be conflicts between the preferences of different groups or classes within the same "community". This can be particularly important in public resource allocation, where the market (however imperfect) does not apply. Consider, for example, the case of a community comprising two distinct social classes (rich and poor), with collective resources to allocate to health care or armaments. The rich prefer most money to be spent on arms, as they profit from this and can buy health care privately. The poor prefer most money to be spent on health care (e.g. a community-built hospital) as they have no effective demand in the market for private medicine. The two class indifference curves and the social production frontier are drawn in Figure 3.6, to reveal two quite different preferred combinations (H_R, A_R and H_P, A_P). Will there be a compromise midway between the two, on some aggregate community welfare contour? In reality the answer is that the preferences of the rich will very likely be implemented, because they have the political power to impose this on the poor: an optimal solution for the one class but far

from optimal for those who may comprise the vast majority of the population.

Critiques of contemporary capitalism by both Marxist economists (e.g.
Mandel, 1962) and Galbraith (1975) argue that the production of weapons,
supersonic aeroplanes, consumer "durables" and the like serves the interests of the large corporations so that these activities continue to grow
while public services such as health and education are relatively
neglected. These macro-allocation decisions are far removed from textbook markets and preference functions. They arise from an economic
system in which what is produced is determined not so much by the independent decisions of consumers and the response of a multitude of
suppliers in competition to please the public as by the autonomous decisions of large producers—often in close association with government.
The objective is not so much the satisfaction of human needs as profit
and business growth. If there is a "sovereign" to be found, often it is
more plausibly the producer than the consumer.

The crux of this argument, and the case in Figure 3.6, is that consumption levels for some goods and services will not be those which many
people would have freely chosen. The combination of health care and
defence is determined by politics and power structure; what some consume is decided by the preferences of others. This can have an important
bearing on geographical variations in well-being. Although part of the
same community, the rich and poor above would probably occupy different territories, so if the local level of well-being is a function of how
far local preferences are met there is no doubt as to which territory's
people are better off. The general allocation of resources among alterna-

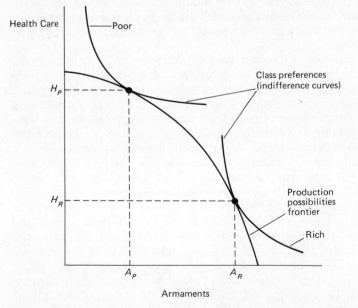

Figure 3.6 Conflicting preferences of two classes within a community.

tive goods and services thus has *spatial* distributional implications, for different people in different places will prefer different things—they have different commodity social welfare functions.

Local levels of well-being can also be affected by the consumption of various sources of *disutility*. Obvious examples are polluted air, the danger of crime or physical violence, dreary neighbourhoods and traffic jams on congested city streets. Exposure to the manifestation of various forms of social pathology or deviant behaviour also fall into this category of reluctant or unintended consumption. Few if any people would freely choose these experiences. They are simply part of the environment of particular places occupied by particular kinds of people, whose choice of residential location may be very limited. Traditional notions concerning consumer preference cannot be applied to these cases with any conviction.

The general condition of one person's well-being arising in part from that of others is covered by the concept of *externalities*. If the consumption of something by one person affects the utility of another, an external effect exists. Thus the smoker's consumption of cigarettes in a bus may harm the passenger with bronchitis or distress the non-smoker. In welfare theory these external effects were for a long time considered exceptions, but they are now becoming much more clearly recognized (e.g. Mishan, 1967). They can be accommodated in theory via the notion of *interdependent utilities*, which provides a reminder that we do not satisfy our needs and wants in isolation. We all affect and are affected by the behaviour of others; the closer we are to people in geographical space, the stronger these interdependencies are likely to be. How externalities are generated is examined fully in Chapter 4.

Consideration of spatial variations in consumption must thus include all the sources of satisfaction (positive and negative) that form part of the human life experience. To confine consumption to material goods is unduly restrictive. When sufficient empirical research into non-material consumption has been conducted, the patterns that emerge will doubtless show substantial territorial inequality at all spatial scales. Inequality in consumption is inherent in the way in which goods and bads are produced and distributed, as will be shown in Chapters 4 and 5. But it must be recognized that spatial variations in consumption also involve *diversity*, because different people in different places may be freely choosing different styles of living. The error is to assume that observed variations necessarily reflect local preferences.

3.5 Welfare in distribution

The neo-classical analysis of individual and collective "choice" offers an abstract view of how a society supposedly maximizes its welfare. Resources and technology constrain what can be produced, while a social welfare function (SWF) expressing collective preferences determines the combination of goods and services consumed. If this is one of the optimal combinations from a technical point of view (i.e. on the production possibilities frontier) it implies that the resources available, including the productive services of labour, have been optimally allocated among alternative uses. A perfect market or planner has thus been able to ensure that no increase in output of one good could be achieved without reducing output of another. Welfare maximization is achieved by virtue of the best possible use of resources, given societal preferences for alternative bundles of goods.

But this analysis involves a restricted conception of welfare, as some function of goods consumed in aggregate. It tells us nothing about distribution among members of society. The analysis of choice between two goods in Figure 3.4 shows the optimal combination of health and education levels with given techniques, resources and community preferences, but it does not reveal that individuals within the community may have different experiences. Some infants survive while others die; some become literate while others do not. As Dobb (1969, 253) puts it: "Some distribution-pattern, implicit or explicit, is crucial to aggregation, and aggregation is involved in any reference to collective *social* welfare." A full SWF specifies how much of everything each person gets—including premature death and literacy.

The tendency in economics to avoid explicit questions of distribution until quite recently stems from the ethical nature of interpersonal utility comparisons. Sidgwick recognized as early as 1883 that consideration of the ideal distribution of income "takes us beyond the limits of the properly separate Political Economy to the more comprehensive and difficult art of general politics ... we can no longer use the comparatively exact measurements of economic science, but only those vague and uncertain balancings of different quantities of happiness" (H. Sidgwick, *Principles of Political Economy*, 397, quoted in Myint, 1948, 128). Pigou (1920) divided welfare economics into its positive aspect dealing with production and remaining scientifically objective, and its distributional aspect which was inevitably political in the sense of involving value judgements. This distinction is well embedded in professional economics (Graaff, 1957, 90–91; Dobb, 1969, 83).

The conventional treatment of distribution in economics is closely tied up with the concept of optimality proposed by Pareto. A social or economic state is *Pareto optimal* if it is impossible to make any individual better off without at the same time making someone else worse off, i.e. each individual is at the highest possible utility level given the level of all others. The major drawback of this concept is that nothing is said about the *existing* distribution. If highly unequal to start with, this could become even more unequal if the rich became richer and the poor no poorer—yet this would be a welfare "improvement" by the Pareto criterion.

The achievement of Pareto optimality and the distribution issue relating to it can be demonstrated in a geometrical construction (Figure 3.7). Assume a community of two individuals or classes A and B, and an economy with two commodities X and Y. Let O_A be the origin of A's commodity space, with axes X_A and Y_A representing the total amount

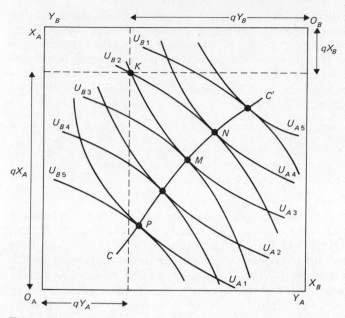

Figure 3.7 Pareto optimality in distribution between two individuals (or territories).

of the commodities available. Let the curves $U_{A_1}, \ldots, U_{A_5}$ be consumer A's indifference curves. Superimpose B's commodity space with origin O_B and axes of the same length as for A (X_B and Y_B) and indifference curves $U_{B_1}, \ldots, U_{B_5}$, in such a way that the axes form a box. Now any point in the box represents a possible combination of X and Y as divided between A and B. (The analysis can be related to what has gone before by assuming that the total quantities of X and Y are the optima found on the community's production possibilities frontier as in Figure 3.4.) Suppose that the distribution of X and Y is as indicated by point K, which gives qX_A and qY_A to A, and qX_B and qY_B to B. Would this be an optimum by the Pareto criterion? The answer is—no, because U_A and/or U_B can be increased without decreasing the other simply by commodity exchange. Moving to point N improves A's utility by taking her or him on to a higher indifference curve (U_{A_3} to U_{A_4}), while B remains on U_{B_2}. Moving to M takes B to a higher level while A is the same. Both moves improve *community* welfare by the Pareto criterion, through A consuming more Y and less X in exchange for B having more X and less Y. *Both M and N show Pareto-optimal distributions*, because it is impossible for further exchange to move one individual to a higher utility level without taking the other on to a lower level.

The problem of the welfare-maximizing distribution should now be apparent. M and N are but two of an infinite number of points of tangency of consumer indifference curves, all of which are Pareto optimal. The *contract curve C to C'* is a locus of such points. Moving from C towards C' increases A's utility at the expense of B and moving from C' to C does the reverse, because the implied transfer of X and Y from one individual to the other makes one better off and the other worse off. What point comprises the optimum? This problem would be simplified if the utility derived by A and B could be measured on some common scale. But interpersonal comparisons of utility involve saying how much satisfaction different people get from the same bundle of goods. Graaff (1957, 167) put the problem clearly:

> If two people disagree on the contributions which various levels of individual well-being make to social well-being, it is extraordinarily hard to think of some objective test which would settle the matter to the satisfaction of both. The question is therefore an ethical one. If, however, two people disagreed on the relative weights of two physical objects, it is extremely probable that they would abide by the verdict of a pair of scales. The question is therefore one of fact.

In Figure 3.7, even if A was very poor and B very rich (e.g. the position P on the contract curve), to say that society would be better off by a move in the direction of C' would be a value judgement. To take an illustration from Sen (1970, 99), how can we judge the consequences on the aggregate welfare of the Romans arising from Nero burning down the city while he fiddled? All reasonable people might agree that on balance community welfare deteriorated, but someone with a set of values placing sufficient weight on Nero's satisfaction (e.g. Nero himself) might find that his delight was great enough more than to compensate for the discomfort of the rest. This is the ethical dilemma that welfare economies finds so intractable.

The conventional solution is found in a "utility space" analysis. Figure 3.8a shows various combinations of utility represented by the contract curve in Figure 3.7, plotted within axes measuring the utility of the individuals (or groups) A and B on an ordinal scale. This locus is referred to as the *utility possibility curve*, or *welfare frontier*. It shows "welfare potential" (Graaff, 1957, 60) and the alternative ways in which utility can be shared, just as the production possibilities frontier shows potential output as different combinations of goods. As on the contract curve, any

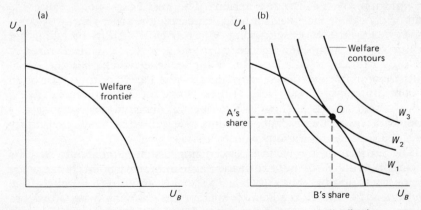

Figure 3.8 The welfare frontier in utility space, and optimality in distribution.

point on the welfare frontier is Pareto optimal; any move along it improves utility for one person, but only at the expense of the other. The frontier is a locus of *exchange optima*, where community welfare cannot be improved by exchange of goods among individuals, while any point inside the curve would be sub-optimal in this sense. Any point beyond the curve is unattainable without more commodities, and this is impossible if the existing collection is one of the *production optima* from the production possibilities frontier in commodity space (e.g. as in Figure 3.4).

Devising methods of analysing welfare maximization through the distribution of utility has occupied the ingenuity of generations of economists. An early approach was based on the consumers' surplus concept (see section 3.1), balancing gains and losses. This can still provide helpful insights, as will be shown in later chapters. A more favoured approach in recent decades has been based on the *compensation* principle, which holds that if a change takes place such that some people gain and others lose but gainers can compensate losers or bribe them into accepting the change, then welfare has increased. The theoretical ramifications of this have been debated at length (e.g. Graaff, 1957, 84–90; Mishan, 1964, 38–62; Mishan, 1969a, 38–66; Dobb, 1969, 86–118; Winch, 1971, 143–150). Its main inadequacy is practical rather than theoretical, however, for in the absence of a mechanism to ensure that compensation takes place it is irrelevant in practice. Even if applied, the outcome will probably favour the rich because they have most money to pay compensation, thus ensuring the pre-eminence of their preferences (Mishan, 1967, 93–4).

The way usually taken to circumvent these problems is to attribute to society a social welfare function explicitly incorporating distribution among individuals. This is usually written as:

$$W = W(U_1, U_2, \ldots, U_k) \qquad [3.3]$$

where there are k members (or groups) identified. A series of community welfare contours are assumed, just as in the commodity-space analysis (Figure 3.4). The optimal distribution is found at the point of tangency with the welfare frontier. In effect, this device ranks all points on the contract curve on the basis of social preferability (Henderson and Quandt, 1958, 218). The graphic analysis is presented in Figure 3.8b. As in the commodity-space analysis, the contours are indifference curves, but here they represent *distributions* providing the same level of community welfare instead of combinations of goods. Point O is the distribution maximizing welfare.

As in the earlier commodity-space analysis, the use of the SWF to generate welfare contours brings in societal values but without being specific. It merely tells us that society makes a choice, without saying what this depends on other than society's preferences. It avoids the issue of whose preferences are really expressed and how conflict is resolved. Specific discussion of the value basis of distribution is circumvented, at the expense of the tautology implicit in the assertion that society distributes its benefits as it chooses to distribute them. This conception of welfare maximization suffers from the same drawback as what Harvey (1973, 157) describes as the "rather unrevealing notion" of revealed preferences, "which simply allows that people behave in the way they behave". The analysis of welfare maximization in utility space also avoids saying anything about the mechanism by which society's preferred distribution is implemented. The only way of finding out how distributions are actually determined is to observe them revealed by society in action.

Our review of conventional welfare theory has now revealed four different optima:

1. *The Production Optimum*, constrained by existing resources and technology, where producing more of any good requires reallocation of inputs and hence producing less of another good. This is represented by points on the production possibilities frontier (PPF).
2. *The Exchange Optimum*, constrained by the volume of goods available, where further exchange of goods will make no one better off without making someone worse off. This is represented by points on the contract curve in Figure 3.7 or the welfare frontier in Figure 3.8.
3. *The General or "Top Level" Optimum*, building on 1 and 2, where greater output is impossible except at greater cost in resources and greater satisfaction for one individual is impossible except at the expense of another. This is the exchange optimum with goods optimally produced, i.e. the bundle of goods represented at the welfare frontier is a point on the PPF.
4. The *"Optimum Optimorum"*, or best of the best, which requires optimality in distribution as well as in production and exchange, and where the conditions of all the other optima are all satisfied. Here the optimum bundle of goods, optimally produced, is optimally distributed among the members of the community, as at point *O* in Figure 3.8.

The necessary and sufficient conditions for these optima are described more fully and formally elsewhere (e.g. Mishan, 1964, 17–20; 1969a, 29–32; Winch, 1971, 77–86). They all relate to just one point in time and space, of course, and for the further development of welfare theory space must be explicitly incorporated.

3.6 Distribution and welfare in geographical space

The focus now shifts from the utility space of the economist to the earth-surface space of the geographer. As in microeconomic theory for generations, welfare economics is implicitly devoid of geographical content, the unstated assumption being of a spaceless or one-point world. Yet without space the process of optimization is incomplete. The discussion that follows explores a few of the implications of adding geographical space to the analysis above. The presentation is mainly confined to what can be demonstrated graphically by extension of the models already introduced, and resembles that adopted in adding geographical space to commodity space in section 3.3.

In utility space, distribution among individuals is found from the superimposition of welfare contours on the frontier of welfare possibilities (Figure 3.8). Obviously, the contours can differ with locality as the values expressed in the SWF change. And the frontier can change with changes in resource endowment and transformation efficiency. Locational efficiency can also be a spatial variable, enabling more to be produced from given resources in some areas than in others.

Figure 3.9a shows three locations, L, L' and L'' on a linear distance axis DD. Each has its own welfare frontier in a utility space with two classes or individuals A and B along the axes. Each has its own optimal distribution of utility or well-being, as indicated by the points of tangency with the highest welfare contour (W, W' and W''). Lines are drawn joining the utility levels at the optimum ($U_A U'_A U''_A$ and $U_B U'_B U''_B$), just as in the health and education gradients in Figure 3.5. How are these to be interpreted, and what can be said about the general level of well-being at each locality's optimum optimorum (O, O' and O'')?

Now the problem of the measurement of utility becomes critical. With ordinal utility axes it cannot be determined whether U_A is better or worse than U'_A or U''_A. So the "gradients" along the space dimension mean nothing, unless cardinal measurement for inter-community comparison can be accepted. The same is true of the interpretation of the general

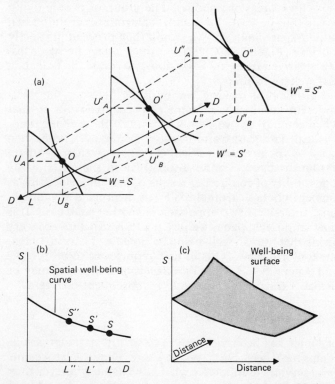

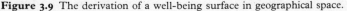

Figure 3.9 The derivation of a well-being surface in geographical space.

level of well-being at each locality. To say whether O is better or worse than O' or O'' requires a general cardinal indicator applicable to all places. If this can be derived, then a *spatial well-being curve* or gradient can be envisaged. This is suggested in Figure 3.9b, where the well-being levels of the three localities are shown on a continuous gradient of change over distance. The addition of a second distance dimension forms a *well-being surface* in space, with the height of the surface (S dimension) proportional to the level of well-being as measured by the uniform indicator. As was pointed out in Chapter 1, the term "welfare" is no longer appropriate to describe the level of collective societal satisfaction (however defined) at different localities, for the inter-locality distribution is part of the general welfare. Thus societal well-being (S) is substituted for welfare (W) in describing what varies spatially.

In conventional welfare analysis the problems of interpersonal utility comparison and the value judgements implicit in cardinal indicators are avoided by postulating a SWF and deriving welfare contours from it, as described in the previous section. *Inter-locality* comparisons could be treated in the same way, by an ordinal SWF relating to distribution among localities. This would take the form:

$$W = W(S_1, S_2, \ldots, S_n) \qquad [3.4]$$

in a system of n localities (areas or regions). The group of people living in a given place would thus be treated as a unit, analogous to the individual in conventional utility-space analysis. We would then proceed in exactly the same way as before (Figure 3.8), with localities along the two axes, and welfare contours derived from the SWF above to reveal the tangency point on the social welfare frontier.

The theoretical problem of making comparisons between the well-being levels of different localities is in some respects analogous to that which appears when comparing two points in time. If the welfare functions have only ordinal significance and if tastes change over time, then as Graaff (1957, 157–8) points out, we can do no more than compare the two years first on the basis of one's tastes then on the basis of the other's, with the possibility of conflicting results. Graaff describes this as one of the few instances where a cardinal SWF has theoretical advantages over an ordinal one. Inter-locality comparison is another such case. It is difficult to see how empirical spatial welfare analysis can proceed very far without requiring that human well-being be capable of cardinal measurement on some uniform scale. This in turn requires us to be specific about the local and general SWF. How local levels of well-being may be identified in practice is considered in detail in subsequent chapters.

3.7 Location and place utility

Thus far, the consumer has been viewed in a spatially static situation. Individuals or groups have been portrayed as expressing preferences for particular goods and services to influence what is available wherever they happen to live, or as largely passive recipients of conditions determined by the acts of others. But people can exercise some selectivity by choice of residence. Alternative locations can offer alternative combinations of goods and bads. The concept of *place utility* provides a convenient means for tying together the discussion of consumption in space.

Place utility, as defined by Wolpert (1965, 162) refers to "the net composite of utilities which are derived from the individual's integration at some point in space" and "may be expressed as a positive or negative quantity, expressing respectively the individual's satisfaction or dissatisfaction with respect to that place". Thus the place utility of any individual i at a place j can be written:

$$_j U^P_i = f(_j q_{i1}, \ldots, _i q_{im})$$
[3.5]

where U^P stands for *place* utility and f is used instead of U to distinguish this expression from that of the conventional utility function. The "goods" $(1, \ldots, m)$ include all sources of satisfaction, positive or negative. Not all people will share individual i's evaluation of location j because they may have different *personal* utility functions, so $_j U^P$ can vary between individuals.

The concept of place utility has been used in geographical research (Brown, 1968; Brown and Longbrake, 1969; Brown and Moore, 1970). A particular focus has been the interpretation of individual behaviour in the decision to migrate and to choose specific destinations. People as decision-makers are viewed as having a set of needs which express their requirements from any given location. This is in turn related to the individual's aspiration level and to the particular societal context in which the decision is being made. A comparison between needs felt and satisfaction derived from the existing place of residence can produce *stress*—the input from the environment into the individual behaviour system (Walmsley, 1973, 50) on the basis of which the person will decide whether to move or whether to attempt to adjust needs and aspirations to the existing situation. If a move is decided upon, then some judgements of the place utility likely to be derived from various alternative locations must be made. This will be based on both imperfect knowledge and uncertainty as to the outcome of any move. Thus choice of place of residence resembles most other consumption decisions: we are not fully informed of the range and quality of goods available and of the degree of satisfaction they may provide. The major difference is that once the location choice is made, a large number of other consumption decisions are also made by virtue of the social, economic and environmental conditions associated with place of residence.

Residental choice is thus tantamount to choice of a particular bundle of goods. It may be viewed as people "voting with their feet" for particular conditions (e.g. Margolis, 1968, 549–51), an idea put forward by Tiebout (1956) twenty years ago. Revealed *space preference* might therefore give a clue to what kind of places and consumption packages people really want. As Wolpert (1965, 162) puts it:

> The individual will tend to locate himself at a place whose characteristics possess or promise a relatively higher level of utility than in other places which are con-

spicuous to him. Thus, the flow of population reflects a subjective place-utility evaluation by individuals. Streams of migration may not be expected to be optimal because of incomplete knowledge and relocation lag but neither may we expect that individuals purposefully move in response to the prospect of lower expected utility.

The caveat is important, because to judge existing locational choices as optimal on the basis of revealed space preference is subject to the same dangers as judging the bundle of goods as optimal by virtue of revealed consumer preference. Among other things, it must be remembered that choice is always constrained. In selecting where to live, individuals may be constrained not only by limited knowledge and ability to choose well, but also by economic considerations (e.g. income) and perhaps even by cultural and political factors. The black ghetto resident in the American city may prefer to live on the other side of the railroad track, but both income and local custom may prevent this. *Apartheid* may prevent the black South African from living in the city; even if allowed in, his choice of residence is confined to his own "group area". To perceive high place utility is not the same as experiencing it: there are repressed preferences in residential choice as well as in choice of goods. Another relevant consideration is that utility derived from location in space may not be as important as social status in determining an individual's life chances: the black or poor may be predisposed to low levels of living wherever their place of residence.

How accurately do people actually perceive the place utility of different territories? People form *mental maps* of subjective geographical reality on the basis of their personal knowledge or ignorance (Gould and White, 1974) and these can be compared with the more objective reality of areal differentiation on the basis of possible sources of utility. Gould (1969) has compared perceptions of the residential desirability of American states with a social indicator derived by Wilson (1969) and incorporating data on a wide range of socio-economic conditions. The relationship was quite close (correlation coefficient $r = 0.78$; $r^2 = 0.61$, i.e. 61 per cent of the variance accounted for), showing that "the overall mental map of the group reflects the variation of relevant welfare measures to a high degree" (Gould, 1969, 39–41). Mental maps may provide accurate surrogates for *residential utility surfaces* (Adams, Abler and Gould, 1971, 519–24).

Research on actual migration behaviour (Cox, 1972, 56–76) suggests that factors related to economic opportunity comprise the single most important group of variables accounting for choice of destination. Evidence can be found in patterns of permanent movement and also in seasonal or short-term migration. Certain groups may seek a place in a particular cultural or ethnic environment in which they can easily become assimilated and feel "at home". The tendency of immigrants to Britain from the West Indies, India and Pakistan to congregate together is a case in point. Availability of housing is another important consideration. Economic status, life style and stage in life cycle are important determinants of the individual's favoured bundle of goods, and these preferences will be more easily satisfied in some places than in others. Thus the person about to retire will have a different mental map of place utility from the young married couple with a living to earn and children to educate.

Once made, choice of residential location may not be easily changed. Then, for many sources of need or want satisfaction, the individual is dependent on *accessibility* with respect to sources of supply. Some sources may be mobile, for example the baker and milkman in many parts of Britain and the itinerant trader or periodic market in many parts of the world. But for most people in most societies, acquisition of most goods involves movement to sources of supply. This is even more generally the case with respect to services such as health care, education, legal assistance and so on. Even when services are partially mobile, as with medical care and police protection for example, location has a bearing on level of service; the more isolated the locations the more costly they will be to serve, an extreme example being Australia's "flying doctor" service.

Recent years have seen a growing interest in spatial accessibility with respect to services. In Britain, it has been shown that even in the welfare state with supposedly free and equal access to certain social services, considerable geographical differentiation exists (Davis, 1968; Coates and Rawstron, 1971). Pahl (1970, 56–8) has stressed that when economic and social constraints on life chances are held constant there still remains "the distinctive constraints imposed by the distribution of jobs, schools, health facilities, shops, recreational facilities, and so on". Even such intangible aspects of life as fulfilling and affectionate relationships with other people are partly dependent on location in space (Axelrod, 1956; Moore and Brown, 1970). In stressing the importance of mobility for the quality of life, Hägerstrand (1974, 44) has stated: "Physical mobility is like income. It is an essential resource for the individual."

Accessibility as a source of "real income" was a major theme of the work of Harvey in the early 1970s (e.g. Harvey, 1971; 1973). He also stressed the other side of the coin—the sources of negative real income arising from *proximity* to sources of nuisance. Cox (1972, 301–4) has stressed the importance of people's receipts of "invisible income" in the city, dependent on accessibility to beneficial locations and proximity to non-beneficial or obnoxious locations. This is closely bound up with the generation of external effects to be discussed in Chapter 4.

Understanding the geographical patterns formed as people satisfy needs and wants is thus a complex matter. The well-being of human populations is not simply a question of deliberate consumption of goods and services, but also depends on exposure to the various intangible goods and bads which go with where people live. Individual well-being is dependent on other people—on what is contributed to the lives of others as well as on what is taken from others in the process of consumption. Thus population movement redistributes well-being spatially, as people seek a better life and bring with them their own potentialities or problems. Each place that loses a migrant loses a contributor to collective well-being, or a source of discomfort to others.

3.8 Conclusion: the utility of welfare theory

Where has this exploration of neo-classical welfare theory and its spatial extensions taken us, in our search for guidance in the analysis of who gets what where and how? The conventional perspective on consumption has certainly not provided the key to understanding that its prominence in economics might have led us to expect. This is because, in certain critical respects, it does not accord with the reality of how economic life is actually organized. A particular weakness is the stress on individual preferences as the origin of collective consumption patterns. Donnison (1975, 423) has summarized the defects of this in a policy context as follows:

> To rely wholly on evidence about short-run individual preferences as the criterion for collective action is *unhistorical*, because it takes too little account of the way in which preferences are shaped (and could be reshaped) by influences extending over long periods of time. It is *unsociological* because it treats people as atomistic individuals, deciding only for themselves, rather than as members of classes, families and other groups which support and constrain them (and could influence them in different ways if the social structure changed). And it is, intellectually speaking, *unurban*, because it regards each choice as independent of every other and pays too little attention to the spatial and other links between the different sectors of an urban economy – its markets for labour, housing and education, and its power structure and value systems – links which together make it difficult to change one sector unless consistent adjustments occur in many other sectors.

When transferred into a specifically spatial context, the assumption of individual free choice can lead to erroneous interpretations. The notion that, as people arrange themselves in space, they are revealing real preferences – maximizing place utility – ignores the constraints on where people can actually choose to live. These are not imposed so much by ignorance or inaccurate place perceptions as by the way society is organized, which in turn depends very much on how the economy works. Research on residential patterns viewed as the outcome of revealed space preference thus fails to provide a full explanation. As Gray (1975, 234) puts it, "By assuming and providing support for the belief that people are free to prefer and choose from a range of options and that individuals and families control their own life chances, urban geographers have, by default, accepted, aided and supported the existing structure of society and hindered a true understanding of reality." We miss the origin of the constraints on choice, and thus help to preserve them. Recent research in Britain stresses that "in the situation of unequal distribution of wealth, prestige, and power, the study of constraints and allocation, rather than preferences and demand, provide the more realistic viewpoint from which to understand housing situations and housing markets" (Duncan, 1976, 10). Contemporary interpretatations are emphasizing the role of institutions such as city housing departments (Gray, 1976) and building societies (Boddy, 1976), operating as an integral part of the broader societal and economic structure.

The point is not that individual preferences and the concept of utility are irrelevant in understanding human society, as some dogmatic Marxists appear to believe. Marx (1867, 48) himself recognized that "nothing can have value, without being an object of utility", i.e. having the capacity to satisfy an individual need or want. He did not deny the operation of demand and utility to consumers in the formation of prices and output levels (Sherman, 1972, 353). The basic objection to neo-classical theory is that it takes as given the major determinants of consumption, failing to ask how preferences are formed, constrained and implemented.

What, then, is achieved by going through the conventional analysis? First, we have been able to expose some of the weakness of a body of knowledge that is still extremely influential. We have learned some of its limited explanatory power, and of its ideological basis. But it has also contributed something more positive. We have discovered that welfare maximization depends on optimality with respect to three distinct conditions, all of which are interrelated in the real economic world: production technique, combination of goods and services produced, and distribution among the population – individuals, groups and areas. We also know that welfare maximization depends on both the purely *technical* relationships of how to get the most output from given resources and the *social* relationships behind the preferences that are actually implemented. But what is perhaps most important, we have found in the formal models of neo-classical theory a number of concepts and techniques that can prove helpful to the analysis of spatial welfare problems and the planning of change. These include market equilibrium, consumers' surplus, the social welfare function, and the graphic analysis of allocation/distribution problems. They figure prominently in some subsequent chapters.

Finally, it must be emphasized that, however abstract the analysis in this chapter may have appeared, it is directly related to the framework set up in Chapter 1 and summarized in the welfare data matrix (Figure 1.1). Each of the three versions of the social welfare function featured above correspond with one dimension of the matrix. Expression [3.2] depicts society's welfare as some function of the goods (and bads) available, thus addressing the "what" question; expression [3.3] shows welfare as a function of distribution among groups—the "who" question; expression [3.4] incorporates the "where" question of territorial distribution. We thus have a formal connection between established welfare theory and our who-gets-what-where theme. Only the "how" question has eluded us. For further guidance on how things actually happen we must now look beyond conventional welfare theory, with its focus on consumption. We must look to the process of production, which holds the key to spatial organization and to the spatial differentiation of human life chances.

4

The Production Process:
The Creation of Value

Sources of human need or want satisfaction have their origin in a process
of production. Just as consumption must be viewed in the broadest possible sense, to include all things from which satisfaction or dissatisfaction
is derived, so the concept of production must be broad enough to cover
the creation of all goods and bads. Thus a geographical view of production
truly relevant to the human life experience must incorporate the creation
of environmental quality, personal safety and security, health and sick-
ness, education and ignorance—indeed everything that contributes to the
spatial differentiation of human life chances. To do this is far more difficult than adopting the more conventional view of production in economic
geography. But to do otherwise is to make the implicit assumption that
material things are all that matter.

4.1 The origin of value

People acquire goods and services in order to satisfy needs and wants.
By being prepared to make a sacrifice for them, in money, time, alternative production possibilities or any other terms, we are implicitly assign-
ing a value. Things thus have value (are "valuable") to us by virtue both
of the satisfaction we gain and of the price we pay.

This commonsense observation is the basis for an important distinction
between two concepts of value. The first is *use value*, which relates to
the utility or satisfaction derived from the object in question. The second
is *exchange value*, which relates to what has to be sacrificed or exchanged,
e.g. the money price required in a market or set by the central planner.
Utility and price may not be the same, as was explained in the discussion
of demand in section 3.1. If use value exceeds exchange value a net gain
accrues to the consumer(s); the aggregate of these value gains with respect
to any good is the consumers' surplus introduced in the previous chapter.

The process of production is concerned with the creation of value.
Whatever the type of society, certain basic features of the production
process prevail. There are three necessary ingredients: human labour,
the subject of labour (i.e. materials) and the instruments of labour (tools,
machines and so on). Only the most primitive forms of economic activity,
such as food gathering, rely on nothing but labour and nature; as soon
as men began to hunt and till the earth they had to fashion instruments
of some kind from the resources of the natural environment. Once the

imperative of keeping alive has been met labour can be devoted to various other forms of activity, from developing better machines, through the production of various goods for personal consumption or exchange, to creative artistic endeavour to satisfy aesthetic needs.

How things of value are actually created can be illustrated by tracing a simplified version of the process of producing shirts, from the cotton-field to the consumer (Figure 4.1). We start with the natural endowment of the soil, the sun and the rain—the conditions that enable seeds to grow

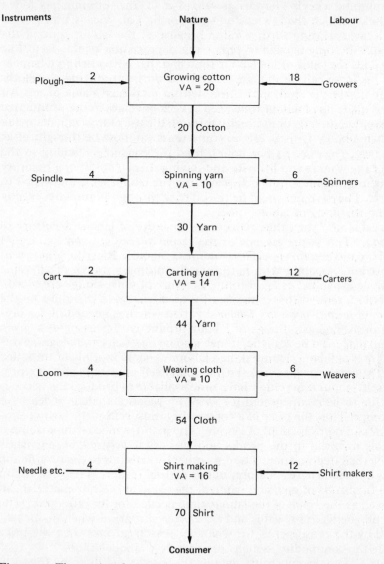

Figure 4.1 The creation of value in a shirt. Note: VA = value added, the numbers representing labour time in hours required to produce a given quantity of shirts.

into cotton. Cultivation requires a plough, which a man can make from the wood that nature provides. Cultivation also requires labour. Suppose that the production of a certain quantity of cotton takes eighteen hours of labour, and that to make whatever part of the plough is used up or depreciated in the process takes two hours. The value of the cotton produced is $18 + 2 = 20$, in units of labour time. Now, the cotton is spun into yarn on the farm where it is produced. This takes a further six hours of labour, to which must be added, say, four hours' worth of depreciation of the spinning wheel. The yarn is valued at 30; the spinning has added 10 to the 20 which the raw cotton was worth. The yarn is transported to the weaver, adding further value because of the labour time of the carter and the time needed to repair the depreciation of the cart. The weaver adds the value of his labour time and that embodied in whatever part of his loom can be thought of as used up in producing the cloth. His wife makes the cloth into shirts, with a total final value of 70. All this 70 is made up of labour time used at various stages in the productive process, either directly or indirectly through the use of instruments made by human labour. If these labour–time units can now be thought of as money (say, £70; i.e. £1 per hour), then the consumer coming to the house of the weaver and his wife and paying them £70 for the quantity of shirts in question is fully compensating the labour time embodied in the shirts. The payment could be traced back through Figure 4.1, exactly reversing the flows of labour time.

The value of a shirt thus reflects the quantity of labour necessary to produce it. This is the essence of the *labour theory of value* associated with Marx and certain classical economists, notably Ricardo, which sees human labour together with nature as the ultimate source of all value and labour expended as an absolute measure of what things are worth. Marx (1867) refined this somewhat by specifying that it should be the quantity of *socially necessary labour*, i.e. that which is needed under prevailing or average conditions of labour productivity existing at a given time and place. To be realistic, it may also be necessary to recognize different types of labour, taking skilled labour as some mutiple of unskilled labour (Mandel, 1973, 19–20). To maintain itself physically and to reproduce itself, labour must either have time available to produce the necessities of life or be compensated for work by wages sufficient at least for subsistence. Thus the price of a commodity must reflect the cost of production (and reproduction) of labour. The maintenance of the machines and tools involved in the production process is assured by payments covering their depreciation. The only other contributor to the production process described here is nature, but as natural resources become useful only in the hands of men and women, the value of the raw material can be viewed as the value of the labour time needed for its extraction. The distinction between use value and exchange value arises when the benefit derived by the consumer is, for whatever reason, greater than the price paid for the commodity, which should reflect labour inputs.

The major alternative to the labour theory of value is to be found in conventional neo-classical theory, which sees the productive factors of capital, land and enterprise, as well as labour, contributing to the creation of value, and thus earning a return in accordance with their *marginal productivity* (see Chapter 5). The question of reward for services rendered makes a critical difference between the distributional implications of the two theories; indeed, value theory pervades the whole of the who-gets-what-where question. This is why the process of production—how it takes place in reality and how it is viewed in theory—is vital to the understanding of inequality.

The main objection to the labour theory of value is that it neglects scarcity of natural resources (von Mises, 1935, 82–3; Desai, 1974, 42; Samuelson, 1973, 739–40). Scarcity can be reflected in a variable labour-time cost, for as easily accessible resources or highly fertile land is used up more labour will be needed to achieve a given increment of production. A particularly fertile area can yield a surplus product, over and above what the same labour input can produce elsewhere; this surplus is reflected in *rent*, or a kind of value bonus that might go to those who work this land. Similarly, if one crop needs twice as much (scarce) land as another, with the same labour inputs, the former may attract a higher market price than the latter; to shift production to the first (land-intensive) crop involves a greater opportunity cost in terms of sacrified output of the other crop than a shift to the second (higher-yielding) crop. The more people want of things that use scarce resources, the more this scarcity is likely to matter in the comparative market valuation of goods and of resources. Where does this scarcity value originate? The answer is in nature, as used by man. Nature cannot be paid, but if scarce resources have owners they can be viewed as contributing to the creation of value by virtue of sacrificing some of their property. "Land has no value . . . Only where private appropriation of land has transformed it into monopoly property does land acquire a *price*" (Mandel, 1962, 283). A similar argument applies to machines or capital equipment: if these have private owners they can command a monetary return, which may bear little relationship to the labour time embodied in them or required to cover depreciation. Neo-classical theory accounts for value in terms of the contribution of privately owned factors of production.

The particular arrangement for paying those viewed as contributing to the production process is basic to who gets what where. It originates in a *mode of production*, or how the creation of goods and services is organized in a broad societal context. The *physical* process of producing things from materials and labour is similar whatever the mode of production, for this is purely a technical matter. The *value* process of production concerns buying and selling—the introduction of exchange values as opposed to use values—and thus implies social relationships (Desai, 1974, 24, 30). The distinction between the labour theory of value and that of the marginalist or neo-classical school is that "whereas Marx and the classical economists start from the social character of the act of exchange, and regard exchange value as an *objective* link between owners (producers) of different commodities, the marginalists start from the *individual* character of needs, and regard exchange value as a *subjective* link between the individual and the thing" (Mandel, 1962, 714). What private owners of productive factors earn is thus traced back to consumer preferences instead of to the structure of society.

This echoes our critique of the conventional approach to consumption, in the previous chapter. But again, it is important to stress that the subjectivist view based on marginal utilities is not inconsistent with the labour theory of value, as Johansen (1963) and Sherman (1972) have argued. The individual evaluations on which demand is based have a bearing on real world prices, which can fluctuate quite independently of the quantity of labour embodied in commodities. Marx (1867, 76) recognized the two constituents of a commodity: "So far as it is a value in use, there is nothing mysterious about it, whether we consider it from the point of view that by its properties it is capable of satisfying human wants, or from the point that those properties are the product of human labour." What Marxian analysis stresses is that effective demand is less an outcome of human needs than of income distribution, with its origin in the mode of production. This is a macro view, stressing the position of social classes, instead of the micro individualistic view of the neo-classical model.

The major contribution of Marxian theory is to place the productive process and the exchanges that go with it in a broad framework recognizing the relationships between people, instead of seeing it as something mechanical. The capitalist mode of production is one way in which societies organize the creation of sources of need or want satisfaction, which enables private owners of resources to realize a return on their use by virtue of rights vested in property. A socialist system ensures (in theory) that whatever value arises from the use of scarce resources, including labour, accrues to the community at large. Again, the discussion

Table 4.1 The creation of value in shirt-making, in an input–output framework

Inputs \ Outputs	Consuming sectors					Final consumption
	Gr	Sp	Ca	We	Sh	
Producing sectors						
Growers		20				
Spinners			30			
Carters				44		
Weavers					54	
Shirtmakers						70
Value added	20	10	14	10	16	70
Labour	18	6	12	6	12	54
Machinemakers	2	4	2	4	4	16
Total value	20	30	44	54	70	

Note: Value is measured in socially necessary labour time, money, or any other common units.

has reached distributional issues (see Chapter 5), a further reminder of the difficulty of separating production and distribution.

4.2 Production and income

The process of production generates *income*. Although by no means all sources of human satisfaction can be reduced to monetary terms, money acts as an important store of value or purchasing power. The relationship between income and value can be explained by returning to the process of shirt production introduced above. Imagine that each stage represents a different *sector* in the economy. Thus cotton is produced by the Growers sector, it is spun by the Spinners, and so on. The flow of material through the various sectors can be depicted in a simple matrix (Table 4.1), with producing sectors along the vertical axis and receiving sectors (the same ones) along the horizontal axis. A producing sector supplies *inputs* to a receiving sector, where they are processed and sent as *outputs* to another sector. Thus the Growers supply 20 worth (e.g. labour time measured in money units) of cotton to the Spinners, who supply 30 worth of yarn to the Carters, who ship it to the Weavers, and so on. The *value added* at each stage in the process is the difference between value of inputs and value of outputs. For each sector, value added is listed (data from Figure 4.1). Thus Growers start with no inputs except from nature and add 20 worth of value, the Spinners add 10, and so on until the Shirtmakers add their 16. Part of the value added is attributed to the machines (labour-time equivalent of depreciation); in fact, Machinemakers can be recognized as a further sector, contributing inputs to each other sector. Taking the machine costs from value added leaves the wages of labour, as the income of the sector in question. *Total* income generated, including that of Machinemakers, is 70 (e.g. £). Note that summing the total value items for each sector would involve multiple counting of value transfers among sectors, hence the blank bottom-right cell in the table.

This *input–output table* describes the linkages among the various contributors to the production process. If further sectors were added and flows between other sectors included (e.g. services of Carters to Growers) it would begin to resemble a real-world economic system. The input–output model can be expanded to accommodate exchange with other places (nations, regions or cities) simply by including imports and exports. Imports are inputs from another place; exports are outputs sent to another place. The general form of an *interlocality* input–output model is shown in Figure 4.2, where sources of imports and destinations of exports are portrayed as specific sectors $(1, 2, \ldots, i, \ldots, m)$ at specific localities $(2, \ldots, j, \ldots, n)$ outside the place (1) featured in the main part of the table. The general input–output model is a very helpful device in understanding various aspects of the production process connected with the creation of value and income. It will reappear at the end of Chapter 7.

If the value-added items in Table 4.1 are summed, they give the total

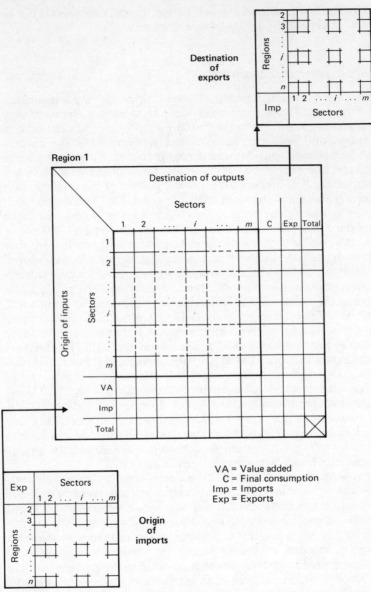

Figure 4.2 A general interlocality input–output model describing linkages and flows among sectors in the process of production.

value added in our simplified economy where every activity is geared to shirtmaking. This is *gross product* or income (Y), and may be written:

$$Y = GP = L + M \qquad [4.1]$$

where L is the direct labour cost and M is the cost attributable to depreciation of machines. Depending on what territory is being considered, this could be gross national product (GNP) or regional, city or neighbour-hood product. Taking away depreciation gives the *net product* (*NP*), or territory income (*Y*) other than for Machinemakers:

$$NP = Y - M = L \qquad [4.2]$$

Gross product may also be defined on the consumption or *final demand* side. This is:

$$GP = C + I \qquad [4.3]$$

where *C* is consumer spending and *I* is investment. In Table 4.1, *GP* = 70 as shirts are the only final demand product. This is, of course, the same as total value added, or *GP* in [4.1] above. There is no investment in this simple case, but if the Machinemakers had produced some new machines this could have been allocated to *I* under final demand, with an equivalent value-added item attributed to labour in accordance with the work involved (this could go in a Machinemakers column, as inputs from the labour "sector").

To open the economy up in a spatial sense requires the incorporation of income from other nations, regions, cities or neighbourhoods as payment for exports, and expenditures on goods and services purchased from outside. The relationship between these two is the *balance of payments* of the territory in question, showing whether it is a net importer or exporter of value in a monetary sense. There are various other compli-cating factors in income accounting described fully in most economics texts (e.g. Samuelson, 1973, Ch. 10; Hunt and Sherman, 1972, Ch. 23; Richardson, 1969a, Ch. 9), but these need not concern us here.

Thus far in this section, nothing has been assumed about the social organization of production except that there is some common unit of value enabling prices to be set and exchange to take place. The general input–output accounting framework is equally applicable in a capitalist or socialist system. Indeed, Marx anticipated the full development of this approach by almost a century (Medio, 1972, 331; Samuelson, 1973, 864–5; Desai, 1974). In Marxian terms, the value of output (*Y*) of any economy or sector is as in [4.1] above, where *M* is *constant capital* in the form of the "dead labour" embodied in the machines or materials from an earlier stage in the productive process and *L* is the value added by labour—further subdivided into the *variable capital* representing payments for labour–power (i.e. the commodity sold by labour) and the *surplus value* which the employer can appropriate under a capitalist sys-tem (see Chapter 5). In a socialist economy (national) income is viewed as originating from employment and labour productivity on the one hand and from stored-up labour or the stocks of means of production and their increase on the other (e.g. Brus and Laski, 1965). The capitalist view, as embodied in neo-classical economics, subdivides *L* (i.e. value added less depreciation) into wages, rent, interest and profits; the social organ-ization of production under capitalism provides owners of land, capital and "enterprise" with payments for the apparent contribution of these factors.

Now, let us turn to the *performance* of an economy. In considering value created as income or gross product, we are accustomed to viewing high figures or rapid increases with approval. Apart from the problem that high average incomes and rapid growth of GNP are not necessarily direct measures of well-being, there are certain technical deficiencies embedded in conventional accounting that further reduce the usefulness of these data. In particular they ignore the fact that certain expenditures are decidedly not subject to the normative interpretation that the higher they go the better off people are. For example, higher outlays on fighting crime show up as higher total police incomes and hence as value added in national or local accounts, yet we would be better off if we could spend less on police. The same goes for defence. Disutilities such as air pollution and urban congestion do not enter the accounts but should really be subtracted in some way from value added. In addition, there are certain sources of positive utility not included in value added, examples being leisure and the contribution of the housewife—perhaps the most undervalued of all workers.

Nordhaus and Tobin (1972) have attempted to address this problem by changes in the conventional accounting system. They reclassify certain expenditures, such as the cost of travelling to work and some government outlays (e.g. police and defence) so as to deduct "intermediates" and "regrettables" from net product. They impute values for leisure and certain non-market activities such as housework, so as to add these to net product. And they make deductions for disamenities of urbanization. As a result, they are able to calculate an alternative to GNP, a "primitive and experimental" measure of Economic Welfare (MEW). Samuelson (1973, 3–5, 195–7) renames this Net Economic Welfare (NEW).

Comparing NEW with GNP suggests a slower rate of progress than that indicated by conventional accounting. In the United States the present level of NEW indexed to a 1929 value of 100 is roughly 160, compared to about 240 for GNP (Samuelson, 1973, 4, Fig. 1.1). The same impression is given by an attempt to calculate NEW in Australia (Gillin, 1974): the average annual growth rate of NEW from 1948–9 to 1972–1973 is estimated at 1·6 per cent compared with 2·5 per cent for Gross Domestic Product. Whether human well-being is really improving and, if so, at what rate, depends very much on how we view the process of production—on our accounting of the creation of value.

The process of production may now be summarized in a simple diagram (Figure 4.3). This relates production back to consumption and raises the major issues to be considered in the remainder of this chapter. The process begins with human needs and wants—with their origin in the biological imperatives of the human condition and in the societal tastes and preferences reflecting culture. Demand or desire is (ideally) expressed and transmitted to the producers via market mechanisms or a planner, though we must also recognize the possibility of production decisions made with little regard to actual consumer wishes (see Chapter 3). Labour and natural resources are called into play, either in a direct form or as capital (machines and goods). Transformation takes place as

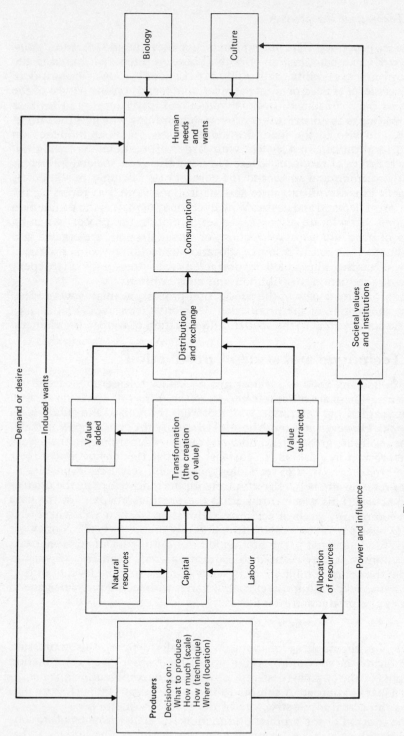

Figure 4·3 A simplified view of the production process.

inputs are processed. The output can be goods (value added), bads (*value subtracted*), or a combination of both. These are then distributed to the final consumers as utility or disutility experienced through consumption. The local level of need or want satisfaction depends on the nature of the goods or bads consumed. Societal values and institutions are shown as contributing to the distribution process determining who gets the output where, and also to the identification of wants via their influence on the cultural milieu. In a system with large corporations exercising not only a measure of producer sovereignty but also great societal influence, or with consumption subject to the control of a planning bureaucracy, producer interests affect values and institutions as well as reversing the direction of demand and desire. Whatever the system, it is the production decisions that allocate resources, to set in motion the process whereby means of need and want satisfaction (or dissatisfaction) are created and distributed. The role of resource allocation in deciding what is produced and who gets the value added or subtracted again stresses the interdependence of production, distribution and consumption.

With this broad view of the production process, we may now proceed to an examination of the production decisions themselves (Figure 4.3), as basic contributors to the spatial differentiation of human life chances.

4.3 Technique and scale of production

To produce any good or service, it is necessary to assemble certain ingredients. These are often referred to as the *factors of production*: land, labour, capital and enterprise, with materials recognized as a subdivision of capital. However, it is more helpful to specify the actual *inputs* needed, for they will vary greatly in number and quantity depending on the nature of the product in question. In socialist societies it is customary to refer to the *productive forces* of technology, skills and resources available.

The relationship between output and inputs is described by the *production function*. This was introduced in the previous chapter, in the case of the community levels of health and education (section 3.3), where output (Q) was portrayed as some function of expenditure (C). Money (or labour time) devoted to the production of health, education, steel, beer, or anything else may be used to acquire different quantities of various inputs; the actual combination chosen will determine the level of output from a given expenditure, as efficiency varies with technique. The general form of the production function is

$$Q = f(X_1, X_2, \ldots, X_n) \qquad [4.4]$$

where X is the quantity of input. When fully defined, this expression can indicate the maximum output attainable from a given combination of inputs or the optimal (cost-minimizing) input combination given a required level of output. A column in the input–output table (Figure 4.2) shows the actual input structure of the sector in question.

The concept of the production function is usually thought of in connection with primary or secondary economic activity. The statement that to produce one ton of pig iron requires a certain combination of iron ore, coal, limestone and labour is an obvious example found in many geography textbooks. However, in theory the technical process of producing any good or service can be described in the same way and attempts have been made at empirical identification of public service production functions (e.g. Hirsch, 1968, 485–92). Drewnowski (1970, 29; 1974, 98–9) refers to "welfare generation functions" in his framework for measuring and planning the quality of life; there are similar suggestions in the literature on social indicators (Smith, 1973a, 75–7). The problem here is that the local level of health or education, for example, can be influenced by major exogenous variables beyond the control of the producers of education or health care. Thus local conditions of housing or family life may operate as constaints on the efficiency of education and health services; to see their output as a purely technical matter risks overlooking the broader societal structure in which they operate.

Nevertheless, it is often helpful to view the creation of social goods (and bads) as the outcome of a production process that might be identified empirically by a production function. For example, studies of variations in educational attainment (see Chapter 7) have consistently identified home background as a more important "input" than certain qualitative characteristics of schools. Other evidence suggests that curvilinear or stepped social production functions may exist; for example better housing may improve health up to a critical threshold of adequate physical protection and sanitation, beyond which further health benefits are slight.

Some of the implications of production techniques and input combination may now be examined by returning to the health and education problem in Chapter 3. If the production possibilities frontier in Figure 3.4 represents combinations of health and education *given the most efficient technology*, then a community might well occupy an actual position inside the frontier by virtue of some production inefficiencies. For example, poorly organized hospitals or schools using sub-optimal input combinations may reduce output levels. If we add local social conditions, such as slums which reduce the effectiveness of health care and education, we may identify a *locally feasible production possibilities frontier* inside the general PPF. It describes the fact that what can be achieved in a particular locality may be less than under optimal conditions. Thus society's actual position represents lower levels of health and education outputs than would be possible with better local techniques and no slums to contend with.

This analysis recognizes that in some places the effort needed to achieve a given level of output will be greater than in others. Similarly, a given technology or combination of inputs will be able to generate more output or value in some places than others. The point has been made in the context of health and education but it is even more obvious in other forms of production; some minerals are harder to extract than others and some soil harder to till, hence spatial variation in the productivity of mining and agriculture. In addition, there is the fact that some inputs will cost more in some places than others. Thus to build the same hospital or school at different locations may involve different expenditures of money, labour time, or whatever the common unit of value sacrificed may be. Other things remaining the same, the local cost will change the position of the production possibilities frontier. And insofar as the combination of inputs chosen varies with their relative costs, production technique will vary from place to place.

These observations underline the inseparability of output (scale), technique and location. This has been recognized in the study of industrial location (Smith, 1971, 231) and readily applies to all aspects of production. At any place there will be an optimal combination of inputs to achieve a given output of benefits; the combination of inputs can vary with the level of benefits required. Thus to halve infant mortality in a poor rural area may merely require the labour-intensive provision of basic antenatal care, whereas the same impact in a city may require major capital investment in new hospitals. Further improvements in both places may depend more on advanced equipment and specialists than on paramedical personnel. Achieving a given result most efficiently calls for a particular technique. Once chosen, the technique will constrain what can be achieved with given resources.

For many goods and services the scale of production or level of output in a particular locality is an outcome of supply and demand conditions in a market. Even in a socialist economy there is likely to be a market for consumer goods, with perhaps only 10–15 per cent collective consumption (Nove and Nuti, 1972, 9). Indeed, in a socialist economy, free from the producer pressures of a capitalist society, "there may be less reason to doubt consumers' ability to choose reasonably for themselves" (Dobb, 1969, 214). A socialist society may be a necessary condition for true consumer sovereignty, making what is produced responsive to real human need. In any event, the conventional analysis of market equilibrium outlined in section 3.1 is relevant to the determination of volume of output in a wide range of actual cases.

But there are many situations in which markets are less effective or quite unsuitable. This is recognized under capitalism as well as socialism. The conventional rationale for not using market mechanisms in capitalist and some mixed economies identifies the categories of "public" and "merit" goods. *Public goods* are those which it is felt must be provided collectively, for to supply only those prepared to pay is impracticable. National defence is the usual illustration: people cannot opt out, nor can they easily be excluded from its assumed benefits. Police, fire protection and certain other municipal services are of a similar kind. *Merit goods* are those for which the effective demand in the marketplace would result in people consuming less than appears desirable. For example, education and some cultural facilities are generally held to have sufficient merit that the desired level of provision would not be freely supported by the public, as individual consumers. Defence is also a case in point: the volume of weaponry produced in most nations of the world no doubt greatly exceeds what the people would freely purchase in allocating personal resources. Public and merit goods are thus produced collectively. Their level of output is related to the general process of public and private resource allocation in society, which constrains what can be spent on public services of any kind. They raise some special distributional issues in a geographical context, as will be shown in later discussions.

The scale of operation of the individual production unit raises different problems. Figure 4.4 summarizes the conventional analysis of the scale decision of the private businessman or entrepreneur. Total operating costs and total revenue earned vary with volume of output, the former reflecting technical production relationships while the latter reflects demand. The greatest positive spread between cost and revenue (*P* to

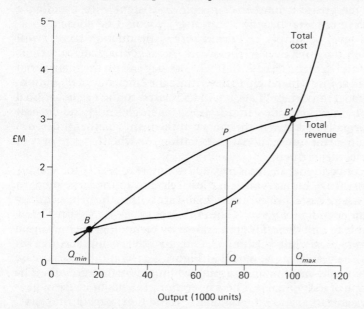

Figure 4.4 The relationship between cost, revenue (or benefits) and output.

P') reveals the profit-maximizing output of *Q*. This corresponds with the point at which marginal cost (i.e. the cost of producing an additional unit) is equal to marginal revenue (earnings from the sale of that unit); further increases in output will reduce total profit because marginal cost exceeds marginal revenue.

This analysis can be applied to a publicly owned production facility in a similar way. If private cost is replaced by *social cost* and revenue by *social benefit* or value, then the output generating the greatest excess of benefits over cost is as at *Q*. Here the marginal social cost and marginal social benefit are equated. Output above this level will begin to incur more social cost than the benefit derived; any lower level implies that net benefits can still be increased.

As well as revealing the optimal scale, where excess of benefits over costs (public or private) are maximized, the analysis in Figure 4.4. shows constraints on the output level. Intersections *B* and *B'*, where $TC = TR$, are "break-even" points, where revenue just covers costs. Between the minimum and maximum outputs (Q_{min} and Q_{max}) defined by these points some financial profit or positive net benefit is possible at any scale. Thus the private producer not motivated by profit maximization or the public producer not bound to maximize excess of benefits over costs has some freedom within which to make the scale decision. For example, the most efficient level of output in terms of inputs used is when average cost is minimized; yet private monopolists tend to maximize profits at a lower level of output and at a higher price to the consumer (Hunt and Sherman, 1972, 248). If the objective is to provide the good or service to the greatest number of people consistent with avoiding a loss (or negative *net* total benefits, output Q_{max} would be chosen.

The actual level of supply or output of any production facility will thus depend on the objectives of the owner, manager or plan, as well as on the supply and demand situation. It will also depend on the managerial knowledge and ability which help to determine the efficiency of operation. But perhaps most important of all, it will be related to the organizational structure—whether the facility in question is a single independent unit of the type normally assumed in the theory of the firm, whether it belongs to a large multi-plant international corporation, or whether it is part of a public service department.

While the conventional analyses may approximate to reality for a single firm in a competitive industry, it is far less relevant to the large modern corporation, where costs, prices, and demand are within the firm's control rather than independently given (Galbraith, 1975, 98–9). As firms grow they will be able to pull their TC curve down by technological innovation and scale economies while pushing TR up by advertising and market domination. The result, in the model in Figure 4.4, would be to increase the optimal or profit-maximizing output, leading to further growth. The increasing scale of individual business operations is a major cause of geographical concentration and integration of production: part of the "law" of uneven development under capitalism recognized in Marxist theory (Mandel, 1962, 163): "The evolution of the capitalist mode of production thus inevitably entails a *centralization* and *concentration* of capital. The average size of enterprise increases uninterruptedly; a large number of small enterprises are beaten in the competitive struggle by a small number of big enterprises which command an increasing share of capital, labour, funds and production in entire branches of industry." As Galbraith (1975, 71, 296) points out, this process has not gone so far in the geographically dispersed activities of the "market system" as in the "planning system" of big business and government. This helps to explain the relative underdevelopment of certain services which are highly consumer-oriented in their location, compared with the growth of the kind of production more effectively organized on a large centralized scale. The national or international corporation tends to develop a hierarchical structure of centralized decision-making and dispersed pattern of productive capacity (Hymer, 1975), with local scale decisions increasingly determined by non-local considerations. This has an important bearing on the space economy (see below), and also on who gains what where from its operation (see Chapter 5).

4.4 Location and the space-economy

In theory, location in space may be considered as a special case of production efficiency. This can be explained by continuing the discussion of the community faced with various production possibilities in the fields of health and education. If we now think of the community as inhabiting a section of geographical space, then the arrangement of production in this space would clearly have a bearing on the level of need-satisfying outputs from given inputs. For example, £10M invested in one new hospital in the major city might be a less effective way to reduce infant mortality than building small clinics in each village. Output is thus some function of the *spatial arrangement* of production, or allocation of investment among alternative locations. There is an optimal spatial pattern of production for any good such as health or education, as well as for commodities such as steel and automobiles. To be on the production possibilities frontier therefore requires efficiency in location as well as in combination of inputs. Indeed, optimal allocation of inputs in a space-economy requires that they be employed in the right place as well as in the right activities and right combinations. At the production frontier the amounts of inputs needed to produce an additional unit of output must be the same in all facilities, otherwise inputs could simply be shifted to the most efficient unit, thus raising production or releasing inputs to be used in the production of something else. Whether the accounting is in money or labour time, economies are effected by shifting production from high- to low-cost locations. Equal marginal costs in all production locations is the basic criterion of spatial *economic* efficiency.

A *socially* sub-optimal geographical pattern can arise from both supply and demand conditions. Production may be in high-cost locations, or badly located in relation to consumer needs. As a sub-optimal pattern will take society away from a frontier position in commodity space, we may recognize a variant of the locally feasible PPF, namely a *geographically feasible production possibilities frontier* in which the location of firms and facilities is taken as fixed, or part of the resource constraint. It will be inside the conventional frontier, unless the location pattern is optimal. If in the imaginary case of Figure 3.4 the location of education facilities was optimal but that for health sub-optimal to the extent of producing at only two-thirds of optimal efficiency at all levels of output (perhaps because people find it difficult to get to sources of medical care) this would generate the geographically feasible frontier shown in Figure 4.5. If the supply of inputs is fixed and they are being used optimally in a technical sense, then progress beyond this constraint can be made only by improving the spatial pattern of production.

The optimal collection of goods on the geographically feasible production possibilities frontier can differ from that under optimal location efficiency. In Figure 4.5 we show welfare contours of a simple linear form,

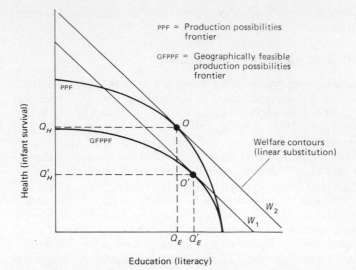

Figure 4.5 The geographically feasible production possibilities frontier (GFPPF), incorporating inefficiencies arising from the spatial arrangement of production.

indicating constant rates of substitution whereby a 1 per cent improvement in literacy and infant survival have the same social valuation irrespective of level of output. The tangency point on the GFPPF is O' in place of O on the PPF. There has been a shift in production in favour of education—the good produced most efficiently—as well as a reduction (from W_2 to W_1) in the general level of welfare.

The form adopted by patterns of production in space has occupied the attention of geographers for many years. The location of the individual producer is much easier to examine than that of an entire spatial pattern: there is a well developed body of theory, beginning with Weber (1929) and incorporating contributions from Hoover (1937, 1948), Greenhut (1956, 1963) and Isard (1956). This work is examined in detail in Smith (1971) and various aspects are summarized in other texts such as Smith, Taaffe and King (1968), Karaska and Bramhall (1969) and Lloyd and Dicken (1972). As well as providing guidance on the circumstances in which single units of production are located, this approach offers some intuitive understanding of how broad features of location patterns emerge.

The theory of the location of the firm may be summarized in a simple graphic model. Although originally designed for a private firm in a competitive economy (Smith, 1966; 1971), this is equally applicable to the public location decision in a planned economy. Figure 4.6 shows the surface of the earth as two distances axes d_1 and d_2. The vertical axis measures cost and revenue or benefits in money, labour time or any other common units of value. A *space cost curve* (TC) and a *space revenue curve* (TR) are drawn—sections through a *space cost surface* and *space revenue surface* along the d_1 axis. Both apply to a given level of output. The form of the space cost surface will reflect differences from place to place in the cost of inputs required, given a technology and given the fact that the optimal combination of inputs can vary in space as differences in input costs lead to substitution of cheap ones for those which are more expensive. The form of the space revenue curve and surface reflects local demand conditions.

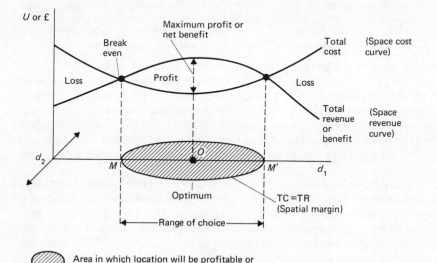

Figure 4.6 A simple model of the location problem of a single production facility, private or public.

The analysis of locational choice is closely analogous to that of scale in Figure 4.5, p. 82. At some point in space the positive difference between TR and TC will be maximized (O in Figure 4.6). It is here that the private entrepreneur will make most profit, and here that net social benefit will be greatest if TC is taken to be total social cost and TR total social return. The two *spatial* break-even points where $TR = TC$ define two points in space (M and M'), between which any location along the d_1 axis offers some profit or net benefit. Extending the analysis into the second distance dimension, an area within which $TR > TC$ is recognized, bounded by a locus of points like M and M'—the *spatial margin* to profitability as Rawstron (1958) termed it. Within this limit there is some freedom of locational choice: the private producer can indulge personal whims and fancies and even locate in complete ignorance, yet still remain in business. Within the margin the central planner, constrained only by a requirement to cover plant operating costs by revenues from sales, has freedom to locate production according to non-economic criteria.

The location of public facilities raises some special considerations.

Teitz (1968, 43–4) summarizes the problem of production where consumer choice is significant but price is zero as follows:

> In general, the larger the scale of a unit in such a system, the more consumers it attracts by virtue of providing better or more varied services, for example [in the case of libraries], by carrying a larger book stock. Since entry is free for members of the community and they commonly travel to the facility for the service, travel cost, including time and inconvenience, represents the major cost to the consumer. Under these circumstances, we would expect to find a distance decay effect on usage. If the budget is fixed but the number of facilities variable, then a larger number of outlets implies a smaller scale at each but greater aggregate access to the population. The scale effect and the distance effect then conflict. An optimal system must solve for both scale and location.

In any productive system with scale economies and spatial costs variations (to producers or consumers), scale and location are interdependent if there are multiple facilities and outlets. In the case of free public goods special problems arise from the distributional impact of differential access. So, as Dear (1974) has emphasized, public facility location must be judged by criteria different from those appropriate to the private sector. Some of the practical issues involved will be considered in later chapters.

An economic landscape or space-economy is formed of an assemblage of production units for all manner of different activities. Every locality, region or nation has its own unique pattern. But two general features are of particular importance: geographical specialization and the spatial concentration or localization of modern economic activity. How these are connected has a vital bearing on who gets what where.

Local product specialization had an early origin. "In primitive society . . . a *regional specialization*, a regional division of labour, can appear in consequence of specific peculiarities of a given territory" (Mandel, 1962, 53). Obvious examples are the local availability of metals for tools or ornaments, and physical conditions favourable for particular crops. Specialization leads to exchange and trade, and to important changes in the nature of economic activity. Gradually, the emphasis shifts from production for local need to production for sale so as to buy other things, and then to buying in order to sell for profit—the activity of the merchant. Trading for profit as opposed to production for use reaches its "highest" form in the capitalist mode of production, the development of which was facilitated by the accumulation of capital in commerce. Trade requires markets, and it was thus that the first tendencies towards spatial concentration appeared—in the market town and port. Large-scale production of commodities for sale led to the first specialized manufacturing centres, at places favourable for the production of particular things. Once local specialization is initiated it often gathers a momentum of its own, as external economies of agglomeration build up further advantage.

The modern space-economy is one of major nodes of production, in complex transportation networks for the physical exchange of goods. Each of the links between sectors, as described in the input–output model earlier in this chapter (Figure 4.2) involves movement between locations.

In a publicly owned economy or a system dominated by large multi-product private corporations, exchange may be little more than a book-keeping operation. But in a national or international market, exchange takes the form of trade between the various participants in economic activity.

The relationship between trade and the geography of production is very important. Trade promotes further specialization, as different places reveal a *comparative advantage* for the production of different goods. Comparative advantage means that some products can be made *relatively* more efficiently than others. A resource-rich region may be able to produce everything with greater *absolute* efficiency (i.e. less inputs used) than every other region, but as long as some regional *comparative* advantage exists some specialization may benefit all. Samuelson (1973, 66) explains this by the case where the best lawyer in town is also the best typist: it still pays the lawyer to specialize in the lucrative practice of law and hire a typist (who has a comparative advantage in typing relative to knowledge of the law) even though the typist may not type as well as the lawyer could.

How trade and specialization can benefit both partners may be illustrated in a simple case of two regions (or nations) and two products. Suppose that beer and wine are consumed in equal quantities of 10M gallons in the North (N) and the South (S), but that different amounts of labour are needed for production. In S a single worker can produce 5,000 gallons of beer each year and 7,500 gallons of wine, where in N the outputs per worker are 4,000 and 3,000 gallons respectively. These differences in productivity are reflected in different prices (Table 4.2); prices are higher in N where each worker produces less of both goods. The South thus has an absolute advantage in the production of both beer and wine. It nevertheless benefits this region to trade, because N has a comparative advantage for the production of beer while S has a comparative advantage for wine, as is shown by each region's prices. These prices simply reflect labour inputs (output per worker multiplied by price is constant for each good in each region) and may be read as units of labour time expended instead of in monetary value. If one worker in S is transferred from beer to wine production this region's output of beer is reduced by 5,000 gallons but 7,500 additional gallons of wine are produced; this wine can be sold in N at £10·00 per gallon to earn £75,000, which can be used to purchase 10,000 gallons of beer (at £7·50 per gallon). The South thus loses 5,000 gallons of beer and gains 10,000—a net gain from trade of 5,000. As long as the prices remain unchanged, it will pay S to transfer all beer workers to wine, and buy all its beer from the North.

The result of regional specialization is shown in Table 4.2. Before specialization the total cost of wine and beer production together is £100M in S and £175M in N, making a total of £275M. Specialization leads to all 20M gallons of wine being produced in S and all 20M of beer in N. Costs now show a saving of £20M in S and £25M in N; total cost is £230M compared with £275M before specialization. In labour-time units instead of £s, the saving is 45M worth of leisure in place of work,

Table 4.2 Product specialization based on regional comparative advantage

		South (S)			North (N)		
		Quantity (Q)	Price (P)	Cost (QP)	Quantity (Q)	Price (P)	Cost (QP)
Before	Beer	10	6·0	60	10	7·5	70
specialization	Wine	10	4·0	40	10	10·0	100
				100			175

Total cost = 100 + 175 = 275

		Q	P	QP	Q	P	QP
After	Beer	0	0	0	20	7·5	150
specialization	Wine	20	4·0	80	0	0	0
				80			150

Total cost = 80 + 150 = 230

		Imports (+) or exports (−) (Q)	Price (P)	Income (+) or expenditure (−) (QP)	Imports (+) or exports (−) (Q)	Price (P)	Income (+) or expenditure (−) (QP)
After	Beer	+10	6·0	−60	−10	6·0	+60
trade (at	Wine	−10	4·0	+40	+10	4·0	−40
prices in S)				−20			+20

Total cost (S) = 80 + 20 = 100   (N) = 150 − 20 = 130

Source: Based on a case in Hunt and Sherman (1972, 528–31). Quantities are in millions, unit prices in £.

or that much more labour released to produce other sources of need satisfaction.

How this saving is actually shared by the two regions after the commodities have been exchanged depends on the *terms of trade*. If 10M gallons of beer from N were simply swapped for the same quantity of wine from S, the allocation of gains would be as shown in the cost calculation: i.e. £20M saved in S and £25M in N. But if trade takes place at the prices actually prevailing in S, this region's beer imports cost £60M while wine exports earn only £40M, resulting in a net loss of £20M which just cancels out S's cost saving from specialization (Table 4.2). All the gains accrue to N. Similarly, trading at prices in the North gives all the benefits to the South.

The actual terms of trade will be determined by market conditions of supply and demand, modified by negotiation and bargaining. The result will tend to favour one region more than another. As Hunt and Sherman (1972, 531) point out, "When two countries engage in trade, the one that is able to exert the greatest bargaining power will succeed in pushing the trade prices closer to the ratio of the prices and production costs of the other country. In doing this, the more powerful country will reap most of the gains from trade." Even in primitive societies, exchange is seldom between equals; in the modern world, trading "partners" such as the USA and an underdeveloped African nation exchanging manufactured goods for raw materials are in sharp contrast from a power point of view. The outcome is explained by Mandel (1962, 477) as follows:

it comes down in the last analysis to the difference in the level of productivity (socially necessary expenditure of labour) between the two types of country. That is, to the "equal" exchanging of *more labour* (less skilled and less productive) on the part of the colonial and semi-colonial countries [e.g. *N* in the case above] for *less labour* (more skilled and more productive) on the part of the industrially advanced countries. International trade "on the basis of world prices" has thus merely perpetrated [*sic*] and in a sense "regularized" the transfer of values from the former to the latter, which is found at the very beginnings of international trade.

Hence the growing world-wide concentration of wealth. This process has important implications for international differences in levels of development (see Chapter 8).

The extent to which trade takes place between any two places will depend on the cost of movement. Only if the price of a good elsewhere is low enough at least to bear the transport cost will it pay to import rather than produce at home. Market equilibrium in space is explained more fully in texts dealing with international trade and spatial price theory (e.g. Richardson, 1969a, ch. 2; Chisholm, 1970, ch. 6; Samuelson, 1973, ch. 34; Hodder and Lee, 1974, ch. 7). Enough has been said here to show that local, regional and national advantages for the production of certain goods can lead to exchange through trade, to the benefit of at least one party. While specialization may be promoted by market competition it can also be induced by planners in the interests of overall national production efficiency.

While the conventional view of exchange concerns material goods, it is also important to consider flows of information and ideas. Distance can impede these movements just as effectively as those of commodities. Research on the diffusion of innovation in space (e.g. Adams, Abler and Gould, ch. 11; see also next chapter) shows that the spread of ideas and the adoption of new ways of doing things is closely related to location. Thus the telephone, television and even innovations in education or health care are likely to reach the small town or the countryside later than the metropolis.

Exchange is facilitated by efficient transport systems. In this context efficiency means movement with low cost or effort, e.g. minimizing the friction of distance. As with the production of goods, transportation efficiency is constrained by resources and technology; a poorly designed or outdated system will limit movement, in just the same way as a sub-optimal pattern of badly run facilities will limit the output of goods and services. Within any territory, the transport system may be viewed as part of the physical constraint conceptualized as the production possibilities frontier; if other aspects of resources and technology remain the same, transport improvements will push the PPF outwards in commodity space (as well as literally in geographical space) and thus reach a higher welfare contour in the analysis introduced in Chapter 3. Research on the form of transportation patterns (e.g. Kansky, 1963; Taaffe, Morrill and Gould,

1963; Cox, 1972, ch. 8) has shown that national levels of economic development are associated with improvements in certain characteristics
of the road and rail network. Efficiency of production in any activity involving mobility will depend to some extent on the transport or communications system. A scattered, rural population with poor road links
can be served less effectively than a concentrated urban community, given
the same resources, whether the goods in question are market commodities or social services such as health care and police protection.

Transport and communications play a vital part in the *integration* of
the space-economy. Innovations in transportation helped the early spatial
expansion of capitalism from Western Europe into new (often colonial)
spheres for investment and market expansion. It relaxed the tendency towards spatial concentration inherent in the process of capital accumulation: "The need to minimize circulation costs as well as turnover
time promotes agglomeration of production within a few large urban
centres which become, in effect, the workshops of capitalist production"
(Harvey, 1975, 12). But the spatial spread of production facilitated by
modern methods of transport is not necessarily followed by dispersal of
control. Improvements in communication and organizational techniques
have enabled large multi-plant corporations to retain central control. The
result is the spatial expression of the corporate hierarchy, recognized by
Hymer (1975, 49) as contributing to "centralizing and perfecting the process of capital accumulation". The pattern is one of dispersed production,
local or national coordinating offices in the regional centre or capital city,
and the central control and planning office in one of the world cities with
access to the capital market, media and government. There are obvious
similarities with the spatial central-place hierarchy familiar to geographers in the work of Christaller (1933) and Lösch (1954). Looking
into the future: "Since business is usually the core of the city, geographical specialization will come to reflect the hierarchy of corporation decision-making, and the occupational distribution of labour in a city or
region will depend upon its function in the international economic system" (Hymer, 1975, 50).

The discussion has now brought us to the dynamics of the modern
space-economy. How this operates in the areal differentiation of human
life chances is a critical welfare matter, to be taken up in the context of
distribution in the next chapter.

4.5 The generation of external effects

It should be clear by now that the process of production, like consumption, does not take place with the deliberation and rationality
implied in much economic theory. Such terms as private, public and merit
goods tend to obscure the fact that we live in an increasingly interdependent world in which virtually all production and consumption has
public *outcomes*, or consequences for others. In Chapter 3 it was pointed
out that consumption is by no means always intentional, for some of the
goods and bads experienced by an individual are a result of the behaviour

of others. Similarly, the production process may generate unintended side-effects, positive and negative, which require accounting alongside the intended outputs as additional value added or (more likely) subtracted. Increasing negative side-effects are inherent in the modern capitalist-corporation economy; as Galbraith (1975, 225) explains:

> it expands numerous types of private consumption with extensive external dis-economies—increased automobile use with its associated emissions and the spreading patina of abandoned and scrapped vehicle carcasses; increased use of packaged consumer goods with its associated litter of bottles, cans, cartons and non-degradable plastics; increased personal wealth with its increased re-wards to larceny and violent assault and hence increasingly unsafe and un-pleasant neighbourhoods. And it accords no similar emphasis and support to the public services which make such increased consumption socially tolerable.

These are the priorities implicit in a mode of production motivated by profit and capital accumulation via economic growth instead of by the imperative of satisfying fundamental human needs. The concept of *external effects* underlines the inability of markets to regulate resource allocation, production and consumption in the interests of civilized exist-ence. The production of new value in the sense of commodities realizing a price in the market does not mean that the outcome is in the general interest of society (Mandel, 1962, 191).

An externality exists when an activity generates side-effects not reflected in costs or prices. Externalities can produce benefits that enhance indivi-dual well-being and also costs in the form of disutilities, but it is negative externalities which attract most attention. The undesirable side-effects of the production process are a matter of great contemporary concern, which are assuming increasing importance in evaluations of real pro-gress. For a long time externalities were virtually ignored in economics as inconvenient exceptions to the general efficacy of market pricing. How-ever, Mishan (1967) and others have recently helped to draw attention to them, and the alternative national income accounting of Nordhous and Tobin (1972) mentioned in section 4.2 above represents a step towards giving hitherto unpriced activities more explicit treatment. As Scitovsky (1971, 269) has put it, "Externalities seemed like curiosa to the economist of barely a generation or two ago; in today's overcrowded world, with its problems of air pollution, sewage and waste disposal, they seem like a characteristic and all-pervading feature of the modern economy." Their importance in a space-economy has recently been recognized by Jackman (1975).

The definition of externalities sometimes includes the fact that they are unintended as well as unpriced. For the most part, they are certainly unplanned in the sense that their precise extent and impact is not deter-mined in the same way as the output and physical distribution of the intentionally produced goods. However, it would be naïve to regard the pollution of the air or the disposal of factory effluents in rivers as uninten-tional, for this is usually a deliberate transfer of part of the real cost of production from the producer to society at large. The difficulty of pricing such things is that their general impact on the environment and on human well-being is virtually impossible to measure. Indeed the wider external effects of some economic activity, for example agriculture dependent on large-scale use of DDT, may be quite unsuspected by the individuals involved and unknown to society at large until revealed by scientific inquiry. Externalities should thus be viewed as including the unanticipated or unsuspected outcomes of behaviour which often has an element of intentionality.

In passing, it might be stressed that these external disutilities are not the sole prerogative of capitalist societies, in which the transfer of real costs from producers to the public is facilitated. Environmental pollution is also a serious problem in socialist systems, e.g. the Soviet Union (Goldman, 1971; Hunt and Sherman, 1972, 618) and east-central Europe (Dienas, 1974). One of the paradoxes of the publicly owned economy supposedly operating in the general interest is that the managers and bureaucrats may have greater freedom than the private capitalist to ignore the problems of pollution if this is given lower priority than increasing output. As the real impact of many externalities cannot be anticipated, undesirable side-effects can be generated under any mode of production. However, a socialist economy has greater power to control these outcomes in the general interest (Dobb, 1969, 149–50).

Most geographical concern with externalities has focused on environmental pollution. However, the quality of the environment is now being viewed more broadly than in purely physical terms, to include its human impact (e.g. Coppock and Wilson, 1974). Emphasis has recently shifted to the urban environment, where certain manifestations of pathological behaviour and social malaise (e.g. crime, delinquency, prostitution, drug addiction and mental illness) appear as increasingly serious side-effects of city life (Michelson, 1970, 148–67). These conditions may be seen in part as external effects of the way in which urban life is managed. Cox (1973) has used the concept of externalities as the core of his interpretation of the interplay of conflict, power and politics in the American city. Harvey (1971) has also stressed the importance of externalities in the redistribution of real income in cities (see Chapter 5).

The concept of externalities is intrinsically spatial. Indeed, externalities are sometimes referred to as "neighbourhood effects" or "spillovers", both of which have spatial connotations. The smoker produces an external disutility for the asthma sufferer only when they are close together; the smell from the abattoir is stronger to those closer than those further away. On the positive side, a beautiful building or garden produces beneficial externalities only for those who see it or know of its existence. The more familiar example of external economies in production, referred to as economies of agglomeration, depends largely on the physical proximity of producers in related activities.

External effects in space become particularly important influences on human well-being in the case of public goods, supposedly equally available to all people in a defined territory. They are in theory *indivisible*, and cannot be split up for the exclusive use of some people and not others.

But geographical space creates *impurity* in public goods, for in reality any good or service available at a particular point will benefit some more than others, even if all people pay equally for its provision. Those particularly advantaged by location will gain benefits not paid for, while those who live far from the facility will be penalized. Fire stations are often cited as examples of this. Similarly, certain nuisances such as noise and air pollution affect some people more than others, including people who reap no gains from the process generating them. In so far as these negative externalities are indivisible and cannot be avoided, they can be thought of as accruing in the nature of a public good (Bish, 1971, 27); they are *demerit goods* (or bads), in the sense that people consume more of them than they would freely choose. The provision of public goods and the problem of externalities are closely intertwined, particularly in the theory of public finance (Margolis, 1968; Netzer, 1968; Bish, 1971).

The most important contribution to the geographical analysis of externalities has been made by Harvey (1971). He stresses that all public goods are impure, and that the consequent externality exists as a "spatial field" effect. Thus (Harvey, 1973, 60):

> We might generalize these spatial fields by distance-decay functions or by diffusion equations (such as those which describe the general field of external costs imposed by a source of atmospheric pollution). These spatial fields of externality effects will vary in intensity and extent, from the influence of a derelict property on the values of the adjacent properties to the extensive field of influence of airport noise. Externality fields can be positive or negative or, sometimes as in the case of an airport, both (since an airport is a nuisance from the point of view of pollution and noise close by but has important benefits for employment and movement). We know very little about the shape and form of these externality fields in an urban environment. But there can be no doubt that their location has a very powerful effect upon the real income of the individual.

The concept of the *externality field* for nuisances is very appealing, and has been examined in some detail by Harrop (1973).

The externality field is illustrated graphically in Figure 4.7. Point i is the source of some utility or disutility accruing to the population of the surrounding area. The level of utility or disutility (U) decreases with distance from i. The general distance-decay function may be written:

$$U_j = f(d_{ij}) \tag{4.5}$$

where j is some place other than i. In Figure 4.7a the utility ($+$ or $-$) at j is the vertical distance i to U_j. Expression [4.5] may be regarded as a special case of the production function, with the level of output of whatever the source of utility or disutility may be depending on distance from the production location (i). At a point in space some distance from i, the external effect will cease. This is Z in Figure 4.7a, or the spatial limit of the externality field. Assuming an even spread or diffusion of the effect in all directions from i, the line i to Z may be rotated about i, to define the externality field in two-dimensional space. This shows the extent of the territory affected. If population is evenly distributed over this territory, the total utility or disutility generated from i will be

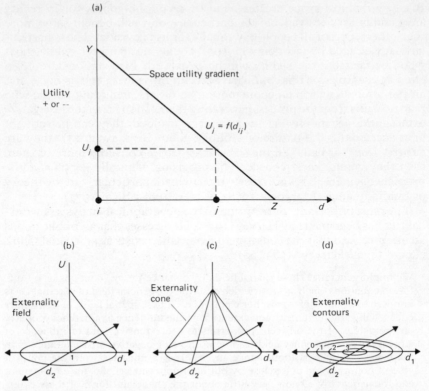

Figure 4.7 The externality field: the spatial expression of certain utilities and disutilities.

proportional to the volume of the *externality cone* formed by the rotation of the triangle iYZ, where Y is the (maximum) level of benefit or nuisance—assumed to be at the source. If population density varies, some parts of the cone will have a denser concentration of utility or disutility than others. The total utility ($+$ or $-$) experienced by the varying numbers of people at any set of places j within the externality field is given by

$$U = \sum_{j=1}^{n} w_j U_j \qquad [4.6]$$

where w_j is the local population weighting and U_j is the local level of utility or disutility from [4.5] above, which is assumed to be measurable on some uniform indicator such as financial cost or benefit. Such a method of calculating the total effect of an externality is analogous to that used in economic geography to identify volume of sales attainable from a market centre, using the concept of the "demand cone" (Lösch, 1954, 106; Smith, 1971, 133). Given appropriate measurements to estimate the distance-decay function, empirical application is feasible.

The idea of a distance decay in externality effects accords with everyday experience. There is evidence to suggest that some of the more serious side-effects of modern transportation facilities are spatially concentrated, for example lead poisoning in populations near a motorway junction and mental disturbance among residents of the area surrounding New York's Kennedy Airport (Michelson, 1970, 159). Certain modern urban disutilities such as robbery and physical assault may be subject to quite regular distance decay from "breeding grounds" of crime in the pits of deprivation on the city well-being surface. In some cases the external effect may diffuse more readily in some directions than others, to distort the regular field suggested in Figure 4.7. Examples are pollution from factory chimneys spreading rapidly downwind, or shoplifters from slums moving along commercial streets while avoiding the intervening residential areas.

At a more general level, there is considerable empirical support for regular spatial variations in the incidence of a number of urban disutilities. Research associated with the Chicago school of urban sociology has demonstrated a distance-decay effect in the level of such conditions as mental disorder and juvenile delinquency, varying in concentric zones around the city centre (e.g. Faris and Dunham, 1939; Shaw and McKay, 1942; Michelson, 1970, 8–11; Smith, 1973a, 41–2). Tomeh (1964) has found social participation in group activities increasing with distance from the centre of the city, all else remaining equal.

The reasons for the existence of crime, mental illness or any other social problem are far more complex than this discussion might suggest, of course. The empirical finding that distance from a certain point is an accurate predictor of a particular condition does not answer the "how" question. It does not tell us what causal mechanisms are at work to produce these conditions and distribute them differentially among groups and territories. To understand this it is necessary to examine the basic functioning of a society, economy and polity, much of which is beyond even the most generous conventional definitions of human geography. As we extend our discussion into distribution in Chapter 5 we will get a little closer to these issues.

5

Distribution in Space: Who Gets What Where

Distribution concerns the sharing of goods and bads among a population. This issue has already emerged a number of times in the past two chapters, as a link between production and consumption. While what is distributed is usually thought of in money terms as income and wealth, we will continue to view it in the broadest possible sense as all sources of value or satisfaction, positive and negative.

The normal context for the discussion of distribution is population groups such as races or social classes. In geography the primary focus is on distribution in space or among territories—on who gets what *where*. To consider place of residence as a distributive criterion runs the risk of over-emphasizing the importance of this single variable and of overlooking the fact that spatial inequality may be largely a result of different population groups living in different areas. The geographical pattern may simply express a non-spatial, class distribution. But there are circumstances when location in space alone has a bearing on what an individual or group gets, as should be clear from the discussion of externalities and accessibility in previous chapters. It is also necessary to recognize that the interpersonal or group distribution may itself vary spatially and that degree of inequality is an important characteristic of place. Indeed, how evenly real income is distributed among the population of a city, region or nation may well be the single most sensitive indicator of the type of society at work.

5.1 Theories of distribution

The discussion of production in the previous chapter began with the concept of value. This provided the necessary link with consumption as the satisfaction of human needs and wants. In developing a theoretical perspective on distribution we will now return to considerations of value, for ultimately this is what is being distributed. In doing so, we shall emphasize again the essential unity of the production–distribution–consumption process and the inseparability of the economic, social and political factors involved. Distribution is very much dependent on how a society organizes production. Power in the political sense of control over institutions and decision-making arrangements is very much dependent on economic power, or control over scarce resources, means of production and mechanisms for the appropriation and disbursement of surplus product.

The creation of value, as described at the beginning of the previous chapter, involves three ingredients: natural resources, human labour and capital goods. The first two are sometimes termed the "primary" factors of production with their supply determined outside the economic system, while capital is an "intermediate" factor generated by human labour within the system, for use in production of further goods and services. The question of distribution in economics is generally posed in terms

Region 1

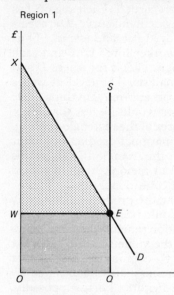

Region 2

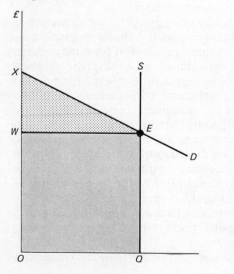

Wages of labour

Rent of landowners

Figure 5.1 Income distribution between workers and landowners in two regions, according to the marginal-productivity theory.

of the relative contributions of these three ingredients in the productive process. If the natural resource of land earns *rent* in recognition of its scarcity, if labour is compensated by *wages* and if capital goods earn a return in the form of *interest*, what share of new value created accrues to each factor?

The solution in neo-classical economics is found in the *marginal-productivity theory of distribution*. This is demonstrated graphically in Figure 5.1, with respect to the rent and wages earned by land and labour. The situation in two different regions is depicted to retain a geographical context, but inter-regional factor mobility is disregarded. Each region has a fixed supply of labour (S) and a down-sloping demand curve (D) reflecting the marginal product of labour as employed by landowners. Thus the money value of the product of the first worker hired is X and each successive worker adds less. The wage of labour (W) is set where D and S intersect (E), as in conventional market analysis. The level of wages is thus determined by the product of the last worker hired; anything more would mean that the product of some workers would be less than what they were paid. The total wage income is the area of the rectangle $OWEQ$. The difference between wages paid and the marginal product of labour is the rent accruing to the owners of land, i.e. the triangle WXE. In this imaginary case, labour is relatively better off in region 2 than in region 1, by virtue of different supply and demand conditions.

The same analysis can be used to show how the product is shared by any pair of factors. For example, landowners could be replaced by capitalists. The general principle governing distribution remains the same, however: each factor will gain the equivalent of the value added by the last (marginal) unit employed. In theory, a perfectly competitive free-market economy will automatically distribute income in shares determined by the interdependent marginal products of all factors. This, supposedly, is how land (owners), labour and capital (owners) get their respective rewards, justified by contribution to total product.

Such a theory of distribution has obvious appeal. If the demand for products, as revealed in the marketplace, truly reflects popular preferences and if prices are equated with marginal costs of production, then the resulting distribution can be thought of as having the implicit approval of society. The fact that such an outcome might be generated by an automatic and self-adjusting mechanism without resort to public intervention and planning adds to its attraction. However, there are serious objections to the marginal-productivity theory (e.g. Hunt and Schwartz, 1972; Dobb, 1973). Some arise from imperfections in the operation of markets and competition as institutions for the promotion of the general welfare. Others come from a confusion between positive and normative features, i.e., between description of the process of distribution and approval of its outcome. But the most serious problem in the present context arises from the treatment of land, labour and capital in exactly the same way—as similar contributors to production, each earning a justified return for their owners.

Land, fixed capital and machines in themselves create no value: this requires human labour. Labour differs from land and capital by its very nature. Land is in fixed supply; labour can reproduce itself. Capital cannot produce labour; yet labour can produce capital. But of critical importance with respect to distribution is the fact that labour-power is assigned naturally to individual human beings while land and capital are not. As Marx (1867, 166) put it, "Nature does not produce on the one side owners of money or commodities, and on the other men possessing nothing but their own labour-power." Ownership of land and capital requires particular institutional arrangements, whether proprietorship is to be vested in private individuals or some public collective. On these arrangements will depend who gets any return attributed to non-human factors employed in production. The size of this return is itself an institutional outcome, whether it emerges almost by magic from the interplay of market forces, or whether it simply appears on paper as "shadow prices" in the accounts of a planned economy. Distribution of society's product thus depends on how society is organized.

The interrelationship between production, distribution and consumption within a particular institutional setting is a basic feature of the Marxian view, which provides the major alternative to the neo-classical theory of distribution. "Any distribution whatever of the means of consumption is only a consequence of the distribution of the conditions of production themselves" (Marx, 1875, 388). The mode of production is fundamental to distribution; to quote Marx (1859, 4) again:

> In the social production of their life, men enter into definite relations that are indispensable and independent of their will, relations of production which correspond to a definite stage of development of their material productive forces. The sum total of these relations of production constitute the economic structure of society, the real foundation, on which rises a legal and political superstructure and to which correspond definite forms of social consciousness. The mode of production of material life conditions the social, political and intellectual life process in general.

A major concern of Marx was to show how the particular mode of production operating in capitalist societies leads to inequality and class conflict. This was achieved largely through an exploration of the meaning of value, as introduced in the previous chapter.

At the core of the Marxian view of distribution is the process of capitalist expropriation of value produced by labour. Under capitalism, those who own the means of production and employ labour are able to gain more from their employees than they actually pay for in wages. The difference is *surplus value*. This is defined as the use value of labour minus its exchange value, i.e. the difference between what the capitalist can get in the market for the product of labour and what he pays the labourer for his work. Thus the total value of output (Y) in any activity is split up as follows:

$$Y = C + V + S \qquad [5.1]$$

where C is the labour embodied in the material or machines used (i.e. "constant capital"), V is the immediate labour input ("variable capital") and S is surplus value. The more surplus value the capitalist can extract in relation to labour used, the higher the degree of "exploitation". Thus the *rate of surplus value* (r) or *rate of exploitation* of the workers is

$$r = S/V \qquad [5.2]$$

The more the capitalist is able to force wages down to subsistence level, the lower will be V, the higher S and the higher r. The capitalist is able to appropriate this surplus because of his power as owner of the means of production: "Labour creates surplus value by virtue of the fact that the unequal class relation operating in the market for labour creates a gap between its use value and exchange value" (Desai, 1974, 22). Labour-power has become simply a commodity: "The seller of labour-power, like the seller of any other commodity, realizes its exchange value, and parts with its use value. He cannot take the one without giving the other" (Marx, 1867, 188). Labour alone can produce *surplus* value; materials are bought from other capitalists and the value produced by machine is simply the rent paid for the use of the machine (Desai, 1974, 21–2). Thus it is only in the labour market that the capitalist can appropriate surplus value.

A simple illustration will help to clarify the distributional implications of the appropriation of surplus value. In the description of the creation of value in shirt manufacture in Chapter 4 (Figure 4.1), suppose that a capitalist is introduced at the stage of spinning the yarn. The spinners earn £6·00 for their work, but can subsist on half this figure. Power in the labour market enables the capitalist as employer to force wages down to £3·00. The product of labour is still worth £6·00; the capitalist takes the balance of £3·00 surplus value as profit. Thus $V = 3$, $S = 3$, and $r = 3 \div 3 = 1$. Suppose now that the making of spindles and the growing of cotton are also in the hands of capitalists, with the same rate of exploitation as in spinning. Table 5.1 shows how payment for value created would be distributed, compared with a mode of production without capitalists ("socialism"). Under capitalism, surplus value is extracted in each sector, to give half the payment to the various capitalists involved, while under socialism all income accrues to labour. The rate of profit (p) is:

$$p = S/(C+V) \qquad [5.3]$$

In the spinning sector, $p = 3 \div (24+3)$ where C is payment to suppliers of cotton and spindles ($V + S$ in these sectors) and V is payment for labour power of spinners. This works out at $p = 0·11$ (approx.), or a profit of 11 per cent on capital advanced.

The taking of profits or returns on investment is justified in various ways in capitalist ideology (e.g. Samuelson, 1973, 619–22). These include: (1) an implicit factor return on the means of production contributed by the capitalist, as explained in the summary of neo-classical distribution theory above; (2) a reward for enterprise and innovation; (3) a reward for risk-bearing; and (4) an abstinence payment for the deferred satisfaction involved in investment instead of consumption. The range of explanations is itself an indication of the ambiguity of the concept

Table 5.1 Distribution of payments in the creation of value under capitalism and socialism

| Sector | Capitalism | | | Socialism |
	constant capital (C)	variable capital (V)	surplus value (S)	labour (L)
Growing cotton		10	10	20
Making spindles		2	2	4
Spinning yarn				
cotton and spindles	24			
labour		3	3	6
Returns to labour (*V* or *L*)		15		30
Returns to capital (*S*)			15	0
Total value added		30		30

Note: The item of 24 under C is value added in growing cotton and making spindles, i.e. $V + S$ or L.

of profit. The Marxian view is that the conventional method of cost-pricing goods and calculating profits disguises the true (exploitive) relationship between people under capitalism. The distinction is between the visible price or exchange domain of relationships between things and the invisible value domain of social relationships between men.

The importance of private property in the determination of distribution should now be clear. Ownership of the means of production enables a capitalist class not only to claim a return on the use of their property but also gives them the power to extract this return from the labour of others. "The apparent productivity of the entrepreneur is a by-product of property rights" (Desai, 1974, 30). The distributional significance of property ownership and its institutional basis is explained frankly by Friedman (1962, 161–2) as follows:

> The ethical principle that would directly justify the distribution of income in a free society is, "To each according to what he and the instruments he owns produces." The operation of even this principle implicitly depends on state action. Property rights are matters of law and social convention. As we have seen, their definition and enforcement is one of the primary functions of the state. The final distribution of income and wealth under the full operation of this principle may well depend markedly on the rules of property adopted.

It would be surprising if the economic power of the property owner was not accompanied by the political power to influence these rules in the interests of the capitalist class. Samuelson (1973, 806) recognizes that "The greatest disparities in income are due to differences in *wealth ownership*", and that "private property, unequally distributed" is not the only twentieth-century mechanism to bring about economic growth via capital accumulation (Samuelson, 1973, 616). He also accepts that the role of power relations as against market relations in determining shares of national income is an open question (Samuelson, 1973, 533), and that recruits to the business elite who have the power are more likely to come from business or professional families than from a farm or a work-ingman's home (Samuelson, 1973, 92), thus perpetuating inequality.

Rent was considered by Marx to be but one manifestation of surplus value under capitalist institutions such as private property, realized in a number of distinct ways (Harvey, 1973, 141, 178–92): a gratuitous payment to landowners, not a return on contribution to production. The scarcity of land (and other factors) can be reflected in prices, but this does not necessarily justify payment of a rent to landowners. To quote Samuelson (1973, 542) again: "charging a rent for God-given land is necessary if such scarce land is to be rightly allocated. But notice that we have not proved that the competitive result is 'fair' or 'equitable': efficiency itself does not necessarily imply justice in distribution." The modern socialist position is, "It is incomes for landlords and capitalists which are contrary to doctrine, not a monetary recognition of the shortage of good land or the most modern machines" (Nove and Nuti, 1972, 15). "Scarcity is socially defined, not naturally determined" (Harvey, 1973, 139), whether it be through the people expressing preferences for particular goods or a monopoly capitalist creating a corner in a market. Thus in land, the value "is completely derived from the value of the product" (Samuelson, 1973, 560).

If value should properly accrue to those who create it, it is not difficult to argue that scarcity payments to factors should accrue to the consuming public and not to private owners. The technical problem arising from the failure of the labour theory of value to explain actual prices as partly reflecting scarcity of non-labour inputs (e.g. Samuelson, 1973, 739–40; Desai, 1974, 41–2) does not necessarily invalidate the proposition that the entire product should be paid to labour.

The crux of the distribution issue under capitalism is summarized thus by Mandel (1962, 709–10):

> The allocation of incomes among capitalists, workers and landowners takes place in the market. But the market is characterized by an *institutional inequality* without which the capitalist regime could not last a single day: the *monopoly* of the means of production in the hands of one social class; the *obligation* to which another social class is subject to sell its labour-power, in order to be able to exist. The "prices" of the factors of production correspond to this inequality of market conditions.

Who gets what where is thus very much a matter of class structure and power, within the institutional organization of production and exchange.

5.2   Class and political power

The ownership of property and the power that it bestows is at the root of class conflict over shares of the social product. The technical controversy in economic theory over the role of capital and the everyday observation of events in capitalist society both suggest that the explanation of who gets what should be couched in terms of " 'relative bargaining power' or class struggle, not marginal productivity" (Hunt and Schwartz,

1972, 20). The essence of the meaning of class in relation to distribution is captured by Weber (1946, 6–7) as follows:

> We may speak of a "class" when (1) a number of people have in common a specific causal component of their life chances, in so far as (2) this component is represented exclusively by economic interests in the possession of goods and opportunities for income, and (3) is represented under the conditions of the commodity or labor markets ... It is the most elemental economic fact that the way in which the disposition over material property is distributed among the plurality of people, meeting competitively in the market for the purpose of exchange, in itself creates specific life chances. According to the law of marginal utility this mode of distribution excludes the non-owners from competing for highly valued goods; it favors the owner and, in fact, gives to them a monopoly to acquire such goods. Other things being equal, this mode of distribution monopolizes the opportunities for profitable deals for all those who, provided with goods, do not necessarily have to exchange them. It increases, at least generally, their power in price wars with those who, being propertyless, have nothing to offer but their services in native form or goods in a form constituted through their own labor, and who above all are compelled to get rid of these products in order barely to subsist. This mode of distribution gives to the propertied a monopoly on the possibility of transferring property from the sphere of use as a "fortune", to the sphere of "capital goods"; that is, it gives them the entrepreneurial function and all chances to share directly or indirectly in returns on capital. All this holds true within the area in which pure market conditions prevail. "Property" and "lack of property" are, therefore, the basic categories of all class situations.

This is basic to the interpretation of distribution—spatial or otherwise—in capitalist societies.

Important though property is, groups with common interests may not necessarily correspond with classes in the narrow Marxian sense of relationship to the means of production. Bell (1974, 53–4) explains this as follows:

> Class categories (or plausible alliances) and political groupings are often imperfectly matched because these are bases of association other than economic loss or gain which mould individuals' perceptions of their interests, but which cross-cut class distinctions. The most obvious and persuasive examples are caste, tribe, race, region, religion and town and country. Whether one of these or class forms the actual basis on which people are politically organized is not a simple empirical question, but a matter of consciousness. For example, a landless laborer may see caste as defining the boundaries of solidarity and division. Simply to label such perceptions of reality as "false consciousness" is unhelpful so long as people continue to see the structure of their world in such ways, though it remains true that a change in the awareness of the poor may have to precede the growth of their political power.

This problem is exemplified in the case of South Africa, discussed in Chapter 9, where race and class are both relevant to the distribution issue.

Who gets what where and how is very much a matter of practical politics. Until quite recently geographers have tended to overlook the importance of political considerations in spatial distributions, confining their studies largely to the more obvious forms of government intervention via regional planning, land-use restriction and so on. The same is true of other disciplines interested in spatial organization and development. As Friedmann (1972–3, 13) says of students of urbanization, they have "tended to explore economic explanations, such as the distribution of natural resources, the location of transport routes, the organization of markets, and economies of scale and agglomeration. With rare exceptions, they have neglected political explanations and, more specifically, explanations given in terms of the spatial distribution of power." However, a number of recent publications have drawn attention to the importance of political power and the resolution of conflict in a spatial setting (e.g. Cox, 1973; Cox, Reynolds and Rokkan, 1974; Hall, 1974a, 1974b). The use of government and economic power is probably the most important single influence on the spatial differentiation of human life chances in the development of urban systems (Friedmann, 1972–3, 49). The significance of politics in determining intra-city distribution has been stressed by writers in geography (Harvey, 1971, 1973; Cox, 1973; Eyles, 1974), sociology (Pahl, 1970) and town planning (Simmie, 1974).

Power is an elusive concept. The only general agreement appears to be that power involves the capacity of a person or group to achieve compliance from others to bring about or resist change (Hawley and Wirt, 1968, 1–2, 215). In other words, power concerns ability to influence the actions and beliefs of others. A distinction is often made between institutional bases of influence and power vested in individuals. In the former, power is attributed to people with access to political parties, business corporations, religious organizations and so on, which have *power resources* in such forms as wealth, votes or prestige; persons able to employ an institution s power resources are considered to have power. In the latter, the compliance of others is based on the power that an individual can bring to inter personal relations, such as those between monarch and subject, employer and employee, union leader and member, or consumer and monopoly supplier.

The exercise of influence over others depends on *power relations*. Dahl (1957) has distinguished five constituents: (1) the *base* of power, provided by economic assets, constitutional prerogative, military force, prestige, etc; (2) the *means* of power, i.e. how influence is exerted through promises, threats, public appeals and so on; (3) the *scope* of power, or the specific actions that one individual can get another to perform; (4) the *amount* of power, defined as the increase in the probability of one person actually performing some specific action due to another's use of means of power against him; (5) the *extension* of power, or the set of individuals over whom power is held. The last three are seen as most relevant to the exercise of great power in a society, i.e. the capacity to influence many people in many respects with a high probability of compliance.

Another important concept is that of *power structure*, or how power is distributed within a society. A familiar dichotomy in political studies is between the elite and pluralist perspectives, ideal types at each end of a continuum. *Elite rule* implies a monopolistic decision-making arrangement, with dominant power exercised by a small, cohesive group often with a common class interest. *Political pluralism* implies a more diffused and less structured pattern, with power dispersed through groups whose interests may conflict and among whom some kind of balance of influence is achieved. The elitist–pluralist distinction can have normative connotations, so a sensible guiding axiom in the study of power is that appearances can be deceptive. Thus a high degree of *de facto* concentration of power may exist in a society with *de jure* dispersal. Institutions which appear on the surface to serve the general interest may in reality be controlled by an elite.

Even in a narrowly based elitist system, conflict can exist. Agger, Goldrich and Swanson (1964, 73–4) have proposed a typology of power structures based on the extent to which the ideology of the political leadership is "convergent and compatible" or "divergent and conflicting", as well as on the distribution of power. They recognize four types of power structure: (1) *consensual mass*, with a broad power distribution and a single shared ideology; (2) *competitive mass*, where power is broadly distributed among groups with conflicting ideologies; (3) *consensual elite*, where the ruling have a common ideology or where different interests are compatible; (4) *competitive elite*, where conflict exists within the ruling group. This and similar typologies developed as simple descriptive models of the political system are helpful in speculating about the likely spatial outcomes of conflict as to who should get what.

Distributional conflict can be explained quite simply, using the utility-space analysis introduced in Chapter 3. Figure 5.2 depicts two communities *R* and *P* comprising a single city; they may be read as "rich" and "poor", "whites" and "blacks", "capital" and "labour", or as "suburbs"

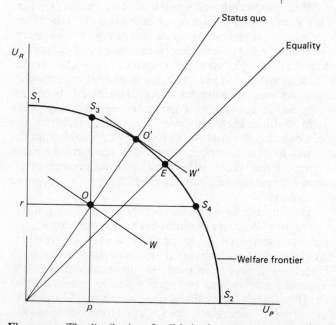

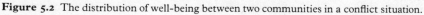

Figure 5.2 The distribution of well-being between two communities in a conflict situation.

and "inner city". The point O shows the distribution of utility or well-being among the two communities, the levels r and p indicating a departure from equality to the extent that the rich have a 3 : 2 advantage. Without postulating a collective distributional preference function, it might be that society operates *as if* the 3 : 2 preference weighting in the slope of the line W applied. Now, suppose that some change such as urban renewal or the construction of a new hospital has the capacity to shift the welfare frontier to $S_1 S_2$ from an existing position running through O. The same relative distribution as before would be at O' on the *status quo* line, or the point of tangency of the line W' (parallel to W) with the welfare frontier. But whether this is the position actually attained depends on the constancy of distributional forces, including the inter-community allocation of power. A dictatorial decision by a new egalitarian ruler might solve the problem at E, which would imply a new preference function of unit negative slope. But there are many other possibilities. Anywhere between S_3 and S_4 is a Pareto improvement on O, because neither R nor P is a loser in the absolute sense; the rich may have the power to appropriate all the additional product and the ingenuity to justify the point S_3 as "better" than O by the Pareto criterion. Any decision of the city government, including where to locate a new facility, implies a distributional position, which could be anywhere on the welfare frontier. The greater the power of the one class, group or community, the more likely a redistribution in their favour unless altruistic motives prevail over self-interest.

The difficulty in this type of conflict situation is lack of a general equity rule for distribution where some gain and some lose. The Pareto criterion begs the question, for at any point in Figure 5.2 other than O' (the *status quo*) there will be a relative if not an absolute advantage to one party or the other. And in reality even Pareto deteriorations (S_1 to S_3 and S_2 to S_4) are very likely if effective power over a decision is in the hands of one party alone. Following Isard *et al.* (1969), a number of approaches to conflict in location decision-making have been suggested, based on inter-community bargaining viewed in a game theoretical framework (e.g. Alperovich, 1972; Salih, 1972). However, these fail to address the fundamental problem beneath the analysis in Figure 5.2, namely that the distributional outcomes have their origin in the allocation mechanisms of the economic system, from which differential political power originates. Novel solutions for conflict resolution are unlikely to be accepted by those who stand to lose.

It is important to distinguish between the actual practice of politics and what happens in theory. Political decision-making is sometimes described in terms of an economic analogy based on consumer sovereignty, in which the vote at elections is an individual resource distributed with perfect equality. The classic form of this model is "to assume that politicians present tax expenditures options to voters so as to maximize the vote they receive. In this search for political support they will discover the preferences of consumers" (Margolis, 1968, 533). However, this view is subject to the same objections as the usual formulations of consumer sovereignty, including consumer ignorance of alternatives and the manipulation of preferences, as well as to the practical fact that a small but well organized minority can often elect their candidate, co-opt the decision-making process and otherwise implement their preferences. In addition, individual votes can be made unequal by those with power, through "gerrymandering", whereby the boundaries of political jurisdictions are arranged so as to ensure minority rule or the disproportionate representation of particular groups or territories (Ginsberg, 1965, 139; Cox, 1973). Power, not votes, is the resource that matters.

The importance of political activity in the redistribution of real income has been stressed by Harvey (1971, 1973). He sees much of what goes on in a city, particularly in the political arena, as "an attempt to organize the distribution of externality effects to gain income advantage" (Harvey, 1973, 58). In the capitalist city the rich and privileged have general allocation mechanisms working in their favour, and also the power to impose their preferences on the poor and weak; wealth provides access to the bases of power and (in Dahl's terms) influences the scope, amount and extent of its application. Large majorities with limited means of power can be excluded from effective participation. "If income redistribution is a 'predictable outcome of the political process' it is not hard to predict the general flow of that redistribution" (Harvey, 1973, 78). Community or neighbourhood differences in wealth, rewards, knowledge and other bases of power are likely to be reflected in differences in well-being, as the redistributive effects of private economic activity and public policy favour those with power to influence the process. This can be self-perpetuating and might even widen the gap between rich and poor. As Pahl (1970, 113) puts it, "The unequal distribution of power, wealth and prestige created by the occupational structure may be simply reinforced in a given locality—so that the less privileged are made even more 'less privileged' by differential access to facilities." Physical planning as well as general income redistribution may help to reduce spatial inequalities in the city. But, as Simmie (1974) argues, planning often proceeds on the assumption of a value consensus when in reality society is made up of conflicting groups who stand to gain or lose differentially by different plans. Territorial equality (or something close to it) seems possible only with a consensual mass or secure consensual elite having equalitarian values and the power to implement whatever redistribution may be necessary.

The territorial-distributional impact of power depends on the spatial arrangement of power. It is therefore helpful to recognize the *spatial extent* of power as a component of Dahl's "extension" concept; space and distance are relevant to the question of who has what power over whom. In some situations power will be limited in its spatial extent by a boundary, beyond which the control of a particular ruler or group will cease by virtue of a change in jurisdiction. Elsewhere, however, *de facto* or informal influence may extend further, as in the case of nations with the power to manipulate events in other nations, or the city with the power to pass on some of its production costs to neighbours in the form of foul air or water. Power may be subject to a distance-decay effect, with fields of influence in space analogous to the urban field or tributary area.

An exploration of the distribution and effect of power at a broad spatial scale has been provided by Friedmann (1972–3). He defines power as "the ability of organizational and institutional actors, located in geographical space, to mobilize and allocate resources (manpower, capital and information) and intentionally to structure the decision-field of others" (Friedmann, 1972–3, 13). He argues that "the spatial distribution of power influences the growth and development of urban systems and, at a higher level of synthesis, also the spatial pattern of integration of a national society". Integration, in its turn, is a major factor affecting the internal cohesion, functioning and survival of a social system. Power is viewed as a stock of resources. In early stages of development, this is likely to be highly concentrated in the capital city and, to a lesser extent, in provincial administrative centres. This will have the effect of concentrating growth, for non-economic influences will weigh heavily in location decisions as (in a private competitive system) management is motivated by a desire for direct access to the relevant centres of government power. The attractive power of the capital will be further enhanced in the process. Subsidiary growth centres spring up in the periphery, frequently following the urban-administrative hierarchy, so that "the initial distribution of governmental power within a country will therefore tend to guide the subsequent evolution of the space economy" (Friedmann, 1972–3, 23). Empirical evidence from a number of countries is offered in support of this generalization. Power in space clearly has an important bearing on the development of the urban and regional system and on distributional inequality between core and periphery.

5.3 The distribution of value among classes

It is now time for some more specific suggestions as to how value is distributed among classes. This can be accomplished via the concept of consumers' surplus, introduced at the beginning of Chapter 3. It will be recalled that consumers' surplus is the difference between what people pay for something and what they would be prepared to pay rather than go without. This is in some respects analogous to Marx's surplus value in the labour market: both identify the difference between use value (or utility) and exchange value (or price). They are not identical, because the portrayal of use value in exchange value terms (e.g. money) is a non-Marxist conceptualization (Harvey, 1973, 169), out of keeping with a more abstract notion of use values which "become a reality only by use or consumption" (Marx, 1867, 44). However, the concept of surplus in the neo-classical sense enables us to catch the spirit of Marxian class conflict, within a familiar graphic model.

Harvey (1973, 169–75) has recognized the potential of consumers' surplus as a device for analysing spatial redistributive effects. It is sometimes used as a measure of consumer "welfare" in location analysis (e.g. Alonso,

1967, 37–8; Denike and Parr, 1970, 56–9). The complementary concept of producers' surplus can similarly provide a measure of rent or profit (e.g. Skitovsky, 1971, 474; Mishan, 1972, 55–6; Samuelson, 1973, 569). The two together might be interpreted as *community surplus* in a system where the producers' share is considered a legitimate return (e.g. Denike and Parr, 1970, 58). The fact that there are methods available for the empirical estimation of the surplus makes these concepts particularly helpful for the analysis of distributional issues associated with development and change.

Figure 5.3 illustrates the general problem of distribution in "value surplus" terms. ("Value surplus" is used here to indicate that the concept

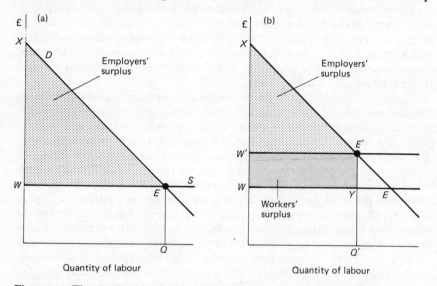

Figure 5.3 The distribution of value surplus between employers and workers.

is close to but not identical with surplus value in the Marxian sense.) In Figure 5.3a we depict the classic situation described by Marx, where labour is paid a bare subsistence wage (*W*). The capitalist can attract all the labour needed at this wage: supply (*S*) is infinitely elastic and the actual number employed (*Q*) is determined by their use value to the capitalist as expressed in his demand curve for labour (*D*). In this situation a surplus equivalent to the triangle *XWE* accrues to the capitalist as consumer in the labour market. There is no producer surplus or rent to labour as there is no difference between what any worker would have worked for and what he or she is actually paid. Thus all community surplus goes to the capitalist employer. Now, suppose that labour is able to organize, exercise some bargaining power, and force wages up to *W'* (Figure 5.3b). All workers accept this wage, nothing less (though if the capitalist exercised the countervailing power of a lockout they might then accept *W* rather than starve). At the new wage level, the consumers' surplus has been reduced to *XW'E'*, the capitalist having lost *WW'E'E*.

There is now a rent to labour of $WW'E'Y$, this having been forced from the capitalist by the power of the workers in the labour market.

While the equity of redistribution does not concern us at this stage, it should be noted that in one sense the community as a whole is worse off with labour market equilibrium at E'. Total employment has fallen from Q to Q', and total community surplus has been reduced by the equivalent of $E'YE$. The transfer from capitalist to labour has occurred at the expense of redistribution *within* the working class. Most workers are better off but some are out of a job—a deterioriation in welfare by the Pareto criterion as well as on egalitarian grounds. The surplus forced from employers may be enough to enable those in work to compensate or support those out of work, but whether such compensation would actually take place depends on the degree of working-class solidarity and on institutional arrangements for redistribution of gains. This raises the important point that in reality conflict over value surplus is not confined to that between capitalist and worker: there may be different interest groups within the working class.

Comparison with Figure 5.1 shows that Figure 5.3 resembles the neo-classical analysis of income distribution. But there is an important difference: in Figure 5.1 *factor* shares are determined by marginal productivity, whereas in the case above *class* shares reflect power in the market. The basic determinant of the wage level or exchange value of labour in Figure 5.3 is the cost of production and reproduction of labour-power. Whatever surplus can be added to this represents real gains to the working class only if the higher wages are not merely compensation for higher costs of the means of subsistence. What comprises a minimum or "reasonable" standard of living for workers is culturally determined and can rise over time—a fact emphasized in Marxian analysis (e.g. Mandel, 1962, 147). Thus the real cost of labour can increase as the economy requires better educated and trained workers or as societal values require the extension of social services. Who meets these additional costs is part of the class struggle.

Our simple model thus recognises the role of class conflict within the labour market in determining who gets what. Marx (1867, 313) described the conflict vividly as follows:

> The directing motive, the end and aim of capitalist production, is to extract the greatest possible amount of surplus-value, and consequently to exploit labour-power to the greatest possible extent. As the number of the co-operating labourers increases, so too does their resistance to the domination of capital, and with it, the necessity for capital to overcome this resistance by counter-pressure.

Capital's bargaining power was assisted by the "industrial reserve army" of unemployed, prepared to take jobs at a bare subsistence wage. During the century since Marx wrote this, the growing power of labour has enabled workers in many countries to increase their real standards of living by successful competition for some of the surplus. However, the *relative* shares of national product going to labour and capital in the USA, for example, remains "surprisingly" constant over the decades (Samuelson, 1973, 541). The general impression from the evidence available is that labour's share of national income in most advanced countries has shown a long-run tendency to rise over time (Atkinson, 1975, 168), and that income has become more equally distributed among workers in different sectors and territories (see section 5.5 below).

The analysis above provides an appropriate framework within which to examine a wide range of distribution problems with a space dimension. Two simple illustrations are offered in Figure 5.4. Case *a* involves the construction of an urban motorway, providing access from suburbs to city centre for a toll charge of £1.50. There are two distinct areally separated communities—poor living in the centre and rich in the suburbs.

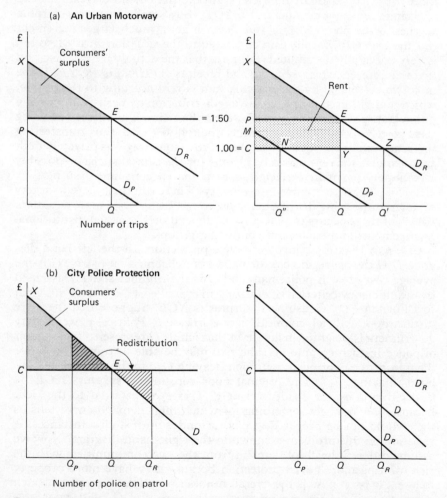

(a) **An Urban Motorway**

(b) **City Police Protection**

Figure 5.4 Redistribution problems in spatial situations viewed from a consumers' surplus perspective.

The demand curve (D_R) for the rich for the new tollroad intersects the price line at E; the triangle XPE identifies their consumers' surplus. The poor have less demand for the facility, as they cannot afford the toll, many of them lack cars and in any case the road does not help them to get to their jobs (it was not designed to); their demand curve (D_P) shows that they do not use the road at all. In this extreme case no value surplus accrues to the poor community, and as part of their neighbourhood has probably been demolished to make way for the road the redistributive impact is almost certainly regressive. It is bound to be regressive if the road has been financed through taxes to which the poor have contributed. Now suppose that the motorway actually cost £1·00 on average per trip (initial construction plus maintenance). A toll of £1·00 would enable more trips to be made by the rich (Q' in the right-hand diagram instead of Q) and a few poor now make trips (Q''). So a small consumers' surplus accrues to the poor (CMN), but the rich get a much larger increment (i.e. the area $CPEZ$); the gain compared to the situation with £1·50 toll is very unequally distributed. Suppose that the actual fare is £1·50 and that the difference between cost and receipts (Q trips) is $PCYE$. If the motorway is owned by the city this sum is rent accruing to the people, which could be used for progressive redistribution by perhaps improving public transport for the poor. However, the rich might succeed in using their power in city politics to reduce the toll to £1·00, thus transferring this rent to their consumers' surplus. If the motorway was privately built and financed, the rent would be income for the capitalist class—possibly a monopoly payment extracted from potential consumers' surplus by virtue of scarcity of routes into the city. There are thus quite a variety of different possible distributional outcomes from this simple situation. Which of these occurs in practice will depend on the actual institutional arrangements and balance of competing groups.

Case *b* in Figure 5.4 involves police protection. In the left-hand diagram D is the aggregate city demand for policemen on patrol, C is the average cost of each policeman, and Q is the number actually assigned by the efficiency criterion of equating marginal cost ($=C$) and marginal social benefit (D). Consumers' surplus is XCE. Suppose that there are distinct poor and rich communities, as in case *a*. Political power in city government is weighted in favour of the rich. If Q represents the number of police in each community, the rich may be able to transfer some of them from the poor neighbourhood (leaving Q_P) to the rich neighbourhood (making Q_R). The original poor consumers' surplus (XCE) is now reduced by the shaded triangle. This is transferred to the rich, because they now get something for which their demand curve tells us they would not be prepared to pay for under normal circumstances. A variation on this problem is shown in the right-hand diagram. Now we assume different levels of demand from the two communities, with the rich wanting more police protection because they have more property to lose. At issue now is the overall number of police in the city, which is set at Q_R if the rich preferences carry, instead of Q_P with poor preferences and Q if the average of D_R and D_P is taken. The fact that the poor will be helping to pay for what, by their preferences, would be an over-supply of police is indicative of the redistribution effects of operating on the basis of rich preferences. One community gains value; the other pays for it.

These imaginary situations are quite representative of actual practice in cities in America and elsewhere. For example, Hirsch (1968, 494) describes the impact of crime as follows: "If those who are hurt are powerful, e.g., in Los Angeles, if they are rich residents of Beverley Hills, Bel Air, Pasadena, or other such communities, as against poor residents of Watts—public remedies might result that incur marginal costs far exceeding the social benefits derived. Thus, the result may be inefficient, yet change the distribution pattern." This is just what case *b* above shows—over-supply by the criterion of equating marginal cost with marginal social benefit, if the general demand curve *D* is the appropriate one for public decision-making. The resulting redistribution helps the relatively rich retain the surplus extracted from the relatively poor by virtue of power in the labour market. Initial class advantage creates further class advantage.

That class conflict over the appropriation of surplus value is inevitably spatial is clearly expressed in the following (Hunt and Schwartz, 1972, 30):

A motorway is to be built through a city displacing thousands of families, inflicting noise, dirt, fumes on nearby residences. Land acquisition, and construction costs are astronomical. Given that the poor and very rich are concentrated, for the most part, in the town centres with middle-income groups in the suburbs and that the latter will constitute overwhelmingly the majority of users, we are in the peculiar situation of *spatially distributed class struggle* [italics added].

Such a struggle has been repeated in many American cities. The outcome is almost invariably the same. The poor are displaced or their environments polluted, the middle-income groups increase their already considerable mobility, and the rich reap most of the additional returns from a more efficient if more unequal city.

To date there have been very few attempts to view spatial distribution explicitly in terms of a struggle over surplus value. The major exception is Harvey (1973). He has shown that in the urban housing market increasing income may enable a group to realize a disproportionately increasing consumers' surplus. They can acquire better housing by the ability just to outbid poorer people, whereas they might be prepared to pay substantially more (Harvey, 1973, 169–70). Externalities are seen as important in this context: "The ability of land to capture benefits, to trap consumers' surpluses, and so on, is exceedingly important and it has to do with scarcity in the sense that both public and private activity create scarcity of sites with favourable access to man-made resources" (Harvey, 1973, 186). Thus the process of jostling for and bargaining over the use and control of the mechanisms for redistribution may be viewed as a struggle to realize surplus value. Recent research from a similar perspective is shedding new light on the operation of the property market in Britain (Ambrose and Colenutt, 1975).

We will now proceed to a more direct discussion of distribution in space, so as to further clarify the origins of inequality at the intra-city and inter-regional levels.

5.4 Spatial distribution within cities

Local differentiation with respect to the benefits of life has its most obvious source in the operation of the economy. Under capitalism the market in the private sector will tend to reward people on the basis of their resource endowment and productive efficiency. As these attributes are unlikely to be distributed at random within a city, we can anticipate spatial inequalities in money income and those amenities or services dependent on income. In early stages of economic growth the degree of inequality among neighbourhoods is likely to be extremely marked, with a small rich elite and the rest of the people very poor. In time there may be a spread effect as the wealthy invest in activities that generate employment and other benefits for the poor, but the degree of inequality may not be greatly reduced. Mobility of factors will be very limited: capital does not flow into poor neighbourhoods in search of cheap labour—it may avoid them because of higher insurance rates arising from the perceived threat to property. Low-paid workers do not migrate to rich parts of a city, except perhaps temporarily as servants; wealthy neighbourhoods are more likely to exclude the poor and attract more rich people. Marked spatial differentiation of per capita income is therefore likely to be a permanent feature of the capitalist city. It will also occur under socialism, if people in different occupations get different rewards and are not evenly distributed among all residential areas.

At this point it is worth distinguishing between "place poverty" and "people poverty". Differentiation of per capita income among subdivisions of a city reflects who occupies particular areas and their role in the economic system. Low-income people may occupy certain parts of a city by virtue of their low income, but their money incomes are not low because of where they live except in so far as poor accessibility reduces employment opportunities. Place poverty emerges when other benefits or penalties compound the advantages or disadvantages of particular groups by virtue of where they live. This is how the spatial distribution of external effects plays its crucial role in the process of areal differentiation.

The more obvious external costs imposed by economic activity in cities have been recognized for a long time. In the capitalist city private business is able to "slough off on society various social costs that its presence imposes, such as its addition to traffic congestion and air pollution" (Thompson, 1965, 80), thus decreasing the proportion of real production costs that fall on business. External costs are very unlikely to be borne by just those people who consume the product in question, so redistribution is at work which benefits some people at the expense of others. If the environmental deterioration caused by congestion, pollution, noise and so on accrues mainly to residents of low-income areas close to the factories (as is often the case) and if their goods consumption levels are lower than those of richer people (as is usually the case), then the normal operation of the private sector in the urban economy will substantially redistribute real income (value, utility or well-being) from poor to rich. How far this is balanced by the higher taxes paid by the richer residents is difficult to establish without measures of the disutility effect of environmental degradation.

It is in the public sector rather than in the operation of private business that the more subtle redistribution takes place. The distributional implications of the provision of public goods and the impurity arising from the reality of geographical space has been recognized for some time in literature on metropolitan government, public finance and urban economics (e.g. Musgrave, 1959; Thompson, 1965; Margolis, 1968; Netzer, 1968; Buchanan, 1968). Netzer (1968, 438) summarizes the problem as follows:

Distribution policies or consequences ultimately concern individual consumer units. One dimension, the usual measure in incidence studies, is the proximate dimension of incidence by income *class*. Another dimension, important in a metropolitan context, is that of *geographic* redistribution within large urban areas. The fragmentation of tax bases among a large number of political jurisdictions of extremely disparate character, the high uneven geographic distribution of expenditure needs (notably, residences of the poor) and the possibility of exporting some tax burdens across jurisdictional lines, together suggest that the metropolitan fisc might have redistributive consequences among communities. The usual variant of this is the "suburban exploitation of the central city" hypothesis.

Although this relates specifically to the American city, where local government organization often facilitates the avoidance by suburban residents of much of the real cost of the generation of their wealth in central parts of the city, it has general implications. Whatever the city, different public resource allocations and different locations of facilities will produce different distributions of real income or well-being.

The covert nature of spatial redistribution in the public sector is particularly important. Shoup (1964, 383) explains it thus:

Little is known about the distribution of government services by location, race, religion, income class, or other category. Usually, no record is made, no estimate attempted. The laws providing for the service are silent in this respect; the authorizing or appropriating committees of legislatures do not discuss it; budgets submitted by the executive say nothing about how a given service is to be distributed among the users. This silence reflects in part a social propensity to discriminate covertly in ways that are not tolerable in taxation, where the pattern of impact is more obvious. For example: education has been distributed unequally, by social class, race or colour, in communities that would not think of distributing the tax bill by those indicia.

Studies of allocation in the public sector often ignore distributional aspects "as if some lump sum transfer could painlessly solve the problem of equity" (Katzman, 1968, 201). The question of equity or fairness of the distribution of benefits and costs arising from public spending exists in any society, by virtue of distance making equal access in real terms impossible. But in the capitalist city the problem is exacerbated by un-equal distribution of the power resources needed to influence public policy.

Harvey (1971; 1973, ch. 2) was the first to raise these problems expli-citly in geography. He refers to the "hidden mechanisms" which connect allocation decisions on transport networks, industrial zoning, the location of public facilities, household and so on with their distributional effects upon the real income of different groups in the population. This works in favour of certain areas of the city: "Force gives way to public policy as a device for securing and maintaining locational advantage" (Lineberry, 1974, 30). The same theme has been developed by Cox (1973). In addition to the more familiar external effects generated by the public and private economy, he recognizes certain more personal sources of well-being aris-ing from the interdependence of utility. *Public behaviour externalities* such as upkeep of property, crime, general public comportment (e.g. quiet, sobriety and tidiness) and child behaviour are strong influences on indivi-dual satisfaction with a particular neighbourhood. *Status externalities* may accrue as positive or negative utility arising from place of residence. These conditions are important in differentiating place utility; people will tend to arrange themselves in space so as to exclude those from whom negative spillover effects can be expected while encouraging those bring-ing positive external effects. The class and race exclusiveness of large tracts of American suburbia exemplifies this. It is a major force behind the emergence and preservation of intra-city inequality in human well-being, for the poor have less freedom than the rich to avoid places with negative public behaviour and status externalities.

The spatial distribution of benefits (value added) and costs (value sub-tracted) may now be considered more specifically. The context is the pro-vision of public goods, where externalities are particularly clear at the local level. We will begin with the problem of *spillovers*, which Musgrave (1968, 569) describes as "the crux of local fiscal theory". In a spatial con-text, these have been defined by Cox (1972, 122) as follows: "Positive spillover effects are unpriced benefits to individuals in areas outside the area commanded by the collectivity. Negative spillover effects are un-priced costs to individuals in areas outside the area commanded by the collectivity." The collectivity referred to is those who pay for the pro-vision of a service in the area in question through local taxes or whatever other system of financial levy is used. There is controversy on which ser-vices exhibit particular spillover characteristics (e.g. Margolis, 1968, 534–5), but some obvious examples should make the point. A tough and effec-tive police force in one part of a metropolis could force criminals to move to another part (negative spillover) or reduce the level of crime city-wide by generally discouraging lawlessness (positive spillover). A good neigh-bourhood school can have positive city-wide spillovers in the form of better citizens or more skilful labour: a poor school can have negative spillover effects by lowering general educational standards.

Any territory or local government jurisdiction can be thought of as

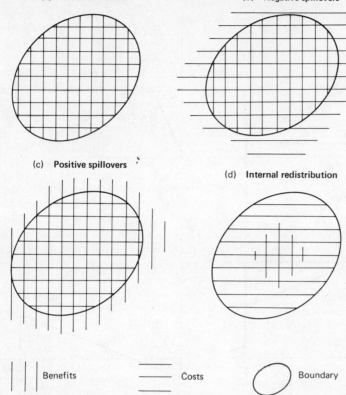

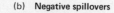

Figure 5.5 Alternative spatial patterns of spillover and spillin effects.

having exports and imports of external effects. It will be in the interests of the collectivity to minimize net positive spillovers and maximize net positive spillins. How space is bounded is thus a critical matter in public finance (Williams, 1966; Buchanan, 1968; Bish, 1971, 45–61; Cox, 1972, 120–24). This is illustrated in Figure 5.5, where a local government area boundary is shown with four possible alternative distributions of benefits and costs. Pattern *a* is the "ideal" situation of all costs and benefits confined to the area in question. In *b* benefits are confined but there are negative spillovers transferring part of the real cost to adjoining areas. In *c* some of the benefits go to people in the adjoining areas who pay none of the costs. Case *d* shows an area-wide cost but benefits confined to only part of the area—an internal redistribution in favour of perhaps a single neighbourhood. Some or all of these spillover/spillin effects will be present in any system of local government jurisdictions, as typified by the spatial organization of the modern metropolis. Even in the case of a single city-wide jurisdiction responsible for all public services, some internal redistribution will take place.

The spatial distribution of costs and benefits depend very much on

(a) **Fire station**

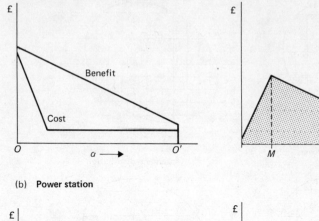

(b) **Power station**

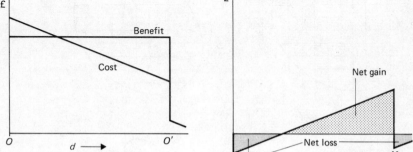

(c) **Park or Swimming pool**

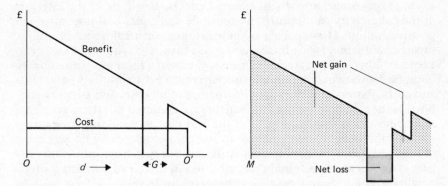

Figure 5.6 The spatial distribution of costs and benefits from public facilities.

the location of facilities. Accessibility or proximity creates an *impact field* within which benefits or costs are imposed (Dear, 1974, 49), analogous to the externality field recognized in the previous chapter (Figure 4.7). Many facilities combine negative neighbourhood effects on those close by with broader spatial distribution of benefits (Alperovich, 1972, 6); all impact must be taken into account in the analysis of *net* benefit or cost.

Three imaginary cases are illustrated in Figure 5.6. A population is evenly spread along a line (*d*); a facility is located at *O*, paid for by taxes contributed by the people within a local government area extending to *O'* to the right (and a similar distance to the left, not shown). Case *a* is a fire station, benefits from which are subject to a distance-decay effect and do not extend beyond *O'*. There is a spatially constant finance charge, to which must be added a negative neighbourhood effect in the immediate vicinity of the fire station as a result of noise and so on. The difference between benefits and costs gives the net gain, which is maximized at *M* some distance from the fire station where the neighbourhood effect ceases. Case *b* is a power station, benefiting all inhabitants of the area up to *O'* equally by reducing their electricity charges. Air pollution is added to the operating costs; total cost near the plant is high enough to more than balance the benefit so there is a net loss to close residents. Spillover of pollution beyond *O'* accrues as a net loss to residents in a neighbouring area. Case *c* is a park or a swimming pool, which costs all residents the same annual charge, disregarding any slight negative neighbourhood effect from use by noisy people. Benefits are subject to a distance-decay effect arising from accessibility. They extend beyond *O'* because visitors from adjoining areas may use the facility. To add a complication, the area *G* is the ghetto of a racial or ethnic minority, who are denied access by virtue of discrimination or lack of transport even though they help to finance the facility through their taxes (black residents in South African cities and some in the USA are in this position). There is thus an area of net loss corresponding with *G*. Maximum net gain is found adjoining the facility in case *c*, while it is on the edge of the jurisdiction in case *b*.

In two-dimensional space and with variations in population density the identification of spatial benefit and cost surfaces becomes more complex than in these simple situations. The problem of calculating net gain or loss is the same as that posed by the utility or disutility field (Figure 4.7). An example of this type of *spatial cost–benefit analysis* is provided by Mumphrey and Wolpert (1973).

While the above analysis has focused on the city in a capitalist or mixed economy, similar if less marked spatial differentiation may be found under socialism. Services are likely to be more evenly distributed among neighbourhoods or other internal subdivisions, but local accessibility will give some people advantages over others. And there may be differences in environmental quality (e.g. proximity to factories or parks) not reflected in rentals, as in the case of Moscow, for example. Restriction on freedom of residential choice may add an element of capriciousness to this differentiation.

The analysis of distribution in the city underlines again the importance of geographical mobility. Personal mobility on a day-to-day basis makes for ease of access to facilities such as place of work, shops, entertainment and hospitals. In most societies it depends on car ownership or an efficient public transport system. The former is dependent on income; the latter may well require a city administration dominated by the interests of the rich approving public expenditure which largely benefits the not-so-rich. In any event the poor are likely to be the least mobile.

On a longer-term basis, mobility implies the capacity to choose place of residence from a range of alternatives. The greater the mobility, the greater the freedom to avoid the effects of negative externalities and to choose the particular mix of local services and so on that best satisfies personal preferences, stage in life cycle, etc. This is the notion of voting with one's feet, introduced in Chapter 3. It is important in the literature on public services (e.g. Margolis, 1968), where attempts are sometimes made to portray territorial differences as a response to consumer sovereignty. But individuals and families are not equally mobile. All manner of considerations promote immobility—from income to ignorance—and this means that many if not most city residents may live in an environment not of their own choosing. As Brazer (1964, 139) puts it:

> If people chose their place of residence freely, it could then be argued that the price paid for living in one community rather than another, in terms of higher taxes paid for a given level of services or a given rate of tax paid for a lower level of services, was voluntarily assumed. It might even be reflected in land values in such a fashion as to be approximately offsetting in effect. But as long as barriers to mobility exist, through zoning regulations, racial discrimination, and so forth, such offsetting will not occur and neither equity nor efficiency can be achieved.

Freedom of residential choice is thus a critical determinant of an individual's life chances. For this reason private and public mechanisms for allocating housing and residential locations are important means of deciding who gets what where, in which economic and political power have a major role (Harvey, 1971; Eyles, 1974, 50–52). Restrictions on freedom of residential choice not equally applicable to all are an obvious *prima facie* indication of social injustice (see Chapter 6).

5.5 Regional growth and inequality

What basis is there for expecting inequality in regional levels of well-being? If the well-being of people in different places can legitimately be compared on some uniform indicator such as money income (an assumption commonly made) what conditions are likely to lead to territorial differentiation? In other words, if who gets what varies with region, how do these variations arise?

Obviously, what can be produced and distributed among the population will vary with local input or factor endowment and transformation efficiency. The uneven geographical distribution of resources and skills might thus be reflected in an uneven distribution of income and wealth.

This is a familiar notion in geography. However, to understand more fully the origins of regional variations in well-being we must look much further than the local resource base and culture.

Economic growth theory provides a starting point. In Chapter 4, expression [4.1], the level of income of any territory was defined as gross product, or depreciation of capital equipment plus value added by labour in the process of production, which in a capitalist system includes the shares attributed to interest, profits and rent. Growth of the product takes place as the amount of labour and capital increases, given the natural resources and technology. Ignoring improvements in productivity, labour supply increases as population grows, and this can be assigned to the production of goods for immediate consumption (e.g. by the new workers and their families) and also to the production of more capital goods. From [4.3], gross (regional) product is consumption plus investment; the more that is consumed, the less there is to invest in capital equipment. Thus how fast the economy grows depends on how much is saved and how much is produced by the new investment.

The proportion of any addition to income spent on consumption is known as the *marginal propensity to consume (MPC)*. As all income is either spent or saved, the *marginal propensity to save (MPS)* is 1—*MPC*. Following Keynesian income theory, any increase in investment will raise income by a *multiplier* given by the reciprocal of the marginal propensity to save, i.e.

$$dY = \frac{1}{MPS} dI \qquad [5.4]$$

or

$$dY = \frac{1}{1 - MPC} dI \qquad [5.5]$$

where dY is change in income and dI is change in investment. The greater a region's capacity or inclination to save and invest, the more rapid its income growth (other things remaining the same). The production possibility constraint imposed by resources and technology may itself change, with investment in research and development to identify new resources and promote technical innovation.

If growth depends on savings and investment, then ownership of the surplus product is important. In a capitalist economy the decision to spend on consumption or save and invest is in private hands, which can be very few in number if wealth and control of the means of production is highly concentrated. In Marxian analysis the rate of growth is determined by how much of the surplus value appropriated by the capitalist class is available after spending on luxury consumption. In a socialist system the people or their planners can select their own balance between immediate consumption and growth-directed investment. Thus the mode of production and the pattern of ownership and control can have an important bearing on national and regional growth rates. The more an economy is in the hands of people predisposed towards consumption of the surplus, the slower the growth of aggregate income is likely to be.

Trade is important to regional growth, just as it is to a national economy. Other things being equal, the more a region can export rather than consume at home, the greater its growth potential. We can write [5.5] above with exports in place of investment, to give

$$dY = \frac{1}{1 - MPC} dE \qquad [5.6]$$

where dE is an increase in exports and MPC is now the marginal propensity to consume goods and services produced within the region. A given increase in earnings from exports will thus generate an increase in regional income determined by the *regional multiplier* (Richardson, 1969a, ch. 10; 1969b, ch. 1; Nourse, 1969, ch. 7). Much research has been devoted to the empirical identification of regional multipliers through *economic base theory*, which distinguishes between basic (export) and non-basic economic activity and uses the proportion of basic to total employment as a surrogate for the marginal propensity to consume domestic production (Smith, 1971, 458–9; Keeble, 1967). Other influences on regional income must not be overlooked, however. For example, the local propensity to spend on imports will cut the growth-inducing effect of export earnings by reducing what is available for investment in new capital equipment.

With these foundations of growth theory we may return to the question of income inequality in a system of regions. If one region has a strong comparative advantage for certain lines of production and is able to find markets in other regions, relatively rapid growth will be initiated. But theory is somewhat ambiguous on the critical question of how far this will continue and lead to marked inter-regional income inequalities Richardson, 1969a, ch. 13; 1969b, ch. 2). Neo-classical growth models which stress factor mobility suggest a convergence of regional per capita income levels: the market will tend to generate capital flows from high- to low-wage regions in response to higher potential returns, with labour flowing in the opposite direction. As factor returns are equalized, regional income levels will converge. In reality the equilibrating mechanisms will be prevented from operating fully, for example by imperfect *spatial* mobility of factors and imperfect knowledge of distant opportunities on the part of both labour and capitalists. This, along with regional differences in natural resources, population growth, technical progress, labour productivity and so on, strongly suggests some inter-regional income differences as a permanent feature of any economy not planned with territorial equality as an over-riding goal.

More specifically spatial approaches to the question of regional inequality show similar conclusions. Myrdal (1957) has argued that once regional growth has been initiated, flows of capital, labour and commodities tend to support it and operate as a *backwash effect*, to the disadvantage of the regions from which inputs are drawn. Subsequent demand from the prosperous core for goods from the stagnant periphery may induce a growth *spread effect*, but continuing regional income inequality is strongly suggested. Hirschman (1958) developed a similar model, with growth having a *polarization effect* and a *trickling down effect*. Polarization includes the depressing effect of the prosperous region's strength on a lagging region, while trickling down spreads growth through investment and the purchase of inputs. Hirschman regarded a trend towards convergence as more likely than did Myrdal, but this was partly on the basis of an expectation that regional balance would be promoted by public policy.

Another view of the regional development process that has attracted recent attention proposes that growth is transmitted through an economy via the urban hierarchy. Innovations initiated in the major cities or metropolitan areas diffuse down to successively lower levels in the hierarchy, thus spreading economic growth from the core region or regions into the periphery (e.g. Berry and Neils, 1969; Pred, 1969, ch. 4; Lasuén, 1971; Friedmann, 1972). Berry (1970, 43) summarizes this process as follows:

(a) The size and function of a central city, the size of its urban field, and the spatial extent of developmental 'spread effects' radiating outward from it are proportional.
(b) The impulses of economic change are transmitted in order from higher to lower centres in the urban hierarchy, in a 'size-ratchet' sequence, so that continued innovation in large cities remains critical for extension of growth over the complete economic system.
(c) The spatial incidence of economic growth is a function of distance from the central city. Troughs of economic backwardness lie in the most inaccessible areas along the peripheries between the least accessible lower-level centres in the hierarchy.
(d) The growth potential of an area situated along an axis between two cities is a function of the intensity of interaction between them.

Research in the United States provides some support for this view (e.g. Barry and Neils, 1969), but Pred (1971) has questioned how far innovation proceeds in this orderly progression down the urban size hierarchy. Certainly Britain provides an obvious exception, with most major innovations in technology during the Industrial Revolution taking place outside London in peripheral locations. Friedmann (1972–3, 25) argues that in the "ideal-type developing country" hierarchical diffusion holds true, with the entry points for most innovations tending to be the largest cities such as the capital or major port.

Even if only partially true as an empirical observation, this process might suggest that differences between centre and periphery would gradually be eliminated and the space-economy integrated by the outward flow of growth impulses and the inward migration of labour to the cities. Troughs of economic backwardness at the intermetropolitan periphery would be eroded (Berry, 1970, 43). Closely tied up with the diffusion argument is the use of planned *growth points* in the poor periphery to stimulate industrialization and thus assist with the reduction of regional inequality. But if change continues, with further innovations in the metropolitan areas, some time-lag differentiation will persist. As Friedmann (1972–3) suggests, political as well as economic conditions will tend to preserve the dominance of the core over the peripheral regions (see section 5.2 above).

The relationship between economic growth and income inequality is clearly not a simple one. There is some empirical support for the view that inequality *increases* in early stages of development and then decreases, among population groups as well as regions (e.g. Ahluwalia, 1974; Reiner, 1974; Stöhr, 1974). Williamson (1965) found such a pattern in a study of inter-regional inequality in twenty-four countries, with maximum inequality in middle periods of development. Myrdal (1957) and Kuznetz (1966) both suggest declines in inequality among population groups in later stages of development. Increasing inequality in early stages of development is supported by various studies, for example Semple and Gauthier (1972) in Brazil. Richardson (1969b, 59–62) cites evidence supporting the convergence hypothesis for regional income in the USA (see also Figure 10.11 below), while convergence tendencies seem weak in Britain where the gap between low- and high-income regions is very small. Atkinson (1975, 250) is sceptical about evidence for convergence: "there are structural reasons to expect an increase in concentration in the early stages of development. Whether this trend will be reversed as incomes rise has yet to be determined.'

The perpetuation of regional inequality under capitalism is a major feature of the contemporary critique of neo-classical theory. Responding to the proposition that "competition tends to eliminate differences in rates of wages for similar workers in different occupations *and geographical locations*" (Stigler, 1966, 257; italics added), Galbraith (1975, 218) claims that "The present system leads, in contrast, to the expectation of an enduring difference in income between workers in different parts of the economy." This he explains as a consequence of the power of the "planning system" of large corporations to organize the economy in their own interests, predominant among which are the status, security and monetary rewards of the managerial "technostructure". Economic growth has thus become concentrated, to the disadvantage of the small producers of the "market system" who tend to be more geographically dispersed and less influential in the corridors of government power.

Marxian theory offers a similar prediction of increasing geographical concentration, driven on by the generation of surplus value, profits and capital accumulation. This is part of the general phenomenon of "uneven development" (Mandel, 1962, 91–2, 371–3). The spatial expansion of capitalism in search of new markets and investment opportunities is highly selective, favouring growth in some cities, regions and nations overseas (and benefiting only some population groups within them), just as at home some regions prosper while others become depressed. Marxian analysis offers a major alternative to conventional regional development theory (see for example de Souza and Porter, 1974; Brookfield, 1975; Slater, 1975), with its failure to penetrate the critical issue of spatial inequality.

The most influential contributions to spatial analysis from a Marxian perspective are those of Harvey (1973; 1975). He argues that location analysis is a crucial link between the theories of accumulation and imperialism: the dynamic of accumulation requires certain geographical structures (Harvey, 1975, 13). Important in this are centre-periphery relations in production and exchange. This builds on an earlier view of urbanism in capitalist societies, analysed in terms of the creation, appropriation and circulation of surplus value (Harvey, 1973, ch. 6). That cities emerge with the extraction and concentration of surplus product from an agricultural hinterland has been recognized for some time. Harvey sees hierarchical systems of cities as providing channels for the circulation and concentration of surplus value. Internal differentiation is associated with the circulation of surplus value within the city. Following Hoselitz (1960) Harvey distinguishes between *generative* cities in which a considerable amount of the surplus is invested to increase production locally or in the surrounding rural area, and *parasitic* cities where the surplus is mainly consumed by the elite. The more effective the integration of the space economy, the easier it will be for capitalists to extract and concentrate surplus value: "Price-fixing markets cannot function, for example, on a parochial basis and require an effective economic integration over space if they are to work" (Harvey, 1973, 237).

Harvey (1973, 238) takes issue with Friedmann's early proposals for generating economic growth in underdeveloped nations via an urban-hierarchical form of spatial organization. This might simply facilitate core concentration of the surplus extracted in the periphery. Friedmann himself provides a clear view of this process in a summary of the theory of "dependent capitalism" (Friedmann and Wulff, 1975, 13):

> Basically, it involves the notion that powerful corporate and national interests, representing capitalist society at its most advanced, establishes outposts in the principal cities of Third World countries, essentially for three related purposes: to extract a sizeable surplus from the dependent economy, chiefly in the form of primary products, through a process of "unequal exchange"; to expand the market for goods and services produced in the home countries of advanced monopoly capitalism; and to ensure stability of an indigenous political system that will resist encroachment by ideologies and social movements that threaten to undermine the basic institutions of the capitalistic system. All three forms of penetration are ultimately intended to serve the single purpose of helping to maintain expanding levels of production and consumption in the home countries of advanced capitalism.

Important in this process is the cooptation of local elites, the local concentration of wealth, and the role of the international corporations.

A particularly instructive view of the emerging world economy and its impact on spatial variations in human well-being is provided by Hymer (1975, 38):

> A regime of North American Multinational Corporations would tend to produce a hierarchical division of labour between geographical regions corresponding to the vertical division of labour within the firm. It would tend to centralize high-level decision-making occupations in a few key cities in the advanced countries,

surrounded by a number of regional sub-capitals, and confine the rest of the world to lower levels of activity and income, i.e. to the status of towns and villages in a new Imperial system. Income, status, authority, and consumption patterns would radiate out from these centres along a declining curve, and the existing pattern of inequality and dependency would be perpetuated.

The relationship between countries would be one of superior and subordinate, head office and branch plants—or "company countries" (Mandel, 1962, 470) like the company towns of the Industrial Revolution in Britain but with a head office in London. This would be the final stage in the classic imperialist-colonialist progression from plunder, through trade and the destruction of indigenous modes of production by competition, to capital investment and the repatriation of profits.

The urban hierarchy now takes on a role somewhat different from that postulated in the diffusion-of-growth theory. Returns on investment in the periphery (national or international) flow up the hierarchy. The material benefits of economic growth trickle down and out to the periphery in the form of new income and consumer goods to absorb it. But these innovations may merely reflect the tastes of the core elite, adopted elsewhere through a demonstration effect: "This group may have something approaching a choice in consumption patterns; the rest have only the choice between conforming or being isolated" (Hymer, 1975, 51). The periphery may become the cradle for discontent on the part of some "counter-elite", perhaps spawning separatist movements (Parr, 1974, 86). These may be suppressed, or mollified by regional development programmes, growth points and devolution of administrative functions. But they may also lead to more revolutionary innovations, as in Cuba and China, to reverse the conventional diffusion process (Brookfield, 1975, 126) and create a new society.

The process of uneven regional development and underdevelopment is sketched out in Figure 5.7. This shows four stages in the emergence of an imaginary urban hierarchy, with suggestions as to the direction of the predominant (net) capital flows. Stage 1 shows the major city (core) disbursing capital accumulated in earlier commercial activity into its hinterland (periphery), via smaller regional centres. In stage 2 the flows are predominantly back towards the core in the form of interest on investment in the periphery, though subsidiary centres still funnel capital out to more distant places. In stage 3 the spatial structure of capital flows has become more complex, but concentration still predominates; the core city now exports capital to its colony previously connected by trade. In stage 4 the colony's hierarchy is developing to channel funds into the periphery and to repatriate profits; at home there is some withdrawal from the periphery, leaving a depressed area, in the modern period of metropolitan concentration. Although this is highly intuitive, it bears a resemblance to the model of transport development proposed by Taaffe, Morrill and Gould (1963). Some evidence that Figure 5.7 might describe actual patterns of capital flows during the development process is provided by Conzen (1975). Returning to our concept of the spatial well-being surface from Chapter 3, the general form will show a falling-away

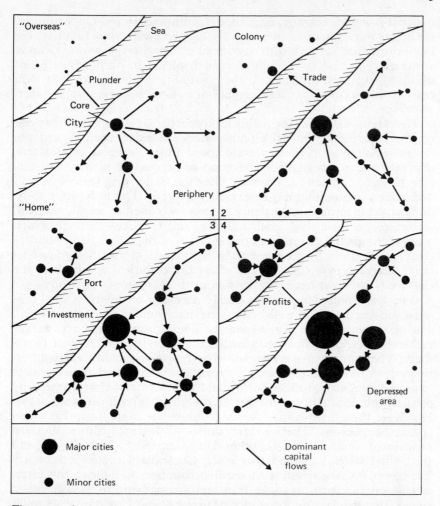

Figure 5.7 A generalized view of the emergence of a space-economy involving a "home" and "overseas" territory, emphasizing the articulation of capital flows via the urban hierarchy.

from the central metropolis towards the periphery, interrupted by local peaks corresponding with regional and sub-regional centres in the urban hierarchy and by depressed areas as troughs of low well-being. Empirical support for this generalization will be found in the case studies of South Africa and the USA in Chapters 9 and 10.

Some of the implications of this process for the British space-economy have been examined by Westaway (1974a; 1974b). He finds the changing distribution of occupational groups and head offices consistent with the theory of hierarchical organization put forward by Hymer (1975). The uneven geographical distribution of social classes associated with concentration of business decision-making is paralleled by inequalities in material rewards, housing, education, health and so on. Opportunities for access to positions of privilege are limited away from London; the less prosperous regions with few head offices have a stunted career structure. External ownership of branch plants in peripheral regions means loss of local control, and the possibility of closure for non-local reasons. It also means a "leaking out" of non-wage income to investors elsewhere.

The extent of regional inequality in any particular situation will depend on the actual geographical circumstances. Marxian analysis and the recent revisions of regional development theory suggest certain tendencies—towards spatial concentration of productive activity and differentiation of human life chances. "But the underlying logic does not, and indeed cannot uniquely determine outcomes. The latter have to be understood in terms of the balance of forces—economic, social, political, ideological, competitive, legal, military, and the like—through which interest groups and classes become conscious of the contradictory underlying logic and seek by their actions to 'fight it out' to some sort of resolution" (Harvey, 1975, 18). This is where the empirical approach of the case study becomes necessary, to fill out the bare bones of theory.

One clear prediction emerges from our review of theory: spatial inequality in real income or well-being is inevitable under a capitalist system. The idea of integration of the space-economy promoting concentration rather than a spread effect casts further doubt on the convergence hypothesis. That capitalism is accompanied by general inequality is recognized by its most fervent defenders: "A capitalist system involving payments in accordance with product can be, and in practice is, characterized by considerable inequality of income and wealth" (Friedman, 1962, 168). However, these inequalities are not unique to capitalism; Friedman (1962, 169) goes on, "There is surely drastically less inequality in Western capitalist societies like the Scandinavian countries, France, Britain, and the United States, than in a status society like India or a backward country like Egypt." Comparison with socialist countries is difficult but Hunt and Sherman (1972, 615–16), in a text sympathetic to radical views, suggest that the distribution of income in the Soviet Union is very similar to the distribution of wage income in the USA; the difference is that there is no upper end of the distribution in the USSR, no profit, rent or interest, and no exploitation in Marx's sense of the term. With respect to *spatial* distribution, socialist societies have greater freedom to disperse investment in pursuit of regional equality and the reduction of disparities between town and country. But even here there may be efficiency constraints to slow down or limit convergence. Investment may be more efficiently deployed in concentrated form, by virtue of economies of scale and agglomeration. Even in a socialist society dedicated to the eradication of differences in living standards among regions, efficiency criteria in national planning may lead to a concentration of effort on regions with the greatest productive potential, as in Chinese agricultural policy (Wilson, 1970, 107), for development of poor regions may depend on the surplus generated in those with a more favourable resource endowment.

Special bonus payments may be made to encourage workers to move to priority development regions, as is the case with Siberia. Nevertheless, socialist countries have the highest degree of overall equality in the distribution of income—or so the available data suggest (e.g. Ahluwalia, 1974, 7–9).

Thus spatial inequalities in levels of well-being—in who gets what—can be expected in societies at all stages of development and under both capitalist and socialist systems. Industrialization, the integration of the space-economy and dispersal of productive capacity will reduce the more marked inequalities of feudal or status societies. But a continuing spread effect may well run counter to the concentration tendencies of capitalism and is likely to be more an outcome of the emerging political power of peripheral regions and changing societal values than a natural economic process. If convergence eventually comes, it is more likely to be under socialism than capitalism. And even then it can conflict with efficiency, in societies where the support of poor, unproductive regions may at first be an expensive luxury. Only in the mature socialist state can we expect to see the spatial equivalent of: "From each according to his ability, to each according to his needs" (Marx, 1875, 388). And even then, needs may still vary with locality.

Part Two

Approaches to Practice

Society is produced by the wants, Government by the wickedness, and a state of just and happy equality by the improvement and reason of man.

Percy Bysshe Shelley, "An Address to the Irish People", 1812

So long as production does not ensure ... satisfaction of fundamental human needs, the central economic problem remains that of *sharing scarcity* (in a more or less relative sense) of consumer goods, a form of distribution which must be regulated by objective criteria.

Ernest Mandel, *Marxist Economic Theory*, 1962

Part One has provided theoretical perspectives on the positive question of how human well-being varies from place to place. The discussion now shifts to the normative question of how things might be arranged better or best. Passing judgements on spatial patterns, like any evaluation of the distribution of life's benefits and burdens, raises complex issues of political and moral philosophy. The word *evaluation* itself is a warning that values are involved and that we must therefore tread with care. Evaluation inevitably leads to the question of change, for once a pattern has been judged inadequate from a welfare point of view the next step is alteration or spatial reorganization.

Part Two provides the basis for an applied human geography concerned with the planning of spatial aspects of social and economic change. It comprises a bridge between the theory of Part One and the case studies of Part Three. The content is rooted in the theoretical framework established in previous chapters, but it responds to real-world problems of evaluation and action. Chapter 6 addresses the question of how alternative spatial distributions might be judged, while Chapter 7 reviews research procedures of special importance in the practical application of the welfare approach. While the focus is on rather abstract concepts of social justice and on the specifics of evaluative and planning techniques, we will not entirely lose sight of the fact that who gets what where is very much an outcome of the broader structure of society. The theme of the interdependence of spatial inequality, spatial organization and socio-economic structure will be subdued for most of Part Two, but it will emerge again strongly in Part Three.

6

Evaluation: Judging Distributions

The evaluation of spatial variations in human well-being is closely associated with *social justice*. While we have become accustomed to judging conspicuous inequality by race, colour, creed or class as unjust, it is only recently that the notion of *spatial injustice* has been aired (e.g. Harvey, 1972a, 1973, ch. 3; Buttimer, 1972). When people refer to "inequalities in the educational opportunities . . . regardless of race, colour and region" (Mack, 1970, 19), the casual reader could well take "region" as a misprint for "religion", so rare is the use of the spatial term in this kind of context (Smith, 1973a, 4–5). Yet the possibility of *discrimination* by place of residence leading to an unjust distribution of income, goods and services is a matter of growing concern. To describe a situation as discriminatory or unjust is deceptively easy—so much so that these terms are in danger of being debased by careless usage. This chapter should help to restore meaning to the concept of spatial or territorial injustice.

How do we go about making judgements between alternative (spatial) states of society? This question is basic to the welfare approach to human geography, which has as one of its major objectives the clarification of the issue of who *should* get what where and how. Ideally, we would like a precise specification of the perfect world against which to compare the existing state. In reality we often find it difficult to make a choice between two apparently simple alternatives, such as industrial concentration or dispersal, more or less money for depressed regions, or alternative motorway routes. But to improve the world, we must have ways of distinguishing better from worse. Specifically, the geographer requires rules whereby existing distribution patterns of human well-being and the redistributions likely to result from social change may be assigned an order of preference.

Before proceeding, a reminder of the scope of our concept of *what* is distributed is again in order. The previous chapter inevitably tended towards a rather more concrete concept of human well-being than was proposed at the beginning of the book; whether the focus is on income or surplus value, the empirical identity is likely to be in pecuniary units. But the evaluation of distribution patterns must as far as possible concern all sources of human satisfaction, positive or negative. This even includes such abstractions as liberty and freedom. These are sometimes portrayed as outside that which is distributed; for example: "The nineteenth-century liberal regarded an extension of freedom as the most effective way to promote welfare and equality; the twentieth-century liberal regards welfare and equality as either prerequisites of or alternatives to freedom" (Friedman, 1962, 5). In other words, freedom is viewed as a causal factor or outcome of the distribution of goods and services, with the possibility of pay-offs between freedom and equality. However, it seems more sensible to regard freedom or liberty as part of what society can distribute, equally or otherwise. This is what Rawls (1971, 62, 303) has in mind in his treatment of justice, with distribution involving "all social primary goods—liberty and opportunity, income and wealth, and the bases of self-respect". Particular conceptions of freedom—for example the one attaching great importance to rights of private property ownership—may be extremely influential in determining the distribution of other things. But this freedom is also unequally distributed: the so-called free-enterprise system limits freedom to be enterprising to those with command over the means of production. Lenin is reputed to have said, "Liberty is precious—so precious it must be rationed" (Samuelson, 1973, 635): liberty is a scarce resource as well as a desirable attribute and if not exactly rationed it is *de facto* enjoyed by some people to a greater extent than others.

6.1 Equality

Equality is the easiest criterion to apply to the evaluation of distributions. It also has strong emotive appeal, with undertones of moral rectitude associated with the egalitarian ideals of much Western philosophy, Judeo-Christian ethics and the rhetoric of democracy. An intuitively attractive rule of evaluation would be to regard territorial equality in distribution of sources of well-being as best, in the absence of any considerations that would convincingly justify differentiation.

The argument for equality of treatment is generally based on the acceptance of certain *rights* (and responsibilities) held by all people by virtue of their common humanity. In a more restricted sense, particular rights and duties might be an entitlement of citizenship of a given nation or territory. The idea of natural human rights is a popular philosophical position, associated with the view of men and women as having some intrinsic worth as ends in themselves or as *beings*, not merely *things* to be used by others as means to their own ends. Attempts to deprive certain groups of people of such basic rights as electoral participation or free choice of sex partner are often accompanied by efforts to portray those concerned as sub-human or possessed of animal characteristics (Kuper, 1974, 11–14). Attitudes to the Jews in Nazi Germany, to Africans in South Africa and to blacks in parts of the American South are cases in point, while the dehumanized state of the slave is the ultimate example of treating people as objects. The Marxian concept of alienation has similar connotations, dealing as it does with the unnatural separation of man from his product and the reduction of human labour to a market commodity. The practices of regarding people as factors of production or "human resources" imply similarly dehumanizing concepts.

Attractive though it is, the criterion of equality is not as easy to apply as might appear at first sight. The practical and conceptual problems are recognized in recent literature on urban services (e.g. Levy *et al.*, 1974; Lineberry, 1974; Lineberry and Welch, 1974). For example, to achieve equality in results (educational attainment, level of health, etc) may require inequality in resource allocation, whether the subjects are people or places. Equal allocation of resources can produce inequalities in living standards. This suggests two alternative views of equality: perfect equality of treatment in the sense of the same quantity of benefits and penalties going to all, and equality of treatment in the same circumstances where the circumstances can justify different quantities. This is, in fact, Aristotle's distinction between *arithmetic equality* and *proportional equality*. While recognizing that arithmetic equality might be the "democratic" ideal, justice is commonly associated with people getting what they deserve (be it rewards or retribution)—a differentiating criterion that can be reconciled with equality by distributing things equally in proportion to desert. "If one who deserves little receives little, while another who deserves much receives much, then the justice manifested in this differential treatment of the two lies in the fact that the proportion of reward to desert is the same in both cases" (Haworth, 1968, 41).

The use of either concept of equality for the evaluation of areal distribution patterns requires methods of measurement. Given a set of territorial units $(1, 2, \ldots, j, \ldots, n)$ among which well-being or real income is distributed, how do we establish the degree of inequality? If S_j is the level of well-being in the jth territory, measured by some appropriate interval or ratio indicator, and $\bar{S}$ is the average level for all n territories, then perfect equality is obviously achieved where:

$$S_j = \bar{S} \quad \text{for all } j \ (1, \ldots, n) \tag{6.1}$$

This would be arithmetic equality. Proportional equality would be:

$$S_j = kD \quad \text{for all } j \tag{6.2}$$

where D is some measure of desert and k is a constant. If in either case the desired level ($\bar{S}$ or kD) is written S^*, then the difference between S and S^* indicates the degree of inequality.

A number of well developed methods exist for measuring inequality (e.g. Alker and Russett, 1964; Alker, 1970; Atkinson, 1970; Sen, 1973, ch. 2; Chisholm and Oeppen, 1973). The degree of inequality experienced by any single territory can be measured by its *difference* from the average or desired level (i.e. $S_j - S^*_j$) and its *ratio of advantage* or disadvantage can be found (from $S_j \div S^*_j$). But in studying a set of territories some measure of overall inequality is usually required. The best known general inequality measure is the *Gini coefficient*, which can compare the percentage frequency of some attribute with an equal distribution. Thus if S_j is, for example, the proportion of total income within a nation going to territory j and S^*_j is the proportion of total population in j (assumed to be the distributional criterion), then the Gini coefficient is

$$G = \tfrac{1}{2} \sum_{j=1}^{n} S_j - S^{\star}_j \qquad\qquad [6.3]$$

i.e. all territorial deviations from the "fair" share are calculated and summed and G is half the result. This coefficient has a range 0 to 100, with the larger the value the more inequality. It may be calculated from raw scores rather than percentages by the following formula:

$$G = \tfrac{1}{2} \sum_{j=1}^{n} \left| \frac{100\,Y_j}{Y_t} - \frac{100\,P_j}{P_t} \right| \qquad\qquad [6.4]$$

where Y_j is the actual income (or whatever) accruing to territory j, Y_t is total (e.g. national) income, P_j is the population in j and P_t is the total population.

The Gini coefficient can measure departures from both arithmetic and proportional inequality. As an illustration, Table 6.1 shows four regions

Table 6.1 Calculation of the Gini coefficient (G) for territorial equality

Region	Pop. (m)	Arithmetic equality % Distribution of income		Difference (+ or −)	Desert weight	Proportional equality % Distribution proportional to $P \times D$	Difference (+ or −)
	P	Y	$Y^{\star}_A$	$\lvert Y - Y^{\star}_P \rvert$	D	$Y^{\star}$	$\lvert Y - Y^{\star} \rvert$
North	1	15	10	5	1	5	10
South	2	30	20	10	2	20	10
East	3	30	30	0	1	15	15
West	4	25	40	15	3	60	35
Totals	10	100	100	30		100	70

$$G = \tfrac{1}{2} \sum \lvert Y - Y^{\star} \rvert = 15 \qquad\qquad G = \tfrac{1}{2} \sum \lvert Y - Y^{\star} \rvert = 35$$

with different populations (P); an equal division of income (or whatever) on the basis of population requires the percentage distribution indicated by $Y^{\star}_A$. Comparison with the actual Y, following expression [6.3], gives a G value of 15, i.e. slight inequality on the 0 to 100 scale. In the proportional equality case it is assumed that there are differential desert weights (D) attached to the regions, so the share must now be proportional to P multiplied by D. The required percentage distribution ($Y^{\star}_P$) differs from $Y^{\star}_A$ and, with the same actual distribution (Y), so does $G (= 35)$. The appropriate measure of regional desert might be anything from infant mortality levels (e.g. to allocate medical care funds) to an indicator of regional social deprivation.

A common way of expressing inequality graphically is via the *Lorenz curve*, which is closely related to the Gini coefficient. Territories are ranked according to their ratios of advantage, and the cumulative percentages of income, or whatever is distributed, (S) are plotted against

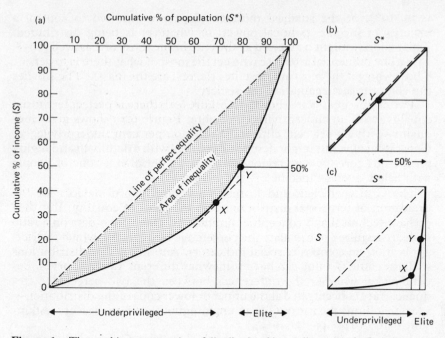

Figure 6.1 The graphic representation of distributional inequality, using the Lorenz curve.

cumulative percentages of population, or whatever the distributional criterion happens to be ($S\star$). Perfect equality produces a $45°$ diagonal plot; the greater the inequality the greater the departure from this line. This technique is familiar to the economic geographer as the localization curve and is often used in a non-spatial context to show inequalities in the distribution of income by classes or other groups within a population (e.g. Wilcox, 1969, 8–16; Samuelson, 1973, 83–9).

The Lorenz curve can reveal a number of interesting properties of a distribution. Figure 6.1a shows an imaginary curve for a set of territories, derived from cumulative percentage distributions of S and $S\star$—say, income and population. The difference between the curve and the line of perfect equality is the *area of inequality*; the Gini coefficient measures this as a proportion of the total area below the diagonal. Somewhere on the curve is a point X, where the change in S is equal to the change in $S\star$, or where a tangent to the curve would be parallel to the $45°$ line. To the left of this point along the horizontal axis the population gets less than under equality (S), while to the right they get more. In Figure 6.1a the proportion of population with less than equality is 70 per cent. Alker and Russett (1964) define this as the *equal share coefficient*, measuring the proportional size of the "underprivileged" population. The larger it is, the less egalitarian the society. Also marked on the curve is a point Y, corresponding with the 50 per cent S level. When projected on to the horizontal axis this indicates the proportion (to the right) accounting for half the total income. This is the *minimal majority* (Alker,

1970, 198), or. the smallest number of people required to control a majority of income, political power, or whatever is being distributed. This majority might be viewed as the elite in the sense of Lasswell (1958, 13): "The influential are those who get the most of what there is to get. . . . Those who get the most are the elite; the rest are the mass." The smaller the elite, the less egalitarian the society.

Two extreme cases are shown. In Figure 6.1b there is perfect territorial equality, with no underprivileged or elite. Figure 6.1c shows great inequality, with a 5 per cent elite and almost 90 per cent underprivileged. Geographically, this might describe a country with a dominant and highly prosperous core (or elite region) and a large peripheral zone of people with below-average income or well-being.

The Gini coefficient and Lorenz curve are helpful devices for the evaluation of territorial distributions on the basis of equality. But they do have technical and conceptual limitations. One is that data on a ratio scale are required to calculate the percentage frequencies, which restricts application on composite social indicators. Another is that distributions with the same G value can have somewhat different Lorenz curves, depending on whether the differences between the two percentage frequencies are concentrated at the upper or lower ends of the distribution—a fact that limits the use of G as an unambiguous welfare measure (Atkinson, 1970; 1975, 45–7).

A particular problem in spatial analysis is that G is sensitive to the level of territorial aggregation. Thus, what is highly unequal at one spatial scale may appear much more equal at another. Consider the imaginary case in Table 6.2, where there are two cities A and B, both subdivided into rich and poor neighbourhoods. To simplify matters, the cities have the same total populations of 100,000. Actual income distribution (Y) among the *four* areas shows a substantial departure ($G=55$) from what distribution according to population ($Y^\star$) would require. But if the cities are taken as a whole, i.e. there are *two* areal units instead of four, income appears perfectly equally distributed ($G=0$). Thus local inequalities can be hidden by measures calculated at broader levels of areal aggregation. This is a difficult problem in the analysis of spatial distributions. Nevertheless, the Gini coefficient and Lorenz curve are quite effective for measuring territorial inequality, providing that they are used with care. They can be applied to problems of judging change as well as to existing patterns.

Table 6.2 Calculation of the Gini coefficient at different levels of territorial aggregation

	P	Y	Y*	|Y–Y*|	P	Y	Y*	|Y–Y*|
City A (Rich)	20	45	10	35 ⎱	100	50	50	0
City A (Poor)	80	5	40	35 ⎰				
City B (Rich)	40	40	20	20 ⎱	100	50	50	0
City B (Poor)	60	10	30	20 ⎰				
Totals	200	100	100	110				0

$$G=\tfrac{1}{2}\sum|Y-Y^\star|=55 \qquad\qquad G=\tfrac{1}{2}\sum|Y-Y^\star|=0$$

6.2 Differential treatment

The principle of to each (individual or territory) according to his or her deserts implied in the notion of proportional equality raises the general question of what circumstances justify differential treatment. Desert implies equity or fairness in distribution, yet there are situations relating to the survival of a society and to efficiency in production that can in practice override more conventional equity considerations. The same distribution may be able to satisfy all three criteria, but conflict between them is far more likely. In this event, the trichotomy of survival, efficiency and equity is likely to represent an ordering of societal priorities with respect to the distribution of benefits and burdens among people or places.

For most societies *survival* is a major national or group objective. Indeed, some argue that it is difficult to envisage a nation having goals other than a consensus on survival (Hoffenburg, 1970, B-779). A distribution not conducive to the survival of a society must have a low or zero preference, assuming that it can be identified as such. Thus in a "primitive" society in which there are just enough people to hold off the neighbouring tribe and just enough food to keep all people alive, an unequal distribution of food would threaten survival. Early urban societies often had an elite religious-political class, supported from the surplus product, to maintain stability. Religious functions making material demands may be regarded as "necessary" for the survival of society, just as large defence budgets with their income-distributional implications are justified by national security today. If, as Harvey (1973, 200) suggests, the survival of a society means the perpetuation of a given mode of production, then the inequalities inherent in the capitalist system might be justified by its supporters under the survival criterion (see the case of South Africa, Chapter 9). Certainly, unequal private ownership of the means of production is necessary for the survival of capitalism. Generally, those who are viewed as contributing most to survival may be recognized as most deserving, whether they be the successful stockbroker and general or the tribe's best hunter and warrior. Thus physical survival or the preservation of the existing social, economic and political order may justify a differential distribution of surplus product. Unless or until survival is ensured, it is likely to transcend efficiency and equity as distributional criteria. However, efficiency and equity themselves contribute to survival. Producing enough food for an expanding population may require efficiency payments to the more productive individuals and areas. And a grossly inequitable distribution of income or blatant territorial discrimination may promote revolution, provincial independence movements and other threats to national stability.

Efficiency concerns the maximization of output from given resources. An efficient distribution of real income from an economic point of view would thus maximize the production of further goods, including leisure, or minimize the cost of producing a given output. This implies incentives. As long as economic incentives are regarded as effective stimulators of individual and group contributions to production, more productive people and localities can be expected to receive rewards of greater real income. Thus levels of well-being will tend to be higher in highly productive regions than in less productive regions. But there are hints of the operation of equity criteria here, for such a system of differential rewards might be considered not only conducive to efficiency in production but also just from a moral point of view. In other words, the most efficient are the most deserving. Inequalities in the interests of efficiency are not confined to capitalist systems, but socialism places more emphasis on the non-material rewards of contributing to the common good. However, efficiency and equity often conflict, and to approve or recommend the efficient rather than the equitable pattern can represent an important practical distributional judgement. Whether the good in question is an industrial product or a public service, the gains from the optimally efficient location pattern may be inequitably shared.

Equity is an extremely difficult concept. The word implies fairness or justice in the distribution of society's benefits and penalties. Its Latin derivation suggests equality and in Western societies greater equity or a "better" distribution is invariably taken to mean a more egalitarian one (Mishan, 1969a, 26, 62), at least in most public pronouncements. But equity is seldom interpreted as perfect equality. Even under socialism, inequality is to be expected as long as labour is compensated by wages; as in a capitalist system, this may compound other personal advantages. Dobb (1969, 229–30) points out that if welfare maximization theories are framed so as to include disutilities involved in work as well as utilities derived from consumption, equality of individual utility may require differences of real income to compensate for differing negative utilities from work. Thus those who enjoy what they do would get paid less than those who do not; those who do society's dirty work deserve more than those in comfortable and congenial employment.

There are few if any societies that do not in fact differentiate in the interests of survival, efficiency or equity. But it is the equity principle that is generally used to uphold the legitimacy of differentiation. As Ginsberg (1965, 66) puts it, "It is as unjust to treat unequals equally as to treat equals unequally. The problem is to decide what differences are relevant." In practice, then, the moral problem of desert becomes that of finding *relevant differences*.

The most common basis for differentiation is that of *contribution to society*, as measured by value of output in the production process. As suggested above, this combines the idea of efficiency rewards with equity: the neo-classical marginal-productivity theory of income distribution referred to in the previous chapter is a case in point. Friedman (1962, 167) suggests that "Even the severest internal critics of capitalism have implicitly accepted payment in accordance with product as ethically fair"; he reads into the Marxian concept of exploitation the assumption that labour is entitled to the surplus value by virtue of the *capitalist* ethic of to each according to what he produces. Marx (1875, 387) explained "equal right" as follows:

The right of the producers is *proportional* to the labour they supply; the equality consists in the fact that measurement is made with an *equal standard*, labour.

But one man is superior to another physically or mentally and so supplies more labour in the same time, or can labour for a longer time; and labour, to serve as a measure, must be defined by its duration or intensity, otherwise it ceases to be a standard of measurement. This *equal* right is an unequal right for unequal labour. It recognizes no class differences, because everyone is only a worker like everyone else; but it tacitly recognizes unequal individual endowment and thus productive capacity as natural privileges. *It is, therefore*, a right of inequality, in its *contents, like every right*.

Marx clearly had proportional equality in mind. The similarity with Friedman (1962, 166) is quite striking: "The man who is hard working and thrifty is to be regarded as 'deserving'; yet these qualities owe much to the genes he was fortunate (or unfortunate?) enough to inherit." The difference is that under capitalism people may inherit property and other class privileges as well as natural endowment, and that under socialism the time may come when the highly productive worker's differential reward is the satisfaction derived from making a disproportionate contribution to the common good. Marx of course recognized payment by product as "bourgeois right", which would eventually disappear in the communist state, though it still prevails as a distributional criterion in the USSR and most other socialist countries.

To each according to his need was what Marx (1875) had in mind as the ultimate criterion for distribution of the product. *Need* is quite commonly held to be a relevant difference today in both socialist and capitalist societies. Although in practice need is hard to define, as was pointed out in Chapter 2, the allocation of resources is often designed so as to give most to those in most need—especially in the social services. Regional development programmes are most obvious spatial examples of the application of the need criterion, though again some efficiency considerations may accompany the desire to achieve "regional balance".

Other bases for differential treatment include *merit, status* and *position in society*. Examples include special rewards for royalty, the nobility and others with inherited privileges recognized by society as entitlements to disproportionate shares of the product—or shares proportional to status. Certain occupations, such as university professors who enjoy congenial work at a high rate of pay, are a case of society recognizing special merit. Geographically, the metropolitan core region or capital city may exercise a special claim for disproportionate expenditure on culture, the arts, and ceremonial structures. Peripheral regions may be discriminated against in public expenditure, particularly if they are occupied by people of low economic, political or ethnic status.

Differential treatment may be either positive or negative. Although special payments according to need are sometimes referred to as "positive discrimination", it is the negative aspects of discrimination that attract most attention in discussion of social justice. The notion of unfavourable or unfair differentiation conveyed by the word discrimination reminds us that "relevant differences" need not have moral approval.

Thus different people and places may be justly or unjustly differentiated in the way society treats them, depending on the basis for differentiation and the moral code to which it is referred.

The most obvious forms of negative discrimination are those practised on the basis of race, colour, religion or sex. These can have important spatial expressions, for example in the differential allocation of resources to neighbourhoods occupied by different race groups. There is widespread though not universal agreement that such discrimination is wrong; in the United States, for example, it has been found to violate constitutional requirements for equal protection under the law (e.g. Salih, 1972; Lineberry and Welch, 1974). Its continuation, sanctioned by local custom and made possible by an initial inequality in the distribution of political power, is often justified by arguments with greater moral force, e.g. that the blacks (or whoever the victims may be) deserve less because they work less or contribute less to society. The real basis of discrimination often goes deeper than the superficial if conspicuous characteristics of race—into a struggle for control of society's product— as will be shown in Chapter 9.

The recognition of *just* differentiation according to *relevant* differences thus accords with the moral principle of equal treatment in the same circumstances, or the substitution of impartiality for arbitrary discrimination. The notion of impartiality may be extended to apply to a wide range of rights and duties, as societies move from guarantees of basic human rights like equal protection under the law, to recognition of political rights such as the franchise, and to equality in certain social and economic rights. Rights and duties are "defined and redefined as we obtain fuller knowledge of the constituents and conditions of well-being" (Ginsberg, 1965, 59). What is regarded as just is thus historically and culturally determined, rather than something with absolute moral authority.

The basic practical problem in geographical research is that of identifying relevant differences within particular societal contexts, and discovering empirically just what they mean in terms of spatial discrimination— positive or negative. Ideally, knowledge of relevant differences would enable us to identify measures of desert and then establish the extent to which the implied proportional equality in distribution is satisfied in reality. Far more likely, however, is an inductive approach by which observed territorial variations in levels of well-being may be used to infer the differences that appear relevant in society's distribution process, or the weights (personal and territorial) in society's distributional social welfare function. This will not provide a magic key to the question of whether the basis of spatial differentiation is right in a moral sense. But it will help in practice to distinguish between differentiation according to criteria that are widely accepted as just and differentiation arising from a societal structure that makes distribution merely respond to economic and political power.

6.3 Constrained inequality

An alternative to perfect arithmetic equality or distribution proportional to desert is to recognize inequality as just, *subject to* the worst-off members of society maintaining a certain level. Thus equity or justice might be conceived of as qualified equality or constrained inequality. For example, to Scitovsky (1964, 251), equity "seems to stand for some minimum degree of equality people would like to see realized and on the nature of which they might be able to agree.... By equity people mean, if not equality, at least something that approximates it closely enough to satisfy them." Equality of access to the necessities of life and to basic social services would be a case in point. Article 25(1) of the *Declaration of Human Rights* states:

> Everyone has the right to a standard of living adequate for the health and well-being of himself and his family, including food, clothing, housing, and medical care and necessary social services, and the right to security in the event of unemployment, sickness, disability, widowhood, old age, or other lack of livelihood in circumstances beyond his control.

Allowing people the freedom to become unequal subject to such rights being upheld would command quite wide acceptance as the specification of a just society. Proposals for a guaranteed minimum income or negative income tax are in this spirit. An early application was the "Speenhamland system" introduced in Britain in 1795, which guaranteed everyone a minimal level of subsistence to be paid through public taxes.

The best-known example of the constrained inequality principle as an approach to social justice is in the work of Rawls (1958; 1962; 1967; 1971). Rawls's theory of justice is widely regarded as the first complete general principle of social choice to command serious interest since the classical utilitarian notion that societal welfare could be measured by summing all individual utility levels (Phelps, 1973, 24–5, 418; Coleman, 1974, 743). Rawls attempts to provide a philosophical basis that overrides the principle of efficiency in resource allocation as a guide to justice in distribution. The fundamental problem posed is that of identifying the conditions in which inequality is justified. Rawls's answer provides a constraint on the degree of permissible inequality.

Rawls's specifications for the just society are deduced from an "original position" of self-interested individuals with complete ignorance as to their subsequent positions in society. He proposes that people will wish to design a society conforming to two principles (Rawls, 1971, 60):

> First: each person is to have an equal right to the most extensive basic liberty compatible with a similar liberty for all others. Second: social and economic inequalities are to be arranged so that they are both (a) reasonably expected to be to everyone's advantage, and (b) attached to positions and offices open to all.

Thus, given an equal initial endowment of the "social primary goods", the state of society could be improved by inequalities if these can be shown to be in the interests of all. In particular, inequalities should make the least advantaged better off, so: "All social primary goods—liberty and opportunity, income and wealth, and the basis of self-respect—are to be distributed equally unless an unequal distribution of any or all of these goods is to the advantage of the least favoured" (Rawls, 1971, 303). Although the practical application of this principle poses problems (Coleman, 1974), the idea of constraining inequality by the interests of the worst-off has much intuitive appeal.

How Rawls's constrained inequality might work out spatially, in a simple two-region case, can be explored graphically. Figure 6.2a shows a welfare frontier indicating how the utility, well-being or real income (U) produced from given resources and technology might be shared between the regions North (N) and South (S). Point E on the $45°$ diagonal

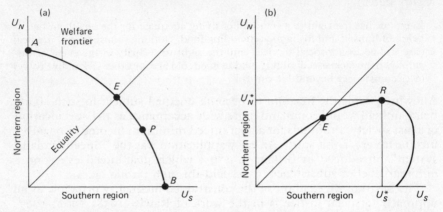

Figure 6.2 Application of Rawls' criterion of maximizing the level of well-being of the least fortunate, in a simple two-region case.

is an equal distribution, P is proportional inequality with S twice as deserving as N. If P is the actual position so that N is worst off, what position would make N as well off as possible? Consider point A on the N axis. Given the shape of the welfare frontier, this would maximize U_N by virtue of giving all to N and none to S. But now S would be worst off, and this would justify a shift to B. In fact, the only legitimate position on the Rawls criterion is E: the worst off are doing as well as they can only when they are doing as well as the best off. However, it is clear from Rawls's theory that the well-being of the worst off is in some way dependent on that of other segments of society. This requires a welfare frontier in parts of which U_N improves as U_S improves, i.e. parts of it must slope positively (Figure 6.2b). Now the highest position for N is at R. Any departure from this in the direction of greater (to the right) or less (to the left) inequality will make N worse off. So the inequality implicit in the distribution U^*_S, U^*_N is justified by the Rawls criterion. Equality (E) would make both regions worse off.

Rawls's constrained inequality (or "maximin") approach figures prominently in the attempt by Harvey (1972a; 1973, ch. 3) to construct a specification for a just distribution in a spatial system. Following Runciman (1966), he proposes that the essence of social justice can be embodied in the criteria of need, contribution to the common good, and merit, in that order. The justice of a particular geographical distribution of real income would be judged by how far these criteria have been followed in arriving at it. Establishing need involves the discovery of minimum requirements for survival and/or the setting of minimum acceptable standards for food, housing, education, and so on. Contribution to common good in a regional system is taken to mean contribution to total aggregate product and inter-regional multiplier effects, i.e. contribution to system efficiency in production. Merit is translated into the idea of allocating additional resources to regions with difficult environments to overcome, if this is required to meet need or contribution to common good. Following Rawls, Harvey (1972a, 98) suggests that "The geographical problem is to design a form of spatial organization which maximizes the prospects of the least fortunate region." How this is achieved concerns the nature of the political process, the way in which collective decisions are made as to inter-regional resource allocations, and the power of the inhabitants of the individual regions to influence those decisions. This resolves into the question of what form of government would make the prospects of the poorest region as great as possible.

The relevance of the Rawls criterion in a regional context is, of course, dependent on a spatially static society. If people can move freely from poor areas to rich ones and thereby improve their lot in life without impairing that of others, a strategy of facilitating mobility could be preferable to one of helping out the poor regions. Placing priority on making the position of the least advantaged region as good as possible gains validity as personal mobility is reduced. One reason for constraining mobility may be that population concentration in the rich region would reduce its efficiency and thereby lower the general welfare. These considerations are at the root of regional development problems, where efficiency and equity criteria often appear to conflict.

In its simplest form, the constrained inequality criterion is not difficult to apply in practice to the problem of judging spatial distributions. Once minimum standards have been set and appropriate territorial indicators developed, it is a matter of ascertaining for each territory that the required level is met. Beyond this, inequality is of no account. The complications arise in determining the minimum standard, or, in the Rawls case, how high the prospects of the least fortunate can possibly be. As Culyer (1973, 86–7) explains, "The degree to which poverty is alleviated will be determined not by what is 'decent' for a man and his family, but by whatever the community, in the light of its desire to help and what it must forego to do so, decides." If the constraint on inequality turns out to be rather weak, the residual inequalities can be substantial.

6.4 Social contracts and distributive justice

The work of Rawls (1971) exemplifies a particular approach to the discovery of a conception of distributive justice capable of commanding wide acceptance. It involves determining the kind of *social contract* people would enter into for their mutual benefit, under varying assumptions about their place in the social order. The institutions and distributional arrangements that can thus be deduced might provide a practical guide to the evaluation of actual situations. In this connection, a useful contribution to the discussion of equity has been provided by Sen (1970, ch. 9). He reviews three alternative approaches to the question of what comprises a just distribution, described respectively as "universalization", "fairness" and "impersonality". Although explored in the context of the distribution among individuals, they can easily be viewed in geographical terms.

The principle of *universalization* requires making the same judgements irrespective of one's place (including location) in society, or putting oneself in the place of the others and seeing society in the same way. It echoes the Christian morality of doing unto others as you would that others do unto you. Geographically, it can be translated into the idea that the just distribution of sources of need and want satisfaction would be the one that would be judged the same by the same person no matter where he or she lived. It would require the suburban resident viewing the existing pattern of territorial differentiation within the city with the same approbation if transferred to a home in the slums, or anywhere else. If what looks good from a suburban home does not look equally good from the slums, an unjust situation would be recognized. This strongly suggests perfect spatial equality as the just distribution. The difficulty here is that the suburbanite might argue that, in the slums, she or he would be entitled to the same treatment as at present; their circumstances (e.g. class or ethnic status) would be the same as before, and location should be irrelevant. This is precisely the problem of relevant differences raised in section 6.2. So the egalitarian expectations initially aroused by the universalization principle are unlikely to be fulfilled in reality, for society sees people as different and treats them accordingly.

Sen's second principle—that of *fairness*—reflects Rawls's idea of making the level of the worst off as high as possible. Whereas the universalization principle involves looking at the social state from *everyone* else's position, the fairness principle requires us to specify the way things should be without knowing whose shoes we will be in. Geographically, we do not know which neighbourhood or region we are destined to live in, so a reasonable response would be to ask that the worst be as good as possible as there is some (unknown) chance that we will be there. Subject to this constraint, conditions elsewhere can rise to any level. If we end up in a fortunate region so much the better for us; some inequality may be to our advantage. This criterion is not as straightforward as first appears, for if we cannot say just what "as high as possible" means, then presumably we must judge a social state as being better if human well-being in the worst region improves. We might thus be indifferent to social states in which the level in the worst region is the same. Real income in a rich region doubles while remaining the same in a poor region: by the Pareto criterion it is an improvement, by the criterion of the level of the worst

off we are indifferent and by the criterion of greater inequality not working to the advantage of all we might judge a deterioration due to interdependent utility functions (i.e. regional envy). Real income in the rich
region falls almost to the level of the poor region and in the latter improves
slightly: this is not a Pareto improvement as many previously rich people
are now worse off, yet by the criterion of the level of the worst region
there is an improvement and inequality has been reduced. What is "best"
is by no means clear.

The third principle—*impersonality*—involves a state in which the individual has an equal rather than an unknown probability of being in
any position. Just geographical distribution would be the one we would
design if we knew that we had an equal chance of living in any neighbourhood or region. On the face of it this again suggests equality. But Sen
(1970, 142–3) argues that the individual might risk being in a very poor
position if the chance was small. In a society with 99 free men and
one slave we might accept the 1 per cent risk of being the slave, given
the 99 per cent chance of being able to share the services of a slave. We
might accept one very poor neighbourhood in our city if it provided us
with cheap domestic labour and if the chance of ourselves living there
was very low. The prospects of the least fortunate region could be much
worse under the impersonality principle than under the other two.

Thus Sen offers three alternative ways in which an equitable or just
society might be conceived. Other similar analogies can be developed, to
explore the distributional implications of alternative societal organizations. One that is particularly instructive is set in an English public
school, where traditional practice requires that the cake on the Sunday
tea table be cut up by the boy who gets the last slice. In this type of
problem it is sometimes proposed that the cutter-up has to divide the
cake without knowing which part he will get, i.e. there is an element of
risk to encourage fairness in distribution (Pattaniak, 1968, 298–9). On
the assumption that all will choose in their own interests, the cutter-up
will be left with the smallest piece, which gives him an incentive to divide
the cake equally. This is equivalent to giving the individual 100 per cent
probability of being in the worst off's shoes and suggests that the just
distribution is what would be arrived at from this position. Geographically, the residents of the poorest region or neighbourhood would determine the inter-area allocation of resources or distribution of income. Perfect equality is a very likely outcome, but by no means certain. The boy
cutting the cake might recognize that the prefects who have first choice
have a claim to larger slices and that it is in his interests to see that they
get them. The expectation of eventually becoming a prefect may have
some bearing on the outcome: the greater the possibility, the more the
junior boy may be predisposed towards accepting the legitimacy of larger
shares for his seniors.[1]

Hints of the Rawls criterion are implicit in this case. With relatively
free social and geographical mobility—positions of privilege open to all—
differentiation seems easier to justify. But the most effective way of

[1] Comments from Michael Chisholm helped to clarify this analogy.

making the worst off as well off as possible is probably to ensure that differentiation has the sanction of society's poorest members. Harvey (1972a, 97) implies a similar arrangement when he suggests that making the worst off region as well off as possible might require that the least fortunate always have the final say, perhaps a "dictatorship of the proletariat". However unpalatable to some, the outcome may be easier to justify than differentiation determined by an elite, or by some hidden hand.

6.5 Ideal institutions

The discussion of justice in distribution inevitably leads to questions of alternative political structures and systems of collective decision-making. Whatever novel arrangements might be devised *a priori* through social contract theory or Utopian dreaming, the real world presently offers the main alternatives of capitalism and socialism. The former allows the "invisible hand" of market mechanisms to perform justice in distribution; the latter places the problem within the conscious control of the people or whoever they choose to perform the task. Between the extremes are various forms of "mixed" societies, in which a greater or lesser degree of redistribution takes place once the market has revealed its hand. Is it possible that some existing set of institutions approaches the ideal, in the sense of generating a just distribution of well-being or something close enough to satisfy us?

The capitalist competitive-market system is often advocated as an effective means of justly distributing society's product. It also has (in theory) the advantage over a planned economy of being self-regulating, with disturbances such as changes in costs or consumer preferences accommodated automatically as new market prices restore equilibrium. The properties of such a system are summarized as follows (Samuelson, 1973, 632):

> Under perfectly perfect competition, where all prices end up equal to all marginal costs, where all factor-prices end up equal to values of marginal-products and all total costs are minimized, where the genuine desires and well-being of individuals are all represented by their marginal utilities as expressed in their dollar voting—*then* the resulting equilibrium has the efficient property that "you can't make any one man better off without hurting some other man".

Production is optimally efficient and the product is optimally distributed by the Pareto criterion. What is produced and who gets it has the implicit sanction of society, as it is determined by the way in which people's money votes are spent, as they satisfy their personal preferences. To say that the result is anything other than a welfare optimum involves value judgements, including that what people prefer is wrong.

The same holds for *spatial* general equilibrium theory, in which the factors, producers and consumers can occupy different locations (e.g. Moses, 1968; Bramhall, 1969). The outcome of a perfect market in a space economy would in theory generate a Pareto-optimal outcome in which no alteration of what is produced and consumed *where* could make anyone anywhere better off without at the same time making someone else some- where else worse off. Location theorists have been much more reticent than other economists in claiming welfare-maximizing properties for par- ticular arrangements, but if they do find an optimal allocation or distribu- tion in space it generally rests on the same intellectual foundations as neo-classical general equilibrium theory.

Enough has been said already, in the discussions of consumer pre- ference (Chapter 3) and of the marginal-productivity theory of income distribution (Chapter 5) to cast doubt on the market as an instrument for social justice. The attainment of the efficient allocation from an eco- nomic point of view depends on the satisfaction of quite a number of unrealistic assumptions (Graaff, 1957, ch. 10). Among the most obvious market imperfections in the real world are the failure of both producers and consumers to behave with perfect rationality, the fact that some buy- ers and sellers are large enough to affect the prices supposedly arrived at in impersonal markets, the fact that people do not have perfect knowledge of all the alternatives open to them, the fact that some goods are provided publicly and in different quantities from those that would be determined in markets, and the existence of external effects whereby certain impor- tant costs and benefits are not reflected in prices. In addition, the un- restrained market-pricing system characteristic of economic *laissez-faire* appears to be inherently unstable and subject to fluctuations that can pro- duce extreme hardship at the times of recessions or slumps.

Extending the free-market model into space creates further problems, recognized in location analysis (e.g. Smith, 1971, 511–13). Richardson (1969a, 391–2) summarizes the objections to the market mechanism as a regional allocator as follows:

> The theoretical base for the free market in regional economics lies in general equilibrium theory. But general equilibrium analysis tends to be static rather than dynamic. It rests on marginalist assumptions, whereas in the space economy locational inertia prevents instantaneous adjustments to marginal changes in costs and revenues. Moreover, even if equilibrating tendencies are strong the path of adjustment may be difficult and have harmful consequences. The efficacy of market forces depends on the assumption of perfect competition, yet oligopoly and monopolistic elements are common in the space economy; distance may be an effective barrier to competition.

The existence of depressed areas is one of the prices society pays for spa- tial adjustments; financial capital is almost perfectly mobile in space whereas labour can be highly immobile. Distance can also be a barrier to the free flow of information, on which markets depend for their alloca- tive efficiency. The general problem of external effects has special impli- cations in a space-economy, as was shown in the previous chapters. With Richardson, we conclude that general equilibrium theory is inconsistent with the realities of a space-economy.

Thus, even if there were sound reasons for anticipating a welfare-maxi- mizing outcome from market competition under capitalism, it will not occur in practice. But there is a more fundamental reason for distrusting the distributional outcome of markets even if working perfectly—*it depends on the existing distribution*. The initial distribution ensures that the market allocation will lean towards the preferences of those who start off with most money, property, power, or whatever else it takes to influence markets. As Nath (1973, 37–8) puts it:

> Depending on what the initial distribution of the ownership of goods and factors is, there is a different point of general equilibrium and a different Paretian optimum—irrespective of whether it is an economy where everything is privately owned or one where everything is state-owned. Each different Paretian optimum has a different distribution of real income or utility levels associated with it.

The difference between private and public ownership is important to the outcome, of course, because upon this will depend who has what factors and who gets what returns.

It is not necessary to cite radical economists in support of this basic flaw in the proposition that free-market outcomes are just or, to be more precise, cannot be deemed unjust without further ethical assumptions. Samuelson (1973, 458, note 10) explains the problem thus:

> If the dollar votes of different consumers represent an "equitable" allocation, so that each peron's dollar represented as ethically deserving a pull on the market as any other's, there would be no need to make the following qualification: Efficient production and pricing does not mean that the FOR WHOM problem of society is being properly solved; it only means that the WHAT and HOW problems are being solved consistent with the *existing distribution* of dollar-voting power and of sharing in natural wealth and GNP. This qualification is vital.

And later (Samuelson, 1973, 632):

> *Laissez-faire* perfect competition *could* lead to starving children; to malnourished children who grow up to produce malnourished children; to perpetuations of Lorenz curves of great inequality of incomes and wealth for generations or forever. Or, if the initial distribution of dollar-wealth votes, genetic abilities, early conditioning, and training happened to be appropriate, perfect competition might lead to a rather egalitarian society characterized by uniformity greater than might please many an aristocratic, ethical condition. Or more likely, lead to inequality deemed too glaring.

Samuelson and his well-known textbook may be a legitimate target for opposition to neo-classical economic theory (e.g. Hunt and Sherman, 1972, 224–5; Hunt and Schwartz, 1972, 25–8), but he makes no claims about the free market as a *just* distributor of society's product.

The present distribution (among persons and places) can hardly be just if it depends on an unjust initial distribution. This has important implications for any attempt to evaluate the distributional outcome of markets in capitalist or mixed economies, in which the initial distribution may be extremely unequal and based on such arguably weak criteria of desert as inheritance and the coercive power of past generations of employers, landowners and other "robber barons". Given an unjust initial distribution and the power of the wealthy to use market imperfections to their own advantage, time may simply compound inequality and inequity. The difficulties raised in welfare economics were recognized by Graaff (1957, 155) two decades ago:

> Much of orthodox welfare theory lacks realism precisely because it assumes that the desired distribution of wealth has already been attained (and is somehow maintained) and then proceeds to regard the price system as a highly specialized resource-allocating mechanism which exercises no influence whatever on the distribution of wealth. Such a view is not easy to defend.

A writer on social justice (Ginsberg, 1965, 69) provides an appropriate conclusion to the argument:

> just as the medieval thinkers took the prevalent status system for granted, so the modern scholastics begin by assuming the justice of the system of free enterprise based on private property. This leads them, I think, to sanction a greater degree of inequality in property and income than might be warranted by a more thorough examination of the principles of distributive justice and its relation to social justice.

A distribution not arrived at by a just process is unlikely to be just.

From the above, it might be assumed that the market mechanism in general should be abolished, if it works so imperfectly and with such unjust consequences. But this does not necessarily follow. "Where there is no income from property and eveyone's earnings are what it is considered right that he should have, the major objection to the market system does not apply" (Robinson, 1972, 263); if it can then be made to work with something approximating to perfection, it can be an effective device for the allocation of resources among alternative uses in alternative places. Allocative efficiency is no less important under socialism than capitalism and can be assisted by market pricing principles embedded in neo-classical theory, in which private ownership of factors has "absolutely no formal or theoretical importance" (Hunt and Sherman, 1972, 154). Even the "dirty word" of profits may come to the assistance of socialist planners, as an index of efficiency in the use of inputs (i.e. cost minimization) given a level of sales or revenue. As Samuelson (1973, 625) recognizes, much of the hostility towards profit is really aimed at the extremes of inequality in the distribution of money income that comes from unequal factor ownership.

If the outcomes of the operation of a market are considered unjust, society may intervene with redistributive programmes of progressive taxation, welfare-state provisions and so on. This is what has happened in all capitalist nations, to a greater or lesser degree. How much actual redistribution of real income and wealth has taken place is a difficult question, complicated by deficiencies of data. Whether the redistribution actually accomplished is itself just is another open question. Any redistribution from the rich (or capitalists) to the poor (or workers) seems very likely to be justified, either on the grounds that capitalists get what is really an entitlement of labour or because the rich get more than they deserve by virtue of their power in politics and the marketplace. But the particular groups who gain most from redistribution are not necessarily the most deserving. The region that gets the valuable public works

project or the neighbourhood given the funds for environmental rehabili-
tation may simply be those with most influence on the redistribution process, just as the larger wage increases may go to the most powerful trade
unions irrespective of any general concept of desert except that "might
is right".

The typical modern social democracy, with its welfare-state provisions
and mixed economy, appears to be an improvement on extreme *laissez-
faire* capitalism from almost any moral point of view. Yet it is difficult
to see the answer to the just distribution in the institutional arrangements
of this kind of society. The capitalist mode of production still predominates, private ownership of wealth, land and other resources remains concentrated, and a combination of economic power and inherited privilege
enables a relatively small elite to retain effective control. Where organized
labour is able to accelerate income redistribution it has to do so within
the competitive power-game ethics predominating in the economy and
society as a whole, which often works to the disadvantage of the weakest
and most needy groups.

What of socialism as the answer to the problem of the just distribution?
The writings of Marx suggest a "total concept of welfare—a relational
norm of human solidarity and cooperation, a major aspect of which is
that distribution becomes communally oriented and need-based"; he
presented communist and capitalist distribution norms as polar or ideal
types—"total welfare and total diswelfare" (Mishra, 1975, 242). But
Marx was not much troubled by specific ethical issues: "Presumably he
believed that his condemnation of capitalism was robust enough as not
to depend upon foreseeable vicissitudes in morality, was not so delicate
as to need a special ethical theory" (Phelps, 1973, 26). As Harvey (1973,
14–16) emphasizes in a reassessment of his earlier attempt to derive spatial principles of distributive justice, Marx viewed social justice and
morality as relating to and stemming from human practice rather than
as independent philosophical matters: social justice is contingent upon
the social process operating in society as a whole. Concepts of social justice are both produced by and producers of social conditions (Harvey,
1973, 300).

There are some quite obvious bases upon which we can anticipate the
superiority of socialism over capitalism as a process for achieving distributive justice—or at least for avoiding gross injustice. Collective ownership of the means of production eliminates the narrow appropriation and
concentration of the surplus generated by labour. The abolition of private
ownership eliminates the question of whether landowners are entitled
to rent. The fact that market mechanisms are used by choice rather than
necessity places resource allocation and distribution of rewards within
the open and conscious control of the people rather than in the hands
of some anonymous hidden device. The major redistribution of existing
wealth accompanying the advent of socialism can remove whatever injustice from the past is inherited in the present allocation of "dollar
votes". All these are sound reasons to expect a more just distribution
under socialism, almost irrespective of the particular ethics of desert that

may be applied to questions of differential rewards and spatial allocations of resources.

While some form of socialism seems a necessary condition for a just distribution, given the evident injustices inherent in a capitalist system, it would be naïve to accept this or any other kind of society as sufficient to guarantee distributive justice. Revolutionary socialism carries with it the possibility of a substantial diminution in the supply of some goods, including liberty, for which people have strong preferences. Human beings appear to like material comfort and the trappings of the affluent society rather successfully generated under capitalism, however misguided an outcome of want-creation some of these things may be. It could be argued that it is better to live in a just society, however poor, than in a rich one rife with injustice, but the spatial preference patterns made by people "voting with their feet" in various parts of the world seem to be predominantly in favour of capitalism. Depending on how the society is run, a relatively enlightened liberal democracy with a mixed economy may be more attractive to the intuitive feelings of ordinary people than the rigorous demands of a socialist state. But these feelings are themselves influenced by existing social conditions.

Distributional issues are not automatically solved by revolutions. In extreme cases, such a change may leave everyone worse off than before or simply replace one privileged elite by another. But no change is without risk. In searching for some ideal institutional arrangement as the best prospect for justice in distribution, the ultimate criterion would appear to be that of how broadly the real power to determine who gets what where is actually spread over the population, whoever and wherever they may be. As Thomas Jefferson (1820) remarked, "I know of no safe repository of the ultimate powers of society but the people themselves." Of all the ideas explored in this and the previous section, the most appealing seems to be that of requiring any inequality to have the sanction of those who are worst off, by virtue of their right to cut up the cake. Given the tendency for men to strive to become unequal in a world where greater emphasis is given to competition than cooperation, and given the tendency for inequality in wealth and power to be self-perpetuating, this arrangement seems the best guarantee of *just* differentiation.

6.6 Welfare improvements

Having explored some of the more abstract problems raised in the evaluation of alternative spatial distributions, the time has now come to be specific. However convincing the arguments for some particular societal arrangements or institutions may be, the immediate practical problem is that of finding some basis on which to judge existing patterns or changes empirically observed. In what circumstances could we say that a particular distribution among territories is an improvement on another? The problem is posed purely in distributional terms; it is assumed that *what* is distributed is an optimal "bundle of goods" (e.g. utility, real income,

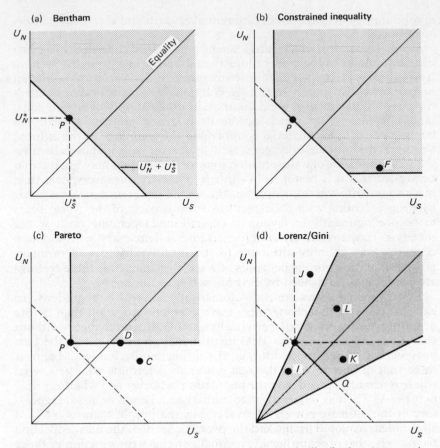

Figure 6.3 Alternative criteria for judging improvements in distribution among regions.

well-being or value) optimally produced, so that the only remaining welfare improvement lies in who gets it where.

Figure 6.3 shows four possible alternative criteria for judging a distributional improvement, implied in earlier discussions. The diagrams portray a two-region utility-space analysis of the kind used in Figure 6.2 above. Case *a* represents the criterion of the classical utilitarians, notably Bentham, who argued that the objective of society was to maximize the *sum total* of individual utilities somehow measured on comparable cardinal scales. Thus if *P* is the existing position with the inter-regional distribution as shown in the figure (twice as much goes to the North as to the South), any position in the shaded area beyond the welfare frontier measuring $U^{\star}_N + U^{\star}_S$ would be an improvement. This criterion would judge anything between the extremes of all to one region and perfect (arithmetic) equality as an improvement providing that the total utility increases. Thus distribution is irrelevant unless additional value judgements are made.

Case *b* is a version of the constrained inequality criterion introduced in section 6.2. Now, there is an improvement if total utility increases, providing that neither region falls below the level indicated by the lines parallel to the axes. As shown, *S* could end up with less than at present—a risky position that inhabitants of the South might accept if they felt that by doing so they opened up the converse possibility of being in a very favourable position such as *F*. The higher the constraints the more likely it is that the worst off region will be better off, though positions like *F* will thereby be eliminated. The practical problem with the application of this criterion is the identification of the appropriate regional minimum.

Case *c* is the familiar Pareto criterion. Like the Rawls criterion, it is a special version of constrained inequality. But it is more specific than Rawls's requirement that the worst off be as well off as possible because the minimum acceptable for each region is its existing level. Providing that no region becomes worse off, any change making one region better off is a Pareto improvement. If cardinal utilities capable of summation is assumed, any Pareto improvement is also a "Bentham" improvement. If we introduce the compensation principle whereby an improvement is recognized by a change (e.g. to *C* where gains to *S* exceed losses to *N*) through which redistributive transfers could lead to a Pareto-superior position to *P* (e.g. *D*) even if such redistribution did not take place, then no significant difference exists with the first case. The compensation principle, introduced to strengthen the Pareto criterion, in practice weakens it by permitting some region to lose unless the required transfers are made to take place.

The final case (*d*) is that of the Lorenz or Gini criterion of greater equality in distribution. If proportional-inequality lines are drawn from the origin of the graph through *P* and *Q*, any position between them is a Lorenz improvement on *P*. This even applies to *I*, where both *N* and *S* are worse off and which is inferior to *P* by the other three criteria. Just as inequality can be constrained, so the achievement of greater equality can be constrained, for example by the requirement that total utility or income should not be reduced. This *constrained Lorenz* criterion identifies an improvement anywhere within the heavier shaded area in the graph. Some Pareto-superior positions (e.g. *J*) will not be acceptable by the Lorenz criterion; similar, this criterion permits some improvements of a Pareto-inferior type, e.g. at *K*, for greater equality is achieved here at some absolute loss to the North. The Lorenz criterion could be further constrained by requiring that improvements also meet the Pareto criterion, as is true of *L*, for example.

What are the relative merits of these various alternatives to the problem of making practical spatial welfare judgements? The first (Figure 6.3a) can be dismissed as ignoring distribution entirely. The second (*b*) may be of some assistance, providing that the regional minimum level can be arrived at. Pareto and Lorenz both seem preferable, however, on the practical grounds that they judge improvements with respect to the existing distribution and not in relation to a minimum level which requires much data and many value judgements to define.

How do the Pareto and Lorenz criteria compare? Weaknesses in the concept of Pareto optimality have already been identified in Chapter 3. Changes that help the rich but do not harm the poor are Pareto improvements, providing that any consequent disutility to the poor generated by envy is allowed for. At the extreme, if one person or region has everything, any redistribution is Pareto-inferior to the existing situation. Using the cake-cutting analogy, Sen (1973, 7) summarizes the problem as follows:

> Assuming that each person prefers to have more cake rather than less of it, every possible distribution will be Pareto optimal, because any change that makes someone better off is going to make someone else worse off. Since the only issue in this problem is that of distribution, Pareto optimality has no cutting power at all. The almost single-minded concern of modern welfare economics with Pareto optimality does not make that engaging branch of study particularly suitable for investigating problems of inequality.

Given an initial distribution, a Pareto improvement requires more cake, i.e. economic growth. Despite the minimal value judgements on which it rests, the Pareto criterion provides a powerful basis for opposition to any measure threatening the existing position of society's most advantaged people or regions, and for support of the distributional *status quo* in a no-growth economy. Thus, far from providing a positive means for evaluation, structures based on the Pareto criterion are now being seen as explicitly ideological: "Welfare economics, particularly in its present Paretian form, has become the last refuge of an unrealistic general-equilibrium approach and a reverential attitude towards the market system" (Nath, 1973, 65).

As an alternative to Pareto optimality, the Lorenz criterion of the more equal the better has obvious attractions. It may be derived directly from the classical utilitarian sum-of-satisfactions concept mentioned above, if it is assumed that the marginal utility of income falls as income rises and that all individuals have similar preferences and capacities to enjoy the good things in life. Then, as Culyer (1973, 64) puts it, "a normative argument for egalitarianism can be made to follow on quite naturally from the utilitarian approach, though it will not follow automatically by market processes". This proposition is to be found in the pioneering work on the economics of welfare by Pigou (1920, 89): "It is evident that any transference of income from a relatively rich man to a relatively poor man of similar temperament, since it enables more intense wants to be satisfied at the expense of less intense wants, must increase the aggregate sum of satisfaction." Thus, in Figure 6.3a, the total *utility* available for distribution can be increased by *income* transfers from rich to poor. Pigou's view is echoed by Mandel (1962, 660), who cites with approval Galbraith's claim that nowhere does the law of diminishing returns apply more than with regard to the intensity of needs. But, as Galbraith (1975, 124) reminds us, "it has always been a prime tenet of the neo-classical model that wants do not diminish in urgency and hence goods do not diminish in importance with increased output". This underlines the tendency of neo-classical theory to place greater emphasis on economic growth than on egalitarian redistribution.

The implications of the Pigovian argument have been debated at length (e.g. Dobb, 1969, ch. 5; Nath, 1973, ch. 1). Experience might lead us to doubt that all individuals have similar tastes and capacities for enjoyment, though some economists prefer to see this as an untestable assumption with no higher status than that of a value judgement (e.g. Nath, 1973, 15–16). Thus the proposition that a millionaire will get less utility from a given sum of money than would a poor man becomes ethical rather than positive. The "new welfare economics" which followed utilitarianism abandoned the notion that utility was measurable in a way that made interpersonal comparison possible. Thus the problem of Nero versus the rest of Rome (see Chapter 3) was recognized as beyond positive theory. The issue of distribution was solved via the social welfare function identified as welfare contours in utility space (as explained in Chapter 3), which simply tell us that society has distributional preferences. What these might be and what criteria might justify particular distributions was ignored in theoretical deliberations. "The new welfare economics, therefore, was almost entirely empty of relevant analysis of income distribution problems" (Culyer, 1973, 72).

Sen (1973) has provided guidance on how this impotence might be circumvented. He recognizes (Sen, 1973, 23) that:

> No practical welfare propositions, i.e. no policy prescriptions about economic problems in an *actual, empirical* context—are possible without making some rough estimates of utility or welfare derived by broad economic and social groups from certain amounts of income, leisure, wealth and certain other aspects of the social set-up. This realization is slowly dawning on economists—so that by now the wheel has turned a full circle and we are back to a position similar to Pigou's.

The difference is that now the estimates and comparisons of utility (real income or well-being) levels are explicitly recognized as having ethical content. Thus new theory is needed. As Nath (1973, 67) sees it,

> it will be essential for this new theory to drop the concept of a Paretian optimum, or indeed any concept of an optimum other than that of *the* (unique) *social optimum*, where the welfare of the society is at a maximum because it has the "right" allocations of factors to different uses, the "right" intensity of their employment, the "right" distribution of incomes, and the "right" policies regarding externalities and merit wants.

Basic to Sen's thesis is a questioning of the "odd and obstinate reluctance to accept the democratic, individualistic ethical premise that different individuals should be treated *as if* they have *equal capacity for enjoying* the economic means to welfare". On this, of course, hangs the argument for a more equal distribution.

Returning to our spatial perspective, the above seems to have even greater force of conviction than at the individual level. While tastes and preferences for particular goods and services are subject to areal variation if consumption patterns are any guide, there seems no way in which different "capacities for enjoyment" might be identified. Treating groups of people in different places *as if* such capacities were equal would, according to the Pigovian argument, require income transfers from rich to poor regions, so that the "more intense" needs in the latter would be satisfied at the expense of the "less intense" needs in the former. Reducing inter-regional (national or neighbourhood) inequalities would thus be a welfare improvement.

All this adds weight to the proposition that the Lorenz criterion is preferable to that of Pareto as an indicator of improvement in spatial distribution. Further support is provided by Sen (1973) in a rigorous examination of the welfare interpretation of various inequality measures. While there are some technical problems preventing the interpretation of any Lorenz improvement as a general welfare improvement (e.g. Sen, 1973, 33–4, 60–61; Atkinson, 1970), Sen (1973, 61) suggests that there is a strong if non-compulsive argument in favour of Lorenz:

> The fact that one distribution has a higher Lorenz curve than another can be taken to constitute a *prima facie* case that it is a better distribution from a welfare point of view.... While the Lorenz ranking is not in itself compelling, the onus of demonstration may well be thought to lie on the person wishing to reject this ranking on other grounds.

The Gini coefficient is the relevant numerical measure; a distribution with a lower G value than another is "Lorenz-superior" as Sen (1973, 64) terms it. The value of G is reduced by transfers of income (or whatever) from rich to poor.

One quite important problem not resolved by changes in inequality measured by G is the possibility of a Lorenz improvement being accompanied by a reduction in the total product available for distribution. This was dealt with above by the constrained Lorenz criterion (Figure 6.3). But it is difficult to justify such a constraint as absolute and inviolable. Sen (1973, 58) sees Pigou's resolution of the conflict between quantity and distribution as follows: "while a really big decrease in the inequality of the distribution of incomes could perhaps be approved even if it was accompanied by a small reduction in the value of national product, few increments in its value could be approved at the expense of increased inequalities". Thus some pay-off relationship is recognized. That in certain circumstances the constrained Lorenz criterion might justly be violated, by sanctioning *either* greater regional inequality *or* a lower total product, but *not both*, is in keeping with the non-compulsive nature of the criterion. In the evaluation of territorial distribution patterns, the onus of demonstration is in justifying greater inequality or preservation of the *status quo*, not in justifying greater equality.

The argument in support of a strong if not complete recommendation for the acceptance of the Lorenz criterion has been built up at some length here, because any conception of improvement as simple as "the more equal the better" may otherwise provoke suspicion of a sweeping value judgement. The argument is not value free, as has been made clear, but neither is it merely a statement of personal preference for an egalitarian society. Even as a personal preference it would hardly be a highly deviant position. Such an attitude is deeply embedded in Christian ethics and Western European philosophy; Aristotle, though favouring some merit rewards, stated that "the democratic conception of justice is the enjoyment of arithmetical equality, and not the enjoyment of proportional equality on the basis of desert. On this arithmetic conception of justice the masses must necessarily be sovereign" (quoted in Alker, 1970, 192). Graaff (1957, 169) suspects that there is "a surprising degree of agreement" on whether a given distribution is good or bad, and that egalitarian ideals are now "extraordinarily widely held". What makes this so surprising and extraordinary is perhaps the persistence of very considerable inequalities within most Western societies. Nevertheless, the contemporary consensus alone is probably sufficient to justify the empiricist measuring the distribution of income or well-being in terms of departures from equality, and interpreting reductions in the level of such an indicator as "good".

Ginsberg (1965, 73) provides a suitable synthesis of the discussion of distributive justice underlying the problem of evaluating alternative spatial arrangements:

> There is general agreement that gross inequalities are unjust, and the right to minimum conditions of well-being is now widely recognized. But there is no agreement as to the distribution of property or the reward of service as above the minimum. Differences in needs, ability, productivity, or effort have all been put forward as relevant. But, apart from difficulties of measurement, none of these is free from objection on ethical grounds. It is arguable, however, that as judged by any of these criteria the wide differences in wealth now accepted are disproportionate and that there is, therefore, a strong case for reducing inequalities, even if there is no agreement as to what would constitute proportional equality. In this, as in other contexts, it is easier to recognize injustice than to define justice.

The axiom of "the more equal the better" implicit in the Lorenz criterion seems to respond perfectly to these sentiments. This criterion provides reasonable grounds for evaluation and action, if not ultimate moral sanction for any particular change.

7

Application: Changing Distributions

The discussion of evaluation leads directly to planning, or the deliberate implementation of change. Planning may be regarded as applied welfare analysis; spatial planning is applied welfare geography. Any urban or regional plan has the capacity to alter the distribution of goods and bads—to change who gets what where by modifying the process of how. Yet it is quite rare to find planning discussed explicitly in welfare terms. This chapter reviews the practical application of the welfare approach to human geography, with special reference to the planning process. Various parts of the theoretical framework built up in Part One will re-emerge, to provide guidance on such matters as the identification of planning goals, the design of policy for the spatial allocation of resources and the evaluation of impact of alternative programmes.

No attempt is made here to offer either a comprehensive view of urban and regional planning or a compendium of planning techniques. Numerous other books on these subjects are available (e.g. Boudeville, 1966; Tinbergen, 1967; McLoughlin, 1969; Chadwick, 1971; Masser, 1972; Catanese, 1972; Lee, 1973; Wilson, 1974; Krueckeberg and Silver, 1974). The intention is simply to show that most of what is required in planning flows logically from the content of previous chapters and that the meaning of planning is itself clarified by being placed in a welfare framework.

7.1 Planning the process of change

Economic and social change can take place in various ways. At the one extreme is the spontaneous action of individuals motivated by self-interest or altrusim, while at the other is highly coordinated collective planning. Some conscious planning is needed in all societies, but the more complex they become the more organization and control is required to run them effectively. Whether in public or private hands, the management of society in pursuit of specific objectives or in avoidance of specific disasters is a growing contemporary preoccupation.

For a long time, planning in the public sense was confined to the control of land use and physical development. This is the "town and country planning" tradition deeply rooted in Britain, with its emphasis on zoning within the city and on green belts to prevent urban sprawl. However, the past quarter of a century has seen the emergence of planning on a regional scale, not only in so-called advanced nations facing problems of differential regional performance but also in countries in earlier stages of growth seeking to accelerate the process of "modernization". Today the inseparability of urban, regional and national planning is widely recognized. Planning is no longer virtually the exclusive province of architects and engineers but a multi-disciplinary activity embracing almost all facets of life from the design of buildings to the control of industrial output.

One of the most influential developments in planning during the 1970s has been a growing awareness of distributional implications. Taking their cue from such writers as Pahl (1970), Harvey (1971) and Simmie (1974), more planners now appreciate that the development of land and the location of new facilities provide powerful instruments for the redistribution of real income or well-being. Equity considerations have always been prominent in planning, but the precise impact of development as differentially benefiting or afflicting different people has tended to be left somewhat to chance. As a result, the benefits have often flowed in the wrong direction, for example from the public purse to the private builder or property developer rather than to the poorly housed people whom the planners were trying to assist. As a not-so-hidden mechanism for the redistribution of well-being, public planning is particularly vulnerable to manipulation in the interests of the rich and powerful.

As who gets what where becomes increasingly a matter of deliberate public choice in many countries, it is important that the planning process is explicitly recognized as a means of redressing existing inequities in the spatial distribution of human life chances. The planning of land use, physical development, public services, transportation systems and so on, can then all be subjected to the guidance of welfare criteria and supporting analytical techniques designed to ensure that redistributive effects are planned to be just rather than fortuitous or an unjust outcome of the existing spatial allocation of wealth or power.

The extent to which planning can effect major changes in distribution will depend on the type of planning used. This will depend on the structure and ideology of the society concerned. Berry (1973, 172–9) has distinguished four modes of planning, evident in different parts of the world. The most common is *ameliorative problem-solving*, confined to "reactive" or "curative" responses to present problems. The implied goal is the preservation of the "mainstream" values of the past by smoothing out the problems that arise along the way. The second is *allocative trend-modifying*, or a future-oriented version of the first mode, with the projection of trends leading to the anticipation of problems and the setting up of regulatory mechanisms to alter undesirable trends. Again, the preservation of existing values is implied. The third is termed *exploitive opportunity-seeking* and involves finding new growth opportunities as, for example, in corporate planning, private entrepreneurial activity and publicly led private economic development. Some problems are predicted and avoided, but there is not much concern for the emergence of new problems. The fourth mode is *normative goal-oriented planning*, under which goals relating to a desired future are set, with policies designed and plans implemented to guide the system towards the goals or to change the system if necessary. The desired future may be based on present, predicted or new values.

Clearly, the normative goal-oriented approach is most likely to lead to substantial spatial redistributive effects. This alone allows for basic changes in the structures and values on which the existing distribution rests. But its implementation requires considerable technical sophistication in the allocation of resources towards specific societal objectives. If there is conflict over goals and means of attaining them, society may have to acquire "sufficient control and coercive power to ensure that inputs will produce desired outputs" (Berry, 1973, 179). The normative goal-oriented planning style is typically the one adopted in socialist states. However, there is a growing interest in such an approach in many countries with capitalist or mixed economies, where the "muddling through" characteristic of the ameliorative problem-solving style is proving increasingly inadequate as a response to contemporary problems.

Whatever the planning style, it will have some kind of objectives. These may be explicitly stated, or merely implicit in how policy is designed and implemented. The discussion in this chapter assumes a planning mode in which goals are explicitly recognized and consciously sought. The question of possible limits to rationality in problem-solving and the planning of human progress is reserved for the final part of this book.

The basic features of a plan are illustrated in Figure 7.1. In the top diagram (a) a *goal (G)* or *target variable* is shown, its attainment level being determined by the operation of some causal mechanism or *system*. There are two different elements within the system: *controlled* variables (*C*) towards which planning policy is directed and *uncontrolled* variables (*X*) not subject to manipulation. The policy (*P*) comprises an instrument or set of related instruments (i.e. a *strategy*) designed to affect the controlled variable(s) in such a way as to achieve the goal expressed as a specific target for a given period of time. The objective of the plan may be to maximize the attainment of the goal as measured by an appropriate *indicator*, subject to a budget constraint, or to realize a given attainment level for the minimum resource commitment. The condition towards which the plan is directed is a system output, while policy operates on or through the inputs. Alternatively, the goal might be attainable only by more fundamental modification of the causal mechanisms involved, i.e. changing the relationships among conditions within the system.

Figure 7.1b shows a specific version of a simple planning situation. Here the goal is to "improve educational attainment" in a city, the achievement of which is to be monitored by average pupil test performance. The plan objective is to raise performance as much as possible, within the constraint of a given addition to the city school budget. The chosen instrument is to improve the schools by providing more books. The uncontrolled variable is the home background of the children, which combines with the school to determine educational attainment.

Figure 7.1c shows a more complicated situation. Here the general goal

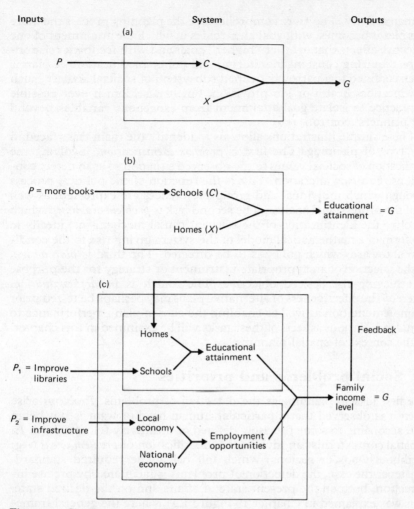

| Inputs | System | Outputs |

Figure 7.1 Simple representations of plans.

is to raise average family income, the target being the national norm. Income is viewed as dependent on the educational attainment of the head of household and on local employment opportunities. These, in their turn, are dependent on other conditions. Two policies are in operation: to raise educational attainment through better school libraries and to stimulate the local economy by improving the city's infrastructure. An added complication is a feedback from the final goal of raising family incomes into the home environment—an uncontrolled variable in the education subsystem. We might have added the further complication of unplanned and undesired outputs from the expanding economy, such as air pollution and traffic congestion. In reality few if any plans are independent of what is going on, planned or otherwise, in other spheres of human activity. The more comprehensive the planning process the more complex it becomes, with goal hierarchies in which the attainment of one objective affects that of other "higher" goals and with feedback relationships requiring constant monitoring and policy modification. A plan is often confined to a narrowly defined subsystem of societal activity, such as education, health or job provision, but it is seldom if ever possible in practice to isolate goal attainment from exogenous variables beyond the planners' control.

These simple illustrations allow us to identify the main tasks faced in any type of planning. The first is *problem identification*, involving the application of societal values to the observed situation so as to detect conditions requiring alteration. This is the function of the political process through which individual and group preferences are expressed, as well as of the professional analyst. The second task is *problem diagnosis*, which involves the identification of the relevant causal mechanisms, ideally in the form of a mathematical model of the system giving rise to the condition(s) towards which policy is to be directed. The third is *plan design*, or the selection of an appropriate instrument or strategy for the purpose of achieving the desired objective. The fourth is *impact evaluation*, whereby the effectiveness of alternative plans may perhaps be tested prior to implementation as well as enabling the chosen plan's performance to be judged. Various aspects of these tasks will be examined in this chapter, in the context of spatial planning.

7.2 Social problems and priorities

The first task in planning is the detection of problems. *Problems* arise when it is observed that a particular human need or want is not being met, according to some precisely defined or intuitively felt standard. In a spatial context, this can involve the identification of *problem areas* (e.g. neighbourhoods or regions) which fall below the required standard. Whatever the case, the detection of problems is facilitated by precise information, both on the present state of affairs and on the desired state. This was explained in Chapter 1 (Figure 1.2), where the general framework for applied welfare geography was introduced. The difference between the existing and desired state indicates the *need gap*, to be bridged by whatever policy instruments are chosen by the planners for the problem at hand.

The identification of the present state of society, the selection of priorities, and the design of strategies for change, all require us to be specific about those things on which human welfare depends. As Mishan (1969a, 62) recognizes, "we cannot move from the conceptual to the real world without first specifying what constitutes a 'better' distribution of 'real' income and, secondly, without adopting some measure of real income". It is difficult to see how any description of spatial patterns of human well-being can be attempted, or any prescription for alternatives proposed, without some criteria of relevance or social priorities. This means reference to an explicit or implicit *social welfare function* (SWF).

The concept of the social welfare function generally adopted in economic theory is subject to serious objections (see Chapter 3). As a formal abstraction that supposedly incorporates all things influencing welfare without making ethical judgements, it does not solve practical problems of social choice: "A formal solution solves nothing if the real problems remain untouched and their solution is only posited in terms of the formalism" (Dobb, 1969, 112). Yet planning requires specific choices. Planners, politicians and other decision-makers may find their own ways of setting priorities and resolving conflict, with little if any reference to the intricacies of welfare theory. As Nath (1973, 34–5) puts it:

> In actual practice, policy-makers do not attempt to maximize social welfare (or its expectation) according to a well-defined social welfare function, but rather try to find policies which are compatible with some given values of a number of social objectives which it is considered desirable to attain in a given period— with only a broad idea of the relative importance of the different objectives in determining social welfare.

However, it can be helpful to view society or its decision-makers *as if* they operated on the basis of a particular SWF, the values in which are revealed by the actual workings of society and the outcomes of its planning policies. Similarly, the practice of planning is itself facilitated by explicitly recognizing a SWF in the form of desired distributive (who-gets-what-where) outcomes. Thus a realistic conception of the SWF is, in the words of Nath (1973, 25), "any general statement of the objectives of a society—with some rough and ready idea of the relative weights of those objectives". This permits the translation of the SWF into forms relevant to empirical research and spatial planning.

As a simple illustration of what is meant by this type of *realistic social welfare function*, Nath (1969, 146) offers the following:

$$W = W(E, \sigma^1, \sigma^2, R, B, G)$$

where E is the employment level

σ^1 and σ^2 are coefficients of the distribution of money income and wealth respectively

R is the rate of growth of national product

B is the balance of payments

and G is a general factor representing non-economic variables affecting welfare.

These conditions bear some resemblance to the major concerns actually recognized in many countries today. However, while there may be a fairly broad societal consensus on desired directions of change in such conditions, the question of priorities will reveal value conflicts. Signs in a SWF are easier to determine than weights.

In the identification of prevailing social priorities, possible research stategies include large-scale attitudinal surveys of the population, content analysis of newspapers or magazines, in-depth interviews with decision-makers, and the examination of policy statements by politicians. As an example, Wilson (1969) based a study of inter-state variations in the "quality of life" in the USA on the "domestic goal areas" listed in the 1960 report of the President's Commission on National Goals. These were: (1) Status of the Individual, (2) Equality, (3) Democratic Process, (4) Education, (5) Economic Growth, (6) Technological Change, (7) Agriculture, (8) Living Conditions, (9) Health and Welfare, (10) Arts and Science, and (11) Democratic Economy. A similar approach has been adopted in attempting to describe the geography of social well-being in the USA (Smith, 1972a; 1973a). From a review of the literature on social indicators and an examination of the content of a selection of textbooks on social problems it was possible to identify seven major conditions of concern to contemporary American society: (1) Income, Wealth and Employment, (2) Environment, (3) Health, (4) Education, (5) Social Order, (6) Social Belonging, and (7) Recreation and Leisure. Each can be subdivided, and defined operationally by appropriate variables for the purpose of empirical research (see Chapter 10).

Having suggested what it is that welfare depends on, it is then necessary to specify the relationships between the variables. From the seven criteria above, a SWF for the USA could be written as follows in its undefined form:

$$W = f(I, En, H, Ed, O, B, R)$$

where f instead of W in the conventional formulation indicates that we are dealing with a realistic SWF, in which welfare depends on the magnitude of numerical indicators measuring attainment on specific criteria. But to use such an expression to derive a single general social welfare indicator for descriptive or planning purposes requires that it be fully defined (see Chapter 10). This brings us back to societal values, for it is here that any system of weighting and aggregation must have its origin. And although there is close agreement on the desired direction of change in the seven conditions embodied in the SWF above, their relative importance to American society is very much a matter of conjecture in the absence of firm empirical data or clear statements of national priorities.

The derivation of a realistic SWF thus requires weighting social goods and bads differentially, according to the prevailing values of society, its decision-makers, or its dictators. The weighted "commodity" SWF is in general:

$$W = f(w_1 Q_1, \ldots, w_m Q_m) \qquad [7.1]$$

where each good $(1, \ldots, m)$ has its own priority or weight (w). Drewnowski (1974, 30–33) suggests that such weights might be derived from an analysis of explicit social aims embodied in actual plans, from implicit or "revealed" social aims, and from an examination of the attitudes of policy-makers. While weightings of items in a SWF would usually be in the form of simple numbers, they could incorporate some kind of sliding scale to reflect decreasing marginal utility with higher attainment levels (Drewnowski, 1974, 32, 49). Examples would be logarithmic transformations or weighting by power parameters (Isard et al., 1969, 178).

In the spatial extension of conventional welfare theory (Chapter 3) we recognize a SWF comprising the levels of well-being in each territorial subdivision. As in the realistic SWF, each territory can be assigned a weight:

$$W = f(w_1 S_1, \ldots, w_n S_n) \qquad [7.2]$$

where S is a territorial indicator of well-being. Such weights can be used in the implementation of policy designed to favour specific neighbour-hoods or regions.

In an equalitarian society every individual, group or territory would have the same (unitary) weight in the SWF, i.e., arithmetic equality in the sense used in the previous chapter. This is the usual assumption in cost–benefit analysis (Pearce, 1971, 26–7), and there are strong arguments for such a procedure in the absence of obvious alternatives (e.g. Drew-nowski, 1974, 32). Any deviation from this would presumably be a result of the prevailing principles of distributive justice, requiring differential treatment for some, i.e., proportional equality related to some criterion of need. Various possibilities have been suggested for giving greater weight to society's poorer members. For example, Foster (1966) proposes the weighting:

$$w_i = \frac{\overline{Y}}{Y_i} \qquad [7.3]$$

where Y is the average national income per capita for all groups and Y_i is the figure for the ith group (or territory). The worse off the ith group, the greater the weight (w) attached to their term in the SWF used to judge between alternative social arrangements or plans. A more general measure of inequality such as the Gini coefficient can also be built into social indicators (Drewnowski, 1974), to favour redistribution in the direction of poorer people or places.

Planning almost always involves a differential spatial allocation of resources. Neighbourhoods and regions with special needs are recognized as *target areas* for policy, the objective of which will be to effect change in the spatial distribution of well-being, real income or whatever satisfies needs. The reference groups are sets of people defined by area of resi-dence. By disregarding distribution *within* the group we avoid problems of interpersonal comparison, which is full of practical and ethical diffi-culties. Within the group we can expect and perhaps accept some vari-ability (Sen, 1970, 100), if only because of the operation of random factors. And in practice judgements tend to be made with respect to sub-groups in society rather than individuals (Nath, 1969, 144–5). But we must not forget that inter-territorial equality may hide intra-territorial inequality, among sub-areas as well as individuals. As has already been mentioned, the level of territorial aggregation or subdivision is critical in welfare analysis. It raises particular problems in policy formulation, for the subsidy of lagging regions out of regressive taxation might end up benefiting the rich in the poor regions at the expense of the poor in the rich ones (Richardson, 1969a, 366). At the regional level a just distri-bution may have been achieved, but it would not have been justly arrived at. And at the intra-regional level distribution would now be more unjust.

7.3 The design of planning policy

The stage has now been set for a more direct discussion of the design of planning policy as applied welfare analysis. The main points of the preceding sections may be brought together in a simplified general model of a social system depicted as a set of interconnected subsystems (Smith, 1973a, 73–7). The model is disaggregated by territories, e.g. neighbourhoods in a city or regions in a nation (Figure 7.2). The general level of welfare is expressed by:

$$W = f(S_1, S_2, \ldots, S_j, \ldots, S_n) \qquad [7.4]$$

where S_j is the level of well-being in the jth territory. In any territory, social well-being *outcomes* are some function of the *outputs* of various subsystems, weighted and aggregated according to:

$$S_j = f(O_{1j}, O_{2j}, \ldots, O_{ij}, \ldots, O_{mj}) \qquad [7.5]$$

where O_{ij} is the output of subsystem i ($1, 2, \ldots, m$) in the jth territory and f is some function by which these outputs are transformed into general social well-being or real income. As [7.5] implies, this would take the form of a "commodity" SWF showing how the people in the place

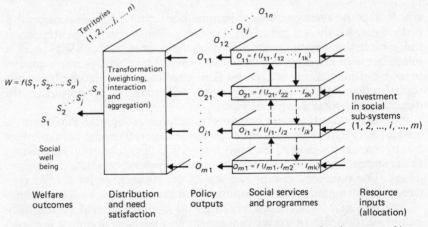

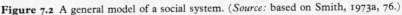

Figure 7.2 A general model of a social system. (*Source:* based on Smith, 1973a, 76.)

in question value different social outputs. The level of output in any subsystem is a function of specific *inputs*. It can be altered by changing input levels or by changing the transformation process to make it more efficient. This is a logical extension of conventional welfare theory, with subsystems and spatial disaggregation explicitly recognized. The use of such a model in a policy context is dependent on two important requirements: a specific SWF and some known subsystem production functions.

The concern is now with a *policy* or *action* SWF, or what Nath (1969) has referred to as a *decision-making social welfare function*. Setting actual goals or objectives in planning is difficult, for the aspirations of the people or policy-makers must be made specific and their attainment measurable, if policy implementation is to be a rational activity subject to performance checks. Some goal statements may be meaningless; for example the objective of the British government's industrial location policy for many years—promoting the "proper distribution of industry"—is quite incapable of evaluation without a definition of what is proper. The aim of "permanently raising the socio-economic and physical standards of living of the most deprived population groups", adopted in the Model Cities programme in the USA, requires a detailed definition of standards of living (see Chapter 11). There may be a difference between the stated goal and that actually pursued, as in South Africa's "separate development" policy (see Chapter 9). The inability of public policy and planning to come up to popular and professional expectation may reflect the frequent failure clearly to state the actual objectives. It is difficult to pursue that which is not defined.

Other problems arise in the selection of the type of numerical target variable or indicator to be used (Smith, 1973a, 72–3). In some cases *relative* figures such as per capita income or average value of housing units owned may be appropriate. However, it must be recognized that general welfare is not necessarily a *linear* function of things like income and housing quality; there may be decreasing returns per unit of increase after a certain level has been reached. *Absolute* indicators would apply where some minimum standard can be accepted. Pigou (1920, 759) was an early advocate of a minimum standard of real income, including "some defined quantity and quality of house accommodation, of medical care, of food, of leisure, of the apparatus of sanitary convenience and safety where work is carried on, and so on". These measures may be easier than relative indicators to rest on some agreed standard. Appropriate measures might be proportion of families above some poverty datum line for income, or proportion of houses with certain amenities. Any attempt to describe the present state of affairs, to design plans and to monitor progress must establish appropriate measures of goal attainment—a matter discussed extensively in the literature on social indicators (Smith, 1973a; Wilcox *et al.*, 1972; Fox, 1974; De Neufville, 1975).

A decision-making SWF need not be very complicated to be useful. A limited set of ordered goals, together with target levels for attainment (if possible, for each territorial subdivision), may be sufficient for practical planning purposes. This need not be in the form of a precise mathematical function; an explicit statement of major policy aims and priorities may be all that is required (Nath, 1969, 227). But if a policy SWF *can* be written as an equation, obvious advantages should accrue. Welfare, well-being or real income can be the dependent variable, with the targets or objectives which the planner seeks to affect as the independent variables. For example, we might have:

$$S = f(aZ_H, bZ_E, cZ_I)$$

where S is a general territorial social well-being indicator
Z represents the target levels for some sub-indicators of Health, Education and Income

a, b and *c* are priority weights

and   *f* represents a functional relationship which indicates pay-offs between the three target conditions and how they contribute to general social well-being.

Then for each target there would need to be a *decision model* (Richardson, 1969a, 358–61) of the form:

$$Z = f(P, X, R) \qquad\qquad [7.6]$$

where *Z* is the goal attainment indicator

P is a set of instrument variables subject to manipulation by policy-makers (*C* in our Figure 7.1)

X is a set of extraneous variables beyond control

R is a set of stochastic or random influences

and   *f* specifies the relationship between the dependent and independent variables.

This is simply a version of the subsystem social transformation function. The aim of policy design is to choose the appropriate target and instrument variables.

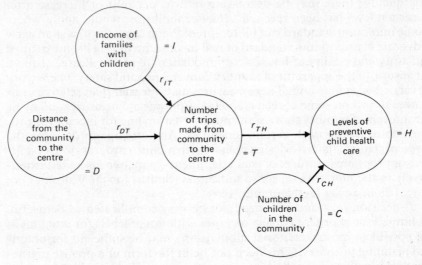

Figure 7.3 An example of a causal structure. (*Source:* based on Krueckeberg and Silvers, 1974, 14.)

The question of appropriate policy instruments is related to what we know about how attainment or "production" levels arise in the subsystem of concern. Once a problem has been identified, dissection of the causal structures in the subsystem in question is an essential prerequisite to policy design. As an example (following Krueckeberg and Silver, 1974, 14–16), Figure 7.3 shows a simple causal diagram relating to child health. The implied production function may be written as:

$$H = f(D, T, I, C)$$

where H is the local level of health and the independent variables are as shown. The r values represent observed correlations. Whether the relationships are linear, logarithmic, exponential or whatever, is part of the question to be answered in finding out how the subsystem operates. This is how the most effectively manipulated control variables are identified— assuming that the relationships are causal and not merely empirical associations.

One actual case will suffice to indicate the problems and opportunities arising from the subsystem approach to the planning of "social production". Suppose that the problem is to find the most effective way of improving educational attainment. The first task is to determine an appropriate target variable, which requires a definition of educational attainment. The obvious indicator may be performance by standard test scores in reading, mathematics and certain other subjects, but these are imperfect proxies for intellectual skills (Rivlin, 1971, 69). Then the independent variables or inputs must be identified, with regard to the effect of conditions outside the education subsystem as well as within it. On this basis a tentative educational production function might be identified as follows:

$$O_E = f(I_P, I_C, I_T) + f(F)$$

where the I represents the inputs of money spent on the physical plant (P), curriculum development (C) and teacher training (T), and F represents exogenous variable of family socio-economic status. For policy purposes the F variable might have to be taken as given or beyond control, if programmes must be confined to the education subsystem. However, socio-economic status of the pupil's family has been found to be the most effective predictor of educational attainment (US Department of Health, Education and Welfare, 1969, 70–71), so this might properly be an instrumental variable in policy. It could be that up to a certain income level the home is most important, after which the school takes over, which implies interdependent and non-linear input–output relationships. The allocation of expenditures to increase educational attainment requires weighting of the independent variables, which can be very difficult (e.g. Little and Mabey, 1972). Where policy includes allocation among territories, those with unfavourable conditions on high-weighted independent variables (e.g. family income) might get a form of positive discrimination (Jackson, 1972, 73). If education is financed from the local tax base, this favours the children who begin with the advantage of a high-income home, and if the policy goal is to raise *overall* attainment as much as possible for a given investment the strategy of favouring existing low-attainment territories will probably be most effective (if attainment is actually influenced by education in these areas). In the USA there is evidence of a shift in values in support of associating equity with equality of educational opportunity *irrespective of place of residence* (Smith, 1973a, 141), and if this is translated into policy the spatial allocation of educational funds will become a major question. The need to identify *local* production relations will then become critical.

Some research has been undertaken on the empirical identification of local production functions for public services, including education (Hirsch, 1968). In a study of ninety-seven school districts in New York State, Keisling (1967) used multiple regression analysis to derive an equation from which he was able to identify intelligence and occupation of head of family as major determinants of a child's achievement test score. In a study of distribution and production in an elementary school system based on data for fifty-six districts in Boston, Katzman (1968) estimated several education production functions by regressing measures of output against measures of school input and local socio-economic status of residents. Katzman found that, overall, school inputs account for a quarter of average level of pupil performance. Thus policy to upgrade educational attainment confined to improving schools, while clearly not ineffective, leaves major causal factors untouched. Prominent among these is the cultural deprivation associated with certain home environments, which are themselves the result of a broader system embracing aspects of society's economic and political structure.

This observation raises a general point of great importance, which must be stressed in any discussion of public policy. To view local levels of education, health and so on as consequences of purely technical relationships obscures the deeper origins of spatial maldistribution. What can be achieved by rational planning is very much constrained by the structure of society and its general mechanisms for resource allocation and real-income distribution.

7.4 Spatial planning strategy

The basic question in spatial planning is what policy or programme to implement where. This will depend on the goals set, the instruments chosen, and the extent to which needs and social production possibilities vary from place to place.

Figure 7.4 illustrates this in the simplest possible way. In Figure 7.4a there is a single territory (nation or region) with the planning objective of reducing infant mortality by 30 per 1,000 live births. The vertical axis measures output (O) in infant survival units, with the target of $Z=30$. The horizontal axis measures inputs (I) in money units (e.g. £M). Two policies are examined: increasing the number of doctors (D) and building more clinics (C). Production functions are established for both of these, O being a simple linear function of I. The intersection of the lines representing the production function and the target variable shows that building more clinics could reduce infant mortality by 30 at a cost of £2·0M, whereas increasing the number of doctors would cost £4·0M for the same result. Building clinics is thus the most efficient or cost-effective policy. If the problem had been to reduce infant mortality by as much as possible subject to a budget constraint (e.g. £3·0M), goal attainment could be estimated from the production functions ($O=15I_C$; $O=7·5I_D$), which show outputs per unit of input. The result is a reduction in infant mor-

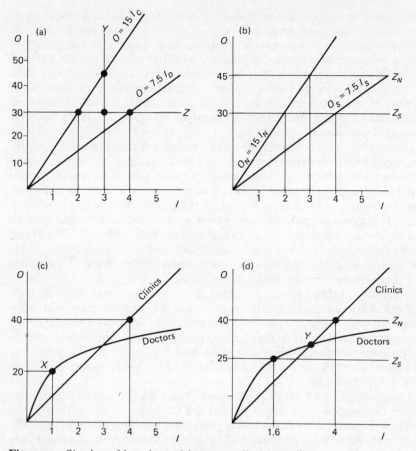

Figure 7.4 Simple problems in spatial resource allocation policy.

tality of 45 with £3·0M spent on clinics, 22·5 if spent on doctors, as can be confirmed from the graph.

In Figure 7.4b we now assume two regions—North (N) and South (S). Infant mortality in N is 75 and in S 60. The objective is to equalize regional rates at 30, so the targets are $Z_N = 75 - 30 = 45$; $Z_S = 60 - 30 = 30$. The policy instrument is the same in both regions, but its production function differs so that it costs twice as much to save an additional infant in S where the rate is already relatively lower than in N. The graph shows that £3·0M must be invested in N to achieve the given target, while in S it costs £4·0M.

The assumption that O is a linear function of I is relaxed in Figure 7.4c. Here infant survival is a linear function of investment in clinics but there are decreasing marginal returns to investment in more doctors. The marginal return or output is indicated by the slope of the production function; it is constant in the linear case but falls with increasing I in the curvilinear case. Suppose that the planning objective is to maximize infant survival subject to a budget constraint of £5·0M, in a single territory with production functions as shown. Up to point X on the doctors curve marginal returns are greater than on the clinics line (i.e. the slope is steeper—less input is needed to produce a unit of output). So the optimal strategy is to invest in doctors up to this point ($I=£1·0M$) and then switch to clinics as they have higher marginal returns once the critical number of doctors is available. Thus the remaining £4·0M is spent on clinics, and the total reduction in infant mortality is 20 (from doctors) plus 40 (from clinics), equals 60.

Finally, Figure 7.4d shows the same production functions but assumes two regions with different targets. Policy is constrained by organizational considerations which means that a region has to put all its resources into either more doctors or more clinics; it cannot combine them as in Figure 7.4c. Now, up to a level represented by the intersection of the two functions (Y) a given output can be achieved with less input by using doctors and not clinics; beyond Y (or $Z=30$) clinics are more efficient. The graph shows that, under the conditions assumed and with $Z_N=40$, $Z_S=25$, the optimal strategy is to provide more clinics in the North ($I=£4·0M$) and more doctors in the South ($I=£1·6M$).

In reality, optimal spatial planning decisions are more difficult than in these simple cases. Generally, input–output relationships are far more complex, with various additional budgetry or political considerations operating as constraints on the strategy chosen. Some kind of mathematical programming is often required to find a solution to the resource-allocation problem, once the necessary data on goals and instruments have been assembled.

The application of *linear programming* may be illustrated by an imaginary two-region case. Suppose that the objective of the planner is to reduce infant mortality in the two regions together by as much as possible, i.e. to maximize the "production" of infants saved from death. There are three possible inputs—doctors, clinics and nurses—with different production functions in each region. Input–output relationships are assumed to be linear, so the output per unit of input can in all places be expressed as a single value or *input coefficient* (Table 7.1). Thus we assume that experience shows that to reduce infant mortality in the South by one requires a (least-cost) combination of £0·25M on doctors, £0·60M on clinics and £1·20M on nurses; the different figures for the North reflect conditions in that region. The maximum amount of each input available is expressed as a set of budget constraints in Table 7.1. The problem is how to allocate resources on the provision of doctors, clinics and nurses *by region*, so as to maximize goal attainment.

A graphic solution is shown in Figure 7.5. Infant survival in each region is measured on the axes, with the three resource constraints plotted as lines. Thus the line for nurses shows that if all the available input (i.e. £10·0M) went to the South the maximum goal attainment would be 8·33 (additional surviving infants), i.e. investment divided by the input coefficient of 1·20 (from Table 7.1). If all the nurses were in the North the result would be $10 \div 2$, $=5$. The constraint lines thus show the saving of life in each region with different resource allocations. Now consider the heavier section of these lines (*ABCD*). This is the *efficiency frontier*—a production possibilities curve summarizing the technical constraints on what can be achieved. Any position inside *ABCDO* (when *O* is the origin of the graph) is feasible; anywhere beyond the frontier is impossible as it violates at least one of the resource constraints.

Table 7.1 Input coefficients and resource constraints in a two-region linear programming problem

Input	Input coefficients: quantity (£M) needed per unit of output		Budget constraint: maximum total expenditure (£M) on each input
	South	North	
Doctors	0·25	0·70	3·0
Clinics	0·60	0·30	4·0
Nurses	1·20	2·00	10·0

To solve the planner's problem now requires the insertion of *equal product lines*. Assuming that one life saved in the South is equal to one in the North, these lines can be drawn in Figure 7.5 with a negative slope of unity. Thus the line labelled 10 shows ten infants saved, all in *N* (where the line intersects the vertical axis), all in *S* (horizontal axis), or in various regional combinations (e.g. 5 in *S*, 5 in *N*). As in the analyses of earlier chapters, the maximum attainable output is where the highest equal product line reflecting society's supposed preferences (i.e. the planner's objective) just touches the outer edge of the production frontier. This is at *C*. Here, infant survival is increased in the North by approximately 1·45 and in the South by 5·85, to give a total goal attainment of 7·3. This is the maximum that can be achieved, given the input coefficients and constraints. The necessary resource allocation by regions (i.e. the planning strategy) can be calculated from the input and output data, as in Table 7.2. All the available resources of clinics and nurses have been employed but expenditure on doctors is £0·5M less than the constraint. To introduce more doctors is impossible without more clinics and nurses, given the production function $O = I_D + I_C + I_N$, where the input coefficients (*I*) are fixed for any level of output.

The implicit SWF underlying the above is $W = S_N + S_S$, where *S* is the regional level of well-being measured by infant survival. But suppose the prevailing values were such that it was desired to give the North double the weight of the South, i.e. $W = 2S_N + S_S$, or $W = 2X_N + X_S$ where *X* is production of infant survival. This would involve changing the slope of the equal product lines in Figure 7.5 so that two infants saved in the North are equal to one in the South. A line drawn from point 5 on the *N* axis to 10 on the *S* axis would be such a line, the slope reflecting the differential regional weights. This would alter the solution of the model, moving the optimal position to *B* in Figure 7.5. There would then

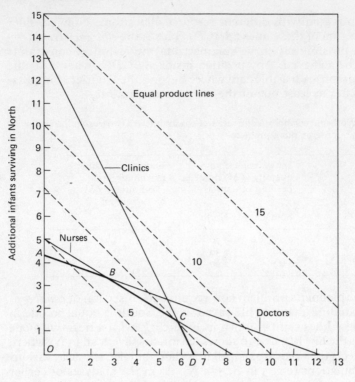

Figure 7.5 Graphic solution of a linear programming problem in regional resource allocation.

be a different regional resource allocation from the original one, which would produce a different result, i.e. infant survival increased in *N* by about 3·4 (instead of 1·45) and in *S* by about 2·6 (instead of 5·85). The total of 6·0 shows less children saved than before, but a higher attainment

Table 7.2 Regional resource allocation in an optimal programme to reduce infant mortality

	South	North	Total
Output (infants)	5·85	1·45	7·3
Inputs (£M)			
Doctors	1·5	1·0	2·5
Clinics	3·5	0·5	4·0
Nurses	7·0	3·0	10·0
Total	12·0	4·5	16·5

Note: Figures have been rounded and are approximate. Inputs are output multiplied by the appropriate input coefficient from Table 7.1.

level *on the new SWF*. The result of putting the new figures in $W = 2X_N + X_S$ is $6\cdot8 + 2\cdot6 = 9\cdot4$, whereas the original result of $X_N = 1\cdot45$ and $X_S = 5\cdot85$ gives $2\cdot90 + 5\cdot85 = 8\cdot75$. The welfare-maximizing solution depends on the weights in the SWF as well as on the technical conditions and resource constraints.

The problem solved in Figure 7.5 may now be stated more formally. The planner has an *objective function* (Z) to be maximized, subject to constraints imposed by the production functions and resource limitations. The problem is thus:

$$\text{maximize} \quad Z = X_S + X_N$$
$$\text{subject to} \quad 0\cdot25X_S + 0\cdot70X_N \leqslant 3\cdot0$$
$$0\cdot60X_S + 0\cdot30X_N \leqslant 4\cdot0$$
$$1\cdot20X_S + 2\cdot00X_N \leqslant 10\cdot0$$
$$X_S \geqslant 0; \quad X_N \geqslant 0$$

The first three constraints relate to the maximum contribution of doctors, clinics and nurses, respectively. The fourth is added to express the condition that production cannot be negative. This format may be generalized into a model involving m activities and n inputs, as follows:

$$\text{maximize} \quad Z = p_1 X_1 + p_2 X_2 + \ldots + p_m X_m$$
$$\text{subject to} \quad a_{11}X_1 + a_{12}X_2 + \ldots + a_{1m}X_m \leqslant b_1$$

$$[7.7]$$

$$a_{n1}X_1 + a_{n2}X_2 + \ldots + a_{nm}X_m \leqslant b_n$$
$$X_i \geqslant 0 (i = 1, 2, \ldots, m),$$

where $X_i (i = 1, 2, \ldots, m)$ is the output of activity i
$p_i (i = 1, 2, \ldots, m)$ is the value of one unit of output
$a_{ij} \begin{smallmatrix} (i = 1, 2, \ldots, m) \\ (j = 1, 2, \ldots, n) \end{smallmatrix}$ is the input coefficient for activity i and input j
$b_j (j = 1, 2, \ldots, n)$ is the maximum available amount of input j.

Linear programming is an extremely versatile device for solving planning problems involving the spatial and sectoral allocation of resources. Application to anything other than very simple cases requires computer solution instead of the graphics adopted in Figure 7.5. Further particulars will be found in more specialized texts, e.g. Isard (1960, 419–31), Chadwick (1971, 234–53), Smith (1971, ch. 20), Reif (1973, 162–73). The various complications that can be introduced include non-linear functions, the time-span required to achieve the goal, and the possibility of multiple objectives.

The infant mortality problem just examined brings to the surface the possibility of conflict between efficiency and equity in the design of spatial planning strategy. The most efficient plan, in the sense of most lives saved (or whatever the output variable) given the technique and resource constraints, may not be the best in the sense of maximizing a SWF incorporating the distributional preferences of the people or their planners. It is important to explore this issue further.

Shoup (1964) has provided an illustration, using the problem of the spatial allocation of policemen to reducing crime. The general principle of efficient resource allocation and the difficulty arising is stated as follows (Shoup, 1964, 384–5): "Minimization of crime, with a fixed amount of police resources available, is achieved when an increment of police input will reduce the number of crimes by the same amount no matter where it is placed within the city, or at what time of day. The marginal cost of preventing one more crime will then be the same everywhere in the city. But achievement of this goal will usually leave some of the city's

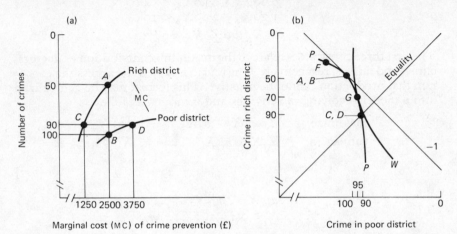

Figure 7.6 The problem of allocating police protection among districts. (*Source:* based on Shoup, 1964.)

districts more crime-ridden than others, ... crime will have been minimized at the cost of distributing police protection unequally." As with infant mortality or any other condition, the same investment can bring greater results in some places than others, by virtue of local conditions encouraging or impeding goal attainment.

Shoup examines an imaginary case of a city divided into two districts with equal population—the one rich (R) and the other poor (P). The objective is to minimize crime in the city as a whole. Crime is higher in P than R; so is the difficulty of crime prevention as measured by marginal cost. Figure 7.6a shows the two district production functions or marginal cost curves plotted against the crime rate (with zero at the top so that attainment rises up the vertical axis). Assume that, as things are, the transfer of one policeman (paid £5,000 a year) from R to P would prevent two more crimes in P and allow two more in R. The marginal cost is the same in both districts (i.e. £2,500) so crime in the city is minimized by the efficiency criterion set out above. The graph shows that at this point crime is 50 in R and 100 in P, as indicated by A and B

on the MC curves. Total crime at the minimum is 150. Now, suppose that police were transferred from R to P to achieve equality in crime rates. Each successive officer moved to P would prevent less crime than he did in R because of the greater difficulty in P reflected in the marginal cost curves. Equality is achieved at rates of 90 in both districts, giving a total of 180. At this position, the marginal cost of preventing a crime in P has risen to £3,750, while in R it has fallen to £1,250. Equality, which might be construed as equity, has been achieved at some efficiency cost because the total crime rate has increased.

Which crime-prevention policy *should* be adopted is an ethical matter of distributive justice, of course (Smith, 1974c, 46–7). In welfare theory society will have preferences expressed in a SWF, which can be drawn as welfare contours or indifference curves of the kind used in Chapter 3. Figure 7.6b follows Shoup (1964) and Dosser (1964) in identifying three possible optimal distributions of police protection measured by crime rates, in a diagram where the rates indicated by A, B and C, D in Figure 7.6a are shown as two points on the production possibilities frontier ($P–P$). Point C, D with 90 in both districts is on the 45° equality axis. Point A, B maximizes total output (i.e. minimizes crime) at the point when a line with a slope of -1 (i.e. equal weight to both districts) just touches the frontier. Point G indicates the distribution where the frontier just touches the highest welfare contour (W) reflecting the preferences of the people, planner or police chief. In practice the policy actually implemented may reflect the preferences of the rich district, giving them most of the protection and leading to a situation such as at F, with low crime in R and very high crime in P, which is sub-optimal by all three criteria illustrated.

One further complication may be introduced, to round off the discussion of inter-locality allocation strategy. This is the possibility of inter-dependence among levels of goal attainment. In the crime case, for example, effective law enforcement in one district might well reduce crime in the other rather than increase it. But a more general case will be developed, to pull together the strands of our view of spatial planning as applied welfare analysis.

There are two regions, N and S. In Figure 7.7 the curve A to D represents the production possibility frontier in cardinal utility space; it can refer to well-being, gross product, real income, or any contributory element such as education, health care and crime prevention. Following Richardson (1969a, 377–8) we make the curve bend back at both ends to reflect regional complementarity (cf. the Rawls case in Figure 6.2b), with very low levels of development in one region tending to hold back the other because of interdependencies. Section B to C on the curve thus covers all Pareto-optimal choices of inter-regional distribution, i.e. those where one region can advance only at the expense of the other, which is not the case on A to B and C to D.

The South is generally the more productive, because of rich resources, and the welfare frontier thus extends further along this axis. Now we add the SWF, such that the welfare contour W is at an angle of 45°

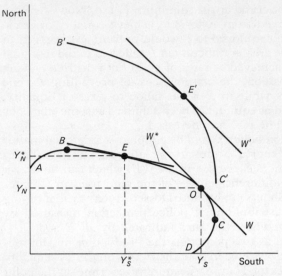

Figure 7.7 The achievement of regional equality, with interdependence of regional income levels.

indicating community indifference between the two regions in so far as distribution of real income is concerned. The point of tangency O reveals the shares Y_N, Y_S. This is unequal, by virtue of the better resources of S—perhaps the tax base supporting the more effective school system. How could regional equality be achieved, if accepted as a desirable objective? One way would be for society's objectives to change, or be changed. If the welfare contour was to change its slope to that shown by W^*, indicating a shift in favour of N, the inter-regional distribution would move to point E on the frontier. This is a point of equality; $Y^*_N = Y^*_S$. Moving society from O to E requires a transfer of real income or whatever it might be, from S to N, achieved by differential taxation or some other measure sanctioned by the change in societal values. Values are vital in moving towards geographical equality, if this is the goal. A ruling elite favouring equality (e.g. a socialist bureaucracy) might use the moulding of public opinion by mass media, education and so on as a policy instrument aimed at creating the social climate for equality, just as an aristocratic or capitalist elite relies on similar methods to maintain non-egalitarian values in support of their own position of privilege.

An alternative strategy is to increase the production capacity of the region with inferior resource endowment. Industrial dispersal policies or positive discrimination in spending on education would be of this nature. Over time, the welfare frontier will advance by a process of technological improvement and the use of new resources, and if in our two-region case it could be arranged that all growth over a given period would be in N, a move towards equality would occur. This is shown in Figure 7.7, where the relevant portion of the welfare frontier at some future point in time (B' to C') has advanced in favour of N only. Regional equality is achieved at E' now, despite the fact that the SWF has not changed and the contour is still at $45°$ (W').

The basic problem in applied welfare analysis is to maximize some preference function subject to a technical constraint. Spatial planning is likely to have territorial equality or the reduction of inequality as a major objective. In so far as society is unlikely to be on its production frontier, increases in efficiency promoted in areas of disadvantage can be used to further the goal of geographical equality. But, as in the case above, this requires the sanction of society, where the interests of the powerful may be in the maintenance of inequality. Those seeking a more equal or equitable geographical distribution, whether in policy-formulating positions or not, may have to regard values as a constraint. The spatial planner must have full regard for both technology and societal values, and keep an open mind as to where the constraints and opportunities lie.

7.5 Location, distance and accessibility objectives

The problem of inter-regional allocation illustrates spatial planning at a general level. At the local level, planning is more a matter of finding the best location for specific facilities, in relation to population needs. Basic to location planning is accessibility. This relates to the ability of people to overcome the friction of distance to avail themselves of services at fixed points in space or, more rarely, the ability of a mobile service to reach a fixed population. As was explained in earlier chapters, access to sources of need or want satisfaction has an important bearing on human well-being; accessibility itself is a scarce resource subject to distribution and redistribution through the planning process.

Accessibility may be measured in various ways. As an illustration, consider the imaginary situation in Figure 7.8, where there are three health-service facilities of different sizes (reflecting different levels of service) and three residential locations with different populations. Real distance (e.g. time) between each facility and location is as shown in the table. Following Schneider and Symons (1971, 11) we may define an index of *access opportunity* (AO) as:

$$AO_i = \sum_j \frac{S_j}{t_{ij}^b} \qquad [7.8]$$

where S is the size of facility j

$\quad\quad$ t is time taken to travel from residential location i to facility j

and $\quad$ b is an exponent describing the distance-decay effect.

Calculating AO for location 1 in Figure 7.8, with the distance exponent as unity:

$$AO_1 = \frac{S_x}{t_{1x}} + \frac{S_y}{t_{1y}} + \frac{S_z}{t_{1z}}, = \frac{10}{10} + \frac{15}{20} + \frac{10}{30}, = 2.08$$

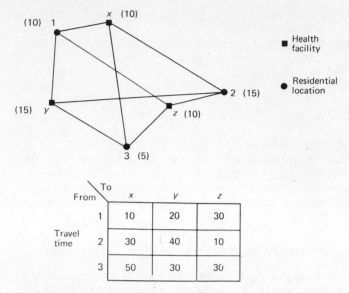

Figure 7.8 A simple accessibility problem. (*Source:* based on Schneider and Symons, 1971, 10.)

The figures for AO_2 and AO_3 are 1·70 and 1·03 respectively. So the people at 1 have the greatest access opportunity to health services.

Expression [7.8] is a version of the *gravity model* commonly used as a measure of interaction over distance. The general form is:

$$I_{ij} = a \frac{P_j}{D_{ij}^b} \tag{7.9}$$

where I_{ij} is volume of interaction or flow to a point j from another point i

P_j is some measure of the attractive power of j or the facility located there

and D_{ij} is distance between i and j measured in real terms such as time or cost.

Describing the actual pattern of interaction requires estimation of the parameters a and b. The former is a constant of proportionality while the latter is the exponent required to measure the frictional effect of distance. The gravity model is an important element in many more complex models designed to solve spatial allocation problems in planning where interaction over distance is a major consideration. Full particulars will be found in works on planning methods (e.g. Lee, 1973, ch. 5; Wilson, 1974; Krueckeberg and Silvers, 1974, ch. 9). The estimation of parameters is also described in texts on quantitative geography (e.g. Adams, Abler and Gould, 1971; Smith, 1975c, ch. 9).

One example is sufficient here to illustrate the empirical identification of distance decay in human interaction. Figure 7.9 shows the number

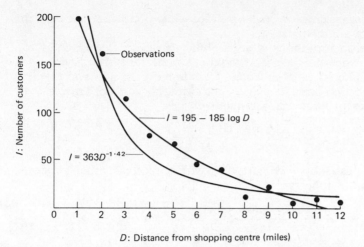

Figure 7.9 Curves fitted to the travel pattern of customers at Chatswood Shopping Centre, Sydney. (*Source:* Smith, 1975c, 293–4; data courtesy of Wayne Bensley.)

of people travelling various distances to a shopping centre in Sydney, Australia, derived from a sample survey of about 750 shoppers (Smith, 1975c, 287–94). The data reveal the curvilinear relationship found in most interaction studies, with greater distances having a disproportionately depressing effect on number of people travelling to the facility. Two different curves have been fitted to the data by regression analysis. The first involved transforming both the I and D variables into logarithms, to give

$$\log I = 2 \cdot 56 - 1 \cdot 42 \log D$$

This is simply a version of the general regression model of $Y = a + bX$. Taking the antilogarithm of the a parameter and using the b parameter as the distance exponent, this can be expressed in the form of the gravity model in [7.9] as:

$$I = \frac{363}{D^{1 \cdot 42}}, \quad \text{or} \quad I = 363 D^{+1 \cdot 42}$$

The a value of 363 is the curve's prediction for the first distance (i.e. 1 mile), while the negative exponent describes the form of the curve. The second curve, in which D alone is transformed into logs, gives a slightly better estimate of the distance-decay effect ($r = -0 \cdot 967$ compared with $-0 \cdot 878$). In research applications it is often necessary to experiment with different functions before the observed pattern of interaction is adequately described.

Returning to the question of accessibility, evaluating AO in [7.8] or I in [7.9] provides a relative indicator of access *potential*. Mapping the results for a set of residential locations can give a graphic picture of spatial variations in accessibility to a set of facilities, in the form of a *potential surface*. In so far as access to facilities contributes to personal utility or real income, any change in such a surface while population remains the same involves a redistribution.

Once a satisfactory index of accessibility has been developed, it can be used in planning as a goal attainment indicator. Multiplying each place's AO index by its population (N), summing for all i and dividing by total population provides a figure for average access opportunity (A), given the present locational arrangement, i.e.:

$$A = \frac{\Sigma(AO_i \times N_i)}{\Sigma N_i}$$ [7.10]

In the simple case above (Figure 7.8), with three residential locations, this works out as follows:

$$A = \frac{20\cdot8 + 34\cdot0 + 5\cdot15}{35} = \frac{59\cdot95}{35} = 1\cdot713$$

This figure can be taken as an indicator of the efficiency of the present location of facilities, measured by accessibility to a given spatial pattern of potential consumers. An alternative location pattern, or a planned change, might be judged an improvement if the value of A increases. For example, improving the transportation system between residential location 1 and facility Y so as to halve the present travel time (from 20 to 10) would raise AO_1 to 2·83, which increases A to 1·927. Average accessibility has been improved. But note that access to health service facilities has also been redistributed relatively: residents in 1 are better off, while those in 2 and 3 remain the same. There has been a welfare improvement by the Pareto criterion but a Lorenz deterioration, for accessibility is now more unequally distributed because those who gained already had the highest AO index.

The possible conflict between efficiency and equity criteria in the location of facilities has attracted much recent attention (e.g. Symons, 1971; Alperovich, 1972; Dear, 1974; Massam, 1974; Morrill, 1974). This reflects a realization that the solution minimizing the total coverage of distance, as generated by most location–allocation models, is not necessarily the best from a general welfare viewpoint. Alternative performance measures have thus been proposed. Of particular interest is an attempt by Schneider and Symons to distinguish between what they term "efficiency", "equity" and "welfare" measures. Suppose that we were able to calculate access opportunity (AO) for the many residential locations comprising a city, plotting the results as a histogram (Figure 7.10a). The mean value of AO might be interpreted as an efficiency indicator: the higher the average accessibility the better. The standard deviation could be a measure of equity: the smaller the better, as this means less variation in accessibility among residential locations. The proportion of people with AO below a certain minimum standard (e.g. the mean) is taken by Schneider and Symons as a measure of "welfare", though it is more appropriately viewed as a constrained-inequality conception of equity.

Figure 7.10b shows how a planned or observed change in the urban

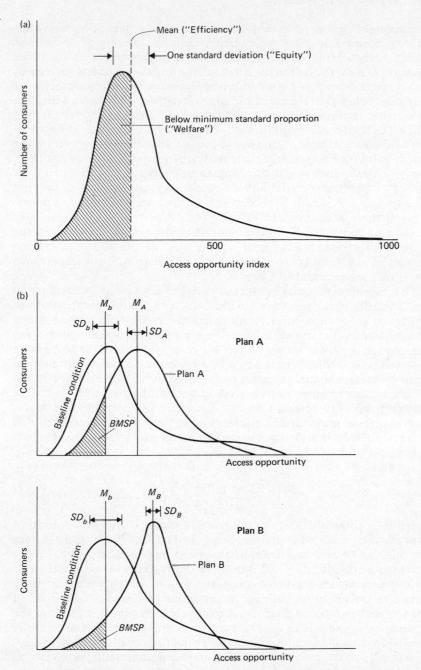

Figure 7.10 Alternative accessibility performance measures. (*Source:* Schneider and Symons, 1971, 22, 24.)

system might be judged in relation to the existing state. The new state could be deemed unambiguously better than the existing or "baseline" state, in accessibility terms, if there is an improvement in all three measures. This is the case in the situation shown: the mean has increased, the standard deviation has been reduced, and a smaller proportion of people are below the original minimum standard in both cases, with Plan B evidently superior to Plan A. Schneider and Symons (1971) provide detailed examples of the application of this method. Evaluation becomes more difficult, of course, if alternative plans reveal different or conflicting relative gains (or losses) on the three performance measures. For example, how much efficiency might the planner be prepared to sacrifice in the interests of reducing variability in access to facilities (i.e. improving "equity")? The solution becomes intuitive unless some trade-offs between these measures can be specified (Alperovich, 1972, 4). This requires a specific SWF or statement of planning goals. However, the approach illustrated at least opens up the practical possibility of judging changes in accessibility by reference to their distributional impact. An actual case is presented in Chapter 11.

The efficiency vs. equity conflict can arise in any facility location problem. Morrill (1974) provides an illustration of the different solutions which can arise when different measures are applied. In Figure 7.11a, a population is distributed in space (e.g. a city), each dot representing the number of people shown. A facility such as a hospital is to be built to serve these people. Where should it be located? Answers can be provided by various spatial statistics or "centrographic" measures, familiar for some time in quantitative geography (Smith, 1975c, ch. 6). One obvious possibility, arising from the discussion of accessibility above, is that the planner might decide on the place at which access potential (AP) to the population is greatest as measured by the gravity model. The location would thus be where,

$$AP = \text{Max}; \quad AP_i = \sum_j \frac{P_j}{D_{ij}} \qquad [7.11]$$

where P_j is the population at residential location j and D_{ij} is distance from j to the possible facility location i. In fact, the point of maximum potential can be well away from what appears intuitively to be the centre of the spatial distribution, as Figure 7.11 shows. This is because the distance exponent designed to express the way in which people actually behave in travelling to facilities incorporates an implied falling off of demand with increasing distance. A relatively high exponent, such as the squaring of distance, can lead to peripheral populations being virtually ignored in the calculation because $P \div D^2$ will be small for these places. As Morrill (1974, 45) puts it: "This model undoubtedly produces an efficient result from the point of view of the supplier of a private good, but since the idea is to maximize sales to the densest areas and ignore marginally located people, it results in great inequity and should certainly never be used for locating public services (or necessary private ones, like health care [in the USA]) to which all people are expected to go." Models and performance measures developed in one context may be quite inappropriate in another—something that should be remembered if land-

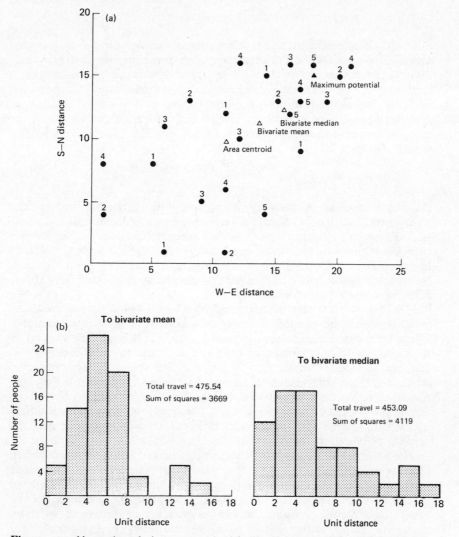

Figure 7.11 Alternative solutions to an optimal facility location problem. (*Source:* Morrill, 1974, 33–4.)

use/transportation models of the Garin–Lowry type are extended into the planning of public facility location (e.g. Breheny, 1974, ch. 1).

An alternative to the point of maximum potential, or harmonic mean centre of the spatial distribution, is the bivariate arithmetic mean. This is generally known as the *mean centre*. It can be found by identifying the appropriate X and Y coordinate values from:

$$X = \frac{\sum\limits_{j} X_j P_j}{\sum\limits_{j} P_j}; \quad Y = \frac{\sum\limits_{j} Y_j P_j}{\sum\limits_{j} P_j} \qquad [7.12]$$

where X_j Y_j are the coordinates of residential location j and P_j is its population. This measure has the advantage of minimizing distributional variability (the variance about the mean), thus introducing a possible criterion of equity. The mean centre is a consumer-oriented measure; potential has more of a producer perspective.

A third possibility is the bivariate *median centre*, otherwise known as the point of *minimum aggregate travel* (AT). The planner's objective would now be:

$$AT = \text{Min}; \quad AT_i = \sum_j P_{ij} \qquad [7.13]$$

As with the median in conventional statistics, this is the point where the total distance to all other observations is minimized. In Morrill's illustration (Figure 7.11b), this produces an aggregate distance to the facility of 453 compared to 476 at the mean centre. But the variance (i.e. $\sum D^2_{ij}$) has risen from 3,669 to 4,119. Total consumer travel has been reduced, but accessibility is more unequally distributed as the histograms show. Efficiency and equity conflict again.

A final possible location illustrated by Morrill (1974) is the *area centroid*, at which the greatest distance travelled by anyone is minimized. The maximum distance some person has to travel might be viewed as the worst possible performance of the system (Church and Revelle, 1974, 101) and to reduce this as much as possible could be an equity objective. At the extreme, this would be achieved when everyone had a hospital, for example, on their own doorstep, which would be a highly inefficient way to supply health care. However, it does raise the important practical question of the mobility of services hitherto fixed in space but perhaps capable of being on the doorstep when needed.

The solution of location–allocation problems of the type discussed in this section is facilitated by the existence of numerous computer algorithms. Many transportation problems, including the routing of mobile services, are amenable to linear programming solutions. As the generalized Weber problem familiar to students of industrial location, the identification of the elusive point of minimum aggregate travel has attracted various algorithms including one by Kuhn and Kuenne (1962), illustrated in a case study in Chapter 11. Reviews of the extensive literature in this field will be found in Revelle, Marks and Liebman (1970), Scott (1970), Smith (1971), Lea (1973) and Massam (1974). Computer programs are available in Rushton, Goodchild and Ostreth (1973).

The vital requirement in using such models in applied welfare analysis is to be sure that they suit the purpose at hand. For example, population may be weighted according to socio-economic status or some other measure of need, to accommodate specific distributional objectives. Whatever optimizing criterion or system performance measure is embedded in the model must properly reflect the planning goals.

7.6 Cost–benefit evaluation

There is much more to the practical evaluation of specific projects or alternative plans. Most of this is beyond the scope of our present discussion and dealt with fully elsewhere (e.g. Lichfield, 1970; Chadwick, 1971, ch. 11; Smith, 1971, ch. 23; Krueckeberg and Silver, 1974, ch. 6; Wilson, 1974, ch. 13). This section is confined to a particularly favoured approach to plan evaluation—cost–benefit analysis and related techniques—in which certain themes introduced earlier in this book will re-emerge.

The disposition of costs and benefits as a spatial-distributional issue was raised in Chapter 5. To make an accurate evaluation of the impact of plans on different people and places is a formidable task in practice. Yet this is precisely what must be done if scarce resources are to be most effectively used to promote specific redistributions. Simple illustrations must serve to illustrate cost–benefit techniques here; more detailed treatments will be found in specialist works (e.g. Prest and Turvey, 1965; Pearce, 1971; Mishan, 1972; Culyer, 1973, chs. 8 and 9).

Mishan (1972, 37–40) provides a suitable case, which we may elaborate a little here. It has the advantage of demonstrating the use of the consumers' surplus concept in cost–benefit analysis. In a city somewhere, a ferry boat provides the service of carrying passengers across a river, charging £2·00 per person. The average cost of running the service is £1·50, so there is a £0·50 per-unit return on capital invested. If consumer demand (D) is as in Figure 7.12a the number of passages purchased is Q. The triangle PXE is the consumers' surplus, while rent or profit to the ferry-owner is $PCSE$. Now suppose that a bridge is built, enabling people to cross by paying a toll of £1·40; per-trip costs of building and running the bridge are £1·20. The ferry is forced to close.

Table 7.3 shows a cost–benefit calculation for the bridge as compared with the ferry. Two population groups are recognized: the consuming public who cross the river and the owners of the means of crossing. Benefits, costs and the surplus or rent have been calculated from Figure 7.12, assuming the number of trips indicated for a given period of time. Building the bridge increases consumers' surplus by 90 but reduces rent or profit by 10. The net social gain is thus 80.

But *net* social benefit obscures distributional impact. Part of the result of the bridge is the shift of $PCSE$ from the former ferry-owner to the travelling public. This is "only a transfer as between one group and another" (Mishan, 1972, 38), but it is these inter-group (often inter-area) transfers that are so important in redistribution. Ownership is also important: if the bridge is privately owned the change has transferred rent from one capitalist to another, whereas if it is publicly owned there has been a transfer from the capitalist class to the rest of the people. In reality,

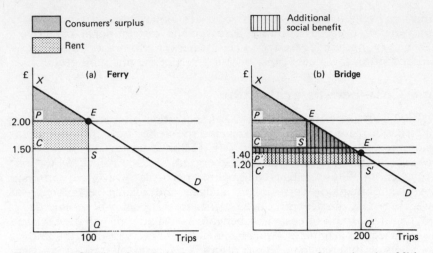

Figure 7.12 Cost–benefit analysis of alternative river crossings. (*Source:* based on Mishan, 1972, 39.)

Table 7.3 Cost–benefit analysis of two alternative river crossings

	Consumers				Owners	
	Ferry	Bridge			Ferry	Bridge
Benefits (use value)	230	400		Benefits (receipts)	200	280
Costs (fares)	200	280		Costs	150	240
Surplus	30	120		Rent (profit)	50	40
Net gain (+) or loss (−):		+90		Net gain (+) or loss (−):		−10

Source: Calculated from Figure 7.12.

of course, the ferry-owner may have the power to block a public bridge contrary to his interests. Alternatively he might come to an agreement with a private bridge-owner to maintain the original fare (i.e. to create artificial scarcity of passages) and share the rents *PCSE*, thus keeping consumers' surplus at the original low level and maintaining capitalist income at 50 instead of 40 as under the bridge plan.

Cost-benefit analysis can be very helpful in evaluating the impact of alternative plans. One of the best-known and most thoroughly scrutinized applications in Britain is in the report of the Roskill Commission which calculated costs and benefits for alternative locations for a third London airport (e.g. Lichfield, 1971). Perloff (1969) has illustrated an elaborate cost–benefit framework for the evaluation of environmental policy measures, and limited applications are certainly possible in the social policy field. As Culyer (1973, 178) puts it, cost–benefit analysis has the great virtue of forcing the decision-maker to concentrate attention on the objectives and the trade-offs which necessarily have to be made. But still, distributional issues are easily overlooked in the calculation of overall net benefit (Mishan, 1972, 4).

There are a number of other evaluation methods similar to cost–benefit analysis. They all involve the search for "value for money". Various *cost-effectiveness* methods have attracted particular interest in the USA in the design of health and welfare policy (e.g. Elkin and Cornick, 1970), and also in Britain (Culyer, 1973, ch. 9). Some use has been made of PPBS (Planning–Programming–Budgeting–System) in the Department of Health, Education and Welfare (Spindler, 1968; Rivlin, 1971). One study was able to establish an order of priorities with respect to the cost of saving a life: the result was first the prevention of motor vehicle accidents, second early detection and control of cancer, third treatment of syphilis, and fourth treatment of tuberculosis (Wilcox, 1969, 369). In the case of traffic accidents it was found that one death could be averted by spending $88,000 on improving driving skills, $45,000 on providing emergency medical services, $13,000 on tightening up on driving licensing, $3,000 on requiring motor cycle helmets, or $87 on requiring seat belts. Expenditure on a programme to get people to use seat belts was thus judged to be a thousand times more effective than improving driving. The important geographical question is whether cost–benefit ratios vary from place to place.

The major practical drawback of cost–benefit approaches is the need to measure things in monetary units. The problem is the same as that raised by conventional accounting of national (regional or local) product: those aspects of life that are difficult to measure in money are left out. Even when attempts are made to measure the intangible, such as loss of life in road accidents, the technique tends towards the extremes of materialist values, with cost measured by loss of potential contribution to national product. The implications of this raise serious ethical issues; as Mishan (1967, 121) points out, "Many of the aged, of course, contribute practically nothing to the national product and, on this principle therefore, their loss to the nation is negligible." One of the more profound paradoxes of the move towards rational goal-oriented planning to improve the quality of life is that it may force upon society a calculus which itself may appear inconsistent with enhanced life quality.

Sooner or later, the evaluation of alternative plans has to confront the problem of multiple and perhaps conflicting goals. Some of the difficulties involved in planning at the regional scale have been outlined by Reiner (1971). A favoured approach in recent years has centred around the *goals-achievement matrix* introduced by Hill (1968; 1973). This is a cost–benefit technique, the basic features of which are summarized in texts on planning methods (e.g. Chadwick, 1971, 269–70; Wilson, 1974, 359–60). It involves differential weighting of various goals and population groups, and is thus easily related to welfare theory.

A simple extension of the ferry and bridge case above provides an illustration (Table 7.4). Assume the two goals of improving mobility and protecting the environment, and the two population groups of poor and rich occupying different districts of a city. The rich have greater influence

Table 7.4 A simple goals–achievement matrix to evaluate alternative plans

| Goal | | Mobility | | Environment | |
| Weight | | 1 | | 2 | |
Group/Area	Weight	Ferry	Bridge	Ferry	Bridge
Poor	1	+ 30	+120	−40	0
Rich	2	+10c	+ 80	−20	−150
Total		+130	+200	−60	−150

Total net benefits: from Ferry = 130 − 60, = 70
from Bridge = 200 − 150, = 50

Note: The figures in the matrix are net benefits (+) or losses (−) in monetary units with goal and group weights applied.

in the planning process, this being reflected in their weighting of 2 compared with the poor's unity and in the double weighting of the environmental protection goal compared to mobility in deference to their value preferences. Under the mobility goal the data from Table 7.3 (p. 188) are inserted, with consumers' surplus attributed to the poor and the rich getting owners' rent multiplied by 2 to reflect their group weight. The figures under environment express the fact that the ferry causes more harm to the poor neighbourhood than that of the rich, whereas the new bridge would have to be built through the rich neighbourhood without affecting that of the poor. The table shows that the total net benefits from the existing ferry (70) are more than from the planned bridge (50), given the weights applied. The planner thus rejects the bridge proposal.

The goals–achievement matrix is generalized in Table 7.5. There are g goals, each with an appropriate attainment indicator with respect to which costs and benefits can be calculated in comparable units. There are n population groups, which may be taken as areas to give a spatial context. Weights are assigned to each goal (a) and group/area (b). Thus

Table 7.5 A generalized goals–achievement matrix

| Goal indicator: | | 1 | | 2 | | ... | g | |
| Goal weight: | | a_1 | | a_2 | | ... | a_g | |
Group/Area	Weight	Cost	Benefit	Cost	Benefit	...	Cost	Benefit
1	b^1	C_1^1	B_1^1	C_2^1	B_2^1	...	C_g^1	B_g^1
2	b^2	C_1^2	B_1^2	C_2^2	B_2^2	...	C_g^2	B_g^2
⋮	⋮	⋮	⋮	⋮	⋮		⋮	⋮
n	b^n	C_1^n	B_1^n	C_2^n	B_2^n	...	C_g^n	B_g^n

Source: based on Wilson (1974, 359).

there are two implicit social welfare functions. The first is a "commodity" SWF of the form:

$$W = a_1 X_1 + a_2 X_2, \ldots, + a_g X_g \qquad [7.14]$$

where X is a goal attainment indicator. The second is a group/areal distribution SWF of:

$$W = b_1 U_1 + b_2 U_2, \ldots, + b_n U_n \qquad [7.15]$$

where U is an indicator of utility, real income or well-being. If we now assume a set of m plans, they can be evaluated by calculating their individual total net benefits. Following Wilson (1974, 359) this can be written:

$$W^m = \sum_g \sum_n a_g b^n (B_g^{nm} - C_g^{nm}) \qquad [7.16]$$

where W^m is the welfare level associated with the mth plan.

The goals–achievement matrix is, of course, subject to the same general difficulty as the more abstract formulations of the SWF. Somehow, goals and weights have to be determined. This is the impasse that leads some to see such a device as unrealistic, and inferior to other more pecuniary ones such as Lichfield's *planning balance sheet* (Chadwick, 1971, 268–70). But any method of plan evaluation yielding an order of preference inevitably involves the weighting of goals and group interests, implicitly if not explicitly. As long as the planning process remains one of the more important of society's redistributive mechanisms it seems as well that whatever weightings are adopted by the planners should be clearly revealed. However they may be arrived at, these practical value judgements are major determinants of who gets what where from planning.

7.7 Towards a general model

A frequent aspiration of academics and policy-makers in recent years has been the development of a macro-scale model of the social system. Inspired by some limited success in the mathematical modelling of economic systems, the proposition is that a social equivalent of an econometric model might be constructed—perhaps an operational version of something similar to that in Figure 7.2 above. Such a device would permit the simulation of social system operation and could greatly assist policy design—or such is the expectation of those who advocate what is sometimes termed the *social engineering* approach.

The most common framework for social systems modelling, borrowed from economics, is input–output analysis. Institutions or social programmes are seen as the producing sectors, contributing outputs to various social objectives. An example is provided by Terleckyj (1970, 1975), who illustrates a table in which a list of activities (vertical axis) is shown as contributing to specific "goal output indicators" (horizontal axis) by means of social production coefficients analogous to the Leontief coefficients in conventional input–output analysis. Very similar is the *social welfare matrix* illustrated by Jackson (1972, 83). This is a table with eight output categories relating to need along the horizontal axis: income flows, financial assets, health, education, housing, social overhead capital, family life, and social relationships. Along the vertical axis are services generating the outputs, including income maintenance, other social services, physical environment services, and so on.

The most comprehensive approach of this kind is that developed by Isard *et al.* (1969). Some of its origins can be found in an earlier work (Isard *et al.*, 1960, 681–721), where a "channel of synthesis" based on a framework of values and social goals is outlined. This involves the setting of political and social goals as well as the economic goals hitherto predominating in regional science, the development of a social accounting system, and an inter-regional linear programming solution to maximize some objective function such as Gross System Product subject to a set of constraints. The constraints include minimum standards of food, clothing, shelter and so on, and also an input–output matrix specifying the technological framework within which society operates.

A much expanded input–output model is presented in Isard *et al.* (1969). This involves the addition of *non-economic commodities* to the conventional input–output matrix, to account for all things produced. It combines the formal framework of inter-industry economics with social and political theory derived substantially from the work of Parsons and Lasswell. The non-economic commodities recognized are as follows (explanations much abbreviated):

> solidarity (integration of diversified perspectives)
> power (ability to influence decisions)
> respect (status, honour, recognition, prestige, etc)
> rectitude (virtue, goodness, righteousness, etc)
> affection (kindness, friendliness, love and goodwill)
> sociality (pleasant feeling generated by interaction)
> well-being (health and safety)
> skill (proficiency)
> enlightenment (knowledge and insight)
> achievement (accomplishment)
> love tendered (giving without expectation of reciprocity)
> sanctions (approval of society, positive or negative)

Any individual or organization is concerned with the production and consumption of some or all of these, as well as the usual "economic" goods and services. The non-economic commodities are also exchanged among territories; for example a region might gain public works projects from central government in return for political support (power). All such exchanges are incorporated within an expanded version of the inter-regional input–output table (Isard *et al.*, 1969, 517).

A somewhat different input–output model has been proposed by Drewnowski (1974). Drewnowski's distinction between level of living and state of well-being was introduced in Chapter 2, and a summary of his synoptic view of the process of human need and want satisfaction provides an appropriate way of closing the circle of our theoretical

Figure 7.13 Interdependence table describing the generation of level of living and state of welfare (i.e. well-being). (*Source:* Drewnowski, 1974, 110–11.)

Column groups (Receiving activities):
- **Accumulation:** L (1), Q (2), K (3), T (4), P (5)
- **Consumption (6):** n (61), s (62), h (63), e (64), t (7)
- **Level of living (8):** n (81), s (82), h (83), e (84), l (85)
- **State of welfare (9):** h (91), e (92), w (0)

Contributing activities	L 1	Q 2	K 3	T 4	P 5	n 61	s 62	h 63	e 64	t 7	n 81	s 82	h 83	e 84	l 85	h 91	e 92	w 0	X^0
Production																			
Labour (1)			$x_{1,3}$	$x_{1,4}$	$x_{1,5}$	$x_{1,61}$	$x_{1,62}$	$x_{1,63}$	$x_{1,64}$									$x_{1,0}$	X^0_1
Quality of labour (2)			$x_{2,3}$	$x_{2,4}$	$x_{2,5}$	$x_{2,61}$	$x_{2,62}$	$x_{2,63}$	$x_{2,64}$									$x_{2,0}$	X^0_2
Capital (3)			$x_{3,3}$	$x_{3,4}$	$x_{3,5}$	$x_{3,61}$	$x_{3,62}$	$x_{3,63}$	$x_{3,64}$									$x_{3,0}$	X^0_3
Technology (4)			$x_{4,3}$	$x_{4,4}$	$x_{4,5}$	$x_{4,61}$	$x_{4,62}$	$x_{4,63}$	$x_{4,64}$									$x_{4,0}$	X^0_4
Goods in process (5)			$x_{5,3}$	$x_{5,4}$	$x_{5,5}$	$x_{5,61}$	$x_{5,62}$	$x_{5,63}$	$x_{5,64}$									$x_{5,0}$	X^0_5
Welfare generation first step — Consumption (6)																			
Nutrition (61)											$x_{61,81}$							$x_{61,0}$	X^0_{61}
Shelter (62)												$x_{62,82}$						$x_{62,0}$	X^0_{62}
Health (63)													$x_{63,83}$					$x_{63,0}$	X^0_{63}
Education (64)														$x_{64,84}$				$x_{64,0}$	X^0_{64}
Needs satisfaction outside consumption (7)															$x_{7,85}$				X^0_7
Welfare generation second step — Level of living (flow of welfare) (8)																			
Nutrition (81)																$x_{81,91}$	$x_{81,92}$		X^0_{81}
Shelter (82)																$x_{82,91}$	$x_{82,92}$		X^0_{82}
Health (83)																$x_{83,91}$	$x_{83,92}$		X^0_{83}
Education (84)																$x_{84,91}$	$x_{84,92}$		X^0_{84}
Leisure (85)																$x_{85,91}$	$x_{85,92}$		X^0_{85}
Productivity effect — State of welfare (9)																			
Health status (91)		$x_{91,2}$																$x_{91,0}$	X^0_{91}
Educ. status (92)		$x_{92,2}$																$x_{92,0}$	X^0_{92}
Wastage and maldistribution (0)		X_2	X_3	X_4	X_5	X_{61}	X_{62}	X_{63}	X_{64}		X_{81}	X_{82}	X_{83}	X_{84}	X_{85}	X_{91}	X_{92}	X_0	

deliberations. Drewnowski's model follows the conventional input–output form (Figure 7.13). Various contributing activities generate inputs to receiving activities, proceeding successively from accumulation and consumption to level of living and state of well-being ("welfare" in Drewnowski's terminology). The symbol x indicates a flow, i.e. that the contributing activity in question exerts an influence on the receiving activity. This is ideally expressed quantitatively as some kind of social production coefficient but need not, of course, be a flow of tangible goods and observable services (Drewnowski, 1974, 107). The time-span of the model can refer to the past or to a future development plan period. The activities included are roughly equivalent to the level of living and state of well-being components introduced in Chapter 2, and can form the target variables for planning.

There are three stages in the operation of the model. The first refers to *production*, with items 1 to 5 representing the factors involved. Their outputs contribute to accumulation (i.e. maintenance and growth of productive capacity) and consumption (i.e. the satisfaction of needs and wants—items 61 to 64). Thus $x_{1.3}$ describes the (direct) contribution of labour to the production of capital equipment and $x_{1.61}$ its contribution to production of sources of nutrition. The symbol X_1^0 in the right-hand column shows the total labour time available during the plan period, X_3^0 the total capital, etc. Total volumes of accumulation and consumption are indicated in the bottom row, by X_3 (total capital accumulation), X_{64} (total education consumption) and so on.

The second stage is *well-being generation*. Two steps are involved: the contribution of consumption to level of living and the contribution of level-of-living flows to the stock of well-being. Thus $x_{61.81}$ is the consumption of food satisfying the need for nutrition, $x_{62.82}$ the flow of services from buildings satisfying the shelter need, and so on. These then contribute to state of well-being; for example the coefficients $x_{83.91}$ and $x_{83.92}$ show how flows of health contribute to stocks of health and education status respectively. The overall state of well-being on these two criteria is X_{91} and X_{92}.

The third stage is *feedback*, concerned with the productivity effect of the state of well-being. Health and education status contribute to the quality of labour through the coefficients $x_{91.2}$ and $x_{92.2}$. These, in turn, enable more sources of need satisfaction to be produced with a given labour supply. Thus the generation of human well-being is a continuous circular process of interdependence.

There are two general measures of system performance. Throughout any plan period the flows into human well-being are measured by the *level-of-living index*. In the terms of the present model, this is:

$$L = X_{81} + X_{82} + X_{83} + X_{84} + X_{85} \qquad [7.17]$$

The increments (d) to *state of well-being* (W) are:

$$dW = X_{91} + X_{92} \qquad [7.18]$$

from which Drewnowski would subtract $x_{91.0}$ and $x_{92.0}$ as flows to "wastage and maldistribution".

Drewnowski (1974, 135–47) offers a formal statement of the model as a linear programming problem. In the short run, the objective function to maximize collective utility (U) is:

$$U = u_{81}X_{81} + u_{82}X_{82} + u_{83}X_{83} + u_{84}X_{84} + u_{85}X_{85} + u_3 X_3^A + u_4 X_4^A + u_5 X_5^A$$

$$[7.19]$$

where X is a level-of-living flow

     X^A is an accumulation increment

and u is a "valuation coefficient" or weight.

This is simply a social welfare function of the form $W = \Sigma wX$. The solution is constrained by the interdependence relationships among the economic and social variables, describing the state of technology and the resources at society's disposal. The optimal plan, in terms of resources allocated to specific goal attainment, is where the magnitude of U (or W) is maximized.

Drewnowski's model is designed for application to a single national or regional plan. It could be disaggregated spatially after the fashion of Isard's model, however. Especially helpful is its conception of development as an interdependent process involving social as well as economic "growth", with the ultimate focus clearly on human well-being rather than on narrow materialist objectives. It also has the important attribute of being institution-free (Drewnowski, 1974, 134), so that it is applicable under any socio-political structure. However, such an approach is more of a practicable possibility in a socialist society. As Mandel (1962, 721) says of input–output analysis and operational research methods, "these techniques will not really find their full application except within the framework of a planned and socialized economy, to which their usefulness would be undeniable, especially where hard mechanical problems need solving (choice between different investment projects with the same priority aim; progressive replacement of current technical processes by new ones; determination of the more or less underdeveloped state of certain regions and of the type of investment most appropriate to overcome this backwardness, etc.)." This is exemplified in the development of models for the design of territorial production complexes within the general framework of economic planning in the USSR, with the objective function of maximizing living standards subject to regional equity considerations (e.g. Bandman, 1976; Granberg, 1976). The application of input–output analysis and linear programming has been of great importance in recent reforms of economic planning in the USSR, in which elements of western or "bourgeois" economics have been introduced to aid the more rational allocation of resources (Campbell, 1974, 186–97).

Despite their similarities in form and in their welfare-theoretical foundations, the models of Isard and Drewnowski provide an instructive contrast in contemporary approaches. Isard *et al.* (1969) offer very much an abstract formalism, with elegant flights into the empyrean of modern regional science; imaginative creativity has full reign, unconstrained by the practical requirements of planning. Drewnowski (1974) is rooted in the reality of world development problems, his model having emerged from United Nations concern with the meaning of development and the search for effective practical ways of achieving it.

If such models could be made operational, they would enable us to trace the origin of regional levels of well-being, gross product or real income, through the system producing and distributing the contributory goods and bads. Isard *et al.* (1969, ch. 13) suggest many possible indicators of the magnitudes to which their non-economic commodities may be related. Drewnowski (1974) is very specific about the composition of level of living and state of well-being and their measurement (see Chapter 2). What is lacking, of course, is a knowledge of social production processes sufficient to specify the coefficients, or functional relationships among inputs and outputs, and a theory of production for non-economic goods comparable with that in economics (Rivlin, 1971). Also a problem is the lack of a common unit of measurement with which to compare and aggregate the production of wheat and corn with respect, rectitude and so on. These are difficulties against which practical research sometimes despairs of making progress. The views of US Department of Health, Education and Welfare (1969, 99) on building a broad national welfare accounting system are relevant here:

> It would be utopian even to strive for a Gross Social Product, or National Socioeconomic Welfare, figure which aggregates all relevant social and economic variables. There are no objective weights, equivalent to prices, that we can use to compare the importance of an improvement in health with an increase in social mobility. We could in principle have a sample survey of the population, and ask the respondents how important they thought an additional unit of health was in comparison with a marginal unit of social mobility. But the relevant units would be difficult even to define, and the respondents would have no experience in dealing with them, so the results would probably be unreliable. Thus the goal of a grand and cosmic measure of all forms or aspects of welfare must be dismissed as impracticable, at any rate for the present.

But despite these and other difficulties, progress is possible. The inter-regional input–output framework, along with theory relating to regional real-income levels, goes part of the way towards providing a model of the process of geographical well-being differentiation. Many non-economic aspects are likely to resist attempts at operationalization for a long time to come, in some cases for ever, but research in the field of territorial social indicators (e.g. Smith, 1973a; Knox, 1975) shows that much can be done that was not envisaged even at the start of this decade. Illustrations are offered below, in Part Three. Against the complaint that even in a limited economic context input–output analysis is of very slight practical use can be offered the argument that at least the idea may help in directing some research effort, possibly into the modelling of restricted social subsystems in input–output terms. The need to design specific programmes to enhance specific aspects of human well-being in specific territories requires the disaggregation of the system into policy-relevant component parts. As attention is focused on specific subsystems (e.g. health, education, criminal justice), knowledge will gradually be built up. As subsystems are understood, they can be connected up within some broader model.

Although the general models reviewed here are very much at the drawing-board stage, they do remind us of the essential unity of the social–economic–political system in geographical space. Society must be viewed as a highly complex aggregation of interconnected subsystems operating in all manner of different spaces if we are to understand how it produces and distributes well-being. As Romanyshyn (1971, 407) reminds us, the religious notion of the common brotherhood of man is now confirmed by our scientific understanding of the interrelatedness of all social systems: "We are in fact interdependent. Our behaviour has inescapable consequences for others for which we must bear moral responsibility. The better science can trace the consequences of our actions the less we can escape the ethical implications of the way we organize social life. Definitions of social welfare that are narrow and parochial must be expanded to embrace the entire family of man." Similar sentiments are expressed in a description by Mandel (1962, 170) of the socialization of production with the development of capitalism: "In place of the fragmentation of patriarchal, slave-owning or feudal society into thousands of little cells of production and consumption, each one independent of every other, with only rudimentary links (particularly exchange links) between them, there has come *the world-wide relationship between men*. The division of labour has become general and advanced not only in a single country but on a world scale. Nobody any longer produces first and foremost the use-values he needs for his own consumption. The work of each is indispensable to the survival of all." As we try to put together our inevitably incomplete and spatially restricted models of parts of the world system, it may be useful to keep in mind its essential unity. No man is an island ...

Part Three

Case Studies

No man is an *Iland*, intire of it selfe; every man is a peece of the *Continent*,
a part of the maine; if *Clod* bee washed away by the *Sea*, Europe is the lesse,
as well as if a *Promontorie* were, as well as if a Mannor of thy *friends* or of *thine
owne* were; any mans *death* diminishes *me*, because I am involved in *Mankinde*.

John Donne, *Devotions*—Meditation XVII, 1624

The stage has now been set for the examination of some real-world problems. As was explained at the outset, the basic objective of the welfare
approach is to contribute to the understanding of human well-being as
a spatially variable condition, in a manner likely to promote improvements in the quality of life. Part One built up a theoretical framework
within which spatial welfare problems may be analysed. Part Two offered
guidance on the more practical matters of evaluation and the design of
improvements in the spatial organization of human activity. This part
of the book demonstrates the application of the approaches elaborated
in the preceding chapters.

In view of the novelty of the welfare approach to human geography,
extensive empirical applications may seem somewhat premature. Perhaps
the theoretical framework should be further refined and extended, before
a sustained confrontation with reality. But geography (and regional
science) already has enough esoteric theory far removed from actual human
life. As Mishan (1964, 89) has remarked of welfare economics, no more
forcibly than necessary, "What the subject badly needs is a strong infusion of empiricism to end its unchecked wanderings in the empyrean
and to bring it down to earth feet first." This part of the present book
thus attempts to anchor Parts One and Two firmly to real-world problems. Sooner or later, this is where any new theoretical perspective must
stand or fall.

The structure of Part Three follows that of the final section of Chapter
1, in which a sample of welfare problems in human geography was introduced. Chapter 8 considers the question of development on a world
scale, emphasizing differences among nations. Chapter 9 examines South
Africa as a case of spatial inequality in a complex situation where economic, political, cultural and moral issues are closely intertwined.
Chapter 10 illustrates various aspects of spatial differentiation at the
national and metropolitan level in the USA. Chapter 11 presents a
number of case studies of location and allocation problems, to demonstrate the applicability of various practical procedures derived from welfare theory.

8

National Development: A World View

Differences among nations with respect to level of development is undoubtedly one of the world's paramount problems. Yet our knowledge of what we call "development" is crude and ambiguous. The manner in which Western societies describe the poor countries of the world has a curious history: "Each of the following adjectives has flourished in succession: primitive, backward, undeveloped, underdeveloped, less developed, emerging, developing, and rapidly developing" (de Souza and Porter, 1974, 1). To these can be added "the Third World", sometimes used to distinguish those countries in a "disadvantaged" economic position in relation to "developed" countries from the other two worlds of capitalism and socialism. Beneath this uncertainty we may detect on the one hand a recognition that some nations are much worse off than others and on the other a reluctance to adopt possibly pejorative terminology. But there may also be an element of wish fulfilment in such an evidently erroneous description as "rapidly developing", arising from a difficulty on the part of more fortunate nations to recognize both the extent of the problem and their share of responsibility for it.

According to most authorities, the "development gap" between rich and poor countries is increasing rather than diminishing (e.g. Myint, 1963; Patel, 1964; Robinson, 1970; Atkinson, 1975). For many of the poor the question of catching up with the rich does not arise, as their rates of progress (in the narrow economic sense of per capita GNP growth) are less than those of developed countries, while for others the time required to close the gap is measured in centuries rather than decades (Donaldson, 1973, 14). And all this despite the avowed intention of most rich nations and international agencies to assist in the creation of a more equal world.

The past few years have seen some important shifts of emphasis in the study of development. The concept of development as economic growth has come increasingly into question, in the spirit of the contemporary concern with non-economic criteria of human progress. The equity issue is gaining recognition. Underdevelopment is now viewed less as a *state* than as a *process*, whereby certain forms of economic and spatial organization can be identified as largely responsible for the condition of the poorer parts of the world. Traditional explanations relating to limitations of national resources and the inadequacy of indigenous culture are at best incomplete. Among nations, as within them, the ability of the

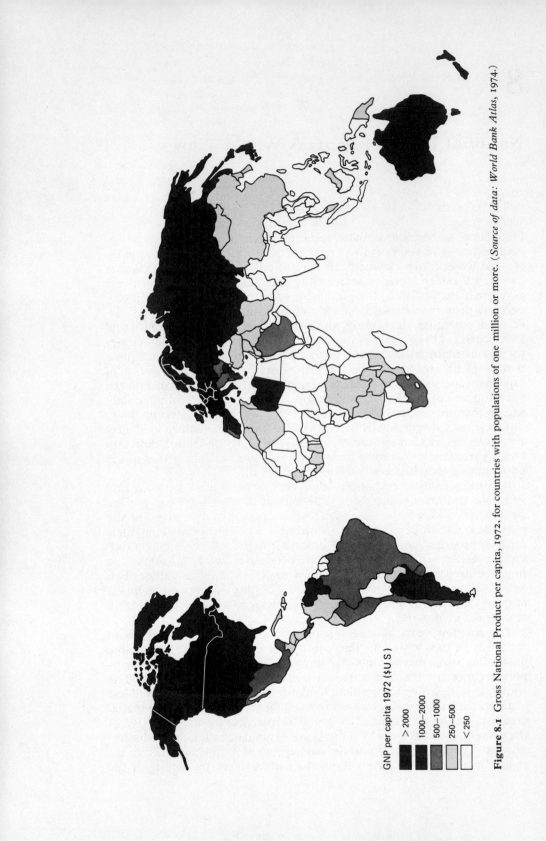

Figure 8.1 Gross National Product per capita, 1972, for countries with populations of one million or more. (*Source of data: World Bank Atlas*, 1974.)

GNP per capita 1972 ($US)

> 2000
1000–2000
500–1000
250–500
< 250

rich and powerful to organize the world in their own best interests must be recognized as an important part of the reason for the extent of inequality. The theme now is *interdependent development*: "the interconnection of the world economy which has been progressively achieved over the last five centuries has brought into existence a set of processes which have operated, albeit in radically different ways, on all points and peoples touched by the interdependent system" (Brookfield, 1975, 189). Level of development or underdevelopment depends very much on geographical position in this system.

This chapter seeks to clarify the meaning of development, within our welfare framework. Various approaches to the empirical identification of national levels of development are reviewed. Some of the the causal mechanisms are identified, to point the way towards a better understanding of the process of development and underdevelopment.

8.1 The meaning of development

Development is frequently assumed to be an economic condition. Indeed, when not described explicitly as *economic* development, "economic" is often implicitly understood. The most common measure of development is an economic indicator—*GNP per capita*. The uneven distribution of production by major world region, compared with the distribution of population, has already been described in Chapter 1 (Table 1.1). The pattern by nations is illustrated in Figure 8.1. The rich are in Europe and North America, with Australia, New Zealand and Japan as outliers; the bulk of Central and South America, Africa and South East Asia is poor. The gap between rich and poor is illustrated by the fact that GNP per capita in the richest country (USA: $5,590) is more than 90 times that of the poorest (Rwanda: $60). Of the 124 nations with one million or more people, only 45 register a per capita GNP more than one-tenth that of the USA.

Another common economic measure of development is the GNP per capita *growth rate*. As Figure 8.2a shows, there is virtually no correlation with level of GNP per capita. Roughly half the countries shown have more rapid rates of economic growth than the USA. The most rapidly growing economies include high-GNP countries such as Japan, Israel and France, and also some of the poorer ones—the Republic of Korea, Papua-New Guinea and Mauritania. They include some centrally planned economies (e.g. USSR and Romania) and some petroleum exporters (e.g. Libya, Saudi Arabia and Iran), but other communist countries and oil-rich states register low growth rates. Whatever development may be, it is not simultaneously measured by both the level and the growth of GNP per capita.

But any development indicator based on monetary value of production is subject to both technical and conceptual shortcomings. The technical problems include the difficulty of compiling accurate figures for countries lacking a sophisticated national accounting system, differences in methods used, and the fact that in underdeveloped countries many goods

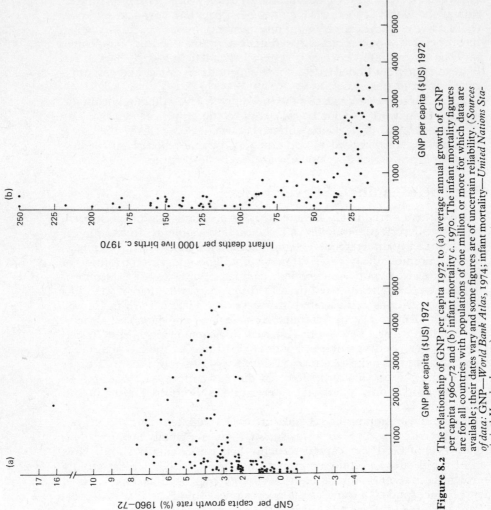

Figure 8.2 The relationship of GNP per capita 1972 to (a) average annual growth of GNP per capita 1960–72 and (b) infant mortality *c.* 1970. The infant mortality figures are for all countries with populations of one million or more for which data are available; their dates vary and some figures are of uncertain reliability. (*Sources of data:* GNP—*World Bank Atlas*, 1974; infant mortality—*United Nations Statistical Yearbook*, 1972.)

and services do not enter the cash economy. The conceptual deficiencies of GNP and similar measures have already been suggested in earlier chapters: whether expressed as the cost of factors employed or as market value of output generated, such a narrowly based economic indicator is most unlikely to capture anything approaching the full range of conditions upon which human well-being depends. And if "development" refers to something less than the broad state of human well-being, the contemporary concern about development may well be misplaced.

A monetary measure such as GNP could act as a surrogate for a broader concept of development if it accurately reflected other relevant conditions. But this is not so. Take the case of infant mortality—a very common health indicator at the international scale as well as more locally. Figure 8.2b shows the relationship between GNP per capita and infant mortality for countries where data are available. In general, the higher the GNP the fewer children die in infancy. But the relationship is markedly curvilinear. At the bottom end of the GNP scale, small increments in national product appear to make no difference to infant mortality; the level in nations with a per capita GNP of less than $500 varies from about 25 per 1,000 live births to 250. Similarly, at the bottom of the infant mortality scale national product seems to make little difference; the Netherlands and Finland have only 11 infant deaths per 1,000 live births compared with about 20 in the USA where per capita GNP is almost twice as high. How far economic growth helps to reduce infant mortality clearly depends on other things, not least of which is the way in which a society supplies health care to its people.

It is only recently that serious attempts have been made to extend the concept of development beyond economic performance. Particularly important in this respect is work initiated at the United Nations Research Institute for Social Development (e.g. Drewnowski, 1970, 1972, 1974; McGranahan *et al.*, 1970; Scott *et al.*, 1973). Rejecting such partial concepts as "economic" or even "social" development, Drewnowski (1974, 94–5) has stressed the essential unity of the development process:

> There is only one socio-economic reality. This is a body of facts about how people use limited resources to satisfy their needs, about the relations between people or groups of people (classes, nations) arising out of that usage, and about the position in which they find themselves as a result. ...
>
> Development is a process of qualitative change and quantitative growth of the social and economic reality which we call either Society or Economy. The close inter-relationship between economic and social elements precludes any purely social or economic development. It is therefore better not to speak of social development or economic development, but of a single process called simply "development".

The conventional economic concept of development is inconsistent with this view. As Drewnowski (1974, 96) explains:

> As long as we express the results of development in terms of the monetary value of goods and services, we take an economic viewpoint. We consider the resources provided but not how they affect people's lives. As the aim of all

economic activity is to improve the conditions in which people live, this means that we have stopped half-way in assessing the consequences of development. To obtain a complete picture of development it is not sufficient to realize the amount of resources brought about by economic growth. It is also necessary to examine the impact of these resources on the life of the people.

Thus per capita GNP or the growth rate cannot show whether the conditions in which people live have actually improved. In particular, such indicators will fail to reflect what Drewnowski (1974, 99–102) calls *frustrated development*, including (in his terminology) maldistribution, wastage and negative side-effects, as well as those components of welfare not produced by economic growth at all. Drewnowski's model of the generation of human well-being described in the previous chapter exemplifies this conception of development as "the unfolding of creative possibilities inherent in a society" as opposed to growth which is merely "an expansion of the system in one or more dimensions without change in its structure" (Friedmann, 1972b, 91–2).

A similarly broad view is advocated by Baster (1972, 1). Her addition of a political dimension to the economic and social realms of Drewnowski's conception helps to stress the importance of the institutional framework in the development process—part of the internal transformation sometimes termed modernization. It is also a reminder that a country's political independence, external economic dependency and general position in the international system is relevant to its degree of underdevelopment.

It should be apparent by now that the meaning of development is very much a question of values, whether it is viewed as a complex, multi-dimensional phenomenon or merely equated with GNP per capita. As Baster (1972, 2) puts it: "Development is necessarily a normative concept, and involves values, goals and standards which make it possible to compare a present state against a preferred one. This raises immediately the question of whose values and goals are to be taken into account in assessing development. Planners' values or people's values? Most national 'welfare functions', as far as they are explicitly stated, are a mixture of these different elements." Seers (1972, 22) explains that "we cannot avoid what the positivists disparagingly refer to as 'value judgments'. Development is inevitably a normative concept, almost a synonym for improvement. To pretend otherwise is just to hide one's value judgments." Among the important value positions hidden in the conventional economic conception of development is that what matters most to man is the production of goods and services measurable in monetary terms, that markets are satisfactory means of arriving at relative valuations and that the distribution of the product is of no consequence.

The contemporary reassessment of the meaning of development is creating an awareness of the value-loaded and culturally biased nature of what most pundits and planners have in mind to improve the lot of the underdeveloped world. Desirable change is almost invariably portrayed as Western-style economic development, assisted by planning but with capitalism as the assumed mode of production. Thus development is rarely considered more broadly. Goulet (1968) captures the essence of development as improvement or human progress in the following statement (quoted in de Souza and Porter, 1974, 3): "Development can be properly assessed only in terms of the total human needs, values, and standards of the good life and the good society perceived by the very societies undergoing change. Although development implies economic, political and cultural transformations, these are not ends in themselves but indispensable means for enriching the quality of human life." The three general goals of development as recognized by Goulet (1971)—life sustenance, esteem and freedom—closely echo the criteria of human need satisfaction proposed by Maslow and others (see Chapter 2). While the necessities for the sustenance of life in a purely biological sense are common to all people, those things on which esteem and freedom depend may be very much culturally specific. Attitude to the ownership and use of land is a case in point: in some of the more traditional societies of South East Asia, for example, "to own land is the highest mark of social esteem; to perform manual labour the lowest" (Myrdal, 1968, 1057). In parts of Southern Europe (e.g. rural Greece) similar attitudes prevail. Thus, "It follows that 'progress' is not necessarily associated locally with maximizing incomes, where these are derived from hired manual work, but often with land ownership, however unremunerative. A change towards more equal distribution of land, or for more people to own land, would be considered progress in this sense" (Scott *et al.*, 1973, 10). In some societies freedom means private ownership and the unrestrained proprietorial right to realize the "highest and best" use of land; in others it means the right of society as a whole to determine the use of collectively owned land in the interests of all. While the consequences of different cultural attitudes can be empirically observed in different patterns of who gets what where, judging them inevitably involves values.

8.2 Development as welfare improvement

What, then, is development? The gist of the argument above is that development is synonymous with progress, as experienced and evaluated by the people involved. Development is a welfare improvement, in the sense explained in earlier parts of this book. Development means a better state of affairs, with respect to who gets what where. Or, to elevate the concept to that of human *being*, development takes place when who can be or become what where improves.

Defining development simply as a welfare improvement runs the risk of depriving the concept of specific meaning, as almost happened to the concept of welfare itself in the abortive search for value-free theory. Thus development might merely be viewed as what the people judge to be an improvement, begging the question of what actual changes are involved and how judgements on them are made. But the practical implications of development are such that the critical questions cannot be begged. If development is to take place, planned or otherwise, and if it is to be judged unambiguously an improvement on the existing situation, it is imperative to be precise about just what development means. To conceive of development as a welfare improvement enables us to bring to bear on development problems not only the formal structure of welfare theory and its spatial extensions outlined in Part One of this book, but also the practical methods for planning and judging welfare improvements reviewed in Part Two. To define development otherwise deprives it of this foundation. It also raises the question of what we leave out if we accept a definition of development narrower than that of a welfare improvement. Any answer to this will be either a value judgement on the part of the observer or analyst, or a specific recognition of what development means in a particular societal or cultural context—i.e. of what constitutes a welfare improvement in that context.

The welfare framework helps us to make a clear distinction between development and other related concepts. Development as a welfare improvement can take place in commodity space, utility space and geographical space, i.e. it can arise from a better collection of goods (and bads), better distributed among individuals (or groups or classes) and among places. *Growth*, in its usual economic sense, simply means more of the same, or a different collection of goods valued more highly by the imperfect evaluation of market pricing or opportunity cost measured by scarce resources used up. Growth means a larger cake, without much reference to its ingredients and with no reference to who gets how big a slice. Other things remaining the same, economic growth may be judged development or a welfare improvement. But the increased product is seldom if ever equally distributed, or its composition universally approved. If a massive growth of GNP accrues largely to an existing wealthy elite as greater opportunities for luxury consumption, a rather extreme value position is required to find this a welfare improvement. As Davidson (1975, 23) remarks in the African context, "we ought to know better, by this time, than to take such statistical abstractions as 'gross national product' as any serious indicator of what is really going on".

Modernization has been the focus of much recent research in development studies (e.g. Inkeles and Smith, 1975). But there are weaknesses in this approach (de Souza and Porter, 1974, 9–14; Brookfield, 1973, 1975, 111–16; Slater, 1973), that are highlighted by the welfare perspective. Modernization usually refers to the spread of Western ideas and institutions in the transformation of traditional societies into something capable of sustaining industrialization and economic development. "The essence of this diffusion process is change—psychological, social, cultural, economic, and political" (Soja, 1968, 1). This includes the creation of a modern infrastructure of transportation and other services, integration of the space-economy, improvements in communication and the spread of ideas, the abandonment of certain traditional attitudes, acceptance of the market principle and capitalist entrepreneurial ethics, and the general adoption of Western concepts of progress. In welfare theory, such changes can be viewed as advances of the production possibilities frontier in commodity space or of the welfare frontier in utility space.

In other words they enhance the possibilities for increased production of particular goods and services. The underlying assumption is that development requires emulation of "advanced" Western economies. If the people's preference is for a different way of life, without some of the supposed benefits of industrialization and without its negative side-effects, then they may be better off without modernization. Modernization, in the conventional Western sense, is neither a necessary nor a sufficient condition for development conceived as a welfare improvement.

Such other concepts as *economic health* suffer similar limitations. Popularized in the 1960s following the initial application by Thompson *et al.* (1962), the identification of spatial variations in economic health involves the analysis of data on local conditions supposedly related to the performance of the economy in conventional output terms (e.g. Lloyd and Dicken, 1972, ch. 10). But the results often provide poor indicators of the broader social performance of an economy. Recent interest in alternative concepts such as *social malaise* and *social deprivation* for the purpose of multivariate areal classification has helped to shift the emphasis away from the narrow economic view, while approaches under the rubric of *social well-being* (Smith, 1973a; Knox, 1975) come close to the broad conception of development as human progress.

The empirical identification of levels of national development has been a focus for much research in a number of disciplines in recent years (e.g. Baster, 1972; Moss, 1973). Its antecedents can be traced to the work of such pioneers as Clark (1951) and Kuznetz (1957; 1959; 1963; 1966), and it is now part of the general social-indicators movement. If development constitutes welfare improvement, then the requirements of a development indicator can be deduced quite simply from welfare theory. The problem is analogous to that of giving empirical identity to the social welfare function (see Chapter 7). A national development indicator should incorporate what a nation produces (in the broadest sense) and should also specify group and territorial subdivisions relevant to the evaluation of distribution. It should incorporate weights reflecting societal preferences or planning goals. The practical problems in devising such indicators for the purpose of empirical research will be obvious from the discussion in earlier chapters. Yet these problems must be faced and somehow solved before even the simplest descriptions of national development patterns can be offered. This is also a necessary prerequisite to explanation and improvement, for it is impossible to explain what is inadequately described, just as it is difficult effectively to pursue undefined goals.

The next five sections of this chapter describe different approaches to the empirical analysis of development at the national level. They illustrate the problems involved and some of the progress made in recent years. Before proceeding, some warnings are required with respect to the special difficulty of cross-national studies. The first is that nations usually comprise large aggregates of people whose life experiences can vary greatly; national data can thus hide the distributional dimension vital for full welfare evaluations—a matter taken up in section 8.7. The second is that international comparison compounds the usual difficulties associated with official statistics, which may have been compiled on a different basis and with different degrees of accuracy in different places. The third, common to all work on social indicators, is that some important aspects of life may not have been measured and will thus be left out of any development indicator: at the national level, what can be included is constrained by data available in the country with the *least* comprehensive statistics, if a composite indicator applicable to all countries is needed. The fourth is that a general cross-national development indicator implies a cross-national value consensus on the meaning of development (Baster, 1972, 3); this contradicts our conception of development as a culturally specific phenomenon unless weights can be assigned to reflect different national preferences. A final point, stressed by de Souza and Porter (1974, 26, 52, 83), is that numerical indicators of development and their manipulation by sophisticated modern techniques may merely obfuscate and obscure more than they reveal, particularly if based on a narrow concept of development determined by data availability. The reality of human life experience may be quite inadequately represented and explanations may have to be sought beyond the data matrix from which the indicators are derived (see section 8.8).

8.3   Economic development and state of technology

The theoretical discussions earlier in this book stressed the importance of transformation efficiency, or technology, in constraining the production of sources of human well-being. The significance of technology in economic development is widely recognized, and the improvement of productive efficiency and service infrastructure is a basic element in development planning. The state of technology figures prominently in the first major attempt in geography at a sophisticated empirical analysis of national levels of development (Berry, 1960; 1961).

Berry set out to put some substantive flesh on our image of the underdeveloped world. Data were compiled for forty-three variables "thought to be significant in the analysis of economic development" (Berry, 1960, 78), the selection being based on theory and intuition modified by data availability. The variables were predominantly concerned with transport, trade, communications and the use of energy (Table 8.1). They thus reflect a technology-oriented view of development, somewhat in the style of later studies of modernization but with little social content.

Figures were compiled for ninety-five countries. These were ranked on each variable, as an ordinal scale demands less of unreliable data than higher orders of measurement. The rank-order 43×95 data matrix was then subjected to a principal components analysis (for an explanation, see for example Yeates, 1974, ch. 9; Smith, 1975c, ch. 9), which distilled certain basic patterns of national variation from the original information. The strongest of these factors was found to account for 84 per cent of all the variance in the data matrix. This was because many of the original

Table 8.1 Indices selected by Berry as significant to the analysis of economic development

I. *Transportation* Kms of railways per unit area Kms of railways per population unit Ton/kms of freight per pop. unit per year Ton/kms of freight per km of railway Kms of roads per unit area Kms of roads per population unit Motor vehicles per pop. unit Motor vehicles per km of roads Motor vehicles per unit area	Petroleum refinery capacity per capita Physicians per pop. unit Newspaper circulation per pop. unit Telephones per pop. unit Domestic mail flow per capita International mail flow per capita V. *GNP* National product per country National product per capita
II. *Energy* Kwh of electricity per capita Total kwh of energy consumed Kwh of energy consumption per capita Commercial energy consumed per capita Per cent of total energy commercial Kwh of energy reserves per capita Per cent of hydroelectric reserves developed Developed hydroelectricity per capita	VI. *Trade* Value of foreign trade turnover Foreign trade turnover per capita Exports per capita Imports per capita Per cent exports to N. Atlantic region Per cent exports raw materials VII. *Other* Per cent population in cities 20,000 and over Per cent land area cultivated People per unit cultivated land
III. *Agricultural yields* Rice yields Wheat yields IV. *Communication and other per capita indices* Fibre consumption per capita	VIII. *Demographic* Population density Crude birth rates Crude death rates Population growth rates Infant mortality rates

Source: Berry (1960, 81).

variables were highly intercorrelated. Thus a single composite index based on the leading factor could satisfactorily stand for most of the conditions initially selected.

The relationship with each of the original variables enables the meaning of the new composite index to be identified. As Berry (1960, 83) described it, "A simple structure is suggested by which countries tend to be ranked similarly on all matters of transportation and trade, energy production and consumption, national product, communications, and urbanization." Berry thus labelled this the *technological scale*. Variables most closely associated with this index included percentage of total energy used commercially, commercial energy consumed per capita, electricity generated per capita, fibre consumption per capita, percentage of population in cities with over 20,000 inhabitants, and national product per capita (see Berry, 1960, Table 5; 1961, Table VIII-2). Variables least closely associated were infant mortality, birth rate, population growth and death rate. The statistical analysis revealed a demographic component accounting for the largest share of the variance in the original data remaining after the extraction of the technology component.

The world pattern of development on the technological scale (Berry, 1960, 86) resembles Figure 8.1 quite closely. Summary figures in Table 8.2 show how major world regions compare with respect to average scores on the technological scale, in which *low* scores show *high* technological performance. The Europe, North America and Australasia group leads, closely followed by the "Soviet Bloc", with a large gap separating them from other parts of the world. Temperate nations scored much higher than those in the tropics; there was a similar difference between those with commercial and subsistence economies.

Regression analysis was used in an attempt to account for national levels of economic development. The result with respect to the technological scale was: "The position of a country varies with type of economy and region, but not with political status; a temperate mid-latitude location is of significance, but a tropical climate and location do not add any significant explanation not already provided by economy and region" (Berry, 1961, 118). No support was found for the hypothesis that less-developed countries frequently are of colonial status or only recently independent: "colonialism, or at least political colonialism, seems not to explain poverty but even in some instances to have countered it" (Berry, 1961, 119). Later research summarized below (section 8.7) suggests a somewhat different conclusion.

Table 8.2 Average values on the technological scale for major groups of countries

Group	Average
Europe, North America and Australasia	173·8
Soviet Bloc	202·1
South America	305·2
Central America	342·3
North Africa	345·4
Asia, except Japan	354·0
Sub-Saharan Africa, excluding South Africa	388·7
"Temperate" nations	176·3
"Commercial" economies	255·5
"Tropical" nations	352·5
"Subsistence" economies	363·6

Source: Berry (1961, Table VII-3).

Berry's findings called into question the common assumption that underdeveloped countries comprise a distinct and separate class. Rather, they occupy the lower end of a continuum from lesser to more developed, just as on the GNP per capita scale (Figure 8.2a). The nature of what Berry (1960, 106) calls the lesser developed countries is summarized as follows: "Lesser developed countries, by virtue of their low technological rank, have inadequate transport networks. They produce and consume little energy, and are poorly provided with such facilities as physicians, telephones, and newspapers. Both internal and external communications are limited, and national products are low. Such nations trade little, and most of their trade is with the North Atlantic region. Only a small percentage of their populations live in cities. Their high demographic ratings indicate high birth and death rates, rapid rates of population increase, high population densities both per unit area and per unit of cultivated land, and large percentages of total area cultivated."

As in any such multivariate analyses, the results are constrained by the data in the matrix analysed. Given the initial variables included, it is not surprising that a technological scale emerged as the major measure of *economic* development. For an exploration of some of the social and political dimensions of the general process of development it is necessary to turn to other studies.

8.4 Society, politics and economic development

Workers outside geography have given more attention to social, institutional and political considerations in the derivation of development indicators (e.g. Russett *et al.*, 1964; Merritt and Rokkan, 1966; Taylor, 1968; Taylor and Hudson, 1972; Rummel, 1969; 1972). A study by Adelman and Morris (1965; 1967) has been selected to exemplify this approach. It covers seventy-four underdeveloped countries at the beginning of the 1960s. The aim was "to analyze the nature of the interdependence between broad levels of economic development and the transformation of sociopolitical institutions and cultural values associated with industrialization and urbanization" (Adelman and Morris, 1967, 149). The results suggest that it is "just as reasonable to look at underdevelopment as a social and political phenomenon as it is to analyze it in terms of intercountry differences in economic structure", revealing in the development process "a systematic pattern of interaction among mutually interdependent economic, social and political forces, all of which combine to generate a unified complex of changes in the style of life of a community" (Adelman and Morris, 1967, 150).

The statistical analysis is similar to that of Berry described above. Data on GNP per capita together with twenty-four political and social indices were subjected to factor analysis. Table 8.3 shows the variables involved and the composition of the first two factors. Also listed is the correlation between GNP per capita and each other variable. The nature of the variables emphasizes the focus on conditions of social and political structure, compared with the strong technological-economic bias of the data in Table 8.1.

The relationship between the original variables and the factors extracted is shown by the factor loadings in Table 8.3. Thus the correlation

Table 8.3 Composition of leading factors derived from political and social indices for seventy-four less-developed countries

Political and social indicators	Factor loadings 1	2	Correlation (r) with 1. (GNP/cap)
1. Per capita GNP in 1961	−0·73	0.31	—
2. Size of the traditional agricultural sector	0·89	−0·21	−0.78
3. Extent of dualism	−0·84	0·14	0·73
4. Extent of urbanization	−0·84	0·13	0·66
5. Character of basic social organization	−0·83	0·24	0·61
6. Importance of the indigenous middle class	−0·82	0·14	0·63
7. Extent of social mobility	−0·86	0·21	0·70
8. Extent of literacy	−0·86	0·32	0·67
9. Extent of mass communication	−0·88	0·28	0·79
10. Degree of cultural and ethnic homogeneity	−0·66	−0·30	0·30
11. Degree of national integration and sense of national unity	−0·87	−0·07	0·57
12. Crude fertility rate	0·63	−0.14	−0·57
13. Degree of modernization of outlook	−0·75	0·31	0·70
14. Strength of democratic institutions	−0·48	0·72	0·63
15. Degree of freedom of political opposition and press	−0·33	0·82	0·51
16. Degree of competitiveness of political parties	−0·32	0·79	0·38
17. Predominant basis of the political party system	−0·43	0·70	0·43
18. Strength of the labor movement	−0·38	0·63	0·57
19. Political strength of the military	−0·26	−0·58	−0·17
20. Extent of centralization of political power	−0·07	−0·65	−0·15
21. Political strength of the traditional elite	0·08	−0·07	−0·17
22. Extent of leadership commitment to economic development	−0·14	−0·02	0·34
23. Degree of administrative efficiency	−0·39	0·37	0·49
24. Degree of social tension	0·22	0·02	−0·14
25. Extent of political stability	−0·07	0·05	0·20

Source: Adelman and Morris (1967, 151, Table IV-1). For details of the derivation of the indices, see Adelman and Morris (1967, ch. 2). Note that the index representing Factor 1 as identified in this table is such that negative scores are associated with high GNP—hence the signs of the loadings.

of GNP per capita with an index representing the first factor is −0·73. The identity of this factor is indicated by the nature of the variables with highest loadings. These are size of traditional agricultural sector, extent of economic dualism (i.e. juxtaposition of a traditional and modern sector), urbanization, measures of social organization including class structure and mobility, literacy, extent of mass communication, national integration, and modernization of outlook. As these increase so does GNP per capita (i.e. the signs of the loadings are the same), except in the case of traditional agriculture. This factor is summarized by Adelman and Morris (1967, 153) as representing "the process of change in attitudes and institutions associated with the break-down of traditional social organization". This takes place through the mechanism of *social differentiation* and *integration of social structure*. Differentiation involves the establishment of more specialized and autonomous social units, as expressed, for example, in the differentiation of the nuclear family from the extended kinship links of tribal life and the breakdown of the traditional self-sufficient family–community economic units. Integration is the process bringing together the specialized social units, represented by improvements in mass communication, literacy and so on. This factor is closely associated with degree of urbanization, reflecting the growth of cities as promoting the specialization of economic activities and the spread of integrative agents such as mass communication and education. Factor 1 expresses the strong interaction between economic development (i.e. GNP per capita) and what Adelman and Morris view as the "rationalization" (i.e. "modernization" or "Westernization") of social behaviour, values and institutions. This dimension accounts for about 40 per cent of variation among countries in the conditions listed in Table 8.3.

The second factor accounts for a further 20 per cent of the original variance. Table 8.3 shows that its highest positive loadings are with strength of democratic institutions, freedom of political opposition and press, competitiveness of political parties, basis of political party system and strength of the labour movement. As these increase, so does GNP, though the correlations are generally not as strong as between GNP per capita and the high-loading variables in Factor 1. Factor 2 has moderate negative loadings with the political strength of the military and with the extent of centralized political power, though these are only weakly related to GNP per capita. This factor thus captures variations in political systems. In particular, it reflects the extent of political participation. "An increase in this factor may be interpreted to represent a movement along a scale that ranges from centralized authoritarian political forms to specialized political mechanisms capable of representing the varied group interests of a society and of aggregating these interests through participant national political organs" (Adelman and Morris, 1967, 155). This movement is usually accompanied by the emergence of organized labour, the weakening of the political role of the military and a decentralization of power.

As in the Berry study and other similar multivariate analyses, Adelman and Morris use country scores on their leading factors as development indicators. The calculation of factor scores weights the original variables in proportion to the strength of their association with the factor, as measured by the loadings. The general form of such an indicator of development (D) is:

$$D = \sum_{i=1}^{m} l_i Z_i \qquad [8.1]$$

where Z_i is the "standard" score (i.e. transformed to zero mean and unit standard deviation) on the ith condition $(1, 2, \ldots, m)$ and l_i is the loading on the factor in question. This formulation is sometimes advocated as a way around the problem of weighting different conditions in a social indicator (e.g. Wilson, 1969, 9–11). To Adelman and Morris (1967, 168), "The use of factor scores therefore automatically provides a criterion for the selection and weighting of various country attributes in the construction of a composite index of economic development. Much of the arbitrariness inherent in index number construction is thereby removed." However, this method is based entirely on empirical association, simply describing how data on certain conditions, combined in a certain way, distinguish nations along a scale. The question of what comprises development is not automatically solved.

With these reservations recognized, Figure 8.3 illustrates the relationship between GNP per capita and scores on Factor 1 (the "sociocultural concomitants of the industrialization–urbanization process"), for the seventy-four countries. The factor score combines performance on the indices listed in Table 8.3 in proportion to the loadings in the first column (with indices 10 and 11 omitted for technical reasons). Adelman and Morris (1967, 169) propose a division into three classes of countries at a more-or-less similar stage of development ("lowest", "intermediate" and "highest") on the basis of the scores: "countries with the lowest factor scores consist of societies that are primarily tribal and that are characterized by a preponderant non-market sector. The intermediate group is made up of countries in which the typical kinship structure is the extended family and in which the exchange sector of the economy is generally much longer than it is in the lowest group. The highest group includes only countries that, although still underdeveloped in the late 1950s, are relatively advanced with respect to both social and economic development." However, they accept that in reality there is a continuum, as the graph shows: "development proceeds continuously and uniformly from the tribal conditions to the fully developed status" (Adelman and Morris, 1967, 265).

The form of the relationship shown in Figure 8.3 is of interest. Although quite closely linear, a curve would describe the scatter more accurately. At the lowest levels GNP per capita increases little with quite substantial moves up the scale of "socio-cultural" development, but at the highest levels GNP seems much more sensitive to the kind of social change reflected in Factor 1. If the relationship can legitimately be considered causal, in the sense that socio-cultural development "produces" increases in GNP, then much greater modernization effort for the same increase is needed at the lower levels than at the higher levels.

Despite the light shed on social and political aspects of development, the Adelman and Morris study has some deficiencies. It is subject to the same criticisms as the intra-national modernization approach, viewing development very much from a Western perspective. Progress is equated with increases in per capita GNP, as the end result of the process of development. The various social and political changes examined are viewed as significant through their association with *economic* development measured by GNP. We must therefore look elsewhere for a broader conception of development that itself incorporates non-economic changes as ends, instead of merely as means to economic ends.

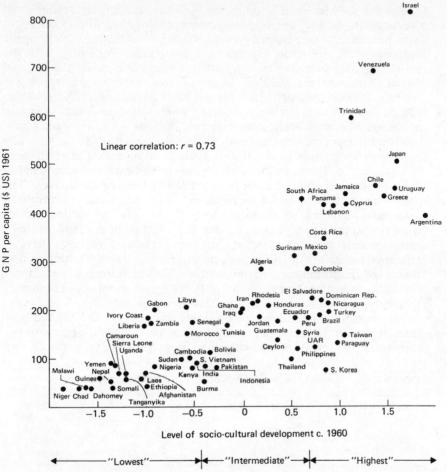

Figure 8.3 The relationship between level of "socio-cultural development" *c.* 1960 and GNP per capita 1961 in seventy-four less-developed countries. The signs of the development scores are such that positive means above average and negative below average. (*Source of data:* Adelman and Morris, 1967, 170.)

8.5 Socio-economic development

Dissatisfaction with economic indicators of development, such as GNP, has been a major concern of United Nations research efforts during the past two decades. The UN Research Institute for Social Development has been responsible for the initial identification and subsequent refinement of a *level-of-living index* to provide a more comprehensive measure of the human life experiences (e.g. Drewnowski and Scott, 1968). Knox (1974a; 1975, ch. 3) has drawn attention to the scope for geographical applications of this approach, which offers the ultimate prospect of a general development indicator consistent with our welfare concept.

The full UN level-of-living index is not yet operational, because all the necessary data are not available. However, McGranahan *et al.* (1970) have been able to construct a general composite indicator incorporating both economic and social aspects of development. Beginning with the UNRISD data bank for 1960 (United Nations Research Institute for Social Development, 1969) a "reservoir" of forty-two variables was assembled, with measurements for up to 115 countries. The selection was made so as to avoid duplication of information and with attention to "balance between social and economic indicators and between structural and development indicators" (McGranahan *et al.*, 1970, 54). The term structural refers to conditions such as composition of the labour force or degree of urbanization, which may be indicative of some kind of development but which cannot be regarded as ends in themselves. The reservoir was then reduced to eighteen "core indicators" on the basis of intercorrelations, so as more concisely to reflect variation among countries in the larger data set (Table 8.4). Although perhaps leaning a little towards structural aspects of the national economy, there is reference to health, nutrition, education, housing and consumption of sources of entertainment and information. To McGranahan *et al.* (1970) these core indicators as a group identify "socio-economic development". In combination, they provide a general *development index*.

The procedure used to generate a single composite index differed from that adopted in the factor-analytical studies reviewed in the previous two sections. First, "correspondence points" were identified from the empiri-

Table 8.4 Core indicators used in the UNRISD development index for 1960

Indicator	Average correlation (r) with other indicators
1. Expectation of life at birth	0·744
2. Population in localities of 20,000 and over (% of total)	0·730
3. Consumption of animal protein per capita per day	0·791
4. Combined primary and secondary school enrolment (% aged 5–19)	0·777
5. Vocational education enrolment (% aged 5–19)	0·788
6. Average number of persons per room	0·783
7. Newspaper circulation per 1,000 population	0·823
8. Telephones per 100,000 population	0·762
9. Radio receivers per 1,000 population	0·737
10. Economically active population in utilities, transport, etc (%)	0·769
11. Agricultural production per male agricultural worker ($)	0·839
12. Adult male labour in agriculture (% of total)	0·809
13. Electricity consumption per capita (kwh)	0·687
14. Steel consumption per capita (kg)	0·769
15. Energy consumption per capita (kg of coal equivalent)	0·760
16. GDP derived from manufacturing (% of total)	0·752
17. Foreign trade (sum of imports and exports) per capita ($)	0·737
18. Salaried and wage earners (% of total economically active)	0·750

Source: McGranahan *et al.* (1970).

cal association among the individual indicators, with GNP per capita added as the conventional economic development measure. Thus empirically, 59 years of life expectation in a country corresponds to a school enrolment ratio of 47 and both of these to a per capita GNP of $300, and so on (see McGranahan *et al.*, 1970, ch. 5). Then the data on each indicator were scaled from 0 to 100, with zero at those values on the different indicators constituting the lowest set of correspondence points and 100 at the highest set of correspondence points. Thus for life expectation $0 = 40 \cdot 0$ and $100 = 71 \cdot 0$, for persons per room $0 = 2 \cdot 5$ and $100 = 0 \cdot 7$, and so on. Intermediate points on the scales were set so as to reflect the non-linear relationships among the various conditions; the 50 point is therefore not necessarily half way between the two extremes of the high and low correspondence points (see McGranahan *et al.*, 1970, ch. 6). Having transformed each indicator in this way, the final problem was relative weighting in the composite index. The average correlation with the other indicators was considered the best empirical method available, somewhat similar to the use of factor loadings (Table 8.4). The score for any country on the final development index thus comprises the sum of its performance on each of the eighteen indicators on the new 0–100 scale, weighted according to their respective strength of association with all other indicators.

Data were available to calculate the development index for fifty-eight countries. The result ranges from 111 for the USA to 10 for Thailand. The median value is 58, for Greece. Although the linear association with GNP per capita is strong ($r = 0 \cdot 89$), the nature of the relationship is distinctly non-linear (Figure 8.4). At low levels of development small increases in GNP are accompanied by very considerable increases in the index value, but at higher levels "socio-economic development" shows little sensitivity to GNP. Thus there is very little difference between the index value for the UK, Canada and the USA for example, despite their respective figures of $1,369, $2,092 and $2,828 for GNP per capita.

The development index is highly correlated with all the eighteen individual indicators on their transformed scales. The value of r is at least $0 \cdot 82$ in every case. For all but two indicators (radio receivers and foreign trade), the index has a higher correlation than GNP per capita: the average r for the index is $90 \cdot 2$ compared with $86 \cdot 3$ for GNP. Somewhat different results are obtained if the countries are split arbitrarily into "developed" and "developing", using the index value of 50 as the division. For the developed group the correlation between the index and GNP per capita is $0 \cdot 86$ compared with only $0 \cdot 67$ in the developing group. Average correlation between the development index and the eighteen indicators is $0 \cdot 78$ in developed and $0 \cdot 64$ in developing countries; the average r values for GNP are $0 \cdot 68$ and $0 \cdot 43$ respectively. This leads McGranahan *et al.* (1970, 141) to conclude that the development index is superior to GNP per capita "particularly in developing countries". GNP per capita is often a poor predictor of the eighteen indicators in the developing countries (eight of the r values are less than $0 \cdot 50$).

It is important to be clear about the nature of the relationship between

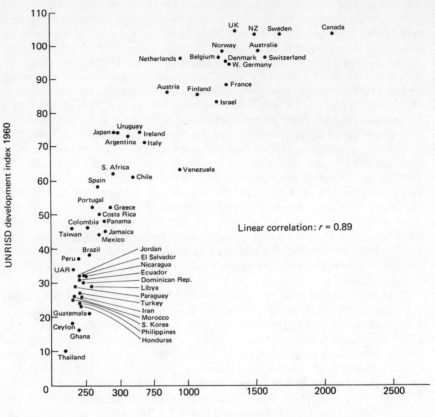

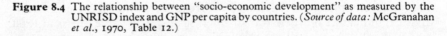

Figure 8.4 The relationship between "socio-economic development" as measured by the UNRISD index and GNP per capita by countries. (*Source of data:* McGranahan *et al.*, 1970, Table 12.)

GNP and general socio-economic development as represented by the composite index. The relationship may be closer in the developed countries, but, as was pointed out above, greater increments of GNP are needed for a given increase in the index at the upper end of the scale than at the lower end (Figure 8.4). Thus if it could be claimed that the relationship was something more than merely an empirical regularity, so that rising GNP could be viewed as producing rises in socio-economic development, the following inference could be made quite confidently: increasing the national product has a somewhat more predictable impact on general level of development in more developed countries than in the underdeveloped world, but the higher the level of development the more GNP will have to grow to generate further development. It is tempting to read into the upper part of the curve in Figure 8.4 a condition of rapidly diminishing returns of general socio-economic development to rising

GNP. As countries get richer, real progress becomes decreasingly dependent on further riches. Whether the end of the curve might turn down, so that the impact of continuing economic growth measured by GNP per capita has a *negative* impact on level of development, is a matter of some interest. The answer depends, among other things, on just how "development" or "progress" is defined; by some definitions the USA may have already reached the point of negative returns to further increases in material affluence.

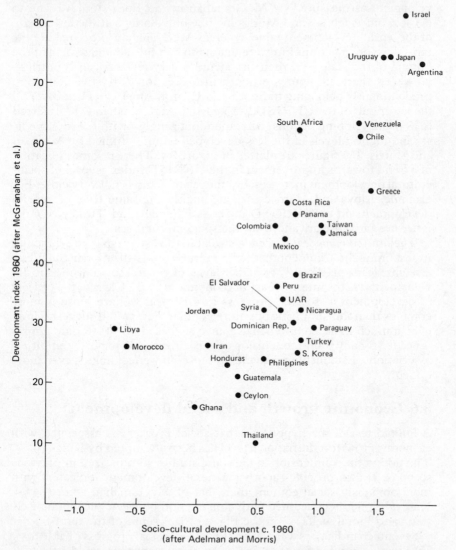

Figure 8.5 The relationship between "socio-cultural development" and the UNRISD development index. (*Sources of data:* Adelman and Morris, 1967, 170; McGranahan *et al.*, 1970, Table 12.)

In the UNRISD index we have a possible measure of *general* development, the level of which might be considered in part a consequence of level of *economic* development as reflected in GNP. The previous section (8.4) revealed an indicator of *socio-cultural* development summarizing conditions that might be regarded as promoting economic development. What can be learned from a comparison between the two? To what extent might the societal transformations captured in the Adelman and Morris scores plotted against GNP in Figure 8.3 be associated with level of development as measured by McGranahan *et al.*? Both studies relate to *c.* 1960, but Adelman and Morris include only nations at the lowest end of the world development table, whereas McGranahan *et al.* include the most developed nations but were unable to compile adequate data at the bottom of the scale (e.g. their list includes very few African countries). However, there are figures on both measures for thirty-five countries, predominantly belonging to South and Central America. They cover all the lower half of the UNRISD list, i.e. what McGranahan *et al.* referred to as the developing nations, corresponding roughly with the intermediate and highest levels of the less-developed nations studied by Adelman and Morris. The figures are plotted in Figure 8.5. There is some indication of a trend towards improvement in the UNRISD index as level of socio-cultural development increases, but the relationship is not very close. For example, Libya and Morocco are at roughly the same level of general development on the UNRISD index as Paraguay and Turkey, yet the latter are far more advanced on the socio-cultural scale.

The limited *empirical* evidence available thus suggests some difficulty in sustaining the argument that socio-cultural modernization in the Western sense leads predictably to higher levels of general socio-economic development, via the intermediary of economic growth. Clearly, the process of development as societal progress in a general welfare sense is more complex than this simplistic but quite popular view would suggest. However, a much more comprehensive analysis based on up-to-date figures is needed for any sound conclusions, even with respect to purely empirical associations. Establishing convincing cause-and-effect links is even more difficult.

8.6 Economic growth and social development

A limited test of the hypothesis that social progress is associated with economic growth at the national level has been attempted by King (1974). This adds a time dimension to the static studies summarized in previous sections. It also provides another general development indicator, with more obviously social content than that of McGranahan *et al.* (1970). King is explicitly concerned with a distinction between "economic welfare" and "total welfare" in the Pigou (1920) sense of the terms.

Seventeen indicators were taken to measure social progress (Table 8.5). Data were compiled for 1951 and 1969 so that changes could be established. The choice of indicators was determined largely by the availability of data for the two bench-mark years. They were intended to measure

Table 8.5 Indicators used to measure "social progress" 1951–69

Indicator	Sign
1. Gross reproduction rate	−
2. Population density	−
3. Dependency ratio	−
4. Illegitimacy rate	−
5. Public expenditure on education as % of GNP	+
6. Students per 100,000 population	+
7. Per cent of students female	+
8. Hospital beds per 1,000 population	+
9. Doctors per 10,000 population	+
10. Protein consumption per person per day	+
11. Infant mortality rate	−
12. Late foetal death rate	−
13. Stomach ulcer death rate	−
14. Suicide rate	−
15. Motor accident death rate	−
16. Telephones per 100 population	+
17. Radio receivers per 1,000 population	+

Source: King (1974). Positive signs indicate that high values are "good" and low values "bad"; negative signs indicate the reverse.

externalities not captured in national income figures and also broader aspects of social development such as trends in health, education and demographic conditions. The reasons for selection of individual indicators is in most cases fairly obvious. The normative interpretation of gross reproduction rate as the lower the better, reflects the fact that the more rapid the growth of population the more rapidly the economy must grow merely to maintain existing GNP per capita. Proportion of students female is an attempt to measure sex equality (the actual figures by nations vary considerably—from 49 per cent in Finland to 22 in Switzerland). As King (1974) recognizes, it would have been desirable to include data on the environment, income distribution, crime, leisure and so on, but figures were not available.

Data were compiled for twenty countries—all European or economically advanced. Two methods were adopted in deriving a single aggregate indicator of social performance. The first involved ranking the countries on each individual indicator in 1951 and summing the ranks, to give a score (S_{1951}) for any country of:

$$S_{1951} = \sum_{i=1}^{17} R_i \qquad [8.2]$$

where R is the country's rank on the ith of the seventeen indicators. Repeating this for 1969 provides the basis for calculating social progress (P) as:

$$P = S_{1969} - S_{1951} \qquad [8.3]$$

The results are listed in Table 8.6. The highest index in 1951 is for Norway while in 1969 Finland takes first place. Greatest positive change

Table 8.6 "Social progress" and growth of GNP per capita 1951–69, in twenty
relatively developed countries

Country	Social Index (S) 1951	Social Index (S) 1959	Change	Change in component score	Average annual growth (%) of GDP/capita
Austria	175·5	127·5	−48	0·214	4·8
Belgium	154	158·5	4·5	0·253	3·0
Denmark	184·5	194·5	10	0·206	3·2
Finland	194	241	47	0·246	3·4
France	171	178·5	7·5	0·228	3·9
West Germany	152·5	157	5·5	0·215	5·1
Ireland	173·5	156	−17·5	0·153	2·5
Italy	157·5	182	24·5	0·252	4·5
Netherlands	191·5	184·5	−7	0·198	3·2
Norway	235	207·5	−27·5	0·155	3·2
Portugal	66·5	94	27·5	0·186	4·4
Spain	132	127·5	4·5	0·201	6·2
Sweden	202·5	224·5	22	0·252	3·2
Switzerland	209·5	184	−25·5	0·126	2·6
UK	186	172	−14	0·161	2·1
Canada	220·5	232	11·5	0·306	2·5
USA	221·5	205·5	−16	0·288	2·3
Japan	114	174·5	−60·5	0·332	7·8
Australia	210·5	176	−34·5	0·167	2·5
New Zealand	218	193	−25	0·180	1·6

Source: King (1974).

indicating most social progress is in Japan; greatest negative change is in
Austria.

The second method of measuring social progress involved a principal
components analysis of the data on the seventeen indicators. This
generated a first component accounting for 36 per cent of the original
data, the loadings showing that it mainly reflects the education indicators,
health and communications. Scores on this component placed the twenty
countries in similar positions as on the S index (rank correlations: 0·77
for 1951, 0·56 for 1969). Changes in country scores 1959–69 on this component were interpreted as social progress (Table 8.6).

To test the relationship between social progress and economic growth,
King found the average annual rate of growth of real per capita gross
domestic product between 1951 and 1969 (Table 8.6), and correlated
these with the two progress measures. In both cases the association is
weak. Statistically, growth of GDP accounts for only 24 per cent of the
variance in changes of rank sums and 16 per cent of changes in component
scores (only in the first case is this significant at the 5 per cent level).
Omitting the USA and Canada was found to improve the correlation to
significant levels in both cases ($r^2 = 0·43$ and 0·26 respectively). King
(1974) thus concluded that "we cannot reject the hypothesis that change
in social score is positively correlated with the rate of economic growth.
We can, however, reject the hypothesis of a negative association."

This study suggests that, at relatively advanced levels of development, the association between social progress and economic growth, though positive, is not strong. However much sustained increases in GNP per capita may be necessary in the initial stages of development (broadly defined), social progress certainly cannot be equated with economic growth in the richer nations. And enough has been said in earlier sections to suggest that economic growth is not an unambiguous indicator of development as welfare improvement at any level.

8.7 Development and inequality

A conspicuous omission from the various attempts to define national development levels outlined above is distribution. Yet who gains (or perhaps loses) from the process of economic and social change is an essential dimension of development conceived as welfare improvement. Building distribution into an operational indicator is more difficult than our earlier theoretical discussions of social welfare functions might suggest. Accurate data on average or per capita conditions are difficult enough to compile for cross-national comparison; disaggregation by class or region is often impossible. However, enough information is available to allow some limited speculation on how distribution relates to development measured in other ways.

In Chapter 5 it was suggested that we might expect a divergence of income levels during early stages of development, with a subsequent tendency towards convergence. Some of the empirical evidence may now be examined. The most thorough analysis at the regional level is by Williamson (1965). He identified inequality by a weighted coefficient of variation; this measures the dispersion of the regional income per capita levels relative to the national average, while each regional deviation is weighted by its share in the national population. The index V_w is defined as:

$$V_w = \frac{\sqrt{\sum_i (y_i - \bar{y})^2 (f_i/n)}}{\bar{y}} \qquad [8.4]$$

where f_i is population of the ith region
$\quad n$ is national population
$\quad y_i$ is income per capita of the ith region
and $\quad \bar{y}$ is national income per capita.

Williamson's calculations of V_w for twenty-four countries at different levels of development are summarized in Table 8.7. With the exception of the Philippines, the results conform to the pattern of highest regional inequality at middle levels of development. The extreme values are 0·058 in Australia and 0·700 in Brazil.

This association between regional inequality and development is given further support by data on changes over time (Williamson, 1965, Tables 2 and 5). Of the nations listed in Table 8.7, Japan, Yugoslavia and India show rising inequality during the post-war period, while Australia, the UK, France and Italy have stable V_w values and in the rest it is falling.

Table 8.7 Differences in regional per capita income inequality by level of development

	Development level (high to low)	Average regional income inequality
I:	Australia, New Zealand, Canada, UK, USA, Sweden	0·139
II:	Finland, France, W. Germany, Netherlands, Norway	0·252
III:	Ireland, Chile, Austria, Puerto Rico	0·335
IV:	Brazil, Italy, Spain, Colombia, Greece	0·464
V:	Yugoslavia, Japan	0·292
VI:	Philippines	0·556
VII:	India	0·275
	Total	0·299

Source: Williamson (1965, Table 1). The data relate mainly to years in the 1950s. Development levels are defined by per capita product, following Kuznetz.

More detailed time-series data for individual nations show the USA, for example, peaking at $V_w = 0·410$ in 1932 to fall to 0·192 by 1961, Canada peaking at 0·237 in 1935 and falling to 0·175 in 1960, and Brazil rising to 0·781 in 1952 to fall to 0·663 by 1959. Further discussions of the USA will be found in Chapter 10. Differences in regional inequality even among underdeveloped countries can be considerable: the ratio of per capita income in poorest and richest provinces varies from one-fiftieth in Kenya to one-third in India, while for the consumption of social goods the difference can be even greater (Elliott, 1972, 44). But it would be wrong to read too much into *regional* inequalities, which may obscure even greater *local* inequalities, particularly in cities.

Another empirical approach to distribution is to examine the shares of population groups. Early attempts were made by Kuznetz (1957; 1959; 1963; 1966), using data on income distribution among sectors of the economy. Although missing some of the detail of inequality among classes or ethnic groups, for example, this method does help to identify the imbalance between the rural subsistence farming sector and the urban commercial and manufacturing sectors of a dual economy characteristic of underdeveloped countries. Taylor and Hudson (1972, 212–14, 263–6) have updated and extended the Kuznetz figures. They use the seven major sectors of (1) agriculture, forestry, hunting and fishing, (2) mining and quarrying, (3) manufacturing, (4) construction, (5) electricity, gas, water and sanitary services, (6) commerce, and (7) transportation etc. Inequality is measured by the Gini coefficient explained in Chapter 6: the higher the coefficient, the more unequal the sectoral distribution of income compared with numbers employed. Data for the early 1960s were compiled for fifty-two countries. These are plotted against GNP per capita for a comparable year in Figure 8.6. There is little sign of the inverted U relationship sometimes suggested, but inequality does tend to fall with rises in GNP per capita. The association is not strong, however, and extreme differences in GNP can be found for countries with similar Gini coefficients. For example, India, Pakistan and South Korea have a GNP per capita of barely $100 yet their G coefficients are much the same as in Finland, Norway, France and Canada. Lorenz curves for

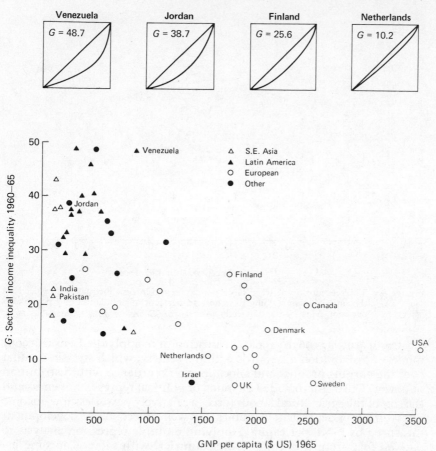

Figure 8.6 The relationship between sectoral income inequality and per capita GNP by countries, *c.* 1963, with selected Lorenz curves of income distribution. (*Source of data:* Taylor and Hudson, 1972.)

selected countries show some of the contrasts in the form of sectoral income distribution.

Another view of the relationship between income inequality and economic development is provided by data from Ahluwalia (1974). These enable the ratio of income of the top 20 per cent of the population to the bottom 40 per cent to be calculated. The results are plotted in Figure 8.7, where GNP is on a logarithmic scale so as more easily to reveal trends in the poorest countries. The relationship now bears some resemblance to the inverted U, but with the bottom filled in by countries with low GNP and also low inequality. The lowest inequality is in four socialist countries: Bulgaria, Poland, Hungary and Czechoslovakia.

The incomplete coverage and doubtful reliability of cross-national data on income distribution makes speculation on cause and effect rather hazardous. However, some statistical tests have been undertaken by

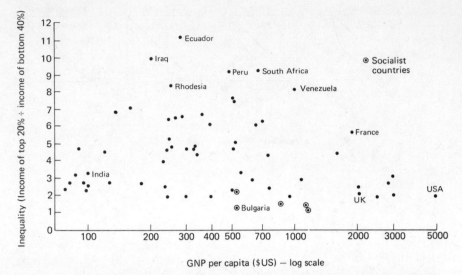

Figure 8.7 The relationship between GNP per capita and income inequality measured by the ratio of income going to richest 20 per cent of population and poorest 40 per cent. Most of the data refer to *c.* 1970. (*Source of data*: Ahluwalia, 1974, 8–9.)

Curtright (1967a; 1967b; 1968), in an attempt to apply the Lenski (1966) model of distribution of rewards within a society, which stresses conflict over the surplus product and allocation in accordance with distribution of power. Curtright included an index of political representativeness and the size of the agricultural labour force (a relatively powerless low-income class) in his independent variables, as well as economic development measured by GNP per capita. Applying multiple regression analysis to data on forty-four non-communist countries, with sectoral income inequality as measured by Kuznetz for the dependent variable, economic development was found to account for 27 per cent of the variance. Political representativeness and size of the agricultural labour force added a further 14 and 17 per cent respectively. Thus advanced economic development coupled with a representative parliament and relatively few workers on the land predicted low inequality of income distribution quite accurately.

More recent research by Adelman and Morris (1973) adds further to our emerging appreciation of the basis of income inequality. As they remind us (Adelman and Morris, 1973, 141): "Even in economically advanced countries, the persistence of significant hard-core poverty for large minorities in the midst of growing affluence for the majority has contributed to serious social tensions and political conflict. Public concern over income inequality has been heightened by both Marxian and contemporary radical stress on forces in capitalist societies that tend to increase the concentration of wealth and income and by more orthodox studies of conflict between distributional justice and economic efficiency." They present a statistical analysis of income inequality within forty-four of the relatively underdeveloped countries in their earlier study (section 8.4 above). Data on various measures of income inequality were compiled, and statistical explanations sought by an analysis of variance that revealed which of a range of economic, social and political conditions were most significant in differentiating countries by inequality group. The results for two distribution measures are summarized here.

The first dependent variable is the proportion of total income going to the lowest 60 per cent of the population. This ranged from 39 per cent in Israel to only 2 per cent in Libya, with an average of 25 per cent for all forty-four countries. The statistical analysis found that share of income to the poorest 60 per cent is "explained", broadly speaking, by the extent of socio-economic dualism, the level of social and economic modernization, and the expansion of secondary and higher education. The poor receive largest shares where there is a predominance of small-scale or communal subsistence agriculture (i.e. the lowest level of economic development in the conventional sense) and where there has been a major effort to improve human skills via education and so on. They receive the smallest shares "where a sharply dualistic development process has been initiated by well-entrenched expatriate or military elites ideologically oriented to receive most of the benefits of economic development" (Adelman and Morris, 1973, 160). In general the results do not support the hypothesis that economic growth raises the share of income of the poorer people; indeed, they suggest that early stages of growth make the poor poorer in an *absolute* as well as a relative sense—so much so that it may take them a generation to recover their original position.

The second measure is the proportion of income accruing to the wealthiest 5 per cent of the population. This ranged from 60 per cent in Rhodesia to 11 per cent in Israel, with an average of 30 per cent overall (i.e. six times what these people would have received with an even income distribution). Extreme concentration of income was found to be associated with the political and economic dominance of expatriate and other elites, especially in countries with abundant natural resources. The share of the richest people is significantly smaller in countries with large public sectors and major government investment than in predominantly private-enterprise economies. Continuing economic growth beyond the initial stage appears to require government initiative in promoting more even distribution of the benefits. The authors see their results as consistent with the view that "very uneven income distribution is a typical outcome of a narrowly based growth process where natural resources are exploited for the primary benefit of a small class of wealthy, usually expatriate, businessmen" (Adelman and Morris, 1973, 169).

The general conclusion drawn by Adelman and Morris (1973, 192) is very important: "The frightening implication of the present work is that hundreds of millions of desperately poor people throughout the world have been hurt rather than helped by economic development. Unless their destinies become a major and explicit focus of development policy in the 1970s and 1980s, economic development may serve merely to promote social injustice." If any major policy inference is justified from their analysis it is that such injustice is most likely to be avoided where the development process is taken out of the control of the capitalist economic and political elite, whether expatriate or indigenous.

Shortage of data on other aspects of life means that inequality is almost invariably measured in terms of income. But income is not a perfect measure of other things that matter to man. It does not even necessarily reflect wealth accurately; for example a Lorenz curve of income distribution shows greater equality in Britain than in the USA, yet for wealth the positions are reversed (Samuelson, 1973, 87). Holdings of wealth tend to be more highly concentrated than income, the redistribution of which may change the distribution of wealth only slightly. And who owns the wealth, in the form of capital, land and other productive resources, has an important bearing on the development process, including income distribution.

Data on the distribution of land in fifty-four countries have been assembled by Taylor and Hudson (1972, 267–70). Those included are substantially the same as for income distribution described above (Figure 8.6). But the overall extent of inequality is much greater with respect to land: the mean Gini coefficient (scaled 0 to 100) is 67 and the range from 35 in Finland to 93 in Peru, compared with a mean G of 26 and a range from 5 (UK) to 49 (Guatemala) for income inequality. The coefficients are plotted against GNP per capita in Figure 8.8 along with some sample Lorenz curves. The relationship is much less distinct than in the case of income, showing that the distribution of land is virtually independent of level of economic development. However, there is a tendency for countries from different world regions to group together, as in Figure 8.6. Thus Latin America has high levels of inequality on both criteria. GNP per capita is lower in the SE Asian countries included, but land and income are more evenly distributed. "European" countries (including Australia, New Zealand, Canada and the USA) are characterized by considerable inequalities in land distribution, in contrast to their low levels of income inequality. The control of most of the land by a small elite typical of Latin America has some parallel in Europe, where relics of the former landed aristocracy still hold considerable political power as well as disproportionate shares of land and other sources of wealth. Systems of land tenure have broad distributional implications, making them an obvious focus of reform in plans to promote development.

One further approach to the empirical identification of social inequality within nations may be mentioned briefly, as a possible way around data deficiencies. UNRISD research has shown that a distributional indicator can be constructed out of the difference between national performance on an affluence measure and one reflecting basic need. An example is the difference between automobiles per 1,000 population and life expectancy, which correlates highly with income distribution where data are available: countries with many automobiles but low health consistently rank low on income equality (McGranahan *et al.*, 1970, 15). Another example is the difference between per capita income or energy consumption on the one hand and infant survival or school enrolment on

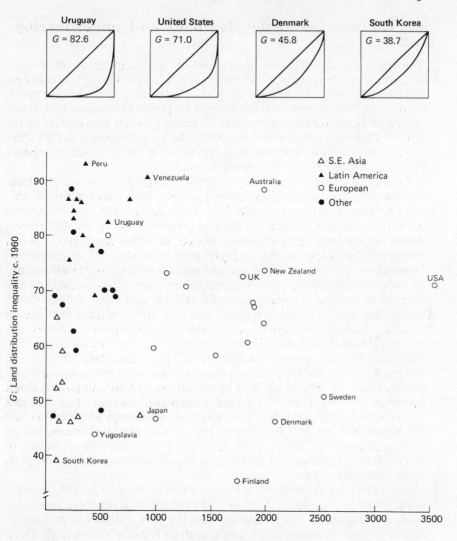

Figure 8.8 The relationship between land distribution inequality and per capita GNP by countries, *c.* 1960, with selected Lorenz curves of land distribution. (*Source of data:* Taylor and Hudson, 1972.)

the other (United Nations, 1961). Experiments with ratios of this kind help to underline the fact that inequality in distribution cannot adequately be explained as some simple function of a country's place on an economic development scale, particularly at lower and intermediate levels.

8.8 The process of development and underdevelopment

The empirical identification of national development levels offers considerable scope for geographical research, guided by our welfare concept. But to understand the process of development and underdevelopment, we must go beyond numerical indicators and their association with other aggregate characteristics of nations. A much broader perspective is required. This can be found in some of the theoretical sections in Part One, where relationships between the organization of production, spatial structure and distribution were explored.

Conventional explanations for inequalities among nations tend to stress the resource constraint, population pressure and transformation efficiency. "Poor countries typically have been poorly endowed by nature. And such land and minerals as they do possess must be divided among dense populations. The romantic notion of overlooked geographical areas, rich in resources, has largely been exploded by geographers" (Samuelson, 1973, 777). Geographers have also stressed the fragile nature of the environment in many underdeveloped countries, subject to the vagaries of tropical climates, uncertain rainfall, and soils easily depleted by careless use. In addition tropical and arid environments pose health hazards which, in combination with malnutrition and poor social services, can greatly limit the work people are able to do. But the local environmental constraint is easily exaggerated. This particularly the case in geography, with its traditional predisposition towards environmental explanations for the state of human affairs. Many underdeveloped countries have vast resources of land, forests and minerals. Thailand and Malaysia have half the world's tin reserves, the Congo and Zambia half the cobalt, Guinea and Jamaica 30 per cent of the aluminium, and so on (Meadows *et al.*, 1972, 56–9). Indeed, it was the natural wealth of Africa, South America and South East Asia that attracted the European empire-builders of the colonial era.

But resources themselves are not sufficient to guarantee economic growth and development. To make use of them requires tools, machines and other instruments of production and the slow indigenous accumulation of capital characteristic of poor countries is a major constraint. Even when resources are exploited the economic and social changes that result cannot necessarily be described as development. For example, the concentration of great riches from oil revenues in the hands of a small elite whose autocratic rule is thereby strengthened by large military expenditure may be a welfare improvement in the Pareto sense but it certainly is not by the Lorenz criterion. External ownership of resources or of the process of transforming them into real income or well-being limits the benefits going to the mass of the indigenous population. The mineral or crop may be exported in its raw state for processing in Europe or North America, thus depriving the producing country of a possible basis for building up secondary industry. Britain's long-time monopoly of the manufacture of cotton textiles is an obvious case in point. Thus many underdeveloped countries remain highly dependent on the export of a few basic commodities for revenue from outside. Three principal commodities account for over 95 per cent of all exports in such countries as Gambia, Mauritius and Zambia as well in the oil producers; for many other countries the proportion is well over 80 per cent (Ingram, 1970, 82; see also Taylor and Hudson, 1972, 366–71).

Many underdeveloped countries are at a disadvantage with respect to trade. Exports of agricultural commodities are often subject to unpredictable fluctuations of world markets, which cannot be met simply by a shift from soya beans to sugar production, for example. The terms of trade usually work to the advantage of the rich, with most power in the marketplace (Chapter 4). As Donaldson (1973, 139) summarizes it: "The overall effect of rich-country international trade policies is therefore to add to, rather than counteract, the natural handicaps involved in over-concentration on primary production by the poorer nations; and when underdeveloped countries try to reduce that excessive dependence on a handful of primary commodities, they encounter still more severe trading problems." During the past two decades world prices for manufactured goods have tended to rise while those for many primary commodities have fallen, thus worsening terms of trade for underdeveloped countries.

Advanced technology to improve transformation efficiency can easily be transmitted from rich to poor countries. This is commonly assumed to accelerate the development process in the less-advanced parts of the world. Certainly the pace of industrialization in Japan, some Eastern European countries and in the modern metropolitan sectors in many parts of Africa, Asia and South America offer evidence of the effectiveness of rapid technological diffusion. But the advanced countries continue to advance and second-hand technology in the underdeveloped world may be second-best by the time it is applied. It may also be based on assumptions concerning entrepreneurial attitudes, administrative skills and working habits that are in part alien to the indigenous culture. Peasants do not become efficient and punctual factory workers overnight, as was discovered in Britain's Industrial Revolution; similarly the social stratification and traditions of ethnic conflict in tribal societies are not immediately conducive to life in an industrial township or mine compound.

Much has been made of the "modernization" of societies as a necessary precondition for self-sustained economic development. The following description by Adelman and Morris (1967, 202) expresses this view with particular clarity:

At the lowest end of the socioeconomic scale the nature of the growth process requires both economic and social transformations. It is apparent that for this group of countries the extent to which the sway of tribal society has been reduced and the degree to which the modernization of social structure has proceeded are important determinants of the rate of improvement of purely economic performance. These social transformations are required for the enlargement of the sphere within which economic activity operates independently of traditional social organization. It is also apparent that the economic process by which growth is induced involves the dualistic development of a modern, foreign-trade-oriented sector based on the exploitation of natural resource endowments. This economic process provides both the opportunities and the incentives for the social changes that are essential for the initiation of economic growth at this level of development. The successful diffusion of the market economy and the continuous expansion of a technologically advanced sector entail significant transformations of social structure because of two concurrent phenomena. First, within the traditional agricultural economy, the spread of production for the market inevitably involves a decline in the sway of tribal society over economic actions. Secondly, the expansion of a distinct modern sector augments the importance of market transactions within a traditional society by increasing wage payments to members of indigenous villages as well as by increasing their cash purchases of consumer goods. Therefore, it is the appearance and growth of opportunities for the exchange of goods and for the sale of labor which stimulate the requisite social transformations rather than social changes internal to the traditional society.

This process is typically initiated exogenously, as for example in sub-Saharan Africa where "a small foreign or expatriate market sector provides a set of economic incentives that continually erode the structure of tribal society" (Adelman and Morris, 1967, 267). Rising GNP per capita is closely associated with this conception of socio-cultural change, as was shown in section 8.4 above. Countries where such societal transformations are well under way are becoming more developed economically.

But it is important to note that the context is that of "purely economic performance", as Adelman and Morris recognize. Our broader conception of development as welfare improvement requires an explicit account of what may be lost in modernization. This includes the transformation of previously reciprocal exchange into pecuniary transactions and labour into a market commodity—basic changes in human relationships that are very often for the worse. Then there is the deterioration of life quality that may accompany "detribalization", as workers try to cope with an abrupt transition into membership of an urban proletariat with no clear code of personal conduct to replace the *mores* of the tribe. This reaches its extreme where the requirements of the labour market are for male migrants, as in South Africa's mines (see next chapter). Even if economic development through industrialization is the right goal, western-style modernization guided by the ethics of the market may not be the most truly progressive route.

The geographer's perspective on modernization and development tends to focus attention on spatial organization of the economy and its infrastructure. This is a special aspect of transformation efficiency, as was pointed out in Chapter 4. The view of economic development somehow spreading with the diffusion of modernization down the urban hierarchy has been particularly influential (see Chapter 5). But caution is required in accepting this as an accurate description of what actually happens. Other observations of the behaviour of a space-economy stress what Ullman (1961, 28) terms the "general localization principle that initial locational advantage at a critical stage of change becomes magnified in the course of development" through external economies of agglomeration and what used to be called industrial inertia. As we have shown already, regional growth theory is unsure as to the extent of the spread effect following initial localized development. There is little empirical evidence to support this as an automatic process; indeed, the reverse may be more likely. Even to induce such a spread through a system of planned growth points rests on a rather insecure foundation, given the importance of linkages and agglomeration economies in modern location theory (Smith, 1971, 452–8, 501–7). If development in the full sense is to have widespread benefits instead of simply enhancing the advantage of the existing urban elite, very positive planning is required. Donaldson (1973, 107–8) put it thus:

> rural progress is vital because that is where the people happen to be. To be meaningful, development must be a participatory process in which the masses are involved and moved. So much of what is commonly termed development—generally measured by increases in national income—is really nothing of the sort, affecting as it does only small groups of people concentrated in a handful of urban areas. If development is to include a general widening of horizons, and if its benefits are to be widely dispersed, then substantial resources *must* be directed into the rural sector.

Few geographers have yet been able to consider development from a non-Western rural cultural perspective, looking *up* the urban hierarchy instead of down it.

One important reason for the inadequacy of the space-economy of many underdeveloped countries as an instrument for general welfare improvement is its origin in the colonial era. Transport networks were designed to facilitate the movement of the products of the interior to the coast; the cities or major ports simply helped the commodities on their way to the European markets. Space was organized for colonial purposes—for the expropriation of surplus value by European powers, with the military might to back up the position of their planters, merchants and factory owners. As Davidson (1975) says of Africa, the colonial economies have changed little since independence, facilitating a continuation of external exploitation and deepening inequality with more and more capital piling up on the one side and more and more poverty at the other. "What already exists . . . is either an inheritance from a world that is past, or the merely peripheral fragment or fragments of an international system built and controlled for the benefit of non-Africans . . . growth [of what already exists] is by no means necessarily the same as development, and may indeed be quite the reverse of development" (Davidson, 1975, 4–5). Tanzania stands as an exception, with its attempts to break the colonial mould and create a system geared to *African* development (de Souza and Porter, 1974, 64–8; Davidson, 1975; Slater, 1975, ch. 3).

This view of the spatial and structural impediments faced by former colonial countries is a major feature of the Marxian theory of uneven development (see Chapter 5) which is becoming increasingly influential in the literature on underdevelopment (Brookfield, 1975, ch. 5). The general process is summarized by Mandel (1962, 372) as follows:

> The industry of the first-industrialised countries destroys the craft and domestic production of the colonial and semi-colonial countries, which are transformed into markets of the advanced countries. The labour-power "released" as a result of this destruction of the age-old equilibrium between agriculture and industry cannot find occupation in an expanding national industry, because it is the expansion of industry in the *metropolitan* country that has made it possible to conquer this market. In consequence there appear the related phenomena of chronic under-employment and pressure of over-population on the land.

McGee (1971, ch. 3) has drawn special attention to the destruction of the "bazaar-peasant" sector in the Third World, under the impact of capitalist penetration—a process with serious implications for economic and political stability in cities with large "informal-sector" service employment closely tied to peasant agriculture.

The existing space-economy cannot match the needs of the people with the underemployed labour that could be used to satisfy them. The spatial structure of colonialism in the African context has been summarized diagrammatically by Slater (1975, 141–2). He shows the initial (pre-colonial) structure replaced by colonial penetration in the form of mines, plantations and railways to the ports, promoting the spatial concentration of an externally oriented economy. The colonial space-economy gradually develops some internal cohesion as it expands, but ultimate control is exercised by the metropolis overseas and the links through which the colony is integrated into the international capitalist system. What is produced reflects external demand rather than local need.

The pace of development in many countries might have been much more rapid but for the indirect colonialism that replaced direct rule from Europe. The situation may be viewed in global core–periphery terms: "peripheral underdeveloped nations are dominated to a large extent by the huge macro-metropolitan center. The biggest center is Europe–North America, standing like an open maw into which the goods of the earth are sucked with a pneumatic inevitability" (de Souza and Porter, 1974, 29; see also 80–82). While much of this represents a continuing attempt to impose capitalist interests in the extraction and concentration of surplus value produced by peasants and workers overseas, China and the USSR have been practising their own forms of neo-colonialism in weaker neighbouring territories.

The role of the United States is particularly important in the process of development and underdevelopment. During the past quarter of a century foreign aid amounted to about 100 thousand million dollars; the USA typically contributes roughly half of all aid to the poorer countries. But more than 40 per cent of the assistance has been military (*Statistical Abstract of the United States*, 1973, 775) and with both military and economic aid comes political dependency. This can be contrary to the interests of the mass of the people, because it tends to take the form of the stabilization of elitist régimes sympathetic to American business and foreign policy objectives. This is particularly true of Latin America (Frank, 1969), where the Central Intelligence Agency has been a major instrument in the promotion of American interests (Agee, 1975). The role of major American-based international corporations, bound up with the activities of the US government through agencies such as the CIA, has helped to perpetuate a narrow economic structure. "This cycle of single-crop export-oriented economies, begun in colonial times, has been continued and strengthened by the great financial groups which control overseas investments and which use the local ruling groups as cogs in the machinery of exploitation" (Buchanan, 1967, 223). The result is a widening of the division in Latin American society between "the core, dependent largely on the external sector, and the marginalized majority. ... Where progress occurred in education, health care and housing it accrued mostly to the core societies in the cities. Flight to cities by rural unemployed continued with the cities unable to absorb them productively" (Agee, 1975, 565). Thus develop the slums fringing so many South American cities—the poor periphery of the rich core within the greater periphery of world poverty.

Gilbert (1974) has stressed the role of *internal colonialism* as an aspect of the economic and social structure through which the privileged exploit the poorer classes in Latin America. "Regional income disparities are only one aspect of what is essentially a social problem. They are caused by factors such as the high concentration of land and property in relatively few hands, by the elite's control of commercial and economic institutions and by the exclusion of the exploited classes from effective political participation" (Gilbert, 1974, 219). Economic growth increases the gap between living standards in rural and urban areas, despite regional development programmes. Indeed, many policies devised to accelerate social and economic development are likely to increase regional disparities; under a capitalist system the differential-generating forces in a developing economy tend to outweigh the equalizing forces. No Latin American government outside Cuba has genuinely attempted to even out major regional disparities (Gilbert, 1974, 235, 281).

The case of Cuba is of particular interest. Beginning with a typical colonial economic and social structure, recent emphasis has been on the rural sector as in Tanzania, with policies designed to benefit the people as a whole rather than the commercial and export producers who dominate the countryside in many other Latin American states. Land reforms have been initiated in both rural and urban areas. Illiteracy is now virtually nil, compared with over 25 per cent in the 1950s. Infant mortality has been reduced to 35 per 1,000 live births (1971) compared with 50 in the Dominican Republic and a figure generally estimated in the hundreds in Haiti, on the neighbouring island of Hispaniola.

The various styles of development under socialism practised in Cuba, Tanzania, China and elsewhere provide the major alternative to a perpetuation of inequality and neo-colonial dependency. But this is not an easy route to follow. In addition to internal resistance, from the conservative poor as well as the elite, it is contrary to external capitalist interests. When backed by the power of the US government, revolutionary change can be held up, as in Chile, the Dominican Republic, Vietnam, Cambodia and so on. Thus external political power relations and the business interests that largely mould them in the capitalist world are critical in determining whether opportunities for development in the broadest sense will be open to a people. An apt summary of the argument is provided by Buchanan (1972, 325):

> Just as, on a global scale, the free enterprise system contributes to the widening gap between the affluent nations and the "have-not" nations, so, too, at the national level does it contribute to the widening of the gap between the elite and the masses, between the restricted areas where modern and diversified economies have been built up and the remainder of the country which remains stagnant economically and little touched by modernization. And in these economic inequalities, which become increasingly glaring with the passage of time, we may find the major cause of the social and political ferment which is involving many of the underdeveloped countries.

8.9 Responsibility and obligation for development

This interpretation of the process of underdevelopment has tended to stress the broader circumstances of political economy rather than the more obvious constraints of local resources and technology. The basic point is that to make the best of the production possibilities available to enhance the general welfare requires institutions operating in the interests of the mass of the people and not dominated by a local elite or some external source of manipulative control. Thus "the organization of world space and political economy by an intrusive industrial capitalism, and a world network of cities which helps the system to function, has created a world in which resources, already unevenly located geographically, are even more unevenly appropriated and consumed socially. Maldistribution is the central fact in underdevelopment" (de Souza and Porter, 1974, 83).

The usual view of development as an economic phenomenon concerned with aggregate material progress itself contributes to the process of underdevelopment. The alternative view of development as welfare improvement with a major emphasis on its distributional impact, as outlined in this chapter, is an explicit challenge to the already weakening conventional wisdom. Development is a multi-faceted qualitative condition, in which who gets what where is of paramount importance. And who gets what in particular places is very much dependent on the activity of people in other places. Underdevelopment is no longer a phenomenon of geographical isolation. No man or group is truly an island in our interconnected world system. Underdevelopment is a specific result in one place of development elsewhere. Davidson (1975, 139) captures the essence of this view, as he describes Africa's position in relation to the Western world:

> Africa's crisis ... is part of a general crisis, and in this general crisis the people of the industrially advanced countries are as much involved with the plight of

Africans as Africans, willy-nilly, are involved with us. What we are watching is not some distant drama far divided from the comforts and concerns of Europe and America, even if that is how it may often seem to be: the drama is as much ours as theirs, and cannot be resolved at the "periphery" without calling into question the posture and prospects of "the centre". The two "situations" are interdependent, intertwined, inseparable in their causes and consequences. If peace is indivisible today, then so is progress.

And, we might add, so is human welfare.

Where does this view take us, in the more practical realm of what to do about the problem of underdevelopment? Above all, it requires the richer nations to recognize their share of the responsibility for the state of the poor nations, and to translate this into a moral responsibility to assist the development process (Donaldson, 1973, 177–8). And this does not necessarily mean leading the underdeveloped nations along the established Western path of economic progress, capitalist or communist. It requires a much more substantial commitment of foreign aid than the one per cent or so of GNP typically allocated to this purpose by the richest countries. It requires a much more sensitive feel for the value of existing culture and institutions, however backward they may seem to Western eyes. It requires aid without political and military strings and without the economic self-interest of the donor nation as a transcending consideration. It requires the rich to relinquish much of their power in the world marketplace by liberalizing trade policies. It may require further changes in the balance of power in the United Nations and other agencies influential in international affairs. It may require those offering financial and technical assistance to by-pass corrupt, elitist governments and deal directly with the counter-elites representing the people in real need. Something of what is required is indicated in a recent statement of British aid policy (Department of Overseas Development, 1975) which stresses help for the poorest groups in poor countries, via basic rural development rather than massive capital-intensive technology. But such a statement of intent begs the question of whether mechanisms exist to ensure the implementation of such a policy, when it may not be in the interests of those who actually control the destinies of much of the underdeveloped world.

To help the underdeveloped world requires recognition that existing national inequalities are patently unjust. As Ginsberg (1965, 210–11) summarizes it:

> The problem that stands most in need of clarification is that concerning the equitable distribution of the means of well-being among peoples. ...
>   There is good evidence to show that in recent decades the economic inequalities between the developed and under-developed countries have been increasing and that within the poorer countries the inequalities between individuals, classes, and regions are as great as they have ever been and that in many of them they are still growing. What has so far been done to diminish these inequalities is pitifully small. Sixty per cent of the world's population are estimated to be in a chronic state of hunger or malnutrition and only a quarter enjoys adequate nutrition. The situation grows worse because the increase of population is greatest in areas where poverty is most acute. The injustice of this is plain

enough, but efforts to deal with the economic and political problems involved have not so far proved effective.

While seeking a contribution to the solution of these problems, the geographer must recognize the limitations of any academic approach, however relevant it may appear to questions of human welfare. Modern methods of spatial analysis provide the means of more rationally attaining specific economic and social objectives. Simplistic notions of the benefits of modernization cascading down a carefully contrived urban hierarchy aside, we have the capacity to plan industrial location and the provision of social services in pursuit of equity as well as efficiency, as the theory of earlier chapters and the cases in Chapter 11 make clear. But until there is a true commitment on the part of the rich to help the mass of the people in the underdeveloped world instead of pursuing narrow economic self-interest, the application of sophisticated spatial planning may simply aggravate existing inequalities. Such a commitment itself requires a truly revolutionary change in the conduct of world affairs.

9

Inequality and Conflict:
The Case of South Africa

Southern Africa is in many respects typical of the underdeveloped world. Its urban cores of advanced economic development surrounded by extensive rural hinterlands where a subsistence system often prevails exemplifies the spatial dualism inherited from the colonial era. This uneven development is particularly marked in South Africa, where a minority white elite still holds political power. While the past quarter of a century has seen almost all the other African peoples attain independence from white rule, South Africa's black population has been offered only the limited prospect of "separate development" under the Nationalist government's *apartheid* policy. However it may be judged from a moral point of view, this grand design for continued racial domination represents a remarkably bold exercise in spatial planning, in total defiance of the direction of the winds of change elsewhere in the African continent.

South Africa provides an interesting context for the exploration of various approaches to the analysis of inequality outlined in the theoretical sections of this book. We shall proceed step-by-step, from the facts of separate development and "race-space" inequality, through an equity analysis from a conventional perspective, and on to a more fundamental critique of the societal structure and space-economy. By this route we should gain some understanding of the different dimensions of conflict in South Africa's struggle over wealth and power. We shall also learn something of the strength and limitation of alternative interpretations.

9.1 Separate development

The Republic of South Africa has a total population of 25 million (June 1974). These include 17·8 million Africans (71 per cent of the total), 2·3 million Coloured people of mixed blood and 0·7 million Asians (mainly Indians), as well as 4·2 million Whites. The Whites may be divided into those of English origin and the Afrikaners descended from Dutch settlers. The ruling Nationalist Party finds most of its support among the Afrikaners, while the largest opposition group (the United Party) is more closely identified with the English. The Whites comprise 16·7 per cent of the total population. There are thus six Blacks to every White.[1]

[1] Racial terminology in South Africa has changed recently. The official government preference of Bantu for African (i.e. negro) has been replaced by Black. However, a growing number of Indians and Coloured now see themselves as Blacks, thus rejecting the pejorative

Table 9.1 Population and GNP in South Africa and its neighbours 1972

Country	Population	Gross National Product ($ US) Total (millions)	per capita
South Africa	23,650,000	20,050	850
Mozambique	7,962,000	2,400	300
Rhodesia	5,690,000	1,920	340
Angola	5,644,000	2,210	390
Malawi	4,711,000	460	100
Zambia	4,515,000	1,730	380
Lesotho	959,000	80	90
Botswana	629,000	150	240
Swaziland	446,000	120	260

Source: *World Bank Atlas*, 1974. The figures for South Africa include Namibia (South West Africa).

The Republic is the most populous country in southern Africa. It is also the richest, in terms of both aggregate and per capita GNP (Table 9.1). South Africa has close economic ties with most of its neighbours, particularly the "BLS" group (Botswana, Lesotho and Swaziland), which has been part of a common currency and customs union with the Republic since 1969. An important element in economic linkages is the flow of migrant labour, especially into the gold mines of the Witwatersrand (Wilson, 1972; Board, 1976): in 1973 they employed almost 350,000 foreign African workers, including 110,000 from Mozambique and 76,000 from Lesotho (Horrell *et al.*, 1975, 285).

Traditionally, minerals form the basis of South Africa's wealth. The Republic produces three-quarters of the world's gold. It also has diamond mines, coal and major reserves of other minerals—including 75 per cent of the world's chromium, half its platinum and almost 40 per cent of its manganese (Meadows *et al.*, 1972, 56–9). The country now has a vigorous manufacturing sector, contributing about one-third of total GNP compared with less than 20 per cent from primary production. Its economic strength and geographical position give the Republic a special strategic importance.

Racial segregation and the domination of Whites over Blacks has been a feature of South Africa society since the eighteenth century. The present policy of *apartheid* has emerged since the Nationalists gained political control in 1948, as a major exercise in planned segregation and spatial reorganization. Faced with the problem of maintaining white control of an economy dependent on black labour, the Nationalists have attempted to create two different dimensions of geographical space: (1) a racially integrated economic space in which the movement of black workers into the white economy is facilitated, (2) a racially segregated social and political space in which the mixing of the races is discouraged

---

implications of "non-White". In this chapter we refer to Africans, Coloured and Indians as the Blacks, along with the Whites (all capitalized when used as nouns).

and the Blacks are prevented from exercising political power where white control would be threatened. The coexistence of these two spaces as separate entities creates difficulties, of course. The greatest are in the industrial cities, where the functioning of the economy demands black residents to provide labour, while the perpetuation of white political control requires that the Blacks be disenfranchised. Hence the so-called Homelands or Bantustans established by the government in rural areas, where all Africans (including those permanently resident in the cities) are required to exercise their political "rights". Within the cities Indians and Coloureds as well as Africans occupy strictly segregated Group Areas. The Indians and Coloureds, with no Homeland, have thus far defied the ingenuity of the government to slot them into the national social/political space, though they live in the same integrated economic space as the Whites and Africans.

The areas designated as African Homelands are shown in Figure 9.1. Their highly fragmented nature is immediately apparent. Nine major African national groups are officially recognized and in all but two cases the territory allocated to them is split up into a number of spatially separated units. Something of the rationale behind fragmentation can be seen from the map, where the African lands form an almost continuous

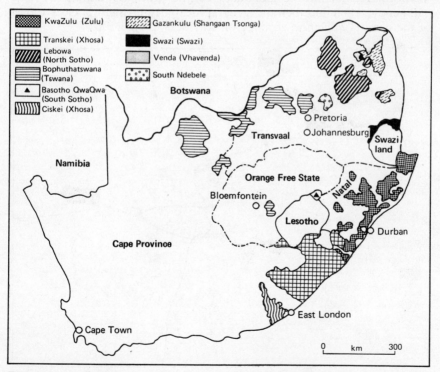

Figure 9.1 Consolidation proposals for South Africa's Homelands as of March 1975. (*Source:* based on a map prepared at the Africa Institute, Pretoria, courtesy of Dr P. S. Hattingh.)

Table 9.2 South Africa's Homelands

Homeland	Area 1973 (1,000 hectares)	Number of blocks (1975 proposals)	Ethnic group population 1970 de facto (1,000s)	per cent of total
Transkei	3,854	2	1,645	55
Ciskei	927	3	512	56
KwaZulu	3,139	10	2,062	51
Basotho QwaQwa	48	1	24	2
Bophuthatswana	3,820	6	597	36
Lebowa	2,144	6	900	56
Venda	639	2	242	67
Gazankulu	676	4	231	36
Swazi	209	1	81	17

Source: Maasdorp (1976, Table 1). Note that this does not include the most recently declared Homeland of South Ndebele.

crescent (with Swaziland, Lesotho and Botswana) strategically placed in relation to the main industrial complex of the Witwaterstrand, centred on Johannesburg, and the administrative capital of Pretoria to the north. While the Homelands recognize actual ethnic groupings among the African people, their number and geographical arrangement is clearly part of the general *apartheid* strategy of "divide and rule".

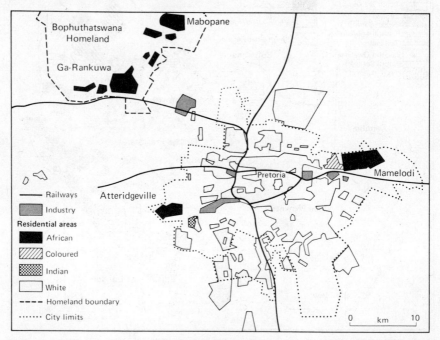

Figure 9.2 The race-spaces of the Pretoria area. (*Source:* Southern Transvaal Land Use Map, 1973, Urban and Regional Research Unit, University of the Witwatersrand; previously published in Smith, 1974b.)

Table 9.2 lists the Homelands, showing their areas and populations. The *de facto* population as proportions of total of the ethnic group in question emphasizes the number of African residents elsewhere, mostly in the cities. Slightly less than half of all Africans live in the Homelands. Despite attempts to attract industry into them or to so-called "border areas" in adjoining "white" territory (Bell, 1973a; 1973b), the Homelands are incapable of supporting even their existing population at anything other than primitive levels of living. The idea that they might in addition provide a home for the almost eight million "expatriates" now in "white" areas, as well as for the natural increase expected to double the African population by the end of the century, is thus quite unrealistic, despite hopes to the contrary expressed by some *apartheid* extremists. The Homelands actually comprise under 14 per cent of South Africa's surface areas, while Africans make up two-thirds of the population.

The race-space pattern of *apartheid* at the metropolitan level is typified by the city of Pretoria. Figure 9.2 shows its separate residential areas for the small Indian and Coloured populations as well as for the Africans and Whites. Similar patterns can be observed in the Witwatersrand conurbation, Durban and Cape Town, and indeed in every town and city in the Republic (Fair, 1971, 342–7). Industry and open space are frequently used as inter-racial buffer zones, to prevent interaction and the mixing of blood. When Group Areas are defined they do not necessarily correspond with the existing racial geography and large numbers of Blacks have been required to move from residential areas decreed to be white.

A feature of the Pretoria map that connects local and national race-space is the section of the Bophuthatswana Homeland shown to the north-west of the city. Here what can eventually be claimed to be an international boundary comes within ten miles of a major white-ruled city, thus legitimizing (in the eyes of the government) the disenfranchising of residents of townships such as Ga-Rankuwa and Mabopane which are in fact dormitory suburbs for many of Pretoria's African workers. A similar situation exists in Durban, where the territory of KwaZulu adjoins the city limits. The Witwatersrand is not so favourably situated with reference to African labour reserves and the political status of its million or so African residents who are foreign citizens of some distant Homeland in *apartheid* theory is a major inconsistency in the government's plan. Increasingly, the Witwatersrand economy is being persuaded to look to migrant labour living in single-sex hostels while retaining family life and political rights in a Homeland (Fair and Schmidt, 1974, 158). Among the more ambitious proposals to overcome the Witwatersrand's labour problem is rapid mass-transit of African commuters over long distances—an indication of the growing difficulty of separating black political and economic space.

In theory, each race group will eventually control its own affairs and institutions within its own race-space, Group Area or nation. No one group would dominate or be threatened by others and in this sense racial equality would exist. It is not uncommon for government spokesmen to deny the existence of racial discrimination in South Africa, on the grounds that *within their own territory* all groups have the same rights. Indeed, Prime Minister Vorster has been quoted as saying, "If I were to wake up one morning and find myself a Black man, the only major difference would be geographical" (*Johannesburg Star*, 3 April 1973). While the credibility of such a statement is clearly questionable, it must be recognized that many of the Afrikaners responsible for the design and implementation of *apartheid* sincerely believe that it is in the interests of the Africans, for whom they have a feeling of paternal responsibility. The hope of the government is that granting independence to the Homelands will bestow legitimacy and external recognition on their spatial subdivision of South Africa and that this, along with diplomacy and military power, can stem the winds of change.

This brief introduction to the policy of *apartheid* sets the scene for the analysis that follows. Further background can be obtained from various collections of papers published in recent years (e.g. Adam, 1971b; Rhoodie, 1972; Barrett *et al.*, 1974; Legum, 1974; Thompson and Butler, 1975), including one on spatial aspects (Smith, 1976). The conventional "pro" and "con" positions are well exemplified by Heerden (1960) and Patten (1963) respectively, while views usually considered "balanced" are offered by Niddrie (1968) and Kahn (1970).

9.2 Race-space inequality

The production of wealth in South Africa is highly localized. As was shown in Figure 1.4, the Witwatersrand comprises the major peak on the GDP surface, with other cities occupying a secondary status. How far is this reflected in general well-being? An attempt to identify a national "welfare" surface has been made by Board, Davies and Fair (1970), using data for magisterial districts. From a principal components analysis of fifteen variables, they derived a general index largely reflecting income and GDP per capita and the "quality of the population" in terms of education, age and employment characteristics. It has correlations (r) of 0·84 with per capita personal income, 0·77 with GDP per capita and 0·81 with percentage of the population having grade 8 education or beyond.

The surface is mapped in Figure 9.3. High levels are associated primarily with the major centres of economic growth, especially the Witwatersrand. The lowest areas (i.e., one standard deviation below the mean) largely coincide with the Ciskei, Transkei and Zululand. Average GDP generated per head in these low areas was about R20 in 1959–60 compared with almost R300 in the country as a whole, while in the major core areas of southern Transvaal, Cape Town, Durban and Port Elizabeth it rose to an average of R567 [2] (Fair, 1965, 61); current differentials are probably in the same proportions. Traverses or sections through the surface (Figure 9.4) show the cities as peaks separated by deep troughs.

The general impression, then, is of high levels of well-being in the

---

[2] R = Rand: 1 Rand = approx. 40p (sterling) or $0·8 (US)—Aug. 1976.

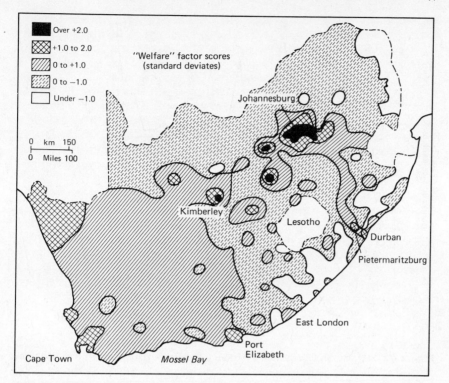

Figure 9.3 A well-being surface for South Africa. (*Source:* Board, Davies and Fair, 1970, 370.)

major metropolitan centres and to a lesser extent along the corridors between them, declining to "economic valleys in the outer periphery" (Fair, 1972, 9). The low level of living in the African-occupied rural periphery is well known, but at this broad geographical scale racial composition is not as effective a predictor of well-being as might be supposed. Fair (1970) shows that at the magisterial district level certain demographic features relating to the black population are better predictors. For example black males aged 20–49 as a percentage of all black males correlates 0·79 with the income variable. This reflects the concentration of working-age African men in the metropolitan centres, mining districts and certain of the more prosperous agricultural areas, where income and general levels of living are relatively high.

However, the existence of large numbers of Blacks in the peaks on the national surface does not mean that they necessarily have high levels of well-being themselves. Shortages of data make it impossible to derive intra-urban surfaces, but it seems safe to assume that they would show the African, Coloured and Indian Group Areas as troughs of relatively low well-being, with only minor local peaks corresponding with the small suburbs of wealthier inhabitants. The lowest levels and the greatest

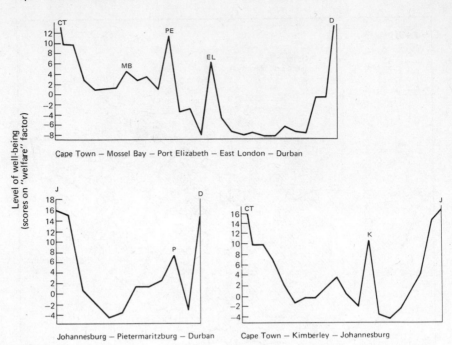

Level of well-being
(scores on "welfare" factor)

Figure 9.4 Sections through the South African well-being surface. (*Source:* Fair, 1972, 10–11.)

homogeneity are in the African areas, where people live in conditions of almost complete uniformity.

In the poorer black areas numerous symptoms of social deprivation can be identified. For example, Duncan (1970) cites two-thirds of Johannesburg's African families living in poverty, with low educational opportunity, high rate of violent crime, long and uncomfortable commuting journeys, overcrowded health services, inadequate recreational facilities, high alcohol consumption, low ownership of household appliances, high incidence of anxiety, pressure, instability, etc. By the criterion of social belonging, important to self-esteem, African and other black areas rate very low indeed, by virtue of their exclusion from many aspects of white-dominated society and because of their zero rating on effective electoral participation. The very existence of Group Areas, as limitations on freedom of residential and environmental choice, reduces life chances in proportion to the degree of restriction imposed, which is much greater for Blacks than for Whites.

In the absence of adequate information by individual territorial units, aggregate data for the major racial groups may be used to infer the extent of the spatial differences in well-being. As the principle of separate development requires that people occupy racially homogeneous areas, both nationally and within the cities, racial differences are necessarily geographical. Thus data for any race group can be taken to refer to those (discontinuous) territories occupied by that group—their designated race-space.

The poverty datum line measuring income required for the basic necessities of life makes possible some estimates of the proportion of people living in poverty. Likely magnitudes appear to be about 2 per cent of Whites, half the Coloureds, perhaps two-fifths of Natal Indians (less elsewhere, where most Indians are traders) and anything from one-third to two-thirds or even four-fifths of urban Africans in poverty together with practically all those in rural areas (Watts, 1971, 43; Horner, 1972, 8; Horrell *et al.*, 1973, 231–41). Within the race group areas there are geographical variations, of course, but the major difference is between the Whites and the other three.

Wage levels in major sectors of the economy are listed by race in Table 9.3. The superior position of the Whites in all cases is clear; they generally

Table 9.3 Average monthly earnings (Rand) in South Africa by major sectors and race groups, 1975

Sector (employment)	Africans	Coloureds	Indians	Whites	A:W
Manufacturing (1,327,000)	102	127	141	489	1:4·8
Agriculture* (830,000)	11	21	33	154	1:14·0
Mining (737,000)†	49	130	179	534	1:10·9
Construction (420,000)	100	186	240	485	1:4·8
Retail (302,000)	64	92	129	218	1:3·4
Central government (267,000)	88	212	327	428	1:4·9
Provincial administration (217,000)	73	116	165	414	1:5·7
Local authorities (205,000)	76	137	137	445	1:5·9
Wholesale (185,000)	72	118	156	389	1:5·4

Source: Horrell *et al.* (1976, 176–99); agricultural data from *Agricultural Census*, No. 43 of 1968–9, Dept. of Statistics, RSA.

Note: * Figures for 1969, regular farm employees, including payment in cash and kind.
† Figures for 1974. African earnings do not take into account value of rations, accommodation and other benefits in kind, which may double the real wage.

receive twice or three times the Coloured or Indian earnings and five times the African wages. The differential is greatest in agriculture, where African workers receive very little cash: typical *annual* payment to regular farm workers in 1971–2 was around R270, including cash and kind (Horrell *et al.*, 1975, 279). As this table covers more than half the national employed population, the data can be taken as broadly representative of general race-space income variations. The figures are more a reflection of the cities than the rural areas, where in African agriculture cash earnings can be virtually nil. The white farmers and traders occupy personal peaks on the local rural well-being surface, as do the often well-endowed African tribal chiefs.

Some other conditions may be dealt with by similar comparisons. Infant mortality (1971) is 20·9 among Whites, 35·6 for Indians and 122·1 for Coloureds (Horrell *et al.*, 1976, 39); for Africans 140 seems a likely figure (Horrell *et al.*, 1973, 64). Life expectation at birth gives a white man 16 years more than a Coloured and 5 more than an Indian; no figures are available for Africans (Horrell *et al.*, 1976, 39). Pensions have maximum monthly payments of R64 for Whites, 34 for Coloureds and Indians, and 15 for Africans (Horrell *et al.*, 1976, 277). Per capita expenses on education 1973–4 were over R500 for Whites, 141 for Indians, 110 for Coloureds and less than 29 for Africans in "white" areas (Horrell *et al.*, 1976, 214). Enrolment in secondary classes is about 33 per cent of all white children in school, 24 for Indians, 11 for Coloureds and 4 for Africans (Randall, 1971a, 32); only 1 per cent of all white children over 15 years of age have no schooling, compared with 17 per cent of Indians, 24 per cent of Coloureds and 52 per cent of Africans (Horrell *et al.*, 1975, 340). These differences, together with others in housing quality, electoral participation, environmental quality, physical security and so on, all have spatial manifestations by virtue of the racial basis of residential location.

Table 9.4 The percentage distribution of population (P) and income (Y) by racial groups in South Africa, 1936–1971

Date	Africans		Coloureds		Indians		Whites		Inequality coefficient (G)
	P	Y	P	Y	P	Y	P	Y	
1936	68·8	19·7	8·0	4·1	2·3	1·7	20·9	74·5	53·6
1946–7	68·5	20·1	8·2	4·2	2·5	1·9	20·7	73·8	53·1
1956–7	68·0	20·6	9·1	4·8	2·9	2·0	19·9	72·5	52·6
1967	69·4	18·8	9·5	5·4	2·9	2·4	18·2	73·4	55·2
1970–1	70·0	19·1	9·4	5·2	2·9	2·1	17·7	73·6	55·9

Source: Randall (1972a, Appendix C, Table 3). Note: Gini coefficient is on the range 0 to 100.

Distributional inequalities by race are summarized in Table 9.4. Here proportions of total population are compared with proportions of national income received. The Gini coefficient is very high—more than half way up the 0 to 100 scale. It appears from these data that there has been no appreciable change in the inter-racial distribution since the 1930s; indeed, since the middle of the 1950s it may have become a little more unequal. The same impression is given by slightly different data on personal disposable income according to Nel (1974), which reveals G values of 49·9 in 1959–60, 50·1 in 1964–5 and 50·7 in 1970. Thus there seems to have been a welfare deterioration by the Lorenz criterion. The latest figures are plotted in Figure 9.5. By the criteria explained in Chapter 6, the African, Coloured and Indian *groups* comprise the underprivileged, while the elite or "minimal majority" controlling half the national income is accounted for by only part of the Whites. This diagram effectively captures the essence of racial inequality in distribution in South Africa.

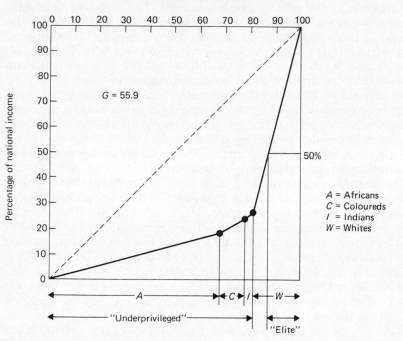

Percentage of national population

Figure 9.5 Lorenz curve showing income distribution inequalities by race groups in South Africa. (*Source of data:* Table 9.4.)

9.3 Equity in distribution

That there is a highly unequal distribution of real income by race-space in South Africa is beyond dispute. But is this necessarily inequitable, or unjust? As was suggested in Chapter 6, some differentiation may be justified by such criteria as societal contribution, merit or need, as well as in the interests of survival or efficiency. What guidance can welfare theory give us, in making an equity judgement on the spatial state of South African society?

Approaching matters from the production side first, the level of well-being in any territory will tend to reflect local factor endowment and transformation efficiency. The rural areas occupied by Africans are deficient in minerals and other resources, and the quality of some of the land is low. In the urban areas the main "productive factor" supplied by Blacks is labour, disproportionately unskilled or semi-skilled and thus lowly rewarded; the Africans and Coloureds, and to a lesser extent Indians, lack an indigenous capital base for local enterprise. On the transformation side, the efficiency of agriculture in African areas is constrained by lack of modern technology. As industrial workers, people drawn from the "tribal" areas into the urban economy are initially inefficient; the productivity of much Indian and Coloured labour as well as that of the

Africans may also suffer from lack of incentives—low wages and limited opportunities for job training or advancement. The effectiveness of some public services such as health and education in the black areas is also low. Thus there are many reasons why the production possibilities in both urban and rural areas occupied by Blacks (particularly Africans) are restricted, when compared with white areas well endowed with capital, skilled labour and a modern service infrastructure.

If the input of Blacks to the national product is relatively small, as might be anticipated from the above, then the existing inequalities could perhaps be justified if the criterion of societal contribution is paramount. Blacks might get out in proportion to what they put in, within a system which gears rewards to productivity. That such an arrangement is just is a commonly held ethical position in a capitalist society. But in South Africa the well-being of Blacks is held *below* the position that might be attained in a normal free-market economy, by discriminatory laws and practices relating to job reservation, wage differentials, limitations on unionization of labour, unequal expenditures on education, and so on. The "productivity" of labour, or value added in the conventional neo-classical sense, is a rather meaningless concept in a capitalist economy if labour is not free to find its price in the marketplace via collective bargaining. The ready supply of cheap black labour in South Africa means that in a competitive system wages are bound to be relatively low, but the readiness with which industry has conceded increases to its African labour since 1973, in the face of strikes, suggests that wages are substantially lower than they would be in a true market. The same impression is created by the relatively high return on investment in South African industry (Biesheuvel, 1972, 15–16), which reflects the low cost of labour. In fact, what might appear to be the low contribution of Blacks to the economy, when compared with white labour and capital, is a false impression created by the way in which the economy and society is organized—a matter to which we will return later in this chapter.

Even if we accept productivity as a just criterion for income distribution, the use of existing "productivity" levels in a restricted labour market is clearly questionable. When applied to matters other than wages, it tends to intensify the disadvantaged position of the Blacks, an obvious example being the requirement that African education be financed largely from the resources of the African people. A similar distributive principle is reflected in the United Party's 1972 proposal for political reform, which includes a federal assembly with members elected by "a formula reflecting the proportional contribution of each community or unit to the Republic, measured in terms of the country's gross domestic product" (Sir de Villiers Graaff, quoted in Horrell *et al.*, 1973, 9). In so far as education and political power are instrumental in affecting what a particular community or group gets, such arrangements simply perpetuate the *status quo*. This is itself unjust, even by the neo-classical conception of contribution to national product, because it is arrived at in a deliberately imperfect market economy.

Holding back sections of a society is generally regarded as wrong. Frankena (1962, 14) puts it as follows: "A society is unjust if, by its actions, laws and mores, it unnecessarily impoverishes the lives of its members materially, aesthetically, or otherwise, by holding them at a level below that which some members at least might well attain by their own efforts." Whether this describes the South African situation hinges on the word "unnecessarily". By the values and priorities of the white "consensual elite" who run the country existing inequalities may seem to be necessary, in order to ensure the perpetuation of the social and economic system on which their status, security and affluence depends. As long as the primary concern of most Blacks is with personal survival, in the sense of growing enough food to live, earning a subsistence wage or avoiding offences against the laws governing urban residence, more abstract questions of equity, political rights and the plausibility of white superiority may seem unimportant. For example, it has been suggested that there is probably no more coveted right (including the vote) anywhere in the world than the qualification of an African to urban residence in South Africa (Horrell *et al.*, 1973, 162). If such rights were freely acquired and assured in the long term by property ownership, along with incomes well above poverty level, aspirations could be expected to turn in other directions more threatening to white supremacy. If Africans could make a satisfactory living in their "traditional" rural Homelands, they would not have to take their labour to the city: migration is the outcome of a spatial differentiation of opportunity.

Race-space inequality must thus be viewed as an integral part of the policy of separate development. The complex apparatus of racial domination is fully described elsewhere (e.g. Adam, 1971a; 1971b; Randall, 1972a; 1972b) and repetition is unnecessary. The point here is that the implementation of the policy itself comprises a major redistribution of well-being or real income, because the costs are exacted disproportionately from Blacks. The consolidation of the Homelands requires the resettlement of hundreds of thousands of Africans but few Whites. The government proposal for KwaZulu in 1972, for example, would involve the transfer of 343,000 Zulu from "excised" African areas, but only about 6,000 Whites would have to move (Best and Young, 1972, 69); the figure may still be as high as 206,000 Zulu in the revised proposal of April 1973 (calculated by Best and Young). Between April 1968 and June 1971 alone about 209,000 Africans were moved under the Homeland resettlement programme (*Rand Daily Mail*, 30 April, 1973). The implementation of the Group Areas Act to create race-space homogeneity in the cities requires (to 1974) the resettlement of 75,500 Coloureds and 40,700 Asians but only 1,670 Whites (Horrell *et al.*, 1976, 69). The number of Africans moved within the urban areas may exceed one million; an index of dislocation of population calculated by Fair and Shaffer (1964) for 1951–60 in the major cities suggested that Africans suffered much more than the other groups. In most cases the quality of housing and physical environment has been improved by relocation in newly built urban townships, though rural resettlement schemes are judged less favourably (Desmond, 1971). But against this has to be set the destruction of community life, including the removal of Coloureds from Cape Town's "District Six" and Indians from their inner-city homes in Durban. Other costs of separate development borne almost entirely by Blacks include long-distance commuting from peripheral townships, lack of amenities for Blacks working in "white" areas, and the relocation of businesses which has affected many Indian traders forced out of existing premises by the Group Areas Act.

Particularly important are the effects of the migrant labour system. This is prejudicial to human well-being both in the cities, where the workers live the unnatural life of the single-sex hostel, and the Homelands where fatherless (and sometimes motherless) families have to remain. The break-up of family life and impediments to normal sexual relationships affect some of the most basic human needs. The use of migrant labour is increasing as a means of preventing Africans from gaining urban residence rights. The system is dangerous by virtue of the social strains created, "even from the narrow perspective of white political survival" (Wilson, 1972, 200).

Against all these costs to Blacks have to be set possible benefits from the current policy. Whatever its shortcomings, a serious programme of geographically separate *and equal* development in which each population group has political autonomy in its own territory may be preferable to the *laissez faire* of the pre-*apartheid* era. The present policy can perhaps be seen as a series of Pareto improvements, where all races have become better off in the absolute sense; i.e. the general welfare has improved if the question of the just distribution of real income is disregarded. The power of the government to implement separate development has enabled advances to be made in the well-being of Blacks that might not have occurred with a continuation of a more pragmatic form of domination exclusively concerned with short-run economic gain. The overall judgement as to whether the Blacks have indeed become better off is complicated by the fact that it requires a balancing of material gains against such intangibles as losses of civil rights and the indignities of "petty *apartheid*" (i.e. trivial acts of discrimination such as separate lavatories and exclusion of Blacks from parks and other public facilities). One credit often claimed is the lack of violent confrontation between the races, an achievement which experience elsewhere in Africa suggests may have substantially benefited the Indians as well as the Whites. Another is the self-determination offered by the creation of racially-homogeneous Group Areas and Homelands. In this case the benefits accrue mainly to the Africans, for the Coloured and Indians have no prospect of the statehood promised by the Homeland concept and no other source of effective political participation. How truly self-determining any black areas can become in an economically interdependent South Africa where effective control of wealth and power is retained by the Whites is a legitimate question, of course, and for the Africans independent Homelands will always be a second-best to the overall control which their numerical strength would give them in a nation-wide multi-racial democracy. Along with territorial separation go the supposed advantages of non-assimilation, racial purity and the preservation of traditional culture and ways of life. Whether the Blacks value these things as highly as the Whites, in particular the Afrikaners, is impossible to say: the Blacks have not had the opportunity to express their preferences for "cultural integrity" as compared with political freedom.

At the more material level, large sums of money are made available for the development of the Homelands through various government bodies. The annual budget is well over R200 M. Other expenditures often portrayed as income transfers to Blacks include grants towards the cost of industrial development in the Homelands and "border areas" adjoining them, and the subsidizing of urban rail services. Financial assistance to the Homelands is sometimes seen as a kind of foreign aid from white South Africa to future independent black states. If the basic objective of separate development is white supremacy, then these expenditures must be seen as part of the necessary price, of course, not as gratuitous income transfers, for the Whites are presumably purchasing something worth at least the amount of the outgoings. They are investing in a system designed to retain black labour without black votes.

This brief evaluation of separated development suggests that most of the benefits accrue to the Whites and most of the costs to the Blacks, the latter thus paying for the maintenance of their own position of disadvantage. The observed inequalities cannot be justified by the criterion of societal contribution even if actually true, because we cannot know what the "just" rewards would be in a free economy without racial discrimination. It cannot be justified by need, for the most needy territories get least, both nationally and within the cities. And merit provides a justification only if belonging to one racial group is more meritorious than belonging to others. If white supremacy or survival is regarded as the transcending criterion the existing race-space distribution could possibly be considered equitable, but this presupposes that the present policy is the best means of achieving that end. The importance of white survival is, of course, an ethical matter and not something which can be demonstrated by factual argument. It is far from self-evident that the physical survival of white South Africa and its distinctive version of Western European "civilization" justifies any inequality of treatment of other kinds of people.

Thus it does appear that the lives of the Blacks are being *unnecessarily* or unjustly impoverished. It requires an extreme value position to believe that the general welfare would not be improved by greater expenditure on economic development, education, health and other social services in existing black race-space, financed by increased taxation on the richer Whites. Some redistribution of income may be in the interests of all: the well-being of the Whites (including their survival) may in the long run be more a function of their treatment of other population groups than of their aggregate consumption of luxury cars, swimming pools, tennis courts and other current benefits of their personal affluent society. The high degree of interdependence of individuals and groups is as much part of the reality of life in South Africa as it is elsewhere.

9.4 Growth, development and welfare

How might things change for the better in South Africa? How might development as welfare improvement take place? A common assumption on the part of both internal and external observers is that a more just society will somehow emerge automatically, from the process of economic growth. Let us examine this position, within the framework of conventional welfare theory.

The existing situation in South Africa can be depicted very simply in a utility–space diagram. In Figure 9.6 well-being or real income (S) in white race-space is plotted against that in black race-space. The welfare

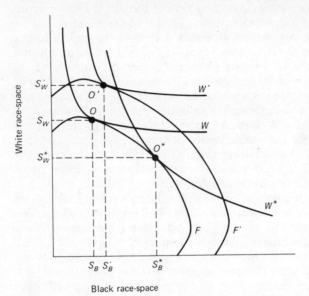

Figure 9.6 A utility-space analysis of distribution between Whites and Blacks in South Africa.

frontier (F) shows the ways in which the national aggregate product could be distributed. The frontier turns down at the ends to reflect the interdependence of the racial groups: below a certain level—perhaps subsistence—the Blacks (or Whites) could not contribute to the economy and this would lower white (or black) well-being. Thus on those parts of the frontier which slope positively, increases in the well-being of one group are accompanied by increases for the other, while on the rest of the frontier all positions are Pareto-optimal because any advance for one group will be at the expense of the other. The implicit national SWF generates a welfare contour (W) embodying the preferences of the white ruling elite, which favour the white race-space. The actual distribution (S_W, S_B) is at O, assuming that society is on the frontier. Apart from the fact that it records substantial inequality, the position of O in the diagram is arbitrary. It might be closer to the vertical axis, on the positively sloping part of the frontier, if increasing black well-being (e.g. wages) would increase productivity enough to raise the well-being of the Whites as well, i.e. the *existing* distribution may not be optimal in a Pareto sense. A redistribution of rewards that stimulates an increase in the productivity of black labour may be to everyone's advantage.

If the existing unequal distribution is unjust, how can the gap be narrowed or eliminated? On the production side, the total output available for distribution can be increased in ways that disproportionately benefit the Blacks. Improving the efficiency of African agriculture is an example. More investment in social services could also help; for instance Barker (1971, 14) claims that infant mortality in the African rural areas could be reduced from 350 per 1,000 live births to around 70 with comparatively little effort—there may be no cheaper way of saving a life in South Africa than to invest in medical care in the Homelands. However, any resource allocation favouring black race-space raises the question of whether the white electorate would sanction it.

Continuing economic growth and the advance of the welfare frontier without any redistribution improves the absolute position of Blacks through increases in earnings. The process of industrialization and modernization is bringing more Blacks into semi-skilled and skilled employment, but will it necessarily bring society nearer a just sharing of national wealth in which race becomes irrelevant as a distributive criterion? If history is any guide the answer is no, for inter-racial income inequality has remained much the same since the 1930s despite South Africa's industrial transformation (Table 9.4). The ratio of white to black wages was almost exactly the same in 1960–61 as in 1915–16: 4·71 compared with 4·84 (Berghe, 1967, 305). During the 1960s per capita increase in real wages was considerably less for Blacks than for Whites (Biesheuvel, 1972, 7), though Blacks have done better more recently. In Figure 9·6 economic growth is shown by an advance of the welfare frontier to F'; with the distribution governed by the same SWF through the same welfare contours (now W'), the income level in both race-spaces improves absolutely but their relative shares remain the same. This may well be the case in reality—continual Pareto improvements but no welfare gain by the Lorenz criterion. In fact, economic growth involving more industrial jobs for Blacks within the existing economic structure may merely help to preserve the *status quo*, i.e. the domination of the mass of the people by a white capitalist elite. As Davidson (1975, 81) remarks, "no rational observer today, I suppose, will care to assert that growth of the white economy in South Africa is equivalent to development of the country as a whole".

It would thus be unwise to rely on the process of economic development as a means of greatly reducing the existing race-space inequalities. Similarly, it would be naïve to believe in economic growth as "the magic defeat of racial discrimination" (Adam, 1971a, 153). And as long as such discrimination exists, substantial race-space differences in well-being can be expected.

In conventional (neo-classical) welfare theory, altering the distribution of a given output or national income requires changing the national SWF. In Figure 9.6, if in place of the welfare contour W we had $W^\star$, a position of equal distribution would be achieved ($S_W^\star$, $S_B^\star$). Perfect equality may be undesirable as well as impracticable, but race-space equity in South Africa clearly requires a substantial move in this direction. Such a strategy resolves into changing the attitudes and values underlying the existing distributional mechanisms of society (Adam, 1971a; Schlemmer, 1971; 1972). How might this be achieved? An obvious way would be to allow all South Africans to contribute their individual preferences: universal franchise is a necessary if not sufficient condition for ensuring that all have their say. And if each say is to be given the same weight, this requires a political structure which guarantees one man or woman one vote, not some federation in which differential weighting of race-space ensures continued white domination. As universal franchise on a national basis would give the existing underprivileged population political control, a rather dramatic shift in the SWF in favour of Africans could be expected. In terms of the general welfare, this could be a high-risk strategy, given the uncertainty as to whether a Buthelezi (Chief Minister of KwaZulu) or an Amin would emerge as leader; the former would probably move society along its welfare frontier, while the latter could move back inside it thus making everyone worse off. But whatever the possible dangers, differentiation sanctioned by the mass of the people is likely to be morally preferable to that determined by a minority elite.

The conventional welfare formulations thus have some light to shed on the problems of South Africa. In particular, they stress the importance of the attitudes and values of those with effective power. These, in turn, are a response to how they view their interests within a distinctive cultural milieu—one in which group interests conflict to such an extent that a general consensus on societal goals (including distributive justice) seems inconceivable. But the theoretical perspectives played out in this section fail to explore the fundamental basis of power and conflict in South Africa, that undermines growth as the panacea. The emphasis on altering the attitudes and values of the dominant group, as expressed in society's implicit SWF, is a liberal notion of the kind that may achieve some success in situations where the (mildly) oppressed are a minority. But in South Africa it requires ultimately relinquishing control to a severely oppressed majority. However comforting to liberals within the white elite the prospect of gradual emergence of a multi-racial democracy may be, this seems most unlikely to be the actual pattern of future events. To understand why requires a broader view of conflict in contemporary South Africa.

9.5 The economic basis of conflict

Thus far in this chapter, it has been implicitly assumed that the basis of conflict in South Africa is racial. This is certainly the form in which South African affairs generally attract attention, with discrimination by Whites against Blacks as the particular manifestation. But other dimensions of conflict have already been implied above. There is conflict, real and potential, among the black groups. And there is an underlying economic dimension in which class conflict might be found to transcend race. The spatial structure of South African society, with its gross inequalities, is the result of a multi-dimensional process of conflict resolution. Who gets what in (and from) South Africa has to be seen as the outcome of a specific historic process, in which capitalist expansion and underdevelopment has taken on some quite distinctive features.

The early economic development of South Africa proceeded in a similar fashion to colonial expansion elsewhere. Land was taken from the indigenous people and their culture was gradually eroded by pressures to work for wages. But as white settlement accelerated in a land with a climate more temperate than tropical, numbers built up so that today the "colonizers" are counted in millions instead of the few thousands of Whites in most other African countries. The evolution of South African society was further complicated by the existence of two distinct white groups, each with its own language and with sufficient conflict of interest at the end of the nineteenth century to lead to the Boer War. From the first intrusion of mining into the essentially agrarian economy of the early Boer republics, the English have posed threats to the Afrikaners' strong feelings of nationalism and cultural identity as a people chosen to perform some special role under divine inspiration. Only since control of the government gave the Afrikaners relative security have common white interests tended to subordinate the old antagonisms. A further complication is that the Afrikaners no longer look to Holland as home, seeing themselves just as much indigenous as the Africans. Added to this is the Coloured population originating from miscegenation among white settlers and the indigenous people, and the Indians descended from indentured labour brought in to work in the Natal sugar industry.

South Africa's spatial structure also has its own variations on the usual pattern of colonialism. As elsewhere, economic development initially focused on agriculture, with penetration of the interior organized from Cape Town and (later) Durban. These ports acted as outposts of European commerce, through which capital was funnelled, control exercised and profits repatriated. But the discovery of gold quickly shifted the economic centre-of-gravity into the interior—to Johannesburg. The core-region of the southern Transvaal was further strengthened by the emergence of Pretoria as administrative capital of the Union of South Africa. It is largely from Johannesburg and Pretoria respectively that the present economic and political dominance of core over periphery is exercised.

We may now see how the South African space-economy fits into the contemporary theory of underdevelopment, outlined at the end of Chapter 5. Frank (1969, 39) views white South Africa as part of the world capitalist metropolis, the "native" population having the same satellite status as in underdeveloped countries. Alternatively, the white-controlled industrial–commercial cores, in particular the Witwatersrand, may be viewed as occupying a secondary level in the world hierarchy of capitalist control and exploitation—an outpost of the Europe–North

America "metropolis", performing its special function in the spatial organization of southern Africa going well beyond the borders of the Republic itself. In any event, the size, wealth and power of the indigenous white-capitalist economic sector distinguishes the country from more typically colonial neighbours such as Rhodesia and (formerly) Angola and Mozambique. Whatever its external links, the South African space-economy has an internal coherence finely tuned to its exploitive role.

Marxian analysis provides the necessary clues to the basic functioning of the South African space-economy, exposing a dimension hidden by the exclusively race-conflict interpretation. The "success" of the South African economy, from the capitalist perspective, lies in the ease with which it is possible to appropriate surplus value generated by black labour. *Apartheid* or separate development is a specific spatial arrangements to facilitate exploitation. The large size of the "industrial reserve army" in the periphery and the degree to which its entry into the labour market is controlled by extra-economic coercion enables employers to realize a use value greatly in excess of wages paid. This produces large profits which, in their turn, have facilitated internal capital accumulation as well as attracting much investment from overseas (Legassick, 1974, 271–4). The capacity to satisfy labour needs in the mines and some other industries largely by the use of migrants is particularly effective in reducing the wages bill, as it transfers some of the real costs of production involved in the maintenance and reproduction of labour to the Homelands, and to other areas beyond the Republic's borders. The mines typify this arrangement: "The workers in the gold sector are important only in so far as they produce surplus-value for the capitalists, their wives and daughters are important only in so far as they manage to maintain, in their allotted 'reserves', the living labour power from which capital derives its surplus-value" (Williams, 1975, 24–5). It is hard to imagine a clearer contemporary case of the power of capital, with the assistance of government, to reduce human beings to the status of a commodity. To quote a Nationalist MP, "it is labour we are importing and not labourers as individuals" (Adam, 1971a, 96).

The traditional role of the rural reserves as sources of cheap labour for the cities has been interpreted by Wolpe (1972; 1974) as a non-capitalist mode of production deliberately maintained to meet part of the cost of reproducing labour-power. The reciprocity relationships of tribal society entitled the returning migrant or unemployed city worker to means of support produced outside the capitalist mode of production. "The extended family in the Reserves is able to, and does, fulfil 'social security' functions necessary for the reproduction of the migrant work force. By caring for the very young and very old, the sick, the migrant labourer in periods of 'rest', by educating the young, etc., the Reserve families relieve the capitalist sector and its State from the need to expand resources on these necessary functions" (Wolpe, 1972, 435). In other words, some of the agricultural production of the periphery outside the market economy is brought into the capitalist sector by the migrant workers—an indirect form of surplus appropriation. The contemporary emphasis on ethnic Homelands as a focus for African political aspiration represents a shift towards more direct control of labour: "the practice and policy of Separate Development must be seen as the attempt to retain, in a modified form, the structure of the 'traditional' societies, not, as in the past, for the purposes of ensuring an economic supplement to the wages of the migrant labour force, but for the purposes of reproducing and exercising control over a cheap African industrial labour force in or near the 'homelands', not by means of preserving the pre-capitalist mode of production but by the political, social, economic and ideological enforcement of low levels of subsistence" (Wolpe, 1972, 450).

While the gold mines are the major beneficiaries from migrant workers, the general low cost of black labour helps all sectors of the white capitalist economy. The rate of exploitation (in the Marxian sense) may be highest in agriculture, where labour is dispersed and unable to exert even the minimal power exercised by metropolitan workers in recent years. The growth of the manufacturing sector has absorbed many African workers within the Republic who would originally have gone to the mines, thus creating some upward pressure on wages through competition. But in general, black labour is sold on a "buyer's market"—literally, in the sense that the employers and their government design and run it. This applies not only to the mining and manufacturing sector but also in tertiary activity, where many Africans, Indians and Coloureds work for low pay in shops and offices. It also applies to domestic service: over 600,000 Africans provide labour in the homes of Whites (and many Indian and Coloured families) for wages of roughly R40–50 a month, cash and kind (Horrell *et al.*, 1975, 245, 312).

The mines are now increasingly looking beyond South Africa's borders for their migrant labour, part of a trend towards a growing economic integration at the international level within southern Africa. "The enormous concentration of capital and labour in a handful of financial and industrial concerns ... has placed South Africa in a decidedly advantageous position in its quest to overwhelm and dominate the countries of Southern Africa" (Williams, 1975, 16). According to this view, capitalist imperialism from South Africa is well underway, with trade relations closely resembling those between developed and underdeveloped countries (the Homelands eventually taking their place in the latter category). Thus the gold mines have continued to accumulate capital on the basis of the high labour content of gold without major mechanization, now relying 80 per cent on non-South African labour. Profits and foreign exchange earned by the mines have assisted the expansion of industry, which now finds markets and outlets for surplus capital in those same countries whose workers generate surplus value for the mine owners. Davidson (1975, 34) sees in this "a new chapter of imperialism", producing something like a "planetary system with satellites" in the form of South Africa's neighbours and Bantustans. The fostering of such dependence is part of South Africa's survival strategy.

In Figure 9.7, an attempt is made to show how the appropriation and flows of surplus value might be viewed, in a simplified spatial structure.

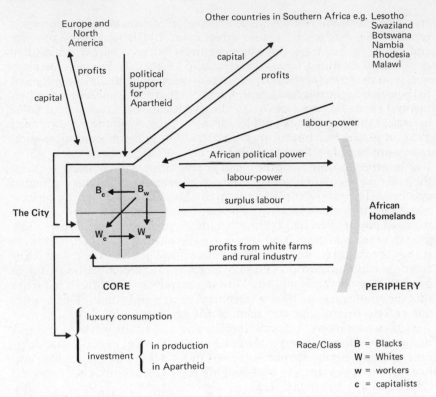

Figure 9.7 Aspects of the spatial circulation of surplus value in South Africa, in a simplified core–periphery structure.

The city core could be taken as the Witwatersrand, with the periphery its crescent of Homelands. Extraction of surplus value takes place in both the urban–industrial core and the rural–agricultural periphery. The former is most important, however, for it is here that the majority of black wage-workers are located. The surplus value accruing to the capitalist class is used partly to finance luxury consumption and partly for investment. Some is repatriated to Europe or North America as profits from investment in South Africa (eliciting external support for *apartheid* in return), some is ploughed back into local industrial expansion, and some is invested elsewhere in southern Africa. Some of the profits are used to finance *apartheid*, so as to ensure the continuing supply of cheap disenfranchised labour.

A major feature of the urban cores in South Africa is the redistribution of surplus value needed to perpetuate the existing system. Compliance of the white proletariat in the internal suppression of the Blacks is achieved through wage differentiation that gives white workers a far higher standard of living than would be the case if they had to compete with black labour on an equal footing. Some state-owned enterprises, for example the railways, traditionally provide protected employment for the least-skilled whites, at substantial inefficiency costs. Thus white workers, as a "labour aristocracy", share with the white bourgeoisie some of the surplus value appropriated from Blacks, but without ownership of the means of production. They often occupy posts supervising the extortion of surplus value from black workers. They have a special role in the day-to-day dehumanization of black labour as a market commodity or inanimate resource—an important element in South Africa's process of racial domination (Kuper, 1974, 14).

Some redistribution also occurs within the black group, as black capitalists and richer households exploit other Blacks. Most of the capitalists who are not white are Indians, and the Group Areas Act whereby residential and business land is allocated to specific race groups has both limited and concentrated Indian entrepreneurial activity. The fact that so little land is available for Indian business has forced up rents and driven many small traders out of business—the process of proletarianization of the middle classes: "their transformation from owners of capital into mere owners of labour-power" (Mandel, 1962, 164). In Durban and other cities, Indian real estate, commerce and industry is increasingly passing into the hands of large syndicates or combines, which are replacing the old family business groups. Meer (1976) suggests that it is from these beneficiaries of capital concentration that the government draws its Indian supporters for separate development. This is another instance of the alliance of capital and government that transcends race.

It should be clear from all this that the spatial structure of the South African economy under *apartheid* is eminently conducive to the functioning of the capitalist mode of production. The interests of capital are consistent with those of the ruling Afrikaner elite, whose first priority is their own survival as a physical and cultural entity. To interpret the existing situation as one of conflict between Nationalist racist ideology and the efficiency of the economy—a frequent feature of the liberal critique—neglects the deeper reciprocal dependence of capitalism and racial domination.

9.6 Prospects for change

As political change engulfs most of the rest of southern Africa, attention is increasingly focused on the Republic, as the last bastion of what appears to be secure white rule. In a geo-strategical sense, South Africa now seems far more vulnerable than at the beginning of the 1970s, following the collapse of Portuguese rule in Mozambique and Angola and growing uncertainty as to the stability of Namibia (South West Africa) and Rhodesia (Zimbabwe). The Republic's position at the southern tip of the African continent gives it a strategic significance to what South Africa likes to think of as its "free-world" allies. But reaction to *apartheid* mutes Western support. The prospects for change within South Africa are related to these external conditions, which are increasingly viewed as putting pressure on the Republic to soften *apartheid* sufficiently to attract greater outside help and build a strong perhaps multi-racial consensus at home.

As has already been implied, an analysis of the likely pattern of change and the success of internal policy depends very much on our view of conflict and alliance. Let us begin our speculations with a core–periphery interpretation of political power relations, of the kind outlined in Chapter 5, ignoring for the moment the economic basis of conflict suggested in the previous section. Following Friedmann (1972; 1973), Schmidt (1975) sees in South Africa a core controlled by the white elite dominating a periphery to which the Blacks are assigned, as the basic features of a spatial system of authority-dependency relations. Blacks resident in the core in geographical space belong to the periphery in a political sense. Conflict over access to political power and the distribution of the national product exists between the core elite and the peripheral counter-elite. The South African government's policy is, in Friedmann's terminology, "suppression" of the counter-elites in the white-controlled core and "replacement" of elite authority in the periphery via the Homelands policy.

As a solution to the present conflict, such a policy suffers from three major inconsistencies—cultural, economic and political (Schmidt, 1975). First, the pressure to retain tribal affiliation and some of its pre-industrial culture, which forms part of the Homelands strategy, is inconsistent with the role of millions of Africans as permanent or migrant industrial workers. "There is a dysfunction, therefore, in a policy which, on the one hand, seeks to perpetuate the migrant labour system without retarding the the rate of urban economic development and, on the other, seeks to inhibit cultural change by direct means without adequate cognizance being taken of indirect cultural change of sub-dominant groups in urban environments" (Fair and Schmidt, 1974, 165). Increasingly, the black urban proletariat will become uneasy with the schizophrenic cultural existence required by *apartheid*. The second inconsistency is that there is no hope of the Homelands becoming viable secondary economic cores in their own right. As Maasdorp (1974) explains, when viewed as nations they possess most of the disadvantages of the less-developed countries, while government policy is quite out of touch with advances in the theory and practice of economic development. Particularly serious is the dependence on industrial dispersal from the white cores to border areas still in "white" territory—a means of tapping black labour across the border without the risk of losing fixed capital to a future independent black state. This is exploitive neo-colonialism, not development of the poor periphery. The third inconsistency is political. The lack of employment opportunities in the Homelands and the labour requirements of the white-controlled urban economy means that Africans are likely to retain their present numerical superiority in the core, yet they are still expected to identify with the periphery as their political space. To this might be added the position of the Coloureds and Indians, with no political space in core or periphery.

Continuing the Friedmann interpretation, as applied by Schmidt (1975), a better strategy would be "co-optation", whereby the counter-elites are drawn into the established structure of authority. Instead of flying in the face of the natural trends towards metropolitan concentration and a more integrated system, a more highly unified space-economy, polity and society would be created. Africans are steadily brought into more skilled and responsible jobs and wealth is thereby redistributed. Gradually some effective political power is given to the Blacks in urban areas as well as the Homelands, possibly leading to some form of multi-racial federation: the conventional liberal solution.

But there are two sides to the integration process. These are explained by Berghe (1967, 274) as follows:

> Participation of disparate ethnic groups in a common system of production is a crucial integrative factor in all African countries, and is one of the major factors which has held such a conflict-ridden society as South Africa together for so long. The utter dependence (at a starvation or near-starvation level) of the African masses on the "White" economy in South Africa has been one of the main inhibiting factors to such mass protest actions as general strikes. There is, of course, a reverse side to economic integration in South Africa. The more economic interdependence there is, the less feasible apartheid becomes. Two major elements of the social structure, namely the polity and the economy, pull in opposite directions, thereby creating rapidly mounting strains.

Now we come to the crux of the matter. The logical end to the process of integration is a transfer of power from elite to counter-elite, which means African control. This threatens not only the survival of the Whites and their position of privilege, but also the entire structure of the capitalist system on which the Whites depend. The extent of the threat of majority rule becomes the greater when it is appreciated that those who gain profits from the present arrangement of South African society include not only the indigenous white capitalists and some black (mainly Indian) businessmen enjoying the fruits of cheap labour, but also the shareholders of the various European and American corporations attracted to South Africa in recent years. Economic considerations and related class interests pervade the conflict between races and cultures in South Africa, as was argued above.

The strict Marxian interpretation of class conflict and revolution runs into difficulty in a society as complex as that in South Africa, however (Simons and Simons, 1969; Kuper, 1974, especially Appendix I). An alternative view is explained as follows by Berghe (1967, 267-8):

> Social classes in the Marxian sense of relationship to the means of production exist by definition, as they must in any capitalist country, but they are not meaningful social realities. Clearly, pigmentation, rather than ownership of land or capital, is the most significant criterion of status in South Africa. The attempt to salvage Marxian orthodoxy by identifying the Whites with the capitalists and the Africans with the proletariat is inacceptable because it does violence to the facts and is, at best, a grossly distorted oversimplification. Conversely, to lump White and non-White wage earners in one supposedly unified, class-conscious proletariat with common interests against the bourgeoisie is obviously nonsensical.

And according to Kuper (1974, 203):

> Economic exploitation, and an intimate relationship between economic and political power, may be almost universal. But there are some societies in which

the relationship to the means of production does not define the political struggle, and in which class conflict is not the source of revolutionary change.

A particular feature of South African society is that the white working class are the most ardent supporters of suppressive policies towards Blacks. To find a common class interest among the proletariat thus conflicts with the same sort of reality as in the USA, where the perceived economic threat of cheap black labour elicits reactionary and racist attitudes from white workers. The failure of the South African Communist Party to be effective in an apparently revolutionary situation must be attributed in part to its emphasis on a class struggle across racial divisions, where social cleavage is predominantly racial and militancy tends to be nationalistic (Kuper, 1974, 271). The interest of Africans is, for the most part, national liberation and not the overthrow of capitalism.

Nevertheless, the Marxian perspective has shed light on the nature of conflict in South Africa. The prosperity of the economy is dependent on the ease with which surplus value can be generated by black labour and appropriated by the capitalist class. The spatial structure of the *apartheid* society can be interpreted quite plausibly as facilitating the continuing supply of cheap and powerless labour—labour with an exchange value so far below its use value that a substantial surplus and high rate of exploitation is virtually guaranteed. Viewed in this way, *apartheid* is a necessary condition for the preservation of the existing economic order. Without it, an effective means of accumulating capital would cease to exist. The basis of conflict in South Africa's complex society is thus ultimately economic. As Kuper (1974, 269) recognizes:

> Plural societies are generally established by conquest, followed by the expropriation of resources, and the exploitation of labour. No doubt ideologies of racial difference, dehumanizing the subject peoples or reducing them to the status of objects, enter into the expression of pluralism. But peoples do not establish domination over each other because they are of different race, but in the pursuit of quite concrete interests in power and other resources.

As Adam (1971a, 21) stresses, the central shortcoming of the pluralist perspective is its failure to integrate ethnic conflict into the broader analysis of political economy.

Does this mean, then, that the conventional expression of conflict in South Africa in racial terms is false, or merely obfuscation designed to hide an underlying class conflict? Does it mean that, after all, the concerted action of an inter-racial proletariat is the most likely revolutionary change? In both cases the answer is—no. The reason for the apparent paradox is that, whatever the underlying economic class conflict, race is relevant if only because the situation is so often viewed in racial terms. Race conflict is part of the reality of South Africa, as lived by its own people and as interpreted by those outside. It is thus a contributor to the direction of change.

African nationalism is in fact a far more potent force for revolutionary change than inter-race working-class solidarity. As elsewhere in southern Africa (e.g. Angola) the struggle against capitalism may have to follow the overthrow of white rule. But it is clear that the true liberation of the African people is ultimately dependent on release from the exploitive system in which they are currently obliged to sell their labour. Social justice ultimately stems from society in action. While militant African nationalism is no guarantee of a just distribution of South Africa's very considerable wealth, perpetuation of the present economic system guarantees injustice.

10

The Geography of Social Well-being: The Case of the USA

In this chapter the focus shifts to a more descriptive approach. In South Africa, as in most other parts of the world, the range and quality of the numerical data available are inadequate for much empirical research on spatial variations in the human condition, broadly defined. Descriptions of the geography of well-being or development, if attempted, are generally far from complete. But in more "advanced" countries with well developed official statistics and other sources of information there is great scope for basic descriptive human geography guided by the general welfare concept. The United States provides a suitable case. This chapter shows how far such an approach may be taken, the kind of results that follow, and some of the problems posed.

10.1 Defining social well-being

The problem of defining the necessary ingredients of human well-being or the quality of life has been considered in earlier chapters. In our welfare formulation, it involves the specification of terms in a "commodity" social welfare function. The task is analogous to that of operationally defining the state of national development, as in Chapter 8, because we view development in the same broad sense as human well-being or life quality. However, in this chapter we will refer to the phenomenon under investigation as "social well-being", to be consistent with the earlier usage of this term in the research on which much of what follows is based (Smith, 1972a, 1973a). Whatever the label and the spatial context, our interest is in the totality of the human life experience—or as close to it as limitations of existing data and measurement devices permit.

To attempt a specific definition of social well-being requires some assumption as to the level of societal consensus. In any pluralistic society with conflicting sub-group aspirations there will be differences on many matters relating to who should get what where. Individuals within groups or as members of a more monolithic society will differ with respect to the composition of the "what"—the ingredients of the good life. The assumption here is that in the USA sufficient consensus exists to enable us to identify a general commodity SWF, specifying a relatively small number of conditions of major concern subject to the normative interpretation that a change in a given direction improves the level of welfare. We do not assume a societal consensus on the priorities to be attached to these conditions, so the weighting adopted for the purpose of aggregation of data into a single social indicator is arbitrary.

Of the various methods available to identify major societal concerns, the one adopted here involves recourse to "expert opinion". As was explained briefly in Chapter 7 (section 7.2), a body of American literature on contemporary social problems and the development of social indicators was examined, to reveal seven major criteria of social well-being. These are listed in Table 10.1, along with certain sub-headings to clarify their meaning. The better the conditions of a population with respect to these criteria, the higher the level of social well-being in the territory in question. A few general comments will help to explain the selection.

Table 10.1 General criteria of social well-being in the United States

I. *Income, wealth and employment*	V. *Social order (or disorganization)*
i. Income and wealth	i. Personal pathologies
ii. Employment status	ii. Family breakdown
iii. Income supplements	iii. Crime and delinquency
	vi. Public order and safety
II. *The living environment*	
i. Housing	VI. *Social belonging (alienation and*
ii. The neighborhood	*participation)*
iii. The physical environment	i. Democratic participation
	ii. Criminal justice
III. *Health*	iii. Segregation
i. Physical health	
ii. Mental health	VII. *Recreation and leisure*
	i. Recreation facilities
IV. *Education*	ii. Culture and the arts
i. Achievement	iii. Leisure available
ii. Duration and quality	

Source: Smith (1973a, 70).

Income, wealth and employment are important means of access not only to material goods but also, in the USA, to such things as health and education. Employment status (e.g. occupation and whether employed or out of work) is important because this affects income and also an individual's status and self-esteem. Income supplements paid as pensions or social security benefits can be significant additions to or substitutes for earned income and accumulated wealth.

The living environment can be viewed at different spatial scales. Housing is important as a source of shelter, comfort and social status; as "home" it performs basic protective and symbolic functions. Neighbourhood quality covers such questions as whether the immediate environment outside the home is attractive or ugly, safe or threatening. The broader physical environment includes air and water quality, noise, odour, and other aspects of pollution.

Health is obviously basic to human well-being. The subdivision into physical and mental is not clear-cut in a clinical sense, but recognizes a distinction between conditions related to physical survival or performance and those with more of a bearing on peace of mind and the functioning of intellectual faculties. Diet and food intake are included under health.

Education, like health, is important in itself as an aid to enjoyment of full human being. It is also relevant to access to employment and income, and also to political power.

Social order refers to lack of social disorganization threatening the functioning of individuals and groups. Pathological behaviour and the breakdown of basic social institutions such as the family are relevant here. Although crime is included, what we term social order goes well beyond the "law and order" issue to which Americans have attached particular importance in recent years.

Social belonging attempts to capture the degree to which people are able to play their full chosen part in society. Exclusion from participation can lead to alienation, undesirable in itself and also conducive to behaviour that threatens social stability. Equality of treatment under the law and lack of discrimination on the basis of race, sex and so on would be indicative of good performance on this criterion.

Recreation and leisure recognizes the importance of non-work activity, including access to opportunities and freedom to enjoy them. In practice, this is difficult to measure, not only because real access in a geographical sense is hard to establish but also because it is probably in recreation and leisure pursuits that people have greatest capacity to express varied personal tastes.

Our general definition of social well-being makes no claim to value-free objectivity. That this would be a contradiction should be apparent from earlier chapters. By no means all experts or ordinary Americans would agree that it captures the essence of life quality. However, it is sufficiently close to what matters most to most Americans to form a basis on which applied research can be initiated. We will use this definition as a guide to the empirical identification of patterns of social well-being at two different spatial scales—national and within the metropolis.

10.2 The national scale

The most convenient units of observation at the national scale are the forty-eight contiguous states. However, areas as large as this are subject in the extreme to the danger of the "ecological fallacy" of attributing average conditions to an entire population. Most of the states are heterogeneous in economic and social character and aggregate per capita data obviously hide internal variations, just as in the cross-national comparisons of Chapter 8. A special problem is that figures for many states are largely a reflection of a single city or metropolitan area. Nevertheless, state data do enable us to map out broad features of the national geography of social well-being—something totally ignored in all textbooks on the United States or North America.

Given the definition of social well-being in the previous section, the first problem is to select variables that can represent the major criteria and sub-headings at the state level. For each variable, measurements are required on an interval or ratio scale. Shortage of suitable data on certain conditions meant that the sub-headings in Table 10.1 had to be modified slightly, but with no significant distortion of the concept involved. Somewhat more serious, the seventh major criterion (recreation and leisure) could not be measured in any satisfactory way at the state level. But generally the variables selected (Table 10.2) provided an adequate if not perfect collective representation of the concept of social well-being built up on *a priori* grounds.

The choice of individual variables is explained fully elsewhere (Smith, 1973a, 80–84). All that is required here is to point out that in some cases measure of inputs had to be used in the absence of output data (examples are medical personnel per capita and educational expenditure) and that in others the actual observations are subject to what may be quite considerable error (e.g. narcotics addicts and incidence of venereal diseases). Variables have been given the normative interpretation indicated by the signs in the table. These are subject to reservations in a few cases, for example in mental health a large number of people in hospital might be bad because there are so many sick, good because they are being treated, or bad because they are not being cured and released.

Before proceeding further, it is worth considering the possibility that the single variable of monetary income might be an adequate surrogate for the general condition of social well-being. The empirical association is shown in Table 10.2, which lists the correlation coefficients (r) between each variable and per capita income (variable 1). Few of the other variables are accurately predicted by income: only eleven coefficients exceed 0·7 and a quarter of the r values are too low to be significant at $p=0·01$. There are some correlations which, according to the sign of the variable, should be the reverse of what they are if poor performance is associated with low income; the most obvious are in mental health, personal pathologies and crime, where low scores are often found in high-income states. Per capita income correlates quite high positively with some variables, particularly in income supplements, housing quality, health and education, but in view of the other findings income cannot be regarded as a satisfactory general state social indicator.

Identifying broad spatial variations in social well-being requires the derivation of a single general indicator or a restricted set of indicators measuring major dimensions of the concept. This necessitates the combination of data on different conditions. In other words, a SWF must be made specific, with respect to the contribution of each variable to the general welfare. This may be done by using a *standard score additive model* (Smith, 1973a, 85–90). Scores on each variable are standardized to zero mean and unit standard deviation (the Z-score transformation) and these are then summed for each state. The SWF thus becomes:

$$S_j = \sum_{i=1}^{m} Z_{ij} \qquad [10.1]$$

where $j(1, 2, \ldots, 48)$ are the contiguous states and $i(m=47)$ the set of variables listed in Table 10.2. This is equivalent to giving each variable

Table 10.2 Criteria of social well-being, and variables used in state analysis

Criteria and variables	Sign	r with 1
I. INCOME, WEALTH AND EMPLOYMENT		
i. *Income and wealth*		
1. Per capita annual income ($) 1968	+	1·00
2. Families with annual income less than $3,000 (per 1,000) 1959	−	−0·86
3. Total bank deposits per capita ($) 1968	+	0·59
ii. *Employment status*		
4. Public assistance recipients per 10,000 population 1964	−	−0·45
5. Union members per 1,000 non-agricultural employees 1966	+	0·56
6. White collar employees (per 1,000 of total) 1960	+	0·72
iii. *Income supplements*		
7. Average monthly benefit for retired workers ($) 1968	+	0·84
8. Average monthly AFDC payments per family ($) 1968	+	0·75
9. Average monthly aid to the disabled ($) 1968	+	0·65
10. Average monthly old age assistance ($) 1968	+	0·50
11. Average weekly state unemployment benefit ($) 1968	+	0·78
II. THE ENVIRONMENT		
i. *Housing*		
12. Median value of owner-occupied houses ($) 1960	+	0·85
13. Houses dilapidated or lacking complete plumbing (per 1,000) 1960	−	−0·84
14. Index of home equipment 1960	+	0·46
III. HEALTH		
i. *Physical health*		
15. Households with poor diets (per 1,000) 1965	−	−0·64
16. Infant deaths per 10,000 live births 1967	−	−0·63
17. Tuberculosis deaths per million population 1967	−	−0·22
18. Hospital expenses per patient day ($) 1965	+	0·29
ii. *Access to medical care*		
19. Hospital beds per 10,000 population 1967	+	0·36
20. Physicians per 10,000 population 1967	+	0·72
21. Dentists per 10,000 population 1967	+	0·73
22. Persons covered by hospital health insurance (per 1,000) 1965	+	0·50
iii. *Mental health*		
23. Residents in mental hospitals etc per 100,000 population 1966	−	0·38
24. Patient days in mental hospitals per 1,000 population 1965	−	0·33
25. Mental hospital expenditures per patient day ($) 1965	+	0·36

Criteria and variables	Sign	r with 1
IV. EDUCATION		
i. *Achievement*		
26. Illiterates per 1,000 population 1960	—	−0·51
27. Draftees failing armed services mental test (per 1,000) 1968	—	−0·54
ii. *Duration*		
28. Median school years completed 1960	+	0·58
29. Persons attended college per 1,000 population aged 25 or over 1960	+	0·56
iii. *Level of service*		
30. Pupils per teacher 1968	—	−0·29
31. Public school expenditures per pupil ($) 1967	+	0·76
V. SOCIAL ORDER (OR DISORGANIZATION)		
i. *Personal pathologies*		
32. Alcoholics per 10,000 adults 1970	—	0·71
33. Narcotics addicts per 10,000 population 1970	—	0·51
34. Gonorrhea cases per 100,000 population 1970	—	0·04
35. Syphilis cases per million population 1970	—	0·01
36. Suicides per million population 1967	—	0·20
ii. *Family breakdown*		
37. Divorces 1966 per 1,000 marriages 1968	—	−0·14
38. Husband and wife households (per 1,000 of total) 1966	+	−0·43
iii. *Crime and safety*		
39. Crimes of violence per 100,000 population 1969	—	0·34
40. Crimes against property per 10,000 population 1969	—	0·62
41. Motor vehicle accident deaths per million population 1967	—	−0·63
VI. SOCIAL BELONGING (ALIENATION AND PARTICIPATION)		
i. *Democratic participation*		
42. Eligible voters voting (%) 1964	+	0·50
43. Registered voters per 100 population of voting age 1968	+	0·15
ii. *Criminal justice*		
44. Jail inmates not convicted (%) 1970	—	0·01
45. Population per lawyer 1966 ·	—	−0·65
iii. *Racial segregation*		
46. Negroes in schools at least 95% negro 1968	—	−0·26
47. City residential segregation index 1960	—	−0·38

Note: Direction of indicators: a plus sign means that high values are "good" and low are "bad"; a minus sign means the reverse

Significance of correlations: $r = 0·28$ at $p = 0·05$; $r = 0·36$ at $p = 0·01$

Source of data: see Smith (1973a, 82–3).

the same weight in the SWF. For any specific sub-category, for example the six major criteria, a sub-indicator of the following form can be derived in the same way:

$$I_j = \sum_i^k Z_{ij} \qquad [10.2]$$

where k is the appropriate subset of m.

Some of the shortcomings of this type of SWF will be apparent from earlier chapters. Equal weighting is a value judgement for which there is no empirical support. The Z-score transformation and the additive relationship among variables assumes linear pay-offs no matter what level is attained; thus an increase of, say, 1·0 (in Z units) in a very high-performing territory would be equated with the same increase in an area of average performance. The assumption of constant marginal social utility implied might be avoided by non-linear transformations, but as the support for this would be intuitive the simpler linear function is preferred here. The equal-weighting assumption implies a negative-sloping $45°$ indifference line in the community's commodity space where any two criteria or variables are plotted in Z-scores along the axes.

Equal weighting can be abandoned if some measures of differential social preference are available. The SWF thus becomes:

$$S_j = \sum_{i=1}^m w_i Z_{ij} \qquad [10.3]$$

where w_i is a weighting parameter for the ith condition, perhaps derived empirically from some attitudinal survey. One experiment on the state

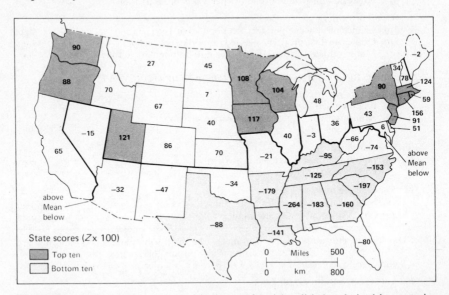

Figure 10.1 State scores on a general indicator of social well-being derived by summing the standard (Z) scores on the variables listed in Table 10.2. (*Source:* Smith, 1972b, Fig. 1.)

data, using weights elicited from a group of American students, produced a result which was very close to that with equal weightings (Spearman's rank $r = 0.977$). Experiments with a weighted index for British regions are reported in Smith (1977). Local variations in values or preferences could be accommodated by allowing w to vary spatially as W_{ij} (Smith, 1973a, 91), but no attempt has yet been made to take the necessary measurements.

Scores on a general state indicator derived from the standard score additive function in [10.1] are mapped in Figure 10.1. As they are expressed in Z units, states with positive scores are above average. The line on the map reveals a clear distinction between the northern and southern halves of the country. The lowest states show a marked geographical concentration in the south-east—the old Cotton Belt, now more appropriately referred to as the Southern Region of Social Deprivation. This general pattern is confirmed by two other similar studies (Wilson, 1969; Liu, 1973).

In Figure 10.2 the data are displayed as a continuous three-dimensional surface. This effectively portrays the quite regular inter-state variations, with social well-being rising from the trough corresponding with the Old South and reaching its highest levels in the eastern end of the Major Manufacturing Belt of the north-east, in the upper midwest, and in parts of the mountain and Pacific regions. The abstract concept of the *spatial well-being surface* introduced in Chapter 3 can thus be given an empirical identity.

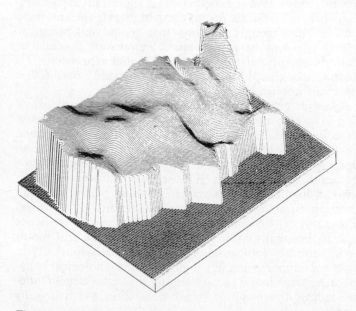

Figure 10.2 A social well-being surface for the USA, generated from the data in Figure 10.1. (SYMVU run by Mr M. N. Mametse, Dept. of Geography and Environmental Studies, University of the Witwatersrand.)

Table 10.3 Correlation (r) between state social indicators from the standard score additive model

Criteria	I	II	III	IV	V	VI	S
I. Income, wealth and employment	1·00						
II. Environment (housing)	0·91	1·00					
III. Health	0·76	0·85	1·00				
VI. Education	0·82	0·85	0·85	1·00			
V. Social order	−0·30	−0·24	−0·20	−0·12	1·00		
VI. Social belonging	0·67	0·67	0·75	0·79	0·11	1·00	
General social well-being (S)	0·88	0·90	0·88	0·92	0·05	0·87	1·00

Note: The criteria are as defined in Table 10.2.

Source: Smith (1973a, 89).

State indicators for the six major criteria of social well-being, derived from [10.2] above, show patterns very similar to Figures 10.1 and 10.2 in all cases but one (Smith, 1973a, 88). The exception is social order, with poor performance in the south-west and in certain northern states containing major cities (e.g. Illinois and New York), while the south-east has higher scores than on the other criteria. This is confirmed by correlations among the six sub-indicators and the general indicator (Table 10.3). Social order has a *negative* correlation with all but one of the other criteria and a very low positive r value with the sixth and with the general indicator; only one of the coefficients is significant at $p = 0·05$. All other coefficients in the table are positive and highly significant, none falling below 0·67. This strongly suggests that social well-being, as defined in Table 10.2, is a multi-dimensional phenomenon in which at least two conflicting elements exist with different spatial expressions. To rely on a single indicator clearly runs the risk of obscuring details that might have important implications.

Principal components analysis has been used to clarify the nature of social well-being as a geographically variable condition. Three major components were identified (Smith, 1973a, 93–5). The first was termed *General Socio-Economic Well-being* (explained variance: 38·65%) loading high on per capita income (0.94), most of the income-supplement variables, housing, health and education. The second was termed *Social Pathology* (13·74%), loading high on crime, personal pathologies and some of the alienation variables. The third has been tentatively identified as *Mental Health* (11·98%), being most closely associated with residence in mental hospitals, hospital expenditure, divorce, suicide and motor vehicle accidents (probably indicative of aggressive behaviour). Thus major concerns of contemporary society in deviant or pathological behaviour and social order were found to vary among the states largely independent of the leading dimension of social well-being which broadly reflects affluence.

As was explained in Chapter 8, the results of a principal components or factor analysis can be used to generate territorial indicators. This has been done in the present case. If I_j designates a component score in the jth state, the implicit SWF is:

$$I_j = \sum_{i=1}^{m} l_i Z_{ij} \qquad [\text{10.4}]$$

where l_i is the factor loading (i.e. r) with variable i. The resulting scores on the two leading components are mapped in Figure 10.3. Two indepen-

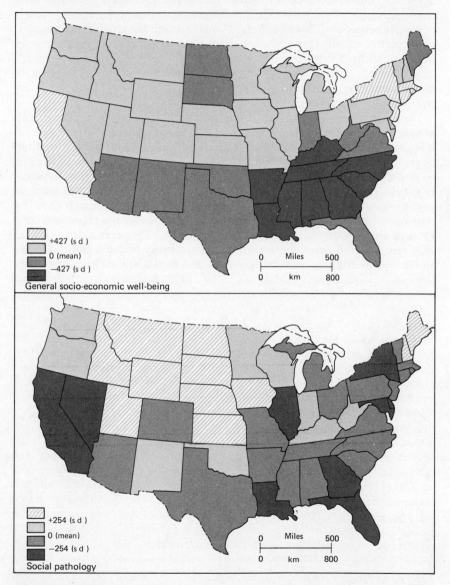

Figure 10.3 State scores on the two leading components of social well-being in the USA. (*Source:* Smith, 1973a, Fig. 7.3.) Note: sd = standard deviation.

dent patterns are revealed, that for general socio-economic well-being closely corresponding with the results of the first analysis (Figures 10.1 and 10.2) while the social pathology pattern largely reflects that of the social order criterion. The difference between the two can be illustrated by the changes in ranks of some states: New York is first (i.e. "best") on component 1 but last on component 2, California drops from 4th to 47th and Illinois from 10th to 44th. The major metropolitan states with their high general *average* affluence levels clearly experience high levels of social pathology. This does not, of course, mean that the affluent *individuals* are necessarily those whose behaviour is pathological, though it may be so for some conditions (e.g. alcoholism and certain stress-related illness). But the analysis clearly shows that *territories* with high aggregate performance on one dimension of social well-being can have very low performance on another.

Data for states can portray the national pattern of social well-being at only the broadest level of generality. But research at the inter-city level has produced similar results. *Affluence* and *Crime* have been identified as the two leading components in a restricted study of the hundred or so major metropolitan areas (Smith, 1973a, 112–18). There is no association between the general level of prosperity of a city and the level of crime—a counter-intuitive result confirmed by further research showing that other social and economic indicators are poor predictors of crime rates at this geographical scale (Smith, 1974c). Property crime can, in fact, rise with affluence, in time and space, simply because there is more to steal. The highest correlations with per capita income are for other

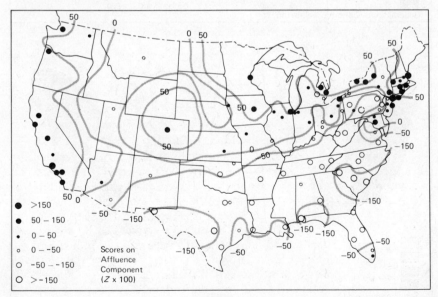

Figure 10.4 The performance of metropolitan areas on the affluence component of social well-being. Contours interpolated by SYMAP. (*Source:* based on Smith, 1974a, Fig. 7.)

measures of income, wealth and property, and with health (Smith, 1973c, 73). In a more comprehensive inter-city analysis Coughlin (1970) found median income and low-income families to be the best single indicators of "goal attainment", measured by sixty different variables, but income was a poor predictor of achievement with respect to physical planning goals (for a summary of Coughlin's study see Smith, 1973a, 108–12).

More detail may be added to our national picture of the geography of social well-being by mapping component scores for metropolitan areas. In Figure 10.4 scores on the affluence component are shown as proportional symbols. High positive scores are generally indicative of high per capita income, property tax, social security payments, retail rates and so on (Smith, 1973a, 115). The most affluent cities are concentrated in the Major Manufacturing Belt of the north-east and on the west coast, while the poorest cities are largely in the South. Contours have been inter-polated to suggest the form of the surface that these data represent, but the relatively few observations in the western half of the country means that a high degree of generalization is involved.

The level of well-being in smaller cities and in the countryside between the major metropolitan areas may be lower than the contours in Figure 10.4 imply. Berry (1968) has identified troughs in the inter-metropolitan peripheral zones, portrayed by traverses based on such variables as family income and school years completed. Examples are shown in Figure 10.5, as illustrations of the empirical identification of spatial well-being gradients.

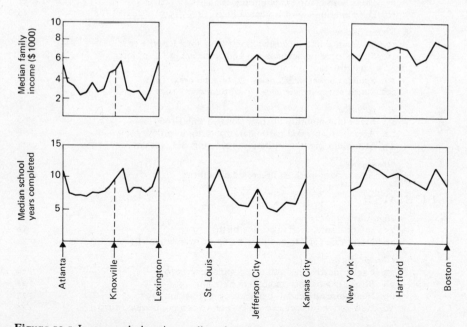

Figure 10.5 Income and education gradients between various American metropolitan areas. (*Source:* Berry, 1968, 20–21.)

Table 10.4 Criteria of social well-being and variables used in Tampa study

Criteria and variables	Sign	r with 1
I. ECONOMIC STATUS		
i. *Income*		
1. Income per capita ($) of persons 14 and over 1970	+	1·00
2. Families with income less than $3,000 (%) 1970	—	0·60
3. Families with income over $10,000 (%) 1970	+	0·93
4. Persons in families below poverty level (%) 1970	—	0·61
ii. *Employment*		
5. Unemployed persons (% total workforce) 1970	—	0·39
6. Persons aged 16–64 working less than 40 weeks (%) 1969	—	−0·35
7. White-collar workers (%) 1970	+	0·88
8. Blue-collar workers (%) 1970	—	0·54
iii. *Welfare*		
9. Families on AFDC program (%) October 1971	—	0·43
10. Persons aged 65 and over on Old Age Assistance (%) October 1971	—	0·50
II. ENVIRONMENT		
i. *Housing*		
11. Average value of owner-occupied units ($) 1970	+	0·88
12. Owner-occupied units valued less than $10,000 (%) 1970	—	0·56
13. Average monthly rental of rented units ($) 1970	+	0·76
14. Rented units with monthly rentals less than $60 (%) 1970	—	0·74
15. Units with complete plumbing facilities (%) 1970	+	0·53
16. Deteriorating and dilapidated houses (%) 1971	—	0·39
ii. *Streets and sewers*		
17. Streets needing reconstruction (% of total length) 1971	—	0·27
18. Streets needing scarification and resurfacing (% of total length) 1971	—	0·13
19. Sanitary sewer deficiencies (% of total area) 1971	—	0·01
20. Storm sewer deficiencies (% of total area) 1971	—	0·08
iii. *Air pollution*		
21. Maximum monthly dustfall (tons/sq mile) 1969	—	−0·09
22. Average suspended particulars 1969 (μgm/m/day) 1969	—	0·28
23. Maximum monthly sulfation 1969 (mg SO_3/100 cm²/day) 1969	—	−0·28
iv. *Open space*		
24. Area lacking park and recreation facilities (%) 1971	—	0·09
III. HEALTH		
i. *General mortality*		
25. Infant deaths (per 1,000 live births) 1970	—	0·18
26. Death rate (per 10,000 persons 65 or over) 1970	—	0·24
ii. *Chronic diseases*		
27. Cancer deaths (per 100,000 population) 1970	—	0·19
28. Stroke deaths (per 100,000 population) 1970	—	0·21
29. Heart disease deaths (per 100,000 population) 1970	—	0·17
30. New active tuberculosis cases (per 10,000 population) 1970	—	0·35

Criteria and variables	Sign	r with 1

IV. EDUCATION

  i. *Duration*
    31. Persons aged 18–24 with 4 or more years high school or
        college (%) 1970   +   0·62
    32. Persons over 25 with 8 years or less school (%) 1970   −   0·78
    33. Persons over 25 with 4 years high school (%) 1970   +   0·55
    34. Persons over 25 with 4 years college (%) 1970   +   0·87

V. SOCIAL ORDER (OR DISORGANIZATION)

  i. *Personal pathologies*
    35. Narcotic violations arrests (per 10,000 residents) 1971   −   0·22
    36. Venereal disease cases (per 10,000 population) 1970   −   0·46

  ii. *Family breakdown*
    37. Families with children, having husband and wife present
        (%) 1970   +   0·48
    38. Persons separated or divorced (% ever married) 1970   −   0·48

  iii. *Overcrowding*
    39. Dwellings with more than 1·0 person per room (%) 1970   −   0·68

  iv. *Public order and safety*
    40. Criminal violation arrests (per 1,000 residents) 1971   −   0·22
    41. Juvenile delinquency arrests (per 10,000 residents) 1971   −   0·32
    42. Accidental deaths (per 100,000 population) 1970   −   0·22

  v. *Delinquency*
    43. Juvenile delinquency arrests by residency (per 10,000
        population) 1971   −   0·47

VI. SOCIAL BELONGING (PARTICIPATION AND EQUALITY)

  i. *Democratic participation*
    44. Registered voters (% population 18 and over) 1971   +   0·48
    45. Eligible voters voting in mayoral election (%) 1971   +   0·05

  ii. *Equality*
    46. Racial distribution index 1970   −   0·38
    47. Income distribution index 1970   −   0·03

Note: A positive sign indicates high positive values are "good" and vice versa.
In calculating the r values, the signs on all negative variables were reversed so that
a positive correlation indicates a relationship in the direction anticipated by the sign
of the variable in question.

Sources of data: see Smith (1973a, 123–4) and Smith and Gray (1972).

How far such patterns would be replicated by data on other important aspects of life quality is difficult to say. But it could well be that the quality of environment, level of stress and so on improves with distance from the large city. Crime rates fall with city size (Richardson, 1973, 97–102) and the same is almost certainly true of other social pathologies such as drug abuse. How much weight these conditions should have in a social indicator, when compared with income for example, is an open question. But it might not require a very extreme value position to give them enough weight to reverse the slope of the gradients identified by Berry. Country or small-town life may be "better" overall than life in the metropolis, at least for most people. The revealed preference of the great majority for the core (or suburb) rather than the periphery is probably an imperfect indication of what people would choose if really free to satisfy themselves. The imperative of the economic system is that they live where employers choose to locate jobs. The actual substitution relationship between income and rural amenity may be such that the price of the latter in terms of the former is prohibitively high for most people. A city location maximizes their utility, within the constraints of the system within which they live and over which their control is minimal.

10.3 The city scale

Empirical relationships can, of course, change with geographical scale. States and cities comprise large aggregates of heterogeneous populations, for whom indicators based on average conditions may obscure as much as they reveal. Within the city, much more social homogeneity can be expected in the areal units for which data are compiled. We also get closer to the individual human being.

An attempt has been made to develop indicators of social well-being by census tracts in the city of Tampa, Florida (Smith and Gray, 1972; Smith, 1973a, ch. 9). The study was guided by the same general concept as in the state analysis above, though data availability required a somewhat different operational definition of the six criteria. In addition the change in spatial scale necessitated some modifications, especially under the environment heading. Table 10.4 lists the variables and their correlation with per capita income. Again, income is an inadequate general social indicator. It predicts occupational status, housing quality and education levels quite well, but general environmental quality, health, and most of the social disorganization and participation variables have low r values.

The data have been subjected to the same analysis as at the state level. A general composite social indicator has been generated via the standard score additive function. The results have been mapped (Figure 10.6) and also transformed into a surface (Figure 10.7). The city has a rather peculiar shape, with its CBD close to the bay and its southern suburbs surrounded on three sides by water. Nevertheless, the pit of deprivation in the inner city shows up clearly. Above it rise the well-being plateaus of the suburban areas.

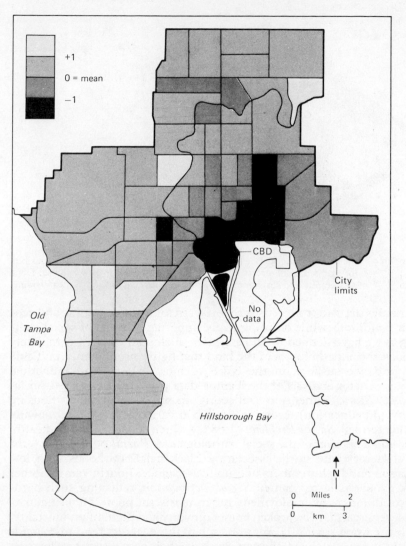

Figure 10.6 Variations in social well-being by census tracts in the city of Tampa, Florida, as measured by an indicator derived from the variables listed in Table 10.5. (*Source:* Smith, 1973a, Fig. 9.3.)

As at the inter-state level, a single composite indicator hides different dimensions of social well-being with different geographical expressions. The conventional view of the spatial differentiation of the city in the USA and other countries with similar cultures is of three major patterns relating respectively to socio-economic status, stage in life cycle and ethnicity. This is the common finding of various studies in factorial ecology, with the three leading factors or components appearing in this order (Berry and Horton, 1970, ch. 10). However, these studies are usually confined

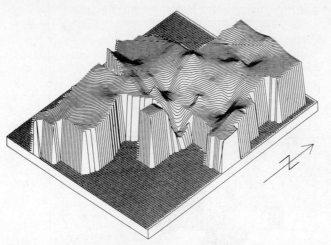

Figure 10.7 A social well-being surface for Tampa, Florida, generated from the social indicator mapped in Figure 10.6. (SYMVU run by Mr M. N. Mametse, Dept.
of Geography and Environmental Studies, University of the Witwatersrand.)

to variables derived from census reports, stressing demographic and economic conditions while omitting many important aspects of social well-
being as we have defined it. In particular, such studies often completely
overlook social pathologies of the kind that figure prominently in Table
10.4 (and, we suspect, in the SWF of most experts and individual
citizens). Factor analysis of the Tampa data placed the expected *Socio-
economic Status* dimension (reflecting income, occupation, housing
quality and education) second in explained variance (11·3%), following
a factor termed *Social Problems* (17·8%) which loaded high on health,
crime and a number of the social pathologies. A *Racial Segregation* (ethnicity) factor came third, associating black neighbourhoods with low
education and high numbers on public assistance. Fourth came another
social problems factor named *Social Deprivation*, reflecting such hard-
core conditions as unemployment, tuberculosis, the poorest housing, narcotics, venereal disease, broken homes, poverty and high infant mortality.
While the worst parts of Tampa on each of these factors tend to coincide
with the inner-city slums, the patterns have their own distinctive features
(Smith, 1973a, 130–1).

The results thus differ from those of the more conventional studies.
The relationship between affluence and social problems at the neighbourhood level is shown to be more complex than is often assumed. However,
too much should not be made of the result of this single study, for Tampa
is atypical from an ethnic point of view (it has a large Latin community)
and there are doubts as to the accuracy of some of the data provided
by local agencies purely as a by-product of their administrative process.
Much more research is needed before intra-city relationships can be clarified. Until then, the textbook generalization of factorial ecology should
be treated with caution.

As a second city example, we may examine briefly the case of Atlanta, Georgia, introduced in Chapter 1. Figure 1.5 showed a high degree of spatial income inequality, closely mirrored by the intra-city pattern of life quality. In this typically segregated southern city, quality of life was shown to be closely associated with the racial composition of population by census tracts. The index developed by Bederman (1974) to measure quality of life in Atlanta is based on a similar but narrower concept to that applied in Tampa. Five criteria were identified and eleven variables chosen to measure them (Table 10.5). To arrive at a general index, each observation on each variable was transformed into deviations from a "base value" for the city as a whole. These scores were then aggregated so as to give each of the five criteria the same weight in the final index. This procedure, set out formally in Bederman (1974, 31), is similar to the standard score additive model in expression [10.2] above. The implied SWF is:

$$S_j = \sum_{}^{5} F_i \qquad [10.5]$$

where F_j is a composite score on each of the five criteria for the jth census tract, each derived from

$$F_j = \frac{100}{n} \sum_{}^{n} Q_j \qquad [10.6]$$

where Q is the standardized score on a variable and n is the number of variables measuring the criterion in question. The final index is such that a value of 0 would arise in a tract with figures conforming exactly to the base values for the city as a whole.

Table 10.5 Variables used to generate a quality of life index for Atlanta census tracts

Variable	Base value	Sign
Health factor		
Infant mortality (1968, 1969, 1970 average)	24·7	−
Public order factor		
Aggravated assaults per 1,000 people	2·4	−
Burglaries per 1,000 housing units	26·4	−
Housing quality factor		
% of housing units lacking all or some plumbing	2·3	−
Median value of specified owner-occupied housing units ($)	17,100	+
Median rent of specified renter-occupied units ($)	82	+
Socio-economic factor		
Median family income ($)	7,696	+
% of families with female as head	21·6	−
% of total population 15 years and under and 65 years and older	44·1	−
Density factor		
Population density per acre	6·8	−
% of occupied units in which the average room occupance is greater than 1·0	11·0	−

Source: Bederman (1974, 30).

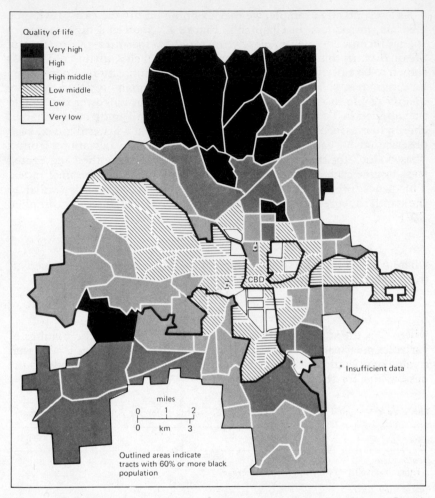

Figure 10.8 Variations in the "quality of life" among census tracts in Atlanta, Georgia, using a composite indicator derived from the variables listed in Table 10.5. (*Source:* Bederman, 1974, Fig. 2.)

The results are mapped in Figure 10.8. As in Tampa, distinct, relatively homogeneous zones are identified, bearing some resemblance to the sector model of urban spatial structure to which reference is made in most urban geography textbooks. The sector dominating the Atlanta map is one of low life quality extending north-westwards from the inner slums just south of the CBD. That this sector has a predominantly black population is shown by the heavy line on the map, enclosing tracts with 60 per cent or more Blacks. The correspondence between life quality (or social well-being) and racial composition is summarized graphically in Figure 10.9. The scatter of dots representing individual census tracts shows three important features: (1) most tracts are almost exclusively

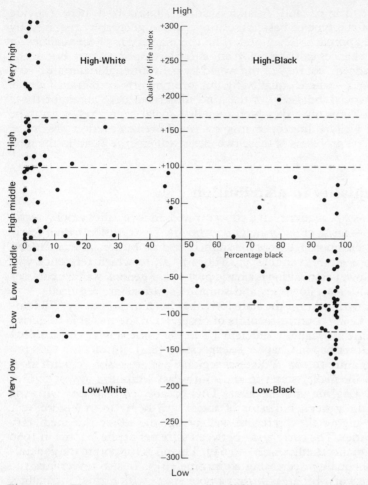

Figure 10.9 The relationship between quality of life and racial composition by census tracts in Atlanta, Georgia. (*Source:* Bederman, 1974, Fig. 3.)

white or black, i.e. the city is highly segregated residentially according to race; (2) both the black and the white tracts display considerable variations in life quality as measured up the vertical axis; (3) most white tracts have above-average life quality while most black tracts are below average. A similar result emerged from a study of Gainesville in Florida (Dickinson, Gray and Smith, 1972). What is described is a sharply bi-polar society, in which race closely determines the general level of well-being of groups of people aggregated on a neighbourhood basis. Statistically, the relationship between the racial composition of a tract in Atlanta and its quality of life according to the six classes recognized in Figure 10.8 is significant at $p = 0.001$, i.e. it would occur by chance less than once in a thousand.

Both the Tampa and Atlanta studies summarized here provide examples of the type of basic descriptive urban geography required by the welfare approach. They underline the magnitude of inequalities in human life chances existing not in an underdeveloped country but in the most "advanced" country of the world by conventional materialist-economic criteria—where equality figures prominently in national ideals. Territorial social indicators of the kind illustrated here highlight those parts of the cities towards which remedial social programmes must be directed if welfare improvements by the Lorenz criterion are to be achieved. The problems of these two cities will emerge again in the next chapter.

10.4 Inequality in distribution

The previous two sections have concentrated on inequality among territorial units—states, cities or neighbourhoods. Distribution *within* territories has been ignored, except for an income distribution index included in the Tampa study (variable 47, Table 10.4), to which reference will be made below. Distribution is a basic part of our general welfare concept at all spatial scales, however, and some illustrations are required.

Income distribution at the state level, has been measured by Williamson (1965). Using counties as units of observation, he was able to derive a state income inequality coefficient V_w in the same way as the national coefficient described in Chapter 8, expression [8.4]. Results for 1960 are mapped in Figure 10.10a. A distinct regional pattern is shown, with most of the high-inequality states in the south-east while the lowest figures are in New England and the west. This broadly corresponds with the pattern of the general indicator of social well-being from Figure 10.1 above: the higher the aggregate well-being, the lower the inequality among counties. The correlation between state per capita income in 1960 and the inequality coefficient is -0.687. This adds support to the generalization of inequality decreasing as income rises. It also underlines the plight of the worst-off areas within a poor state: with greater inequality, the poorest counties will be poorer relative to their state average than in the richer states with less internal income variations.

The level of living of the poor will depend to some extent on the degree of income redistribution achieved through taxation and the provision of social services. Booms and Halldorson (1973) have calculated an index of net redistributive impact in each state, measuring the ratio of public expenditure benefits to tax burdens for people in the lowest income classes. The results (Figure 10.10b) show a market tendency for less redistribution in southern and upper-midwestern states than in the north-east and west. The index is highest in high-income states ($r = 0.65$ with median income) and low where there is relatively great inequality ($r = -0.43$ with Gini coefficient and -0.56 with proportion of incomes under \$3,000). The spatial pattern of redistribution thus reflects the ability to pay in the richer states instead of the needs of the poor in the poorest states, a fundamental failing of America's federal political

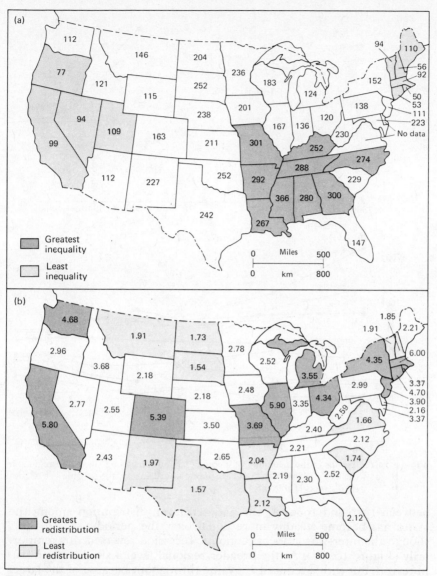

Figure 10.10 Two views of inequality among American states: a. index of inequality in income distribution by counties 1960; b. index of income redistribution via taxation and the provision of services. (*Sources:* a. Williamson, 1965, Table 4a; b. Booms and Halldorson, 1973, Table 3.)

structure. Similarly, welfare payments in cities are much lower in the poor South than elsewhere. *National* redistributive policies are required to accomplish any major impact on inter-area inequality.

Williamson (1965) also provides some historical perspective on income inequality. Most states showed a reduction in V_w on a county basis

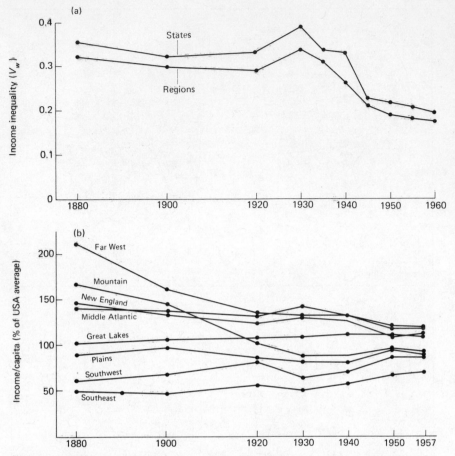

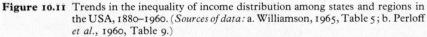

Figure 10.11 Trends in the inequality of income distribution among states and regions in the USA, 1880–1960. (*Sources of data:* a. Williamson, 1965, Table 5; b. Perloff *et al.*, 1960, Table 9.)

between 1950 and 1960. At the national level, distribution among the states has become steadily more equal over the period 1880 to 1960, though the inter-war years of economic recession reversed this temporarily (Figure 10.11a). At the broader regional level a similar trend was observed, but with a reduced V_w value throughout because of the larger territorial units of observation. Deviations of individual regions from the national average income per capita, calculated by Perloff *et al.* (1960, 27), show the same convergence tendencies (Figure 10.11b): in 1880 the ratio of highest regional per capita income (Far West) to lowest (Southeast) was 1 : 4·2 whereas in 1957 this had been reduced to 1 : 1·7. These observations provide support for the hypothesis of convergence in regional income levels at advanced stages of economic development. They also show that the simple view of a relatively rich industrial heartland and poorer periphery does not hold historically in the United States.

In the latter part of the nineteenth century it was the peripheral regions of the Rocky Mountains and Far West that had the highest per capita incomes; the poorest regions have been the predominantly agricultural Plains and Southwest, with the lowest income levels of all in the South-east with until recently an economy resembling the plantation-and-sub-sistence dualism of colonial countries.

Two cases illustrating inequality within cities may be examined briefly. The first involves *intra*-community distribution. In Tampa, like any other city, each neighbourhood (i.e. census tract for operational purposes) has its own internal distribution of income. An index of income distribu-tion has been calculated for each tract, from census data on the proportion of families in each of fifteen income classes. The $9,000–9,999 class, which includes the national average, is considered the "norm"; the index measures the extent of the local departures from this. It is calculated as follows:

$$I = \sum_{i=1}^{15} P_i w_i$$

where I is the index of income distribution in a given tract

           P_i is the proportion of all families in income class i (1, 2, ..., 15)

and w_i is a weight arrived at by taking the difference between the mid-class value of the class i and the mid-class value of the norm class (i.e. 9,500) and dividing by 1,000.

The resulting index falls on a scale from 0 to about 2,400, though it can be transformed to a more convenient scale if necessary. The higher the value of I, the greater the inequality.

Tract scores on this index are mapped in Figure 10.12. For compari-son, per capita income (Z-scores) is shown beside it. Although the areas with the greatest income inequality tend to be the richest neighbourhoods where most families are well above the norm, poor neighbourhoods can also show up with quite high indexes because most of their families are below the norm. So the two maps differ considerably; the correlation ($r = 0.03$) between distribution inequality and per capita income is very low. The use of departures from a general norm rather than from the individual tract norms as a measure of inequality is a value judgement, which implies that overall equality is desirable rather than equality within unequal neighbourhoods. This is an example of an index developed with a particular conception of equity in mind.

The second case illustrates the more conventional measurement of dis-tribution using the Gini coefficient and Lorenz curve. Data on people receiving public assistance, infants dying before the age of one and per-sons over 25 years of age not graduating from high school have been ana-lysed for six major subdivisions of San Diego, California. The extent to which these conditions are unequally distributed is shown in Table 10.6. This lists the ratios of advantage, calculated by dividing the percentage of total city population (or births, or people over 25) in the division in question by its proportion of total public assistance recipients (or infant

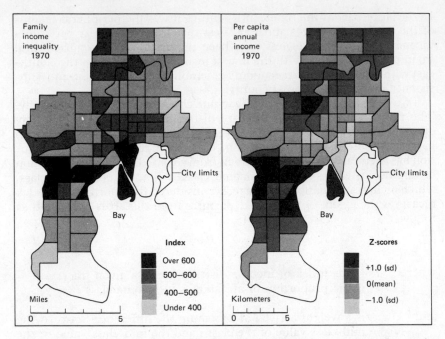

Figure 10.12 A comparison between the spatial pattern of income inequality and per capita income in Tampa, Florida. (*Source of data:* Smith and Gray, 1972.)

deaths, or high school non-graduates). The higher the ratio, the more advantaged the division. In general the coastal strip, the Kearny Mesa and the new northern suburbs are the advantaged areas, central and south San Diego being those most disadvantaged.

Table 10.6 Ratios of advantage in distribution for major subdivisions of San Diego, California

Division	Population on public assistance 1972	Infant deaths 1969–71	Persons over 25 not high school graduates 1970
Central	0·52	0·96	0·66
Coastal	2·56	1·33	1·56
Eastern	0·80	0·91	0·94
Kearney Mesa	2·13	1·02	1·32
North San Diego	6·29	1·24	2·44
South San Diego	0·66	0·93	0·75
Gini Coefficient (0 to 100)	25·9	4·0	13·4

Source of data: Ontell (1973, Tables 17, 20 and 72).

Note: A ratio of 1·0 would indicate a division experiencing a condition in exact proportion to population at risk. The higher the ratio above unity, the more advantaged the division.

The ranges in the ratios of advantage give a first clue to the fact that the degree of inequality differs among the three conditions. Gini coefficients confirm that people on public assistance are more unequally distributed in relation to the population at large than persons without a high school education. Infant deaths are the most equally distributed. Lorenz curves show the situation graphically (Figure 10.13).

In Chapter 6 it was suggested that the Lorenz criterion provided a

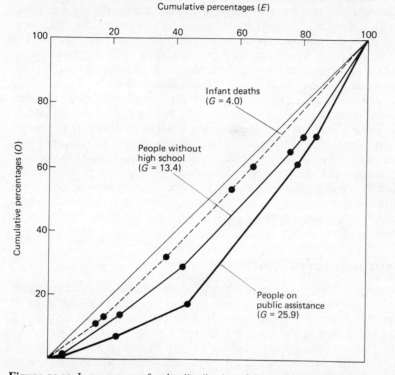

Figure 10.13 Lorenz curves for the distribution of three social conditions among six areal subdivisions of San Diego, California. Cumulative percentages expected (*E*) are those for total population, total births and total over 25, observed (*O*) are population on public assistance, infant deaths and people not graduating from high school. (*Source of data:* Ontell, 1973).

strong if not compulsive basis for welfare evaluations. Applying this to San Diego, we could say that the spatial distribution of infant health is *better* than that for education, both of which are *better* than the distribution of capacity for economic self-support.

The same criterion could be used to evaluate change over time. For example, the Gini coefficient for infant mortality in 1960–62 was 5·78 compared with 4·04 in 1969–71, indicating a distributional improvement, i.e. greater spatial equality. However, the six subdivisions used are rather large for the purpose of making such judgements. The distribution of infant deaths among thirty-four smaller sub-areas of the city shows virtu-

ally no change between 1960–62 ($G=11\cdot46$) and 1969–71 ($G=11\cdot42$)—
a reminder of the sensitivity of this coefficient to territorial aggregation.
While infant mortality for the city as a whole has been reduced from
25·4 per 1,000 live births to 18·6, local extremes still exist. The 1969 rate
in La Jolla, where family income averaged $22,000 in 1969, was only 5·8,
compared with 36·8 in a section of south-east San Diego with an average
family income of $7,000. There have been improvements in some low-
income areas, but deteriorations in others. Differences among economic
groups have strong racial overtones: infant mortality for Blacks is 31 compared with 17 for others (Ontell, 1973, 41). Thus we cannot find clear
evidence for a general improvement in the infant mortality figure. On
average the people of San Diego are better off, but a Lorenz improvement
is uncertain and there may well have been a deterioration by the Pareto
criterion because some areas are worse off than before.

Possible avenues along which this kind of research might be extended
include the measurement of actual distributions against specific equity
criteria. This would involve determining criteria of distributive justice
on the lines suggested in Chapter 6, and calculating the distribution that
should be found if the criteria are fulfilled. Ethical questions arising here
make this approach difficult, of course, but it is one that must be faced
if judging distributions as just or unjust is to become more than a question
of arithmetic equality. If we are to deal with welfare in its full sense,
we must explicitly incorporate equity of distribution in territorial social
indicators.

10.5 Some interpretations

Research into welfare geography in the USA has not yet reached the point
of definitive explanations. Description seems enough of a challenge at
the moment. However, some informal interpretations may be offered
briefly, guided by the theory at our disposal.

Welfare theory requires that we look to both the social production process and the values embedded in the economic system determining what
is produced and how it is distributed. We may not be in a position to
identify actual social production functions of the kind discussed in earlier
chapters, but some empirical relationships may give a clue to the conditions influencing local levels of well-being. Although not accounting for
everything by a long way, income is clearly the major determinant of
the dimension of well-being that includes environmental quality, education and health as well as more material aspects of living standards. At
the macro spatial level, per capita income will tend to be high in areas
producing goods and services in high demand and thus paying relatively
high wages and dividends (in so far as the latter are retained locally).
In the USA average wages of production workers in manufacturing in
some northern states are twice that in the south. Areas of economic decline can be expected to have low levels of well-being by virtue of the
unemployment and loss of income created as entrepreneurs move out,
writing off their fixed capital and transferring their funds and skills to

more profitable activities and locations. Labour tends to be less mobile than enterprise and money; people unable or unwilling to seek employment elsewhere are left behind in the deepening troughs of social deprivation exemplified by Appalachia.

As the national economy becomes steadily more highly focused on the major cities as centres of control (Pred, 1975), the peripheral regions are at an increasing disadvantage with respect to the maintenance of living standards. Local levels of well-being may be some function of proximity to the main cities, within which economic decision-making is increasingly concentrated. At the regional level spatial variations in affluence may therefore be seen as a fairly predictable consequence of differences in comparative economic advantage in a metropolis-orientated competitive system, where factors of production vary in their mobility and where there is no institutional mechanism to ensure equal access to social services. With respect to private production the nation may be close to its social production frontier, but in services such as health and education there are considerable locational inefficiencies and great inequities in distribution. It seems certain that the general welfare by such indicators as educational attainment and health levels (e.g. infant mortality) could be considerably improved by spatial reallocations of investment favouring places with inferior services.

At the micro spatial level, within the individual city, what we have termed "general socio-economic well-being" is subject to extreme spatial variations. A steep gradient rising from the poverty pit of the inner city to the peaks of affluence in the outer suburbs is a repetitive feature of the American metropolis. In making their residential choices people arrange themselves into relatively homogeneous income or status groups, geographical differentiation being further promoted by the operation of the real-estate market, the creation of estates or subdivisions catering for one income group and the use of zoning to maintain class or race exclusiveness in the suburbs. As groups within the population compete for shares of the social surplus generated in the city, the well-off neighbourhoods are at an advantage for their wealth brings political power. Cox (1973) provides a full discussion of the implications of this process, theoretical dimensions of which were analysed in Chapter 5. The middle class are able to avoid much of the social cost of generating the surplus, which has to be met increasingly by the central city areas (as opposed to the often politically autonomous suburbs) from their often decreasing tax bases. The location of urban services and other facilities tends to favour the middle class who have the money and power, rather than the poor who have the greatest need. Much public expenditure is regressive, in the sense that it involves a *de facto* redistribution of wealth from poor to rich. "It is thus quite possible that the poverty-stricken inner-cities are supporting the affluent suburbs rather than the other way round" (Harvey, 1972c, 28).

Bunge (1974) has distinguished between an outer "city of superfluity", an inner "city of death" (e.g. high infant mortality and road accidents to children) and an intermediate "city of need", as an alternative to the conventional concentric-zone pattern of the American city. Money generated in the inner city, at great social cost to local residents, is transferred across the working-class residential areas to the wealthy suburbs, in the form of business profits, rent and so on. This might be interpreted as the spatial transfer of surplus value from inner-city workers to the suburban capitalists and bourgeoisie. The present inter-community distribution of real income within the American city can be socially just only if it is right that the individual gets what he or she can earn in the marketplace, within a system where wealth and power facilitate redistribution in favour of the rich and enable them to escape some of the ill-being generated along with the well-being.

The second ("pathology") dimension of well-being is largely reflected in the problems of the big city—in the social deprivation and degradation of the urban under-class. Although at the inter-state and inter-city levels the magnitude of the social pathology indicator is not well predicted by racial composition (Smith, 1973a, chs. 6 and 7), at the more local level there is a fairly close coincidence between concentrations of Blacks (and other dark-skinned minorities), poverty and personal pathologies such as crime, family breakdown and drug abuse. The traditional discrimination accompanied by restriction of educational and employment opportunities for Blacks is an obvious explanation. The lack of geographical mobility for Blacks within the city promotes extreme spatial concentration of social pathology. Empirically, there seems to be a fairly clear set of interrelated conditions, with their roots in poverty and social exclusion, predisposing a neighbourhood to low performance on this dimension. Behind it all is an economic system in which vast resources can be allocated to space exploration and sophisticated weapons, while basic needs for health care, education and employment are denied to millions of people for whom the economy cannot provide adequately remunerated work.

The third ("mental health") dimension of social well-being, tentatively identified at the inter-state level and also possibly suggested within the city, raises some interesting questions. Poor performance on this condition appears to be related to a high proportion of transients in the population; the geographical pattern by states corresponds quite closely with that of the proportion of people who moved their homes between 1965 and 1970 (Figure 10.14). The association of certain social pathologies or symptoms of social disorganization with population instability is well known—the immigrant ghettos of the American city in the earlier years of this century are a classic case—but what seems to be emerging now is a different set of pathologies disproportionately afflicting the mobile, affluent and achievement-oriented middle class. Packard (1972) reminds us that mobility is often associated with both physical and mental illness. He suggests that mobility fosters the "nomadic" values of hedonism and a tendency to live for the moment; people become more aggressive when they are in anonymous roles and increasingly indifferent to close personal associations and group membership. The predominance of such conditions as alcoholism, suicide, divorce and stress-induced illness (physical

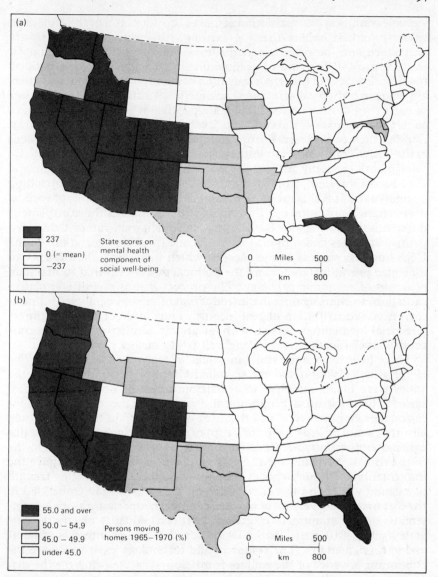

Figure 10.14 The pattern of a "mental health" component of social well-being (high positive is "bad") compared with that of population mobility. (*Sources of data:* a. Smith, 1973a, Table 7.7; b. US *Census of Population,* 1970.)

and mental) among the economically *advantaged* groups should perhaps be taken as a further warning signal that all is not well with the affluent society. As was suggested earlier in this book, we may be failing to count the disutilities along with the more obvious benefits of economic growth, thus mistaking *net* social regress for progress.

Turning from the production of well-being or real income as a spatially variable condition to distribution requires consideration of the American value system. It is here that the existing distributive mechanisms are sanctioned and the resulting inequalities condoned if not always positively approved. Striving to become unequal or advantaged is basic to the American way of life; the acquisition of money is the way this is generally achieved. High value is placed on individual initiative or being master of one's own destiny and welfare-state provisions of the kind that have come close to equalizing access to such services as medical care and education in much of Western Europe are poorly developed or non-existent in the USA. Traditional values that decry any "interference" with *laissez faire* in both economy and society are reinforced by the mass media and the education system, which largely serve the interests of the controlling business elite. It is this group that has most to lose from a shift of societal preferences away from the Protestant work ethic and the conspicuous differentiation of the successful, towards equalitarian rather than competitive attitudes and support for "socialistic" welfare legislation. In the USA business success brings wealth, which buys both the capacity to influence prevailing values and the political power required to maintain positions of economic privilege. The process is thus one of cumulative causation, working against the introduction of effective policies for non-regressive redistribution of real income. Thus interpersonal and inter-territorial inequalities persist, without greatly conflicting with the concepts of social justice held by the well-to-do majority.

There have been some shifts in values in recent years, however. The civil rights legislation and the so-called Great Society measures of the 1960s were major attempts to redistribute well-being in its broadest sense. This took on a geographical aspect with the programmes for regional economic revival and the "war on poverty" in the cities. There also appears to be growing public support for the principal of equal educational opportunity irrespective of place of residence, though the Supreme Court has declined to make a decision that would require the implementation of such a policy. But opposing these trends is the strength of existing values and the distributive mechanisms deeply embedded in the corporate-state version of modern capitalism, operating as major constraints on the attainment of greater territorial equality or equity. The state itself is little more than a facilitator of capitalist interests at home and in foreign affairs. The resources and technology exist to ensure the continuing advance of the welfare frontier, even accounting for the disutilities, but until or unless there is a major shift in the national priorities existing inequalities are likely to persist.

As in South Africa, such a shift is not likely to take the form of a unified proletariat mobilizing to overthrow the exploitive capitalist class. Many aspects of American life exemplify the Marxian critique of capitalism, including not only the domination of the indigenous working class by business interests but also the neo-colonialist activities in the underdeveloped world referred to in Chapter 8. But as in South Africa, race complicates the class structure. By some recent estimates, half the black population of the United States is now "middle class", with a growing number of entrepreneurs. Yet millions of Blacks still live in poverty, with working-class Whites in northern cities as well as in the South often opposing moves towards improved education and job opportunities for Blacks. While in South Africa the black proletariat is large enough radically to change society on its own, the American under-class is in a minority and has much less potential power.

There is a more fundamental reason than racial pluralism for not anticipating radical social change in America, however. This is that the working class, black as well as white, are usually supporters of the capitalist system. In part this can be explained by the high material living standards provided by the economic efficiency of capitalism built on a rich resource base. But it is also an outcome of the power of the ruling business classes to influence general societal attitudes and values. This helps to explain the lack of compelling support for modern welfare-state programmes, such as a national health service, that are taken for granted in other "advanced" industrial nations. The most impressive achievement of American capitalism may well be its capacity to maintain a contented and compliant proletariat to whom revolutionary rhetoric is anathema and likely to remain so as long as a major economic catastrophe is avoided.

11

Location and Allocation Problems: What Should Go Where

Changes in areal distribution of the goods and bads on which human well-being depends seldom occur in a revolutionary manner. More often this takes place gradually, as a result of a succession of minor spatial reorganizations. A new motorway is constructed, a factory relocated, a hospital opened, a pattern of police patrol altered—these and many similar events of day-to-day change in the private and public sectors all contribute to the geographical redistribution of human well-being. This is how most modern societies function, with individual and institutional behaviour guided to varying degrees by some general planning strategy. As each location decision is made, some people in some places gain while others lose. Yet, as was stressed earlier in this book, such decisions are seldom evaluated with specific reference to their spatial redistributive impact.

This chapter brings the discussion down to the level of the individual location decision or planning project. A series of cases demonstrate the application of the general welfare approach to location/allocation problems, via some of the techniques introduced in earlier chapters. Together, they should show that the spatial perspective has a distinctive contribution to make to the field of planning as a redistrubutive activity. In particular, the question of access to sources of human need or want satisfaction stresses the importance of location and distance. But as we proceed through these cases we will see that the geographical point of view does not hold the key to all that matters, even in the specifically spatial differentiation of human life chances. The broader structure of society in all its dimensions continually constrains what can be achieved by spatial reorganization alone.

11.1 Location of industry

We begin with perhaps the best-known location problem in human geography—where to set up a factory. Industrial location is one of the most fully developed branches of modern human geography, with an extensive body of theory and many operational models to guide plant site selection (Smith, 1971). Industrial location analysis can provide guidance on a wide range of problems where it is required to satisfy some efficiency objective such as minimizing operating costs (e.g. section 11.4 below).

The case to be described here is a simple application of *comparative-*

cost analysis. It is derived from work of a leading American plant location consultant (Fantus Company, 1962; Smith, 1971, 320–26). The problem is to determine which of twelve Canadian cities would be the best location for a firm manufacturing small electronic devices, by the criterion of minimizing annual spatially variable operating costs for a given volume of output. The relevant input cost items are divided into five main categories—labour, freight, occupancy, taxes and utilities.

The evaluation of labour costs was confined to wage earners, on the assumption that the salaries of managerial personnel do not vary significantly with location. The likely wage bill in each city was established from published data and on-the-spot inquiries. Calculation of fringe benefits proved to be particularly important, as they comprise about 20 per cent of total labour costs. The calculations were made on the assumption of a labour force of 140, divided into five occupations.

Freight costs include inbound and outbound items. The production process requires five materials—steel strip, laminated plastic sheets, screw machine parts, brass and copper strip and aluminium strip. But as the last two are sold on the basis of equal delivered price irrespective of location they can be disregarded. Freight costs on the required quantity of the other three were calculated for each city, from the known sources of supply. Outbound freight costs were worked out on the basis of sales estimates for seventeen major Canadian cities and the freight rates from each possible location to each of these markets.

Occupancy costs consist of expenditure on acquisition of land, construction of premises, financing and the maintenance of the property. All these were subject to some variation among the twelve cities. Municipal and provincial taxes also varied. The utilities item included the cost of known quantities of electric power, fuel, water and sewage disposal.

The cost of the five major items in each city is listed in Table 11.1.

Table 11.1 Annual spatially variable operating costs for an electronics firm in twelve Canadian cities ($1,000)

City	Cost categories					Annual operating cost
	Labour	Freight	Occupancy	Taxes	Utilities	
Winnipeg	636	24	43	21	18	741
Brandon	592	30	38	15	21	695
Portage la Prairie	561	27	38	14	21	661
Montreal	691	22	66	37	15	830
Toronto	759	19	61	22	18	879
Vancouver	798	49	50	28	19	945
Hamilton	856	19	51	37	14	977
Calgary	768	30	43	21	19	881
Edmonton	738	31	48	21	20	857
Windsor	874	24	47	35	14	994
Regina	751	31	40	21	23	866
Saskatoon	673	38	40	21	19	790

Source of data: Fantus Company (1962); Smith (1971, Table 17.11). Figures rounded to nearest $1,000.

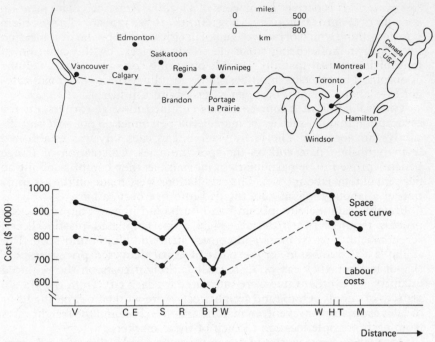

Figure 11.1 Space cost curve for the manufacture of electronic devices in Canada. (*Source of data:* Table 11.1.)

Summing them gives total spatially variable operating costs. The least-cost location is Portage la Prairie, to the west of Winnipeg in Manitoba. The saving over Brandon, its closest rival, is about $35,000. The highest costs are in Windsor, where they exceed Portage la Prairie by about $330,000. Such differences are important for a business with an estimated pre-tax net revenue of about a quarter of a million dollars. Spatial variations in costs are enough to make the difference between profit and loss.

In Figure 11.1 cost differences are depicted as a space cost curve of the type introduced in Chapter 4. The twelve locations in question come close to providing a traverse across Canada; in the bottom part of the figure costs are plotted against distance as though these places formed a linear section through a space cost surface. The data reveal a trough of relatively low spatially variable costs in the prairies, with higher figures in the east (particularly Ontario) and in the west. As Table 11.1 shows, the total cost level is very much dependent on the wage bill as the major item of expenditure; labour costs closely mirror the form of the total space cost curve.

To interpolate a cost surface data for these twelve locations would be impossible. But with more control points this concept can be given an operational identity. Figure 11.2 illustrates a surface of total spatially variable costs in the USA, for a firm manufacturing electronic equipment. This incorporates data on various cost items for 57 city locations (Smith,

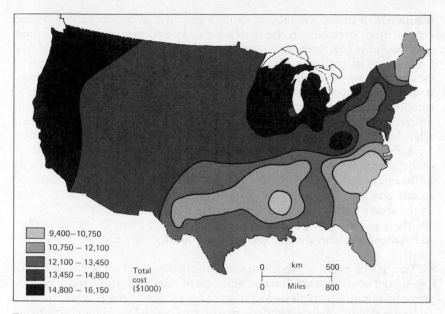

9,400–10,750

10,750 – 12,100

12,100 – 13,450

13,450 – 14,800   Total
                     cost
14,800 – 16,150   ($1000)

0   km   500

0   Miles   800

Figure 11.2 A cost surface for the manufacture of electronic equipment in the USA. (*Source of data:* see Smith, 1971, 377–83.)

1971, 374–87). As in the case above, spatial variations in operating costs can be very considerable: the least-cost location here has a figure of $8·20M, just about half the $16·15M at the location with highest costs. The surface shows the South to be particularly advantageous as a location for the electronics industry, largely by virtue of its relatively cheap labour. However, the high-cost areas of the west coast and the major manufacturing belt have certain externality benefits associated with existing concentrations of the industry—something difficult to measure (thus not reflected in the surface) yet important enough in practice to offset some of the local cost penalties. Real costs in alternative locations are not as easily established as might appear at first sight, even when the concept of costs is confined to these to be met by private business.

This illustration shows that it is not difficult in practice to undertake the kind of analysis suggested by location theory. The necessary data can be compiled, though the time and effort involved is often considerable. Further examples will be found in Smith (1971, Part Four) where other space cost surfaces are shown. Attempts to identify a space cost curve and spatial margins to profitability empirically include those of McDermott (1973) and Haddad and Schwartzman (1974). Such applications are limited to the location problem of single plants, however; the planning of integrated production complexes requires more sophisticated models allowing for economic and social interdependencies, as suggested in the latter part of Chapter 8.

The capacity to evaluate alternative locations accurately with respect to efficiency criteria is extremely useful. In the private sector it helps businessmen to make money or avoid a loss, which benefits those whose employment depends on the firm's viability and also customers whose satisfaction is determined to some extent by the price they have to pay for the goods. In the public sector or in a system where the means of production are owned by the people, comparative-cost analyses can help to ensure that society gets the most out of its investment or that the production required is achieved at least expense of public funds. But such efficiency evaluations are unduly restricting, as should be apparent from what has been said in earlier chapters. The costs and benefits generated by a factory are not confined to the individuals directly involved as owners, employees or customers. They can include disamenities such as pollution (see section 11.7). In the case of employment, jobs generated in one city are a potential loss to people seeking work elsewhere. Thus in the study of the Canadian cities above there may be a greater "need" for the 140 jobs to be created by the electronics plant in Toronto than in Portage la Prairie, despite the greater potential profit in the latter location.

This is the point at which the planner generally enters the scene in the mixed economies of Europe and North America. Regional development programmes are designed so as to try to induce the private investor to locate where jobs are needed, by offering subsidies sufficient at least to compensate for loss of profit attainable at the optimal location from the private point of view. Industrial location policy has been the subject of extensive discussion in economic geography (e.g. Smith, 1971, Part Six). Much less thoroughly researched is the problem of employment generation at the local level, where individual accessibility to the places of work may be a critical determinant of who gets the jobs and whether they are really the people in most need. We will now consider access to employment at the level of the single city. The more basic question of the geography of need will be reserved for the final section of this chapter.

11.2 Employment and accessibility

The location of a new source of jobs can affect access to employment in two ways. First, existing residents will be advantaged differentially, depending on where they live in relation to the facility and the connecting transportation system. Secondly, demographic and economic growth resulting from the new source of employment will change the general pattern of residence–workplace relationships; any addition to the urban economy will set in motion other changes, as new employees and their families join the existing population and contribute their incomes to the demand for goods and services that generate further expansion of production and employment. Mathematical models make it possible to simulate the operation of the urban system so as to predict the impact of changes in the location of employment. Alternative planning strategies can thus be evaluated.

The best-known of these devices is the Garin–Lowry model. In its usual form, this takes the location of "basic" (i.e. non-service) employment as the principal input and arrives at a spatial allocation of additional residents and service employment. This is done on the basis of certain characteristics of the existing urban structure, such as basic : non-basic employment ratio and parameters of individual travel behaviour. In the case to be examined here, the model predicts the impact of change on accessibility or *spatial opportunity* to scarce urban resources (Breheny, 1974, 87). In so far as spatial opportunity determines an individual's real income, the simulation of changes in accessibility allows us to predict the redistributive effects of alternative plans, applying evaluation criteria of the kind discussed in Chapter 7.

The specific problem is to compare the impact of two alternative strategies for the location of an increase of 10,000 in basic employment in the city of Reading. One plan concentrates the new jobs in and around the city centre, the other disperses them about the fringes of the urban area. The relevant performance criterion generated by the model is the *employment opportunities indicator*. For a given part of the city, this measures the distance within which residents can reach a given number of job opportunities. Thus in the existing situation residents of the central part of the city, where access to places of employment is greatest, have 75 per cent of all jobs within just over $3\frac{1}{2}$ km; in certain fringe residential areas it is 11 km. For any change in the spatial pattern of basic employment the model simulates the consequent changes in urban form and calculates new figures for the employment opportunities indicator. These can be compared with the existing situation and with alternative plans.

The results are summarized in Figure 11.3. The relevant distances

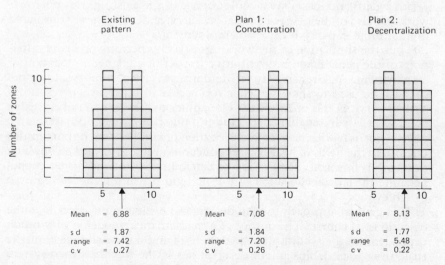

Accessibility to employment opportunity: distance (km) to 75% of jobs

Figure 11.3 A comparison of the performance of alternative patterns of employment in Reading, using an employment opportunity indicator. Note: sd = standard deviation, cv = coefficient of variation. (*Source of data:* Breheny, 1974, Table 2.)

enclosing 75 per cent of employment opportunities have been calculated for 60 zones comprising one-km square cells (Breheny, 1974, 118, 128–9). Following the procedure of Schneider and Symons (1971) illustrated in Figure 7.10, we have plotted the zone data as frequency distributions and calculated overall performance measures. Average accessibility to jobs deteriorates with both the concentration and decentralization strategies, as is shown by the increase in mean distance enclosing 75 per cent of all jobs. This is almost bound to happen when a city expands, with new residential development and associated service expansion on the fringe whatever the location of the initial growth impulse. However, concentration increases the mean distance far less than decentralization of jobs, so by this criterion, which we might term aggregate efficiency of access, Plan 1 is preferable. But on the two other summary measures shown, Plan 2 is preferable both to concentration and to the existing situation: the standard deviation, the range and the coefficient of variation of individual zone accessibility figures have all been reduced. Thus decentralization of employment opportunities may be less *efficient*, but it is more *equitable* in the sense that differences among zones have been reduced.

Figure 11.4a shows the locations of employment under the two plans. Figure 11.4b identifies the zones most disadvantaged—the ten that have the greatest increases in distance enclosing 75 per cent of employment opportunities. Under concentration most of the losses are in fringe areas, as might be expected, but there is also some reduction in accessibility in three central zones. Under decentralization the losses are in the central and northern parts of the city. The details of the spatial distribution of relative gains and losses are a consequence of the existing transport network and also of the new residential and service development stimulated by the initial expansion of basic employment.

Thus the simulation of the workings of a city permits precise evaluations of the general and redistributive impact of a change in location of employment. As Breheny (1974) demonstrates, accessibility indicators can also be used to show the effect on access to other urban resources such as services and open space. The ability to disaggregate likely gains or losses spatially enables us to judge redistribution under alternative plans—not only with respect to the location of employment opportunities but also in the fields of health care, education, recreation and so on. The next step is to specify the desired redistributive effect and have a model generate the spatial allocation of public (and private) facilities required to achieve it.

This general approach to plan design and evaluation is open to some objections, of course. The output of a mathematical model is very much dependent on the accuracy of the data used and on the adequacy of the structural relationships as true descriptions of the way the urban system actually operates; improvements in model-building are dependent on both better methods of measurement and better theory. But there are other less technical problems. One is to be found in the assumptions concerning variables that affect the outcome but are beyond the control of the

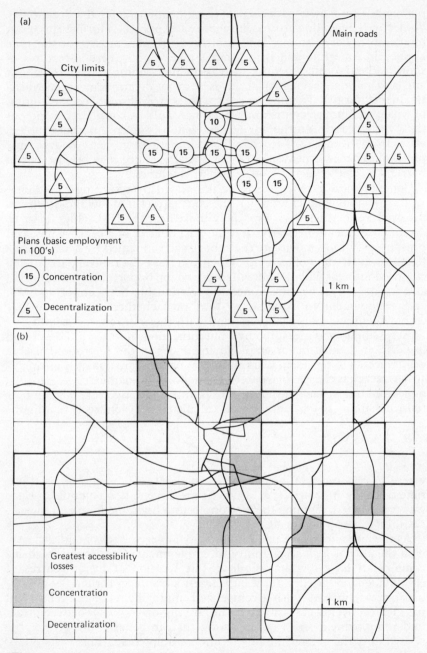

Figure 11.4 Alternative plans for the location of additional employment in Reading, showing zones with greatest losses of accessibility as measured by an employment opportunity indicator. (*Source of data:* Breheny, 1974, Table 2.)

planners. This is where ideological considerations enter the deceptively "objective" modelling process, implicitly accepting certain institutions as unalterable. For example, land-use/transportation models of the type applied in American and British cities take as given certain features of economic and social structure, such as the functioning of the local labour and land market, that may themselves be major determinants of inequalities in real income. To improve the spatial distributions of opportunities, of whatever kind, all contributory factors should be considered as potentially within control and not for ever exogenously given. Another problem arises from the notion of accessibility as merely the capacity to overcome physical distance, when economic or social distance may be just as real barriers to employment or other urban resources.

Some of these problems may be illustrated by returning to Atlanta. In the previous chapter we noted the concentration of low life quality in the black residential areas, especially those near the CBD (Figure 10.7). As in most other American cities, the past quarter of a century has seen prosperous Whites moving to the suburbs accompanied by decentralization of industry and office employment, to leave the central parts of the city predominantly black and with reduced job opportunities. Bederman and Adams (1974) have examined the relationship between job location and employment in Atlanta, to find out whether areas of under-employment and poverty correspond with those of low accessibility.

Accessibility was measured by a potential model of the kind described in Chapter 7. Five major employment nodes in the metropolitan area were selected to represent workplace destinations and a sample of thirty-seven tracts was chosen for workers' residences. From travel times between nodes and tracts, a magnitude V representing "relative aggregate potential accessibility to job centers" was calculated for each tract, as follows:

$$V_i = \sum_{j=1}^{5} \frac{P_j}{T_{ij}} \qquad [11.1]$$

where P_j is number of jobs in the jth node $(1, \ldots, 5)$ and T_{ij} is travel time from the ith tract $(1, \ldots, 37)$. From these data a potential surface was constructed, dividing the metropolis into high, medium and low accessibility areas (Figure 11.5).

As the map shows, the major inner-city poverty area coincides closely with the area of *high* accessibility to employment. Conversely, high-income tracts have low accessibility. The location of major centres of employment on the edge of the city clearly advantages certain fringe suburban areas, but even with decentralized employment the city centre still has greatest overall accessibility. The correlation ($r = 0.55$) between tract underemployment and V score shows that, in general, the greater the accessibility the greater the rate of underemployment. This casts doubt on the common assumption that inner-city poverty can be alleviated by improving physical accessibility to jobs. Almost half the workers from Atlanta's "Model Cities" poverty area already travel to suburban jobs (Bederman and Adams, 1974, 379). Thus the reason for under-

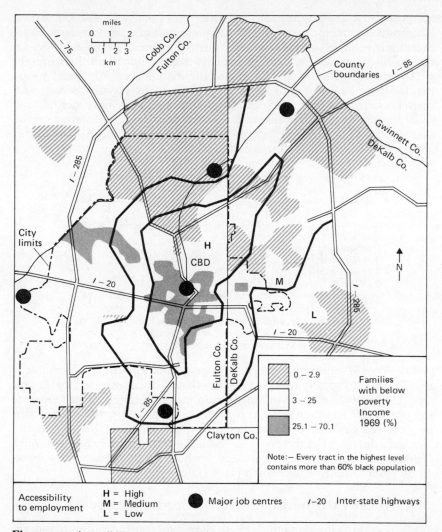

Figure 11.5 Accessibility to employment and the spatial incidence of poverty in Atlanta. (*Source:* Bederman and Adams, 1974, Figs. 2 and 4.)

employment and poverty in the inner city must be sought elsewhere, as must solutions to this problem of spatial inequality in life chances.

The correlations between underemployment and other conditions reveal something of the real problem (Table 11.2). The most critically underemployed are predominantly female heads of families who are black, poorly educated and have several children to support. They lack skills and are often qualified only for low-paid jobs as cleaners or domestic servants. Such people normally walk to work or use public transport. The urban freeways that greatly facilitate the car-owning suburbanite getting to a CBD office job help the inner-city poor only if accompanied by improvements in the usually inadequate public transit system. Even then their economic condition may not be altered. Some may get to reasonably paid suburban jobs previously inaccessible, but others merely get to existing low-paid jobs faster and slightly cheaper. The basic problem for these people is thus not accessibility in the physical sense: "no matter where they live in the metropolitan area they have neither the skills to qualify them for most of the new jobs being created, nor the opportunity to acquire marketable skills" (Bederman and Adams, 1974, 386).

Table 11.2 Correlation (r) between percentage underemployment and selected variables in Atlanta, by census tracts 1970

Variable	r
Accessibility to employment (V)	0·55
Median school years completed	−0·74
Labour force in service related jobs (%)	0·84
Population black (%)	0·62
Families with female head (%)	0·92
Average number of children in families with female head	0·56

Source: Bederman and Adams (1974). An "underemployed" worker is a household head or unrelated individual earning less than $4,000 a year in 1969 (i.e. a poverty-level wage).

The roots of inner-city poverty thus go deeper into the social and economic fabric of society than simply the spatial disposition of homes and jobs. Developments in urban transportation are superficial improvements in a purely efficiency sense; in an equity sense they may well be regressive in their redistributive impact, assisting the well-to-do but not really touching the plight of the poor. To help the poor requires a much more fundamental restructuring of society, with different attitudes to jobs as employment and to employment as a right.

11.3 Access to social services: medical care

While access to employment tends to dominate transportation planning, increasing interest is being shown in access to social services. Medical care has attracted particular attention (Shannon and Dever, 1974), with distance recognized as a major determinant of use of facilities (e.g. Shannon *et al.*, 1969; Morrill *et al.*, 1970). The question of access in the physical sense is now viewed as part of the general efficiency of medical care (e.g. Schneider, 1967; Gross, 1972). Two illustrations have been selected—one from the underdeveloped world and one from the USA.

Inequality in geographical access to medical care is inevitable, by virtue of the discrete location of facilities. This is a particularly serious problem in underdeveloped countries, with the dual drawbacks of limited facilities and low personal mobility. Jolly and King (1966) offer some empirical data on the effect of distance on utilization, as an illustration of the dis-

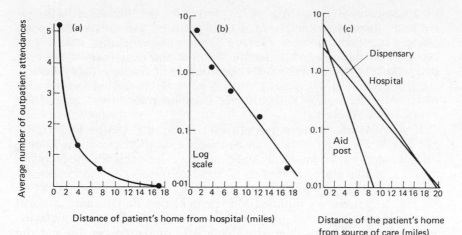

Figure 11.6 The relationship between utilization and distance from health care facilities in Uganda. (*Source:* Jolly and King, 1966, Figs. 4, 5 and 6.)

tance-decay relationship discussed in Chapter 7. Figure 11.6a shows the average number of outpatient attendances per person per year, according to distance from patient's home to hospital. The relationship is exponential negatively, as is made clear when a logarithmic scale is used on the vertical axis (11.6b). A comparison with inpatients shows the same log–linear relationship with distance but with less of a slope; people will travel further for greater care. This point is underlined in Figure 11.6c, where

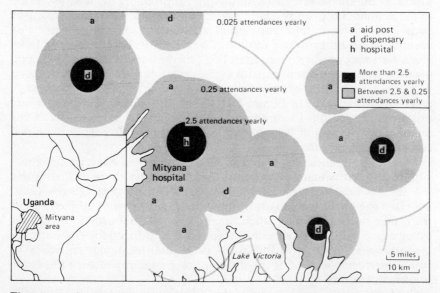

Figure 11.7 An outpatient "isocare" map for the Mityana area of Uganda. (*Source:* Jolly and King, 1966, Fig. 7.)

the distance-decay relationships are plotted for three types of facilities: aid posts, dispensaries and hospitals (outpatients). For the local aid post, offering minimal treatment, average number of attendances halves with every additional mile, while for the hospital and dispensary it is every two miles. The main reasons for the severity of distance decay here is the effort involved when many patients have no choice but to walk and when costs rise steeply with distance if motor transport is used (Jolly et al., 1966, Figure 24).

If distance affects utilization of facilities and this can be interpreted as "care", then level of care can be mapped on the basis of the known distance-decay gradients. Jolly and King have done this for the Mityana area of Uganda, plotting contours of equal utilization (or "isocare lines") as concentric circles about the aid posts, dispensaries and hospitals (Fig. 11.7). The pattern is simplified to the extent that they assume uniform communications throughout the area and the same gradients for all facilities of the same type. They also disregard population density and the fact that the areas within the highest isocare lines may contain most of the people. However, such a map helps to highlight spatial inequalities in care (or, to be more precise, in the probability of a person attending a facility). In only a small proportion of the area shown does the level reach a suggested standard of 2·5 attendancies per person per year. Close to the hospitals as many as six attendancies per year can be expected; in the most distant areas some people will not receive care once in six years.

In this situation, where the real costs of overcoming distance is a major barrier to care only a few miles from a facility, the most effective way to correct the spatial imbalance or inequity is probably to take the service to the people. This can be done by setting up local health centres. But even here distance and population density act as constraints. For example, a health centre of optimum size with respect to output from given staff may require a hinterland or "market area" of 10,000–20,000 people; with population densities as low as ten per square mile, a catchment-area radius of 20 or more miles would be needed. As the distance-decay gradients in Figure 11.6 show, this could mean little if any utilization by persons living towards the edge of the service area. Thus mobile facilities would be required to ensure that all people have real access to medical care.

Moving from underdeveloped rural areas to urban America produces a quite different situation. In many American cities there is a complete hierarchy of health care facilities similar to that of shopping centres, ranging from the major teaching hospital with highly specialized facilities in the centre to the doctor's "office" at the local neighbourhood level. But proximity is still an important determinant of utilization. Accessibility measures may thus act as indicators of general locational efficiency or system performance and of the differential availability of care to people in different places.

Shannon et al. (1975) provide an illustration. In Cleveland, Ohio, thirty-five hospitals are subdivided into five groups, from the major teaching and research hospitals with an average of almost 700 beds to small community or inner-city hospitals. Together they may be viewed as a nested hierarchy in terms of size and specialization. A sample of 859 adults was taken to measure accessibility to different levels of service in four different zones of the city identified on the basis of socio-economic and land-use characteristics (Figure 11.8).

Accessibility may be depicted graphically, using a variation on the Lorenz cumulative-percentage curve (Figure 11.8). In the graph on the left showing accessibility of the total population to each of the five levels of service, each curve traces the proportion of people (vertical axis) within specific distances (horizontal axis) of the level in question. (Note that, as in a shopping-centre hierarchy, each facility provides the services of lower-order facilities as well as its own special services.) The closer the curve to the left of the graph, the closer people are to the facility. The lower levels of service are shown to be most accessible, as would be expected in a central-place hierarchy.

Each of the four zones has its own accessibility pattern. For example, the median distance differential between hospital services of level 1 and level 5 is only $1\frac{1}{2}$ miles for zone 1 (inner city) compared with 9 miles for zone 4 (outer suburbs). Seventy per cent of the population in zone 1 is within 3 miles of the most comprehensive range of hospital services, while for zone 4 the distance is 15 miles. Ninety per cent of the inner urban population are closer to a top-level hospital than 42 per cent of outer suburban residents are to any hospital. The graphs in Figure 11.8 show these differences in detail. As Shannon *et al.* (1975) explain, accessibility measures can be used to evaluate the differential impact of any proposed change, such as the closure of a hospital. Like the Breheny (1974) study described above, this provides a means of judging the redistributive effect, in so far as accessibility is reflected in utilization and actual receipt of care.

But as in the case of employment, reservations must be made about the use of accessibility as a system performance indicator when there are important non-physical barriers to real access. By the accessibility measures of Shannon *et al.* (1975) inner-city residents might appear better off than suburbanites more remote from the hospitals. But to get into a hospital and to be treated in the USA usually requires money. Thus to the poor inhabitant of the inner city, unable to pay or to find the way to financial help through the bureaucratic maze of the "welfare" system, the nearby hospital might just as well be in Uganda in so far as real accessibility is concerned. The nested hierarchy of facilities for those with the means of access may well dissolve into one single public facility, such as Cook County Hospital in Chicago's *"apartheid"* health service examined by de Vise (1973). And when the poor (usually black) get to hospital, the quality of care is likely to be inferior to that enjoyed in private facilities in the fee-for-service sector. The poor also lack the same access to doctors as the rest of the population, for it is extremely difficult for doctors to earn a living from a location in the ghetto, or even in a small rural community.

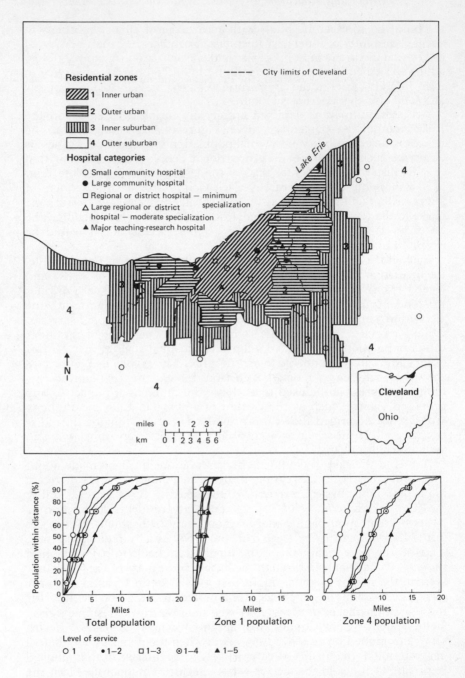

Figure 11.8 Differential accessibility to hospitals in Cleveland, Ohio. (*Source:* Shannon *et al.*, 1975, Figs. 2, 3 and 4.)

The situation in Chicago, typical of that in most American cities, is summarized by Morrill *et al.* (1970, 170) as follows:

Social and economic distinctions according to race and income effectively reduce access to physicians and hospitals for the Negro and for the poor in general. Consequently, these patients must travel much farther on the average than more affluent white patients; perhaps the majority travel beyond intervening opportunities not open to them. These constraints can be overcome, given appropriate financial measures to encourage physicians to practise in or near hospitals in poor areas, in addition to the new programs to enable hospitals to care for poorer patients.

As in the case of underemployment, the problem is one of societal and economic organization rather than of geographical accessibility. Replacing the free-enterprise medical business by a public service is the only effective solution to inequity in real access to health care. This is recognized by Shannon and Dever (1974, 140):

Health care is a fundamental human right. The problem is one of ensuring this right. The fulfilment of this belief is embodied in numerous and diverse international health care systems. The United States, however, stands alone as the only developed country that has not yet attempted to deliver care equitably. It is apparent in the uneven distribution and accessibility of health resources (facilities and services) when compared with other modern countries. Attempts to determine parameters associated with physical location are inconclusive and have little utility in light of the current laissez-faire attitude towards the delivery of medicine and the present framework of non-commitment to a philosophy of health as a human right. Adam Smith's "invisible hand" is not operating to redress problems related to health delivery.

That this "advanced" nation should still rely on market forces for the distribution of such a basic determinant of human well-being is a reflection of the power of vested economic interests in professional medicine, as represented by the American Medical Association. Only in a true public service can race and class discrimination be reduced to the point that spatial discrimination revealed by measures of physical accessibility emerge as the major problem.

11.4 Service facility location: hospitals

With the ability to plan the provision of services in the public interest, standard techniques can be used to solve problems of facility location. Health care again provides an appropriate case, demonstrating the application of a model familiar in economic geography.

The problem is where to locate a new hospital in the Sydney metropolitan area in Australia. As with many other cities, disproportionate growth in a certain direction means that the existing location of medical facilities may be far from optimal with respect to the present population distribution. In Sydney, expansion has spread the built-up area inland thirty miles westwards from the original harbour site, but hospitals and other services have not decentralized to the same extent. Thus there is an "over-provision" of hospital beds in the City of Sydney and the inner suburbs, and a substantial "under-provision" in the outer areas (Lawrence, 1972, Table 5.5). The optimal location for a new facility planned to serve the entire metropolis would clearly be to the west of the major existing concentration of hospitals in the City of Sydney.

The problem posed here is imaginary, but uses real data. Suppose that a single maternity hospital is required, to be visited once for every child born. Figure 11.9 shows the pattern of live births; the technical problem is to locate a facility so as to minimize total coverage of distance by this population, i.e. at the minimum aggregate travel point as

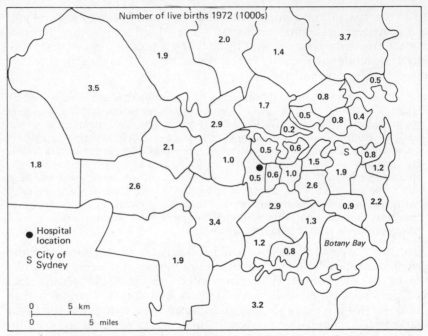

Figure 11.9 The distribution of live births by local government areas in Sydney metropolitan area: data for the problem of maternity hospital location. (*Source of data:* births from *Statistical Register of New South Wales,* 1972.)

in expression [7.13]. This is analogous to the generalized industrial location problem originally described by Weber (Smith, 1971, 114–19), in which each of a number of points of origin exerts a pull in proportion to the quantity of goods to be shipped from that point and the cost of overcoming distance. In the present case, expectant mothers are the quantities to be "shipped". They are assumed to originate from thirty-seven points corresponding with the mean centre of population in the municipalities for which data are mapped in Figure 11.9. For simplicity it is assumed that transportation costs are the same in all directions, so that what is required is to minimize the linear distance to the facility multiplied by number of births, summed for the thirty-seven origins.

There are various computer algorithms that can identify the point of minimum aggregate travel accurately enough for practical purposes. The one used here (Kuhn and Kuenne, 1962) has been modified so as to reveal not only the optimal location but also the extent to which aggregate travel rises away from this point.[1] The model located the hospital in the Municipality of Strathfield, seven miles west of Sydney city centre.

In Chapter 7 it was explained that the point of minimum aggregate travel is an efficiency solution, not necessarily revealing the most equitable location. Other centrality measures could be calculated (as in Figure 7.11) and compared with the distance-minimizing solution. But here we prefer to explore the effect of differential weighting of the population, in accordance with two criteria of need: infant mortality rates and mobility measured by the population-to-car ratio. Multiplying the number of live births in an area by infant mortality or persons per car increases the pull of the areas with greatest need by these criteria. In the analogy with Weber's industrial location model, this is equivalent to shipping more goods from the heavier-weighted origins or making the transport cost per unit of distance greater. Formally, the problem as stated in expression [7.13] becomes:

$$\text{Min } AT; \quad AT_i = \sum_j P_{ij} w_j \quad (j = 1, \ldots, 37) \qquad [11.2]$$

where i is a possible facility location and w_j is the need weighting for origin j.

The solutions are shown in Figure 11.10. This depicts a 7×7 mile section of the Sydney metropolis in which the three alternative points of minimum aggregate travel identified by the Kuhn and Kuenne algorithm are plotted. They fall within less than one mile of each other. Thus the application of a need weighting makes very little difference to optimal facility location, because areas of great need are not spatially concentrated in a manner that would markedly alter the relative pull of different sectors of the city. Aggregate travel values (in millions of miles) for points on a 2×2 mile grid are shown in Figure 11.10. The figure at the locations revealed by the model is roughly 5·45 M miles; the difference between the three is negligible. Away from the optimal locations aggregate travel rises very little at first, but the gradient steepens with increasing distance. Aggregate travel contours interpolated from the data show the basin-shaped form of the surface typically revealed in industrial applications of the Weber model.

Figure 11.11 illustrates sections through the aggregate travel surface. These have been drawn right across the metropolis, from west to east and from north to south. This diagram is analogous to the space cost curve through a cost surface in an industrial location problem, as illustrated above in Figure 11.1. It shows the distance-coverage cost to Sydney's expectant mothers, as it would vary with alternative hospital locations. The steep rise from the shallow basin bottom is revealed clearly. The practical implication of the form of the surface is that within an area

[1] This illustration was developed with the assistance of Jean Taylor, who was responsible for the program modification (Taylor, 1976).

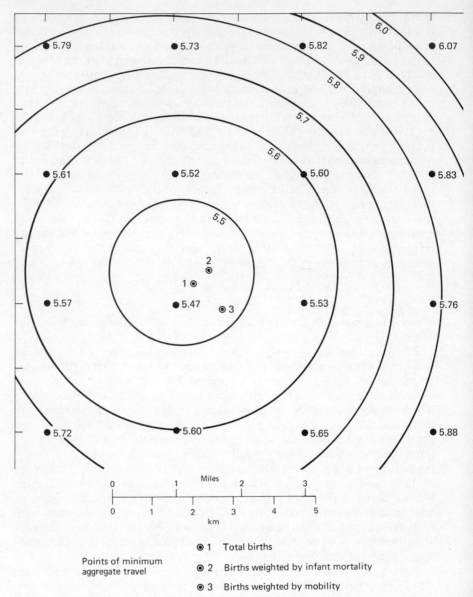

Figure 11.10 Points of minimum aggregate travel for the location of a hospital in Sydney, under alternative assumptions concerning need. The data shown and contours interpolated from them represent total aggregate travel (millions of miles) in the case of population unweighted.

around the optimal point, locational choice is not particularly important from a cost point of view. In any event, exact choice of site at this level of detail will depend on local considerations of land availability and so on. Again, the analogy with an industrial location problem is close. As

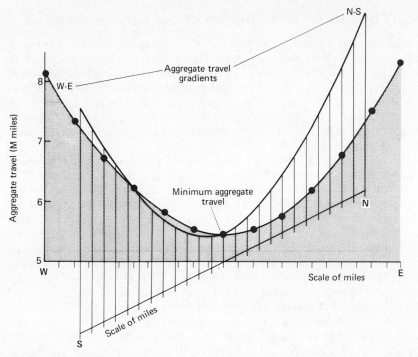

Figure 11.11 Sections through the aggregate travel surface for the Sydney hospital case (unweighted data).

long as the facility is located somewhere within the low-cost zone, the exact site is of little importance from the cost (distance) minimizing point of view. Heuristic methods that identify the optimal location approximately are quite satisfactory for most practical purposes, as long as they are accurate enough to find the low-cost zone. If two different measures can be used, one reflecting efficiency and the other equity, a close spatial correspondence within a highly favourable zone by both criteria would reveal a good location. This is so in the Sydney case.

If the problem is one of multiple facility location, alternative methods are required. Again, various algorithms are available (Lea, 1973; Rushton, Goodchild and Ostresh, 1974). The most commonly used is linear programming, as explained in Chapter 7 in the context of choice of an optimal plan. An illustration of how this method may be applied to a problem in service facility location is provided by Adams, Abler and Gould (1971, 538–43): the objective is to assign three hospitals to five potential locations so as to minimize the aggregate travel (cost) to the population. Godlund (1961) provides another illustration of how to design a pattern of medical-service facilities and hinterlands. Morrill (1967) has examined the service areas of physicians as a transportation problem. A case of linear programming applied to school-district boundaries will be found in Yates (1963; 1974, 258–61). Massam (1975) also provides guidance on this type of problem in social administration.

11.5 The spatial distribution of benefits: recreation

One of the major practical problems in applying the welfare approach is the estimation of who gains or loses what where. Accessibility is merely a surrogate for utility, satisfaction, value or some similar abstraction. A more direct but more difficult procedure than comparing physical access to facilities is to calculate the consumers' surplus accruing to people in different places. As was explained earlier, the consumers' surplus measures the extent to which utility or use-value gained exceeds cost, thus reflecting net benefit.

The case chosen to illustrate this relates to recreation. The problem is to calculate the benefits generated by recreation trips to the Lake District National Park and Morecambe Bay in northern England, following the analysis of Mansfield (1971). Similar methods have been used by others in recreation research (Clawson, 1959; Knetsch, 1963) and also in the evaluation of transport developments (Wilson and Kirwan, 1969).

To estimate consumers' surplus requires a demand curve. In recreation, it is assumed that demand will fall off with increasing distance from the facility because of the increased cost or effort of getting there. Thus we may envisage a demand curve of the kind illustrated in Figure 11.12a, with the number of trips to a facility at j falling as cost and distance rise. The point C_0 represents cost where distance is so great that demand ceases (i.e. no trips are made), while Q_{max} shows demand at the site itself where costs are zero (C_j). At any travel origin i, consumers' surplus is proportional to the area under the demand curve D and above a line representing cost C_i. Given knowledge of the actual travel costs incurred and a monetary figure for the value or utility of the recreation experience (a major research problem in itself), an estimate of consumers' surplus per trip can be made. If this is multiplied by number of trips known to be made or predicted from a given origin i, the total surplus accruing to people at that place can be calculated.

The relationship between distance and number of recreation trips can be found by a survey of actual travel behaviour. It conforms to the negative exponential distance decay in other realms of spatial interaction. This is illustrated in Figure 11.12b, where the number of trips per 1,000 people to the Lake District National Park is plotted for various distance bands. The log–linear version of this relationship can be used to simulate a demand curve of the kind shown in Figure 11.12a.

With this technique, Mansfield (1971) calculated the consumers' surplus (in £ units) accruing to people in different geographical zones, from an average day's visits to the Lake District (Table 11.3). An estimate was also made for 1981, based on a figure for expected trips from each zone derived from forecasts of car ownership as well as distance. The results (Table 11.3) show a marked spatial spread effect, i.e., utility or real-income redistribution. Much more of the benefit in 1981 accrues to people beyond the immediate vicinity of the Park, especially outside Lancashire.

Mansfield (1971) used the same procedures to estimate the likely

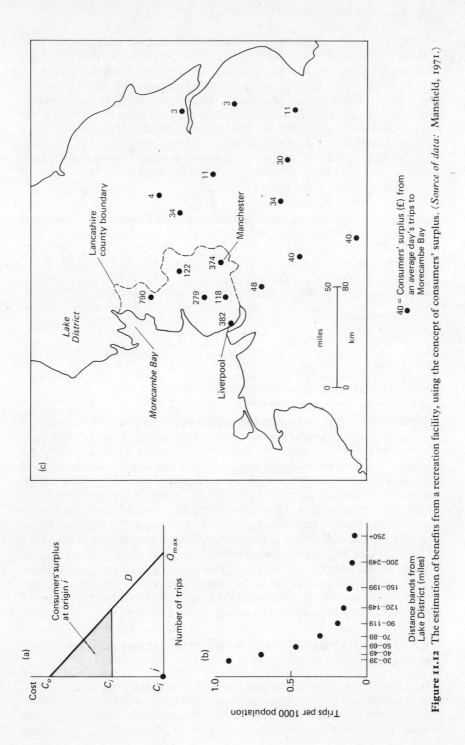

Figure 11.12 The estimation of benefits from a recreation facility, using the concept of consumers' surplus. (*Source of data:* Mansfield, 1971.)

benefits from an expansion of recreation facilities on Morecambe Bay. Taking into account trips diverted from the Lake District and new ones generated, predictions of trips in an average day were made for seventeen geographical zones. The consumers' surplus was calculated for each zone. Data for full-day trips are mapped in Figure 11.12c. The main beneficiaries are the people of Lancashire, especially those in the north of the county close to Morecambe Bay and the inhabitants of the major cities of Manchester and Liverpool. The overall benefits estimated to come from Morecambe Bay in an average 1981 week were somewhere between £22,880 and £33,650—relatively small compared with the figure of £227,510 from the Lake District.

Table 11.3 Estimated consumers' surplus from trips to the Lake District National Park in an average day, 1966 and 1981

Zone	1966		1981	
	£	%	£	%
Within 25 miles of Park	1,988	40·8	3,715	14·6
Lancashire	2,047	42·0	11,793	46·3
North-east England	320	6·6	2,839	11·2
Yorkshire	412	8·4	4,960	19·5
Rest of England	109	2·2	2,137	8·4
Total consumers' surplus	4,876	100·0	25,444	100·0

Source: Mansfield (1971, Tables 1.1 and 2.1).

Thus despite technical difficulties, some attempt can be made to calculate benefits as consumers' surplus. Disaggregating total benefit geographically makes it possible to say who gains *where* from a facility. At present, project evaluation rests largely if not entirely on the question of how total benefits compare with costs. But the spatial distribution of benefits can also be taken into account in overall recreation planning. In the case under review, the substantial gains from Morecambe Bay to people in northern Lancashire (£790 per average day for full-day trips) compared with smaller figures for the much larger population of the cities of Liverpool (£382) and Manchester (£374) point to the limited opportunities for the average city dweller. This might encourage the planning of more recreation areas closer to the major centres of population, or steps to improve the mobility of people currently deprived of the means of ready access to Morecambe Bay or the Lake District.

11.6 The spatial allocation of resources: police protection

The spatial allocation of resources in the form of money or personnel can have an important bearing on the distributive outcome of alternative plans, as well as on efficiency of general goal attainment (Chapter 7). This section examines the problem of how best to allocate police protection among different areas. Crime is a matter of major concern to society as well as a topic growing in geographical interest (e.g. Harries, 1974; Smith, 1974c; Peet, 1975), yet there has been relatively little research into the effectiveness of different policing strategies. The studies summarized here represent first steps towards serious spatial planning in the police service in the United States.

The first case is set in New York—a city that epitomizes the problems of rising crime in the affluent society. The level of criminal activity varies considerably from place to place, as in any city, and it is worth considering how far this is sensitive to the number of police on patrol. Figure 11.13a shows the rate of reported robberies per 1,000 population by precincts, plotted against the ratio of police to population. There is some tendency for the crime rate to vary with police per 1,000 population, but instead of showing low crime associated with high police protection the reverse is the case. The data suggest that in general more police are allocated to high-crime precincts, not that level of crime goes down as a result of a high police-to-population ratio. The productive efficiency of a policeman, as reflected in the crime rate, will be low in areas where local economic and social conditions favour criminal activity, for the effort involved to get crime down to a given level will be relatively great there. Figure 11.13b shows another possible view of police efficiency—the proportion of robberies leading to an arrest is plotted against the ratio of police to population. Now it is impossible to detect any association. Clearly, the relationship between areal deployment of personnel and effectiveness of the police is not straightforward.

Another possible approach is to examine the change in crime rate associated with actual changes in manpower. Figure 11.13c shows the relationship between percentage change in number of patrolmen in each precinct in 1966–7 and changes in the robbery rate. With some imagination it might be possible to detect a negative exponential curve, with reduction in patrolmen accompanied by high increases in crime. But the overwhelming impression is of no obvious regularity of impact: precincts with virtually no change in crime include some at all levels of change in patrolmen.

To identify the impact of an increase in personnel more exactly, an experiment was conducted in 1966–7 involving the 20th Precinct (Press, 1971). This is an area with about 100,000 inhabitants of diverse economic and cultural backgrounds. It is on Manhattan Island adjoining Central Park (Figure 11.13d) and has a moderate level of crime in a predominantly high-crime zone, as revealed in the robbery pattern. In October 1966 the number of patrolmen here was increased by 40 per cent (from about 200 to 300)—a much greater change in manpower than in any other precinct at this time. Comparisons were made between rates of various crimes reported before and after this change.

The results are summarized in Table 11.4. In the case of robbery, grand larceny and total felonies, the observed decreases compared with the changes that could have been expected with manpower remaining the same are significant at the 95 per cent confidence level, for both

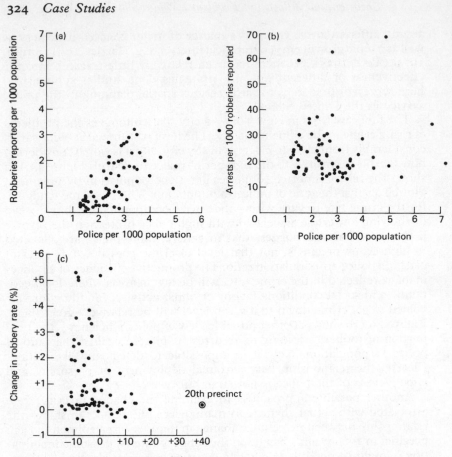

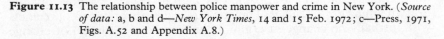

Figure 11.13 The relationship between police manpower and crime in New York. (*Source of data:* a, b and d—*New York Times*, 14 and 15 Feb. 1972; c—Press, 1971, Figs. A.52 and Appendix A.8.)

"inside" and "outside" offences. There were decreases in certain other crimes, but generally not great enough to be significant. In some cases the data were regarded as suspect because of the small number of crimes involved and no judgements were passed on these changes. The conclusion was that, "In general, results are not counter-intuitive, and in a few cases, indicated changes in reported crime associated with the manpower increase in the 20th Precinct appear to be fairly substantial" (Press, 1971, 10). The findings are, of course, subject to reservations arising from the difficulty of measuring the incidence of crime accurately when about half those committed go unreported. And no attempt was made to relate benefits to the cost of providing the additional personnel.

One cost was identified, however, in the form of a "displacement effect". This is an increase in crime in neighbouring areas attributable to the more effective law enforcement in the 20th Precinct—an example

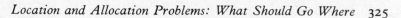

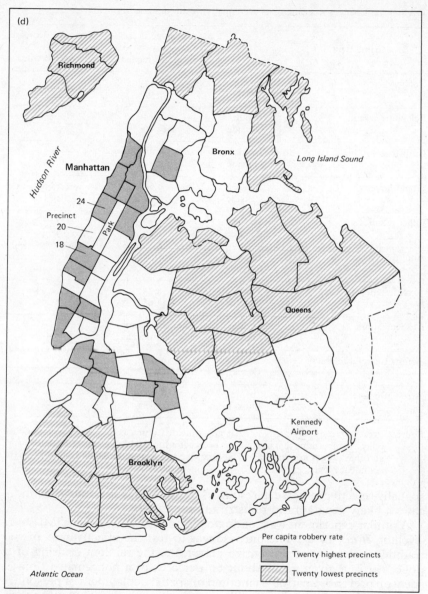

(d)

Richmond

Hudson River

Manhattan

24

Precinct

20

18

Park

Bronx

Long Island Sound

Queens

Kennedy
Airport

Brooklyn

Atlantic Ocean

Per capita robbery rate

Twenty highest precincts

Twenty lowest precincts

Figure 11.13—continued

of the spillovers discussed in Chapter 5. The strongest displacement was found in Central Park, but there were also indications in the adjoining precincts 18 and 24. The increases found were less than the decreases (relative to expected rates) in the 20th Precinct, but no account is taken of other displacement effects that might have occurred beyond the precincts adjoining the 20th. Whatever the precise net gain or loss from a

Table 11.4 Changes in crime rates accompanying an increase in manpower

Crime type		Net average decrease in crimes per week in 20th Precinct	Per cent decrease relative to expected value
Robbery	Inside	1·92	20·91
	Outside	2·59	33·26
Felonious assault	Inside	suspect	—
	Outside	suspect	—
Burglary	Inside	not significant	—
	Outside	suspect	—
Grand larceny	Inside	6·64	28·65
	Outside	17·14	49·15
Other felonies	Inside	suspect	—
	Outside	1·89	38·45
Auto theft	Inside	suspect	—
	Outside	7·71	49·28
Total felonies	Inside	4·43	4·99
	Outside	23·68	35·67
Misdemeanors	Inside	not significant	—
	Outside	not significant	—
Arrests for total felonies	Inside	suspect	—
	Outside	suspect	—
Arrests for total misdemeanors	Inside	suspect	—
	Outside	suspect	—

Source: Press (1971, Figure 2). Note that an "outside" crime is one that allows a police officer to determine that a crime has been committed without leaving his patrol car; all other crimes are "inside". The quantified decreases are significant at the 95% confidence level.

spatially selective increase in resources, the evidence from this case indicates a likely geographical redistribution.

A similar experiment was conducted in 1972 in Kansas City, Missouri (Kelling *et al.*, 1974). The purpose was to test the effectiveness of the traditional strategy of preventive patrol, i.e. the random cruising of a police car in a given area. About 60 per cent of a policeman's time is spent on preventive patrol—a method of spatial deployment of personnel that costs about $2 thousand million each year in the USA. Despite such a heavy commitment of resources, preventive patrol rests on two widely accepted yet unproven hypotheses: (1) that visible police presence prevents crime by deterring potential offenders; (2) that the public's fear of crime is diminished by such police presence. The Kansas City preventive patrol experiment was designed to test these hypotheses—a rare example of the spatial allocation of mobile resources being subjected to scientific evaluation.

For the experiment, fifteen police beat areas were divided into five groups of three on the basis of similarity in crime and population characteristics. Within each group, one "reactive" beat had preventive patrol eliminated, one "proactive" beat had its patrol level intensified by two to three times, while in one "control" beat preventive patrol was maintained as before. By comparing conditions before and after the change, in the five reactive, control and proactive beats, the effectiveness of this strategy could be judged.

The general conclusion was that routine preventive patrol had no significant impact either on the level of crime or on the public's feeling of security. Statistical tests of "before" and "after" conditions revealed few instances in which the different experiences of the three types of beats were significant at the 95 per cent confidence level. For example, the city Police Department crime reports showed only one statistically significant difference among fifty-one comparisons between the reactive, control and proactive beats. A crime victimization survey showed no significant differences in sixty-nine comparisons, while the rates of citizen and business reports of crime revealed only five significant differences in forty-eight tests. Similar results were found in community response to various survey questions designed to measure changes in fear of crime, attitudes to the police and so on.

The finding that preventive patrol is not an effective use of police manpower, if generally accepted, could release vast resources for other purposes more directly related to real prevention of crime. It could also reduce the visual presence of what might be perceived as repressive authority in neighbourhoods where the police are not held in high esteem. In Kansas City, experiments are being conducted into other strategies, such as the "interactive patrol" designed to improve relations between police and the citizen in low-income black neighbourhoods. A change in spatial deployment of personnel could be accompanied by a general shift towards a less aggressive police role, which could have a real impact on subjective life quality in parts of the American city where police action often reinforces feelings of alienation.

It is often suggested that poor parts of the American city get less police protection than the rich suburbs. While the effectiveness of preventive patrols is an efficiency question, the spatial distribution of services raises equity issues. Very few attempts have been made to find out whether police protection is in fact unequally distributed. Brief reference may be made to two studies that cast doubt on the conventional wisdom.

The first takes us back to New York. As part of an investigation into crime and the police in 1972, the *New York Times* made a comparison between precincts grouped into four major categories on the basis of socio-economic status of the population. There is certainly more crime in low-income areas, but is this because the police force is smaller or less effective? Table 11.5 provides a partial answer. There are more policemen per 1,000 people in the two low-income precinct categories and if any group are obviously under-served it is people with middle incomes. Arrests per 100 crimes reported, as a possible measure of police efficiency,

Table 11.5 Variations in police assignment and effectiveness in New York, 1971

Type of precinct	Policeman per 1,000 population	Arrests per 100 crimes reported	
		Robbery	Burglary
High income	2·68	22·9	6·5
Middle income	1·87	20·5	6·1
Blue collar	3·56	23·0	12·0
Slums	3·44	17·6	11·2

Source: *New York Times*, 15 Feb. 1972. Based on data for 26 of the city's 72 police precincts.

show a lower rate for robbery arrests in the slums than in the other areas but almost twice as many burglary arrests in the two poorer precinct types than in the middle- and high-income areas. In addition, large variations in police performance were observed among precincts in the same economic group; for example the two Puerto Rican slum areas of East Harlem and Hursts Point in the Bronx had 14 and 30 arrests respectively for each reported robbery. Thus, from these data it is difficult to sustain the view that poor areas are less well served. However, taking such figures at face value may lead to an erroneous conclusion. For example, a larger proportion of the burglaries that occur in middle- and upper-income areas are reported because more people have insurance and think well of the police, so the arrest rate recorded in the blue-collar precincts and the slums should be reduced to allow for under-reporting. It could also be argued that as long as there are marked inequalities in local crime levels some inequity exists, however much low-income areas may seem better served on paper. The optimal spatial allocation of policemen is a complex matter in which efficiency and equity can easily conflict, as was explained in Chapter 7.

The second study is set in Washington, DC. Equal protection under the law is a right guaranteed to all American by the Fifth Amendment to the Constitution, and on this basis unequal provision of services among different parts of a city have been challenged in the courts in recent years. Residents of the Anacostia section of Washington filed a suit claiming that a variety of municipal services are allocated unequally, with people living west of Rock Creek Park receiving superior treatment. Anacostia is 90 per cent black with 13 per cent of its families below the poverty level and a median income only a little over $8,000 a year; the "West of the Park" area is 97 per cent white with only 3 per cent in poverty and a median family income approaching $20,000. Block (1974) has attempted to judge the situation with respect to distribution of police services.

Various measures were compiled as indicators of level of inputs and police effectiveness. The main findings were that police inputs in terms of personnel assigned are in fact equally distributed (i.e. not significantly different in a statistical sense), that property crime rates in the two areas are almost equal (more robbery in Anacostia but less burglary), that violent crime reported is higher in Anacostia, that clearance rates (i.e. success in identifying and apprehending criminals) are roughly equal, that citizen perception of neighbourhood safety and opinions about police effectiveness (as measured in a survey) are the same, and that Anacostia appears to have poorer services with respect to police response time. In general, it was concluded that the District of Columbia is following "acceptable management standards" in distributing police services between the two communities. In other words, the claim of discrimination by Anacostia Blacks could not be sustained by the facts.

The results of this study underline the difficulty of making a firm judgement as to the equality or otherwise of the distribution of a public service. Input measures such as manpower deployed are not accurate surrogates for performance, as was made clear earlier in this section. Data on the incidence of crime, which are notoriously inaccurate and difficult to interpret, are imperfect indicators of police effectiveness. Even victimization and attitudinal surveys are of dubious value in communities distrustful of the police and any other people associated with officialdom.

If the evaluation of alternative strategies of service provision on efficiency or equity grounds is to proceed in a truly scientific manner, much more accurate indicators of performance are required. This is particularly true of crime, where existing data provide poor social indicators (Smith, 1974c). The extent of spatial disparities in the level of crime and the essentially spatial nature of manpower deployment in crime prevention makes this a particularly fruitful topic for further geographical inquiry. But, as with other social problems, it must not be forgotten that the roots of crime extend deep into the structure of society: redeployment of police personnel attacks symptoms, not causes.

11.7 The incidence of nuisance: pollution

Pollution is a major source of disutility in "advanced" industrial countries. It differs from other undesirable conditions such as crime in that pollution is amenable to measurement by instruments of physical science. Its spatial incidence should therefore be quite easily identified from readings on pollutant matter in the air, water and soil. The concept of pollution can also be extended to incorporate noise levels— another condition subject to physical measurement.

Studies of pollution are commonly confined to a single aspect. Yet for planning purposes it is more helpful to have a comprehensive view of the impact of all media within a given area. An example of such an approach is provided by a detailed analysis of the geography of pollution in Greater Manchester by Wood *et al.* (1974). The territory under review extends from the edge of the Pennines in the east to Wigan in the west. It has an area of about 520 square miles and a population approaching 3 millions.

As a large industrial region, Greater Manchester has a variety of pollution-generating activities. The major contributor to atmospheric pollution is the burning of fuel to generate heat and power, including domestic

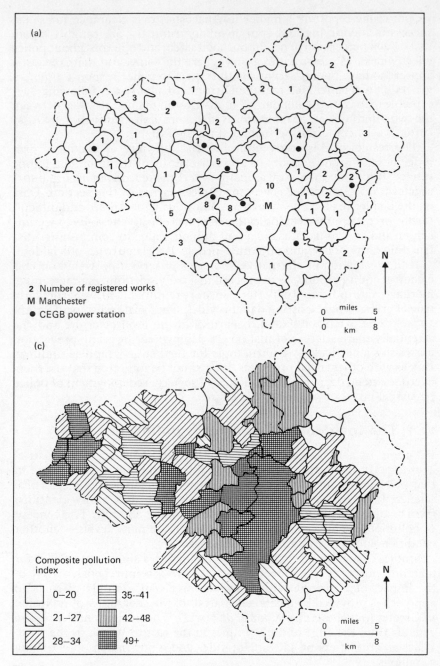

Figure 11.14 The geography of pollution in Greater Manchester. (*Source:* Wood *et al.*, 1974, Figs. 6, 11, 15, 31.)

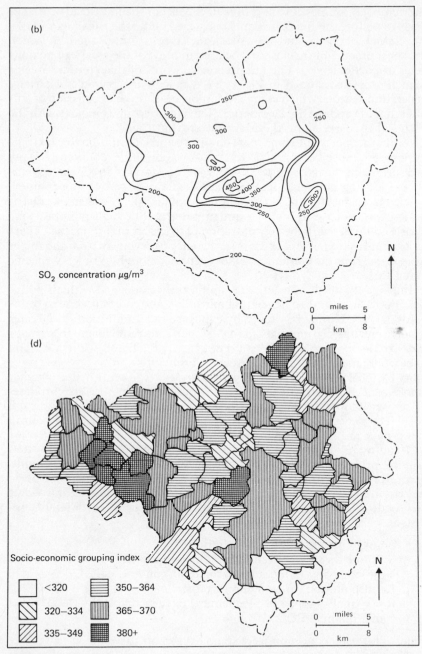

(b)

SO₂ concentration $\mu g/m^3$

N

0 miles 5
0 km 8

(d)

Socio-economic grouping index

<320 350–364
320–334 365–370
335–349 380+

N

0 miles 5
0 km 8

Figure 11.14—continued

and vehicular sources as well as industry. Most of the industrial processes likely to pollute the air are in plants registered under the Alkali, etc Works Regulation Act 1906 and the Alkali and Works Order 1966, in which the "best practicable means shall be used to prevent the escape of noxious gases or particulates". The hundred or so works of this kind in Greater Manchester are mapped in Figure 11.14a, with the region's electricity generating stations which comprise important sources of emission of sulphur dioxide and particulate matter. The major group coincides with the chemical industry along the Manchester Ship Canal.

As in other parts of Britain, data on smoke and sulphur dioxide concentrations are more comprehensive than those on other pollutants. Daily measurements have been taken at over 100 stations in Greater Manchester during the past decade. Figure 11.14b shows contours interpolated from data for 1963–4 on sulphur dioxide; the broad smoke distribution was thought to follow a similar pattern. The high-pollution area clearly coincides with the concentration of works in Figure 11.14a. There is some indication of an exponential distance decay away from the upper Ship Canal, but the contours are not accurate enough to be very specific about this.

Important aspects of health are significantly associated with air pollution. Between 15 and 20 per cent of morbidity and mortality due to bronchitis in the UK may be caused by exposure to air pollution; in Greater Manchester the figure might be 15–25 per cent, equivalent to perhaps 400–650 deaths each year (Wood *et al.*, 1974, 56). These deaths will tend to be where the pollution is most severe: bronchitis and emphysema mortality by local authority areas (1970) correlate 0·84 with winter average smoke concentration (1963–4) and the same pollution measure correlates closely with total mortality ($r = 0·60$). The impact of pollution on health is subject to a time lag, so recent improvements in air quality control can expect to be reflected in mortality figures in the future.

Wood *et al.* (1974) also considered the pollution of land and water, and the problem of noise. They then constructed a *composite pollution index*, for each of the 71 local authority areas. The problems involved in deriving such an index are the same as for any social indicator—data standardization, weighting and amalgamation. Data for six different conditions were obtained or estimated:

1. Smoke concentration (air pollution)
2. Sulphur dioxide concentration (air pollution)
3. Traffic density (a measure of air pollution and noise)
4. Land pollution (area of spoil heaps, etc)
5. River quality (level of biochemical oxygen demand—BOD)
6. Canal quality (BOD).

Figures for each condition were standardized on the range 0 to 100 (= greatest pollution) and the six sets of scores were then summed to give the composite index. The equal weighting implicit in this procedure reflects lack of knowledge of the relative importance of different forms of pollution with respect to harm caused. Although based on data of questionable accuracy for some areas, the index does provide a fairly comprehensive picture of the geography of pollution.

The pattern is mapped in Figure 11.14c. The two main areas of high overall pollution are in the centre of the conurbation around Salford and in the Wigan area in the west. The lowest levels are on the Pennine fringes north-east of Manchester and in the Cheshire suburbs to the south. The disutilities from pollution are quite unevenly distributed among the population of the region. A comparison with Figure 11.14d suggests that the level of pollution bears some relationship to the socio-economic composition of local-authority populations, as measured by occupational structure (a low index means high occupational status). This is confirmed by a correlation of $r = 0.57$ between summer smoke concentration 1966 and the socio-economic index: the more unskilled workers in an area, the higher the level of pollution and its consequent threat to health. A similar result is obtained by correlating car ownership with winter sulphur dioxide concentration 1965–6 ($r = -0.61$): the more affluent areas tend to have less pollution.

As Wood *et al.* (1974, 119) recognize, "This feature raises questions of equity which are central to public policy, not only because the 'disadvantaged areas' are experiencing the highest levels of pollution but because part of this pollution is originating from other, often higher income, areas." Pollution easily generates spatial spillover effects via the flow of air, water, noise and traffic. The fundamental question raised is why those affluent suburban residents who gain most from the regional economy should experience less of that part of the real cost represented by pollution.

A special aspect of pollution that highlights this distribution issue is noise from airports. Wood *et al.* (1974) identified the pattern of noise contours from Manchester's Ringway Airport, based on the Noise and Number Index (NNI) that takes into account the peak noise level of individual aircraft and the total number of aircraft movements. Figure 11.15 shows the typical form of such airport noise surfaces, elongated in the direction of the runways. The exponential distance decay is characteristic of transport noise levels generally (e.g. Stevenson 1972, 210). The peripheral location of Ringway means that the Cheshire suburbs suffer the bulk of the nuisance in this case. Daytime noise in the 40–50 NNI range becomes "intrusive" or "annoying" in residential areas, with a maximum "acceptable" level between 50 and 60. Thus noise levels would be "very annoying" in parts of Cheadle and Gatley UD, Wilmslow UD, Bucklow RD and the city of Manchester. The resident population within the 35 NNI daytime contour and likely to experience some annoyance is about 100,000.

Similar data from estimates made in connection with the Roskill Commission Report on the siting of a new airport for London show that the number of people living inside the 35 NNI contour would range from 94,000 for an airport at Nuthampstead to 25,000 for the Thurleigh site (Lichfield, 1971, 165). People within the 55 NNI contour reached 1,900 for Thurleigh. More severe problems exist around major American city

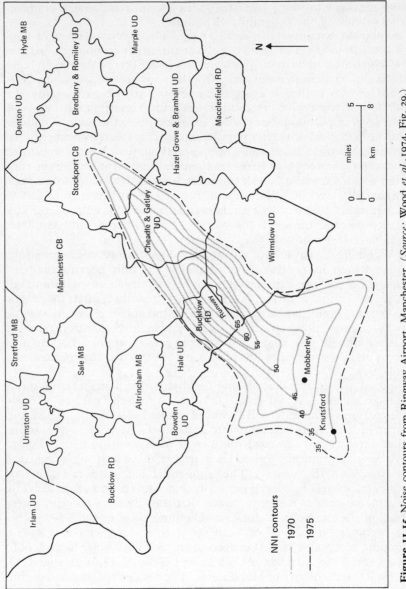

Figure 11.15 Noise contours from Ringway Airport, Manchester. (*Source:* Wood *et al.*, 1974, Fig. 29.)

airports. Noise Exposure Forecast (NEF) contours for Chicago's O'Hare Airport estimated for 1975 show 432,000 people, 142 schools and 6 hospitals subjected to "objectionable" noise; for Kennedy Airport in New York comparable figures are 1·7 million people in 1975 and (in 1968) 112 schools, 37 public parks and a dozen hospitals (Stevenson, 1972, 214–17).

As airport traffic continues to grow in response to the demands of businessmen, affluent holidaymakers and an increasingly mobile general public, noise pollution is becoming a major problem. Steps to restrict its impact implicitly or explicitly recognize that a basic issue of social justice is involved in the disparity between those who enjoy the benefits from air travel and those who bear the brunt of the nuisance caused. The Anglo-French supersonic airliner *Concorde* is an extreme case of slight advantage to those rich enough to use it being purchased at a very high noise and air-pollution cost to others.

11.8 Spatial patterns of need: problem areas

Basic to the rational planning of resource allocations is the identification of spatial patterns of need. Territorial social indicators provide a means of measuring the extent to which various human needs are met. For many practical purposes it is necessary to define "problem", "priority" or "target" areas and recent years have seen the emergence of attempts to put this aspect of applied geography on a more scientific footing (e.g. Smith, 1973a; Knox, 1975). The conceptual and practical problems have already been discussed at some length in the theoretical sections of this book, and the development of territorial social indicators at broader spatial scales has been illustrated in Chapters 8 and 10. This section demonstrates two aspects of the use of indicators in city planning—general problem-area identification and the delimitation of priority areas for specific programmes.

Tampa, Florida, provides the first case (Smith, 1973a, 120–5). As with most American cities, various attempts have been made in recent years to define problem areas. Four different methods are illustrated here, with the results compared in Figure 11.16.

In the middle of the 1960s the US Department of Commerce, Bureau of the Census (1967) carried out a classification and mapping of "poverty areas" in metropolitan areas with populations of 250,000 or more. Five poverty-linked socio-economic characteristics were used, as follows:

1. Per cent of families with cash incomes under $3,000
2. Per cent of children under 18 years old not living with both parents
3. Per cent of males 25 years old and over with less than 8 years of school completed
4. Per cent of unskilled males (labourers and service workers) aged 14 and over in the employed civilian labour force
5. Per cent of all housing units lacking some or all plumbing facilitated or dilapidated.

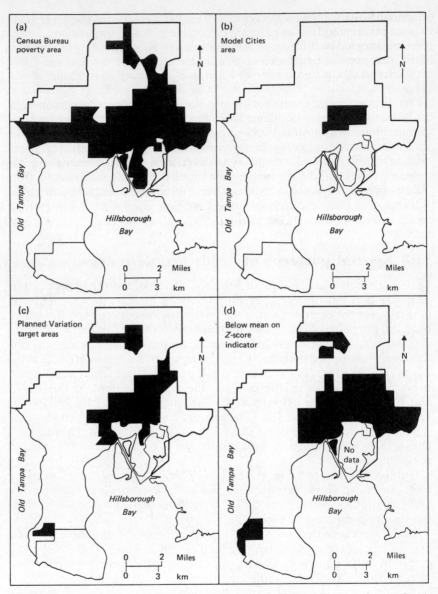

Figure 11.16 Alternative definitions of problem areas in Tampa, Florida. (*Source:* Smith, 1973a, Figs. 9.1, 9.3.)

Tract data from the 1960 census were used to produce a composite poverty index; tracts falling into the lowest quartile were designated "poor". By this method, roughly half of the city of Tampa was defined as a poverty area (Figure 11.16a).

In 1967 Tampa entered the Model Cities programme. A Model Neighbourhood Area (MNA) was identified (Figure 11.16b), as the target for various projects aimed at permanently raising the socio-economic and physical standards of living of the most deprived population groups. It had a total population of almost 35,000, two-thirds of them black. The problems of this area are severe, with 45 per cent of households at or below the poverty level, one in five dependent on "welfare", almost 14 per cent of the labour force unemployed, almost 40 per cent of all residential structures substandard, an above-average incidence of social pathologies such as juvenile delinquency and venereal disease, and low levels of health and education. The MNA was thus the city's hard-core problem area. The precise definition of the MNA involved a combination of numerical analysis and on-site inspection of physical conditions.

In mid-1971 Tampa was selected as one of twenty cities to participate in a new programme called Planned Variation. This was, in effect, an expansion of the existing Model Cities programme to facilitate implementation of "revenue sharing", through which further Federal funds were made available to help combat urban problems. One requirement of the new programme was that plans should be carried out on a city-wide basis, and not confined to the existing MNA, which necessitated the redefinition of target areas. A preliminary delimitation was made by the City, using the general criteria of housing conditions, physical conditions, health, crime and delinquency, unemployment, and welfare services. Data on twenty-one variables were used to rank census tracts, supplemented by detailed knowledge of local conditions. As a result, Primary Target Areas were identified (Figure 11.16c).

The initial definition of these areas was done rather hurriedly to meet a deadline for the allocation of funds. As a check on the results, a more detailed investigation was commissioned (Smith and Gray, 1972). Data were compiled by tracts for forty-seven variables chosen to reflect the general well-being of the population as broadly as possible (they are those listed in Table 10.4). The general social indicator derived from summing standard (Z) scores (see Figure 10.6) provided a basis for problem-area identification. Tracts with below-average scores on this indicator are mapped in Figure 11.16d, which corresponds closely with Figure 11.16c. The earlier definition of target areas was thus generally confirmed, with some minor adjustments around the edges as the only change recommended.

Of course, the definition of target areas on a map is no guarantee that the problems within them will be effectively solved by the programme in question. In the case of Model Cities, performance varied, with active local citizen participation and a feeling of achievement in some cities but domination by the existing power elite in others. In general, "inability to achieve quality of life goals set out in the legislation" is recognized by the US Department of Housing and Urban Development (1973, 6). The reasons lie not in the failure to identify the problem areas in the cities concerned but in an inability to get to the root causes of low life quality, which are not necessarily localized in the deprived areas themselves. The neighbourhood "facelift" operations that characterized much of the activity of Model Cities were quite literally superficial assaults on one of the symptoms of social deprivation. The broader economic mechanisms that create the slums remain unaltered.

Two cases from Los Angeles have been chosen to illustrate the application of territorial social indicators in the context of particular planning problems. The first concerns health and shows how a general community health index might be developed to highlight areas in special need (Donabedian, 1973). Such an index can serve as a programme evaluation device as well as for descriptive or diagnostic purposes. The measurement of levels of health tends to focus on illness, as data on morbidity and mortality are generally available while the number of healthy people (whatever this may mean) is not recorded.

Eleven conditions were selected to measure illness in 141 sub-areas of Los Angeles county. Six are vital statistics, five are rates of communicable disease. The composite indicator was derived by the now familiar standard score (Z) transformation of each variable, the final index value being the area average for the eleven sets of scores. Table 11.6 lists the conditions and the scores for the healthiest area (Beverly Hills) and the unhealthiest (Watts) other than the CBD where the concentration of social deviants in the local "Skid Row" produces freak figures. The contrast in the data for the two areas shows something of the range in life chances between the epitome of the rich American suburb and the site of one of the worst ghetto riots of the 1960s. The data for infant deaths, for example, shows Beverly Hills better than the County average by 2·63

Table 11.6 Composition of community health index for Los Angeles County, 1970, with scores for the most healthy and least healthy areas

Condition	Beverly Hills	Watts
Vital statistics		
Infant deaths	2·630	−0·997
Foetal deaths	1·443	−0·584
Accidental deaths	1·075	−1·463
Alcohol deaths	0·442	−0·404
Narcotics deaths	−0·016	−0·794
Live births	2·163	−1·542
Communicable disease		
Gonorrhoea	0·423	−3·063
Syphilis	0·405	−2·534
Hepatitis	0·688	−1·594
Tuberculosis	0·264	−1·086
Childhood diseases	0·769	−3·407
Average score	0·936	−1·588

Note: the index is an average of the standard (Z) scores on each of the conditions listed, measured as rates to population at risk. High negative values are bad, positive good.

Source: Donabedian (1973).

standard deviations while Watts is one standard deviation below. Watts scores badly on all conditions. Beverly Hills scores very well on some but no so well on deaths connected with alcohol and narcotics and on incidence of venereal diseases and tuberculosis—presumably the hedonistic life of Hollywood exacts its price. .

Figure 11.17 shows the areas with scores on the general health index below the average for Los Angeles County. Nine areas with at least one standard deviation from the mean are recognized as in "poor health". They are mainly in the central part of the city. Fifteen areas with scores of −0·5 to −1·0 are in "moderately poor health"; again they tend to

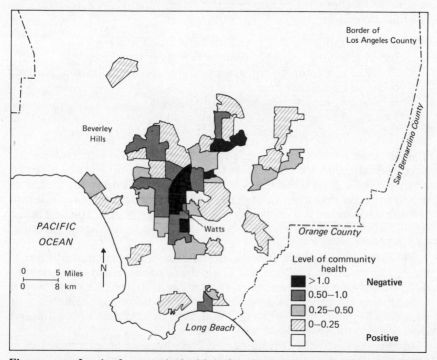

Figure 11.17 Levels of community health in Los Angeles County based on a composite indicator. (*Source of data:* Donabedian, 1973.)

concentrate around the centre. The two other categories of areas below the County average are more scattered. The districts with greatest need for improved health care can be identified quite clearly. How these needs might be met is not considered here, but it should be apparent from what was said about access in section 11.3 above that the solution to severe health problems such as in places like Watts is very unlikely to emerge from the present organization of health care in the USA along business lines. A public national health service is a necessary if not sufficient condition for equalizing access to medical care.

The second case addresses the problem of where to locate new subsidized housing projects in the City of Los Angeles (Department of City

Planning—Los Angeles, 1973). One of the goals of the city is "to increase the supply of sound and desirable housing for low and moderate income residents". The preferred strategy is to scatter relatively small developments throughout the city, in the light of likely resident preferences, rather than to build large concentrations of public housing of the type that has generated so many social problems in Chicago, St Louis and elsewhere. The task of the planner is to find suitable sites. A two-stage process is required—first, favourable districts have to be identified by criteria relevant to resident needs, then the exact site must be determined.

The city is divided into thirty-five planning areas. Their suitability as general locations for public housing was evaluated with reference to the following criteria:

1. Transportation (walking and waiting time for a bus)
2. Job availability (average number of jobs per person)
3. Physical environment (measures of climate, air pollution, aircraft noise and ambience)
4. Education (reading test scores in schools)
5. Land cost (assessed cost of suitable land)
6. Density of existing subsidized housing (units per capita).

The rationale for choice of criteria is fairly obvious. Low-income people have special needs for easy access to employment; they are as entitled as anyone to a good environment; education is an important means of access to better opportunities for their children. Land costs are relevant to budget constraints; increasing the existing density of subsidized housing in an area was considered undesirable on community planning grounds.

For each of the first five criteria, an indicator was calculated and transformed into standard (Z) scores. The density variable had to be treated differently, but it was measured in such a way as to have the same overall weighting as the others. A general indicator of the relative suitability of each area for subsidized housing could then be calculated by summing the six indicator scores.

In this case we may introduce the complication of alternative plan objectives. Ten plans with a different emphasis are listed in Table 11.7, each requiring different weights to be assigned to the six indicators. Thus we have an example of a SWF or goal attainment indicator of the form:

$$S = \sum_{i=1}^{n} Z_i w_i \quad (i = 1, \ldots, 6) \qquad [11.3]$$

where the w reflect weights given to different objectives. Plan 1 weights the six criteria equally, Plan 2 emphasizes transportation by double-weighting this criterion, Plan 3 double-weights job availability, and so on. Differential weighting can change the priority areas: for Plan 1 the best location would be Planning Area 20 while for Plan 2 it would be Area 25. However, the results are substantially the same for most alternative plans, with a few areas recurring.

Table 11.7 Alternative planning strategies for the location of subsidized housing in Los Angeles

Plan emphasis	Indicator* weights						Priority areas†		
	T	J	P	E	L	D	1st	2nd	3rd
1. Equal weight	1	1	1	1	1	1	20	15	17
2. Transportation	2	1	1	1	1	1	25	15	17
3. Job availability	1	2	1	1	1	1	30	15	20
4. Transportation and jobs	1·5	1·5	1	1	1	1	30	15	17
5. Transportation, jobs and density	1	1	0	0	0	1	31	30	26
6. Education	1	1	1	2	1	1	20	15	17
7. Education and no job	1	0	1	2	1	1	20	15	17
8. Needs of the elderly	1	0	1	0	1	1	25	17	28
9. Land costs (slight emphasis)	1	1	1	1	1·5	1	20	15	17
10. Land costs (great emphasis)	1	1	1	1	2·5	1	25	17	1

* T = transportation, J = job availability, P = physical environment, E = education, L = land cost, D = density.
† See Figure 11.18 for location of these Planning Areas.

Source: Department of City Planning—Los Angeles (1973).

Some of the results are mapped in Figure 11.18. This identifies the highest-priority areas under Plan 1 (equal weighting) and the best areas for each of the other plans. The technique used tends to eliminate most of the inner-city areas and also the northern suburbs.

The second stage in locating subsidized housing is to identify a specific site in the top-priority area (e.g. Brentwood–Pacific Palisades for Plan 1). This is the stage at which physical site characteristics and actual land costs have to be considered. Also relevant at this point are political factors, including the power of local residents to oppose the introduction of low-income housing—a major consideration in many American cities. Once a site has been selected and funds allocated, the new density datum can be used to modify the existing density in the area in question. Then the indicators can be recalculated to find the priority area for the next housing project. This technique is still at an experimental stage, but it provides a rare example of territorial social indicators built into a dynamic allocation model for spatial planning.

As the idea of using territorial social indicators in planning spreads, practical applications are becoming more frequent. For example, the Inner London Education Authority identifies Education Priority Areas to allocate extra financial assistance to areas of special need, on the basis of poor education performance and associated social deprivation. The method used follows the standard score additive technique, with data on ten education and social variables (Little and Mabey, 1972; Knox, 1975, 14–15). The Greater London Council has also identified areas of "housing stress" based on an index incorporating seven census variables measuring housing quality and occupancy characteristics (Knox, 1975, 16–17). Somewhat similar, though broader in scope, are studies of spatial variations in multiple deprivation, social malaise or stress in British cities such as Liverpool (Amos, 1970) and Belfast (Boal *et al.*, 1974).

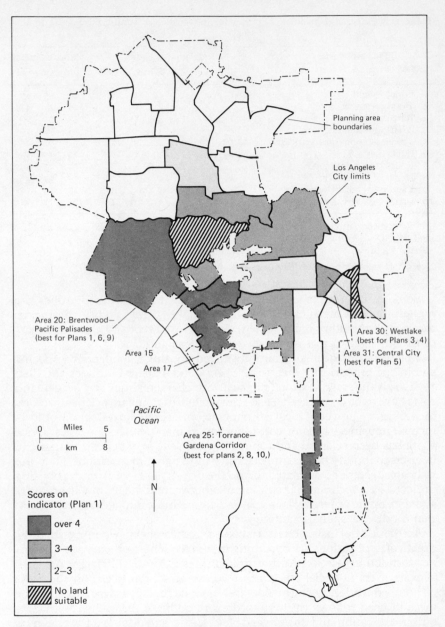

Figure 11.18 Priority areas for the location of subsidized housing in Los Angeles. (*Source of data:* Department of City Planning—Los Angeles, 1973.)

Text labels within the figure:

Planning area boundaries

Los Angeles City limits

Area 20: Brentwood—Pacific Palisades (best for Plans 1, 6, 9)

Area 15

Area 17

Area 30: Westlake (best for Plans 3, 4)

Area 31: Central City (best for Plan 5)

Pacific Ocean

Area 25: Torrance—Gardena Corridor (best for plans 2, 8, 10,)

0   Miles   5
0   km   8

N

Scores on indicator (Plan 1)

over 4

3—4

2—3

No land suitable

The identification of who needs what where offers enormous scope for applied geography. But this specifically spatial approach carries with it the danger of localizing problems that have their origin in general societal allocative and distributive mechanisms rather than in the people or environment of the particular territories found to be in need. Thus people are poorly housed in parts of Los Angeles and London because the economy does not provide them with incomes sufficient for effective demand, in a situation where private supply of housing may be limited by more profitable avenues for capital investment elsewhere. Similarly, public funds to house those in need may be limited by pressures for greater spending on mass transit, supersonic airliners, weapons systems and so on, from which the poor gain little. Thus we return to our underlying theme of the interdependence of spatial organization and the structure of the economic–social–political system. What can be done for the needy is very much dependent on the nature of society at large.

Part Four

Conclusions

Life is not determined by consciousness, but consciousness by life.

Karl Marx, *The German Ideology*, 1844–5

life doesn't *start* with a form. It starts with a new feeling, and ends with a form.

D. H. Lawrence, *Kangaroo*, 1923

The conclusions to this book can be brief. Previous chapters have set down the conceptual framework for a welfare approach to human geography and demonstrated its application to a wide range of problems. The case for this approach rests on what has already been said. It now remains to review a few of the broader issues raised. Chapter 12 considers the general significance of spatial reorganization to the improvement of human life, with a measure of circumspection to balance the practitioner's faith in the efficacy of his own disciplinary contribution. Chapter 13 considers the significance of disciplinary reorganization to the improvement of geography. While the emphasis remains on the spatial perspective, it is necessary to recognize that the study of "geography" is but one of many intellectual pursuits devised to shed light on the reality of life. To be constrained by a single discipline, or even by the practice of science, risks missing some deeper truths about the nature of man. Like any human activity, understanding comes from living and feeling as well as from analysis.

12

Spatial Reorganization and Social Reform

It is often observed that people are not born equal. Whatever the inherited differences in intellectual and physical capacity may be, the chance of birth into a particular family or group *in a particular place* immediately constrains a child's opportunities. Whether the difference is between Beverly Hills and the slums of Watts or between suburban America and rural Africa, the contrasts in quality of life to be enjoyed or endured assail our intuitive notions as to what is right, or just. How far can the reorganization of human activity in space help to make a more equal world?

Obviously, there are limits to our capacity to improve the world. We cannot yet make all deserts fertile, eliminate drought and create mineral resources where none exist in nature. As long as some people live in harsh environments with poor resources, we can expect them to have relatively low material levels of living. Whatever the rest of us may gain from such peoples remaining where they are instead of joining us to share the good fortune of a favourable natural endowment and the technology to utilize it effectively, we seem unlikely to compensate them through a major redistribution of the world's wealth. We cannot immediately eliminate human greed. We may eventually come to understand that, in Europe and North America, our own children have no more right to long, healthy and fulfilled lives than those of the poorer parts of the world. We may eventually begin to repay our debts to the underdeveloped countries, as we recognize the extent of our responsibility for their condition. Spatial reforms, however important they may be in some contexts, must be accompanied by basic change in our feelings towards other people in other places. And how we feel is very much a product of our own situation.

12.1 Spatial administrative reforms

Local government reform is very much a matter of concern today in countries like Britain and the USA. This in itself is an indication of dissatisfaction with present spatial administrative structures. The situation in the United States is summarized in the following description by Higbee (1970, 9–10; quoted in Symons, 1971, 66), which echoes some observations from earlier chapters in this book:

> The jurisdiction of local governments are limited by their geography. These boundaries produce inequities in the public environment. School districts, water

districts, sewer districts, police and fire districts are distinguished by wide disparities in the amounts and qualities of taxable real estate within their territories. Some districts are almost exclusively composed of low-cost, utilitarian structures in a mediocre state of repair. Other districts are high-class exclusive communities—too rich for the poor to get into. Since the quality of public services is directly related to the quality of real estate, some communities enjoy the very best in the way of schools, parks, streets, etc. Others are forced to get by with inferior everything. An American child's chances for future development and well-being depend not upon his nationality but upon his locality. There is no such thing as equality in the public environment because localities are primarily responsible for public services. There is no such thing as being born equal. It depends upon whether the address is good or bad. Good schools go with a good address, bad schools with a bad address—it is as simple as that. America is not a democracy when it comes to its public services. There is not even the semblance of equality between the public services of its Scarsdales and its Harlems.

Spatial aspects of administrative systems have been explored at length by Massam (1972; 1974; 1975). The major issues have been recognized for some time in the literature on public finance and urban government, as was indicated in Chapter 5. The conventional answer to spatial disparities in services, as provided by small administrative units, is metropolitan-scale government via the consolidation of jurisdictions, or the imposition of some control by an upper-tier authority. Uniform standards of service provision can be established and economies of scale realized, but at some cost in terms of lost community control and restriction of choice in the local structure of services.

An analysis of this problem will help to highlight fundamental issues of choice, efficiency and equity in the provision of public services and other aspects of local life quality. Suppose that there are three groups of people (say, rich, middle-class and poor) occupying distinct segments of a city. Demand for a public service (say, education) varies among the groups—the poor want most because they cannot afford private education—but within groups there are identical tastes so that a single demand curve (D) holds for all individuals. The groups occupy three different local government areas. Assuming that the average cost (AC) of providing the service is the same in each area and constant irrespective of scale (Q), the situation for each group would be as in Figure 12.1a. The intersection of the demand curves with cost indicate the quantity of education (X) provided in each area. The net benefits derived from education in each case are as shown by size of consumers' surplus.

Now, suppose that the three local government or education authority areas are consolidated into one (Figure 12.1b). The same level of public educational provision must now apply to all—say X in Figure 12.1c corresponding with the previous middle-class preference. The other two groups now lose some of their original consumers' surplus. In the case of the poor this is because they get less education than they would prefer, while for the rich they get and have to pay for more than before. Even if consolidation reduces average cost to AC', to increase output to X', some losses will still remain, for conflicting preferences cannot be met

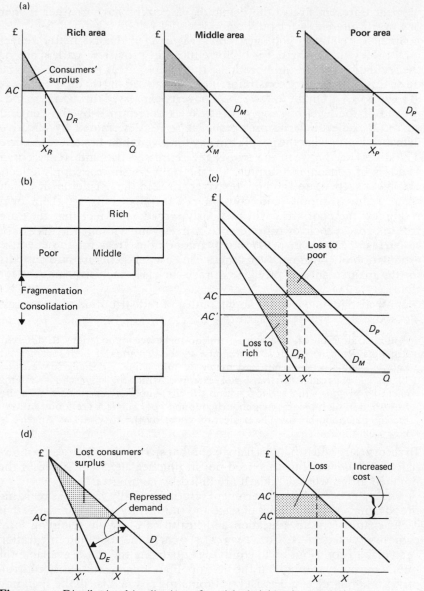

Figure 12.1 Distributional implications of spatial administrative reorganization.

simultaneously. Hence the common conclusion that "when it is necessary to combine individual demands for a public good the most efficient political unit for articulating the demand is a relatively homogeneous one" (Bish, 1971, 49). An examination of two major American metropolitan-scale government units—the City of Los Angeles and Dade County centred on Miami, Florida—leads Bish (1971, 102) to conclude that both "appear unresponsive to the demands of citizens having either higher or lower preferences for public goods and services".

Smaller, relatively homogeneous areas can (in theory) better reflect local preferences, whether it be for education provision, park space or the regulations of bars and brothels. But in poor areas preferences come up against the resource constraint. This is analysed in two different ways in Figure 12.1d. On the left, we show poverty expressed through demand: instead of the level of supply being X, as determined by the demand curve (D) reflecting true preference, it is X' determined by effective demand (D_E) or what the people can pay for given their limited resources. The difference between the two is the repressed demand, represented as a loss of consumers' surplus. On the right we show a supply effect: average cost (per pupil and per taxpayer) rises in the smaller area, which again reduces supply and consumers' surplus. Left to their own resources, the poor areas will be poorly served. The fact that they are free to express their own preference is irrelevant without the necessary resources. The argument for small, autonomous areas for the effective articulation of consumer preferences can easily degenerate into support for the maintenance of privilege in race- or class-exclusive suburbs for the rich.

But consolidation alone is no guarantee of redistribution of resources. To quote Bish (1971, 92) again:

> Administrative bureaucracies may and do make accommodations to different demands—but usually, it is in response to the demands of high-income and knowledgeable persons, not to demands of minorities, especially low-income Blacks or Mexican Americans. For example, while big city school systems allegedly provide equal services within the city, superior services are normally furnished in high-income neighbourhoods and poor services are found in low-income neighbourhoods. The neglect of Watts by the City of Los Angeles is now well known.

In theory, large jurisdictions help to combat spatial externalities by internalizing spillovers, but this need not in practice alter who breathes the polluted air or whose children are killed by commuters' cars.

The challenge in local government reform is usually viewed as realizing the advantages of economies of scale and uniformity of the standards that really matter (e.g. in education and health care), while retaining local community control. As Cox (1973, 114) puts it, metropolitan integration "can make a contribution to equity by equalizing the funds available for public purposes throughout the metropolitan area. Community control, on the other hand, could assist by eliminating spatial bias in the spending of those funds." This implies a two-tier system of local government. A third (upper) tier may also be necessary, to ensure that each metropolis meets basic standards for provision of services and effectively implements national redistributive policy favouring the poor and socially deprived. This is the kind of régime under which Netzer (1968, 453–4) considers that output of public services might be maximized.

The Americans are only just beginning to face the problems of spatial reform in local government. Fragmentation suits the rich suburbs, which can thereby cut themselves off from fiscal responsibility for the problems of the inner city from where much of their wealth is drawn. How successful the reforms elsewhere (Britain, for example) will be is uncertain— and likely to remain so in the absence of any mechanism to monitor the performance of the new and larger local authorities compared with the old. Economies of scale may be lost in expanded bureaucracies, while greater equity in distribution depends on who has control. Spatial organization is, of course, only one of many variables affecting the performance of government in satisfying human needs—and the idea of local government "performance" is itself relatively novel even in political science (Fried, 1973; Fried and Rabinovitz, 1975).

The same problems arise with regional government. Currently, there is much interest in the idea of *devolution* of administrative functions and political power from the capital city to regional centres. Britain is a case in point, with dispersal of power to some extent a recognition of independence movements in Wales and Scotland. The argument for devolution rests largely on the proposition that decentralized power is more democratic and responsive to specific regional needs. In addition, the region may be the most efficient territorial unit for resource allocation and planning. The case against devolution is similar to that used to oppose metropolitan fragmentation, stressing the difficulty of maintaining equality of treatment of people in different, largely autonomous jurisdictions. As Craven (1975, 16) puts it: "The absence of powerful regional governments in the past has meant that national resources could be distributed, in part at least, on an objective and egalitarian assessment of need. If regional government did exist, the distribution of resources from the centre would become, much more than now, a process of political horse-trading in which the political strength rather than the objective needs of regions would play an important part." Regional government can also have a *local* redistributive effect, with political power able to pull resources into well-off suburbs or country towns instead of to the inner-city poor whose protection is traditionally the role of central government social policy.

We are still a long way from designing ideal spatial administrative structures. And we still do not know just how important spatial form is likely to be. *Local* government itself may be a side issue, diverting attention from the broader societal structure really responsible for the local problems (Lee, 1976). As Eversley (1975, 55) recognizes in the context of devolution, "The serious problems of our time are mainly those concerned with economic failure, and with the inadequacy of our distributive system which even in periods of growth leaves some sections of the population seriously disadvantaged."

Similar issues are raised by supra-national administrative organizations, such as the European Economic Community. Centralization of decision-making can lead to loss of political sovereignty, and to conflict between the interests of individual nations and the bloc as a whole. European economic (and ultimately political) integration may promote greater efficiency in production, in a system already to a large extent organized

on an international scale by private business institutions. But it is far
from self-evident that this is in the real interests of the people of Europe,
whose destinies are being increasingly removed from local control. The
critical question of who should control what, and at which spatial administrative level, is far from being solved.

12.2　Spatial planning reforms

Planning has undergone important changes in the past three decades.
From its early preoccupation with architecture and engineering problems, city planning has become steadily more explicitly spatial. In the
1960s regional planning expanded the geographical frame of reference
and in certain countries this approach became an integral part of national
economic planning. The 1970s have seen social planning emerge, to
broaden the scope of what we attempt to control and guide with rational
deliberation. The current interest in spatial income-redistributive aspects
of planning, strongly reflected in this book, is part of the geographer's
response to changing societal concerns stressing quality of life instead
of quantity of goods and equity instead of efficiency.

It has been explained at length in earlier chapters that who gets what
where is susceptible to control through spatial reorganization. The location of employment, public facilities, roads and so on can be evaluated
with respect to its spatial redistributive impact. More important still, new
locations or spatial structures can be designed to satisfy particular goals
with respect to who *should* get what where—who deserves or needs what
where. While we recognize the difficulty of setting societal goals and planning for their attainment, the capacity to enhance human welfare through
more rational spatial resource allocation certainly exists.

The role of spatial planning can be both restrictive and creative. Restrictive planning includes the zoning of land for particular purposes,
perhaps preventing development in green belts and National Parks. This
type of land-use planning has a long tradition, especially in Western
Europe. More positive or creative planning includes choice of sites for
new towns and cities, industrial growth points, transport routes, service
facility location and the direction or inducement of industry to places
of special need. At the more local scale it includes various aspects of environmental design such as the layout of a housing estate or a children's
playground.

Two basic questions arise from the practice of spatial planning, at the
local, city or regional level. The first is whether we really do enough imaginative and creative planning, as opposed to restrictive activity. The
second is (again) to what extent we achieve the desired outcome and how
much planned spatial organization really matters to the differentiation
of human life chances.

As an example of more creative spatial planning, we may return to
the idea of individual preferences being most effectively met in areas of
homogeneous tastes. This is already part of our daily life experience in
some respects, e.g. the "smoking" and "no smoking" compartments in

railway carriages—a superior arrangement to mixed compartments in a general welfare sense because, if all together, either non-smokers suffer the negative externality of polluted air or the smokers suffer because they cannot smoke for a while. Mishan (1967, 144–6) extends this idea: separate parts of a beach can be allocated to those who like to listen to transistor radios and those who do not, those who prefer life without motor vehicles could have an area set aside for their exclusive use, and so on. Similar solutions to other problems of conflicting preferences or activities generating potential harm for others readily come to mind. Nude bathers can be accommodated on a special beach, for the benefit of participants and voyeurs whose preferences would otherwise be frustrated. Drug abuse might most effectively be dealt with by legalization for adults, thus reducing the extent to which addicts are exploited by monopoly suppliers and harassed by the police, subject to zoning regulations to protect minors from contact with adult users (e.g. Culyer, 1973, 240). A similar case is the public purveying of pornographic books and films (a particularly successful form of business exploitation of human sexuality): perhaps the old days in London of a few shops and cinemas in Soho where they could readily be found by those who wanted them were preferable to prominent displays on the corner of Oxford Street and Tottenham Court Road to any ten-year-old who happens to be passing. Perhaps the old informal zoning of the red-light district was preferable to the "massage parlours" and telephone "escort" agencies, that now spread prostitution on demand to all parts of a city.

Such cases of course raise difficult moral problems. Some individual freedom is restricted by any kind of spatial zoning, just as it is by *laissez-faire* attitudes—whether to property development, the use of drugs or pornography. More practical difficulties include that of real access or freedom: the asthmatic traveller may not be able to get into the no-smoking compartment; the poor parents may not be able to leave the neighbourhood where their children experience the depravity of the Skid Row or red-light quarter. Zoning to satisfy conflicting preferences assumes either homogeneity to begin with or spatial mobility. A common proposition in literature on urban government and public finance is that people with particular preferences will tend to move to places where these are best satisfied (e.g. Netzer, 1968, 85; Bish, 1971, 49), but we know that the poor are effectively excluded from living in many parts of the city. Movement works another way: to create homogeneity where it does not presently exist requires the non-conformists to move out, an obvious example being the creation of racially homogeneous areas in South African cities. Nevertheless, there is probably more scope than is generally recognized for broader creative zoning of urban and regional space for people with particular preferences, life-styles or needs likely to generate negative externalities for others.

Another example of more creative spatial planning is provided by networks of personal interaction. Much of the pleasure of life for many people comes from their contact with others—physical and mental. Perhaps planners should transfer some of the effort currently expended on designing motor-transport networks to the creation of environments in which human beings can interact and relate to one another in fuller and more fulfilling ways than is currently possible in the modern metropolis. Axelrod (1956) and others have drawn attention to the importance of networks of "affectionate" relationships. Perhaps planners should try to improve these through the creation of environments conducive to the exchange of love and affection in all its forms. This would help to complement aspects of spatial structure that tend to promote aggression, as for example on the roads of modern cities where commuters in their

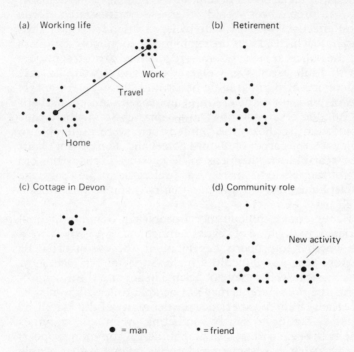

Figure 12.2 Spatial linkage and personal affectionate relationships.

motorized capsules behave towards others in a manner almost inconceivable in face-to-face interaction.

Figure 12.2 shows an imaginary case of a network of affectionate relations. An urban man tends to find his contacts with others primarily in the home, the neighbourhood and his place of work, to which might be added a few between these focal points—the bus conductor, regular fellow traveller, newsagent and so on. The man has a well developed system of contacts producing for him what Isard *et al.* (1969) would describe as the commodities affection, sociability and perhaps respect. Then the man retires. Abruptly, he loses his workmates, his fellow traveller and so on (Figure 12.1b). At home all day and missing the self-esteem derived from his job, he relies much more heavily than before on his wife—and he may not be an altogether welcome infusion into her established social networks and general way of life. To add to this traumatic change, the couple may retire to the long-dreamed-of cottage in Devon, to be almost totally isolated from existing friends and relatives. To some people these changes are a challenge and they successfully adjust by making new friends or developing new pastimes. To others it is a beginning to life's end. Many so-called primitive societies have solutions to such problems, with a purposeful role at all stages in the life cycle—including old age when grandchildren can be cared for and perhaps the cattle minded. But in "advanced" societies no such opportunities may exist. The grand-children may be many miles away and the cattle are gone. Planners might possibly assist, by seeing that old people (for example) may, if they choose, be so located as to find a new role in the community—part-time jobs, baby-sitting for working wives, and so on. All too often, accommodation for old people restricts contact with others rather than making for new or extended affectionate relationships. All too often, redevelopment destroys the spatial networks on which people depend for important social needs, so that "development" in this context is a misnomer.

This is just one example of an aspect of life where creative planning might help people to participate, to belong and to relate to others, if they choose to do so. Similar instances readily come to mind. But just as they raise a challenge to our ingenuity and imagination as manipulators of space, so they raise the question of how effective such planning can be and whether it is people rather than space that is being manipulated. There is no need here to debate the ethics of "social engineering" and the associated dangers of deliberately moulding people's lives to patterns not necessarily of their own choosing—important though these issues are. More to the point in the present context is that there are limits to our capacity to promote change in people's life chances, however desirable, whether the chosen instrument is spatial reorganization, new social services or even perhaps a cultural revolution.

Examples of the failure of physical spatial planning to achieve social goals are not hard to find. The ideal of social interaction among classes aided by building mixed housing in Britain's new towns is an obvious case, suggesting that most people prefer to live with their own kind what-ever the planners may consider desirable. Improving communications into a depressed peripheral region may assist outward migration as much as promote economic revival. Well intentioned plans may misfire or even backfire with quite undesirable consequences. Friedman (1962, 179) gives the following description of the effect of the public housing pro-gramme in the USA:

Once the program was adopted, it was bound to be dominated by the special interests that it could serve. In this case the special interests were those local groups that were anxious to have blighted areas cleared and refurbished, either because they owned property there or because the blight was threatening local or central business districts. Public housing served as a convenient means to accomplish their objective, which required more destruction than construction.

Possible reactions to this differ: Milton Friedman would eliminate public housing, we would eliminate the power of the vested interests. But it does typify the kind of problems arising when the planning process is easily coopted by a local business clique to further their own interests. This is common in the USA and not unknown in Britain. Corrupt city governments allocate construction contracts to the firm who pay the bribes or finance the election campaigns and the poor are (eventually) rehoused in blocks of high-rise flats not of their choosing and quite unsuited to normal family life. The real-income transfer from poor to rich is thus completed.

Regressive public policy is not always quite so transparent. It may arise from the very nature of bureaucratic organization and the more personal, professional objectives of the "public servants" concerned. Simmie (1974, xi) comments as follows: "The paradox has developed that, where the demonstrated effectiveness, from its clients' point of view, of the outputs from town planning is the only criterion of success, all too often town planners measure their success in terms of plan inputs and the esteem they acquire among their professional colleagues." The organizational environment predisposes its members to certain attitudes, rewarding conforming behaviour on behalf of existing interests. Its supposedly neutral decision rules thus have a class bias, so that when applied to the allocation of a city's resources they encourage a pattern of "the more, the more" (Levi, Meltsner and Wildavsky, 1974, 227–32). One result of all this in recent years has been the emergence of more informal organizations acting as pressure groups on behalf of the poor and powerless.

Planning at the regional scale can run into similar problems of not in fact benefiting those in most need. The development strategy of growth points and the integration of the space-economy is an obvious case. On the one hand, we have a vision of the benefits of Western civilization and material affluence cascading down the urban hierarchy to peasants eager to exchange the idleness of underemployment for the benefits of full-time wage labour. On the other we have uncertainty as to whether all that is passed down from core to periphery is necessarily good and, if it is, whether the spatial spread effect is as predictable as proponents of growth point "theory" and the hierarchical diffusion hypothesis would have us believe (see Chapter 5). Harvey (1973, 238) puts his suspicions as follows:

> Liberal policy suggestions of the sort advocated by John Friedmann envisage generating economic growth in underdeveloped nations through the creation of "effective space" within which products and people can be mobilized in a hierarchical form of urbanism: clearly this policy would create a form of spatial organization which would serve merely to increase the rate of exploitation and to create the necessary conditions for the efficient and irresistible extraction of even greater quantities of surplus for the ultimate benefit of the imperial powers.

Planners really concerned with the well-being of peripheral people might profitably look to rural development strategies, where the benefits of better health services, schools and so on can be produced in a cooperative social structure in which people do not need to become wage labourers for a private manufacturer or landowner. All too often, the outside adviser and indigenous power elite collude to see that "development" proceeds under a mode of production that may greatly benefit the few and merely substitute one misery for another for the mass of the people.

Clearly, we need to be much more open-minded as to the manner in which urban and regional planning might be used to enhance human well-being. We need to be prepared to question the type of planning strategy, and also the activity of planning itself. We can easily overestimate our capacity consciously to control people's lives through planned spatial reorganization. So much of what is good in life stems from spontaneous human interaction. We may be able to build environments in which good human relationships are fostered. But no planner can guarantee the outcome; indeed we would be justifiably suspicious of any form of planning that had a mechanically deterministic impact on human behaviour.

The crucial point to the geographer is that space and distance may not matter quite as much as we are inclined to believe. Certainly, such things as accessibility and facility location do have a bearing on human life chances. Certainly, there is scope in spatial reorganization for the more efficient production and more equitable distribution of sources of human well-being. But within certain limits, location may be barely relevant. In industrial location it has been recognized for some time that a range of choice exists within what Rawstron (1958) first termed the spatial margin to profitability; within somewhat narrower limits neither private profits nor net social gains may vary significantly with precise location. Similarly in the delivery of services: Massam (1974, 185) cites the case of ambulance services in a city, which may be largely insensitive to facility location as far as its actual performance (e.g. response-time) is concerned. It is perhaps natural that any discipline will tend to exaggerate the importance of its own special variables, in our case space and distance. In doing so we run a particularly serious risk in welfare studies, that of overlooking the wider societal context in which the broad features of human inequality are really decided.

12.3 Societal reforms

The organization of society at large operates as a constraint on what can be achieved by spatial reorganization. If institutions unresponsive to basic human needs cannot be changed, then the location of their physical plant may be largely irrelevant to many people. An obvious case from Chapter 11 is medical care in the United States: the present fee-for-service system is far more important in excluding the poor from treatment than the spatial arrangement of facilities. If we wish to see medical care more equally or fairly distributed the initial assault must be on private-enterprise medicine as an institution, which may require a more general assault on private enterprise as a philosophy. Only when the practice of medicine becomes a public service does planned spatial organization become a relevant issue.

It will be apparent from both the theoretical sections of this book and from some of the case studies that the capitalist mode of production is at the root of much social inequality—spatial or otherwise. An initially favourable factor endowment generates income and the capacity for further concentration of wealth in the form of capital and land; this in its turn helps to buy the political power needed to maintain or further expand economic advantage. The ethics of capitalism stress aggressive competition and the conspicuous differentiation of the successful from those who fail. Inequality is a natural consequence. The great illogicality of the usual liberal position is to bemoan the undesirable outcomes of such a system without seeking the cure in the only way it can really be found—in the nature of the system itself. As Harvey (1973, 140) says of ghetto housing, "if we accept the mores of normal, ethical entrepreneurial behaviour, there is no way in which we can blame anyone for the objective social conditions which all are willing to characterize as appalling and wasteful of housing resources". In this case, the only effective solution will require the replacement of market forces as the major distributor of housing, the public ownership of urban building land and the elimination of opportunities to use land and buildings for speculative purposes that bear no relationship to human needs for space and shelter. If we are not prepared to consider this type of solution, then it is probably a waste of time for geographers and others to analyse and criticize the social degradation of the slums, wherever they happen to be.

Similarly in the problem of underdevelopment, we cannot simultaneously claim concern for the poor of Latin America, Africa and Asia while our own high living standards in Europe and North America are in part dependent on obtaining cheap primary products. We cannot resist rises in the price of sugar and tea and still maintain that we care about low wages in the plantations of Jamaica or Sri Lanka. We cannot reasonably advocate independence and self-determination for the ex-colonial territories while remaining indifferent to the exploitive and manipulative roles of some international corporation operating in these countries. We cannot assume that the type of industrial revolution under private enterprise that transformed the economies of Europe and North America, at enormous social cost, is necessarily appropriate for the Third World.

The geographer should at least be open-minded enough to see that there may be greater merit to some of the development strategies practised with evident if not painless success in the USSR, China, Cuba and so on. Planning *development* instead of underdevelopment requires a spatial structure stressing internal cohesion, with the resource-rich regions integrated into the national economy, not into some external system of domination and exploitation. In an interdependent world economy motivated by greed, self-reliance may be the key to self-determination. And the form of the space-economy is central to this objective; as Slater (1975, 158) puts it:

An organic link must be forged between the structure of production and the structure of needs of the society as a whole. One of the achievements of countries such as Cuba, North Korea, Vietnam, and China is that their previous spatial disintegration has been replaced by a system of spatial organization which utilizes to the full the resources of all the various zones of their territories so as to satisfy internal needs. And as a result, inter-regional interdependencies and exchanges have evolved and matured as an important solidifying agent of national economic integration. So long as a space-economy is internally atomized and externally tied, such development is not possible. To plan is to choose, and to choose in the context of socialist transformation is to reject the contradictory combination of internal disintegration and external integration.

Samuelson (1973, 616), that favourite target for radical critiques in economics, recognizes that there are alternatives:

> When we consider what great amounts of plant, equipment, and inventories could do for developing countries like India, Brazil or South Korea, for planned economies like Russia, China, or North Korea, for advanced economies like Japan, Italy or the United States, I am led to think that *great gains in the size of the social pie to be divided up in the future can be hoped for from capital accumulation at the expense of present-day consumption.* But this does not mean that private property, unequally distributed, is the only twentieth-century mechanism to bring this about.

The effective socialization of production under capitalism, with all its real and potential material benefits, stands in supreme contradiction with private appropriation (Mandel, 1962, 170)—with the affluence of the few and the poverty of the mass of the world's people. The latest stage of capitalist development, with its trans-national network of giant corporations, reveals again, in the words of Hymer (1975, 61), "the power of social cooperation and division of labour which so fascinated Adam Smith. . . . It also shows the shortcomings of concentrating this power in private hands."

If we prefer not to consider these general issues of political economy, we might at least think about the role of spatial reform in its wider context. An over-preoccupation with spatial reorganization may serve the interests of the existing rich and powerful by helping to obscure the more fundamental issues. Lee (1976, 47), in writing of the advantages of a separate urban level of government to the ruling class, captures the essence of the dangers implicit in purely spatial reform:

> First an emphasis on spatial reformism transforms *allocational structures* into *distributional problems* and so suggests *distributional solutions* to *structural conditions*. But allocational causes are not area based and cannot be cured by spatial reformism. Indeed the superficial (distributional) inequalities between *areas* obscure, in an area-based approach to reform, fundamental (allocational) *class* divisions. Redistribution by area may be necessary as part of the equitable distribution of real income but class structure (the distribution of the ownership of the means to produce) remains the fundamental cause of inequality and the distribution of economic power. Secondly, if urban government is (falsely) perceived as something in its own right it can be used to offload and localize political discontent.

If as geographers we are interested in space relationships, the demands of scholarship require that we trace their implications as far back into the fabric of a society as they go. We must miss nothing, hide nothing, and have nothing hidden from us.

While seeing space in its proper perspective, we may recognize more clearly that spatial reform can contribute to societal reform. In our modern, interconnected societies, the impact of our behaviour on the quality of life of others is calling into question basic assumptions as to how we deal with space—with segments of the earth's surface and the scarce resources or other valuable attributes embodied in them. That spaces and natural resources should be privately owned, with their use subject to the chance of individual avarice, altruism or whim, is increasingly an anachronism. This is especially true in the contemporary city, in which external effects of proximity and accessibility are so important. "It becomes increasingly difficult to maintain the distinction between public and private. . . . Traditional concepts of property rights no longer appear adequate and have to be supplemented by the creation of collective property rights through the political organization of space" (Harvey, 1973, 308). The collective management of space from a general welfare viewpoint is a major challenge to geography, requiring the most creative and imaginative thoughts that we can muster.

There is a sense in which some novel and effective solutions may be thrust upon us by geographical space in a world of steadily diminishing real distances. Our knowledge of other people in other places is growing—not so much by virtue of the popularity of the study of geography but by modern communications media bringing the rest of the world, almost literally, into our living rooms. Thus the television shows us in the well protected West the reality of starvation and the brutality of war, just as newspapers and the transistor radio open up an awareness of the world outside and its opportunities to hitherto isolated people in the underdeveloped world. The closer people are, or appear to be, the more we may care about them. For example, when some catastrophe occurs people tend to give less to those in need who are far away (Culyer, 1973, 87); human concern may be subject to distance decay. The closer we are in space, the closer we may be in a more fundamental human sense, whether as travelling companions in a railway carriage or people on different sides of the globe who begin to understand their shared concerns and aspirations. Out of our common experience as inhabitants of the fragile and contracting "space-ship Earth", we may find the new feeling to give the world a new form, if we can only break free from the limits of consciousness imposed by our present way of life.

13

Human Welfare and Geography

The main points of the argument in this book are as follows. The well-being of society and its individual members is a proper and necessary topic for geographical analysis, which has been neglected in the past. It raises difficult problems of both description and interpretation, associated with the evaluation of spatial states of society against criteria that include equity as well as efficiency. As is generally the case in human geography, the welfare approach relies on other social sciences for its theoretical foundations. Economics provides a helpful starting point; other fields such as sociology and political science can also make contributions, though there has not been the opportunity to do much more than hint at these possibilities in the present work. Difficult though the transition from theory to reality may be, the case studies should have been sufficient to reveal something of the scope for empirical research and for an applied geography concerned with major societal problems in human welfare.

Underlying the actual substance of the welfare approach are some fundamental issues concerning the nature and purpose of geographical inquiry. Brief comments on these are offered by way of conclusion and as a final justification for the direction taken in this book.

13.1 On welfare in geography

As was suggested at the outset, professional geography is in a state of flux. Major advances in techniques and research methods have been made in recent years, as the quantitative-models-theory paradigm of a more scientific geography has largely replaced the traditional approaches. But scarcely had the "new" geography of the 1960s become established than another wind of change began to blow. Its message was "social relevance"; its direction towards more professional concern for the problems of the world.

The reaction has been predictably varied. Some see the call to relevance as just another fad, though perhaps more uncomfortable than previous ones because of its political implications. In time, many opponents of the quantitative revolution developed some admiration for numerical analysis, which could be appreciated as an intellectual advance in line with the traditional yearning in geography for scientific status. But "problem solving" is not quite the same. It may be viewed as conflicting with deep-seated assumptions concerning the societal role of scholars and universities, threatening the tradition of academic detachment and objectivity and even involving the danger of the politicization of students. Something of the opposition is reflected in the reaction of Trewartha (1973) to a plea for more professional involvement in public policy which closed with the question, "What shall it profit a profession if it fabricate a nifty discipline about the world while that world and the human spirit are degraded" (White, 1972, 104). Trewartha sees in this "the manifesto of a social and political activist", and concludes that White apparently advocates classes becoming "indoctrination sessions, which the individual instructor uses to promote his personal views concerning the social order" (Trewartha, 1973, 79). This captures the essence of the conflict precipitated in geography by the era of social activism.

Another reaction is that we have in fact been applying ourselves to human problems for years. "That geographers are, and should be, socially aware is no new American discovery.... Many British (and American) geographers had devoted their research to an investigation of the social, political and economic problems of [the Third World] long before the new revolution broke" (Dickinson and Clark, 1972). This is true, of course, and it may well be that those working in the field in such areas as Africa and Latin America are closer to the problems of real people than most of the quantifiers or activists. The main distinguishing feature of the new "relevance" movement is a questioning of whether the nature of geography as presently structured is really appropriate to the task of problem-oriented research, whether textbooks and teachers deal directly enough with contemporary social issues, and whether geography can avoid implicit support of particular policy measures or social orders. It invites the applied geographer to examine more critically her or his training, motivation and *modus operandi*.

Some of the innovators of the 1960s have also reacted to the call for social relevance with lack of enthusiasm. They may see their position threatened by a new generation, who take regression models, factor analysis and so on as given, and ask—what next? They also see a real danger that the value judgements implicit in the activist approach might impair objectivity of research and threaten the hard-won scientific status of the new geography. However, many of those who promoted the quantitative revolution have now moved into policy-oriented research and are playing a role in the search for constructive involvement in social change. Many of the tools and techniques fashioned in the 1960s and sharpened on what were often inconsequential problems have obvious application in research directed at major social issues. The relevance movement seems, in fact, to provide just what the quantifiers and model-builders need—something to get their feet back on to the ground occupied by real people, whose lives might be enhanced by a resurgence of applied geography.

Where does the welfare approach fit in? In Chapter 1 it was argued that the well-being of society as a spatially variable condition should be *the* focal point of geographical inquiry. Accepting this is not an "activist" position, implying dedication to a particular political ideology. It simply requires recognition of what is surely the self-evident truth that if human beings are the object of our curiosity in human geography, then the quality of their lives is of paramount interest. Demographic characteristics, economic activity, organization of space, diffusion of innovations and so on, though not without interest in themselves, are ultimately significant as things that contribute to the differentiation of territory with respect to the well-being of those who inhabit it. The theoretical framework and the empirical studies in this book have demonstrated that welfare analysis necessarily involves economic, social, cultural and political considerations, whatever the spatial level of inquiry. It also involves the physical environment, in so far as this is part of the resource constraint. Welfare is thus a natural integrating theme. It provides a contemporary equivalent of the regional concept, to which geographers once looked as a means of tying together their disparate subject matter. It also asks that we cross disciplinary boundaries much more often, thus contributing to integration within the social sciences at large. In short, a welfare focus provides a centripetal force to counter centrifugal tendencies in the study of human existence.

But the difficulties must not be overlooked. For example, the use of welfare economics as an alternative point of departure for location theory (Chisholm, 1971a) proves much more difficult than the conventional approach based on microeconomic theory of the firm—and this is difficult enough, as the paucity of convincing empirical applications of location theory testifies. At the very least, we have to be specific about what "welfare" might be, if we are to avoid living in the clouds. The identification of societal goals and of the causal mechanisms determining their attainment poses a multitude of conceptual problems. It also raises the question of the limits of human capacity to improve the world through the rational, managerial approach that pervades modern organization and planning theory. We are soon brought up against the reality that there are no hard and fast laws in human behaviour—no general theory and no working model to simulate and ultimately control human life in all its aspects.

The welfare approach does not stand or fall by its ability to effect immediate reformulations of theory, however. It can play a vital part in the revitalization of description in human geography, including the conventional regional synthesis. It is the prospect of opening eyes and minds to the realities of a world in which millions of people suffer an unnecessarily deprived existence that the initial benefits from the welfare approach are likely to arise. We cannot accept the proposition that "mapping even more evidence of man's patent inhumanity to man is counter-revolutionary" or irrelevant (Harvey, 1973, 144) until the real state of the world is the central disciplinary focus. However, it could well be counter-developmental if we were merely led into another decade of abstract theorizing, model-building and measurement, even with a welfare focus, if this did not have some fairly early practical pay-offs in the creation of a more equal world.

But pursuit of the welfare approach does not necessarily require a personal or professional commitment to the promotion of social change. It follows logically from any of the traditional definitions of geography—areal differentiation, location analysis, spatial organization, and even man–environment relationships. All necessarily involve human welfare. Welfare analysis can be undertaken with little relaxation of our present level of academic detachment, or what the individual scholar might see as objectivity or neutrality. But it does require us to look the world's problems in the face, rather than as something properly the province of politics, sociology or ecology and purely peripheral to geography. And if this experience leads us to a more active participation in policy-related research, or to the role of agent or facilitator of change, then the welfare approach should also be able to provide a sound base for positive knowledge on which to proceed.

13.2 On neutrality and commitment

One of the major questions raised by the welfare approach is that of ethical neutrality. Suspicion about the introduction of personal values is at the root of much of the opposition to a more socially activist or problem-solving geography. As long as we confine ourselves to such fields as geomorphology and quantitative methodology, we can probably avoid value judgements up to the point of asking whether the project is worthwhile. But as soon as we turn our attention to human welfare, particularly to questions of distribution, ethical considerations cannot be avoided and political controversy inevitably arises.

This has been a problem in economics for decades. On the one hand are those who see their role confined to providing positive knowledge, while on the other it is argued that even here ethics are not totally excluded and that there is an obligation to make recommendations to society. Graaff (1957, 170) puts the former position as follows:

> the job ... is not to try to reach welfare conclusions for others, but rather to make available the positive knowledge—the information and the understanding—on the basis of which the laymen ... can pass judgement.

Rothenberg (1961, 331) expresses similar sentiments:

> Anyone is free to criticize currently prevailing values. The welfare economist is neither uniquely nor even especially qualified for such a task.... The welfare economist, *qua* welfare economist, is not concerned with criticizing either the old or the new values themselves.

Recent writers seem less inclined to accept this apparent neutrality. Nath (1969, 130), reacting to Rothenberg, finds it totally unacceptable, saying:

> it is the right, if not the responsibility of every economist, *qua* economist or welfare economist, *and* of every other adult, to enter into such a criticism. Further, in our opinion, "to help reconstruct institutions in accordance with the newly formed values" is exactly the task of applied economics.

Applied geography might be viewed in the same light. Unless we confine our role to that of mapping out policy alternatives from which society makes a choice, it is difficult to see how we can ever approach neutrality.

And even leaving the decision to "society" has value connotations, for we are not entirely ignorant about how choices are made and whose interests are likely to be served.

The insistence that the social scientist's role be confined to the provision of positive knowledge is itself a value judgement. And the extent to which it is upheld cannot be divorced from the fact that it is in the interests of those who might be threatened by a more activist stance. We are taught to revere objectivity, rationality, quantitative precision, theoretical sophistication, rigour, and so on, and to decry the insertion of emotion or feeling into our research. Hurst (1972, 1) puts the situation in geography thus:

> The current positivist stance and scientistic approach leads to the view that knowledge is inherently neutral and that the standard and exactness of the physical sciences is the only explanatory model for knowledge; this leads in turn to a refusal to view geography as a humane enterprise basically concerned with the human condition.

Hurst (1972a, 1972b) argues that contemporary economic and urban geography is largely supportive of the *status quo* and predisposes people to acceptance of the social ills accompanying capitalism. The present author (Smith, 1973b, 3) has suggested that the bias of geography towards the production of goods and the exploitation of resources, and also the current preoccupation with numbers and computers, may induce an indifference to environmental degradation and to human satisfaction or suffering. The plea by Harvey (1972b) for a new revolution in geographical thought—for knowledge which helps to solve problems instead of perpetuating them—is in a similar vein.

Participation or involvement in social change inevitably poses the question of who gains from our contribution. The following observations by Bish (1971, 150) are to the point:

> The achievement of any particular public interest usually results in benefits for some individuals and costs for others. It would appear that identification of benefits and costs in relation to the individuals who bear them would be more useful than the designation of programs that result in specific benefits to particular individuals as being in the "public interest". Too often, the public interest, as expressed by political reformers, coincides with policies that benefit non-minority groups, middle and upper-middle-income class individuals, to the neglect of minority preferences—and most political reformers are of the upper middle- and upper-income classes.

While a scholar is unlikely to attempt to bestow a special status on a preferred plan simply by deeming it to be "in the national interest", he or she may be powerless to prevent a politician from doing so. And scholars may themselves be guilty of unconscious elitism in their prescriptions as to what may be "best" for people. The ideal of spatial equality of life chances may be an academic elitist concept, which most "ordinary" people might judge inferior to personal (spatial) mobility in an unequal geographical state. The role of custodian of the interests of the people is not an easy one to play, or to learn.

But even more important than the ethics of involvement is the question of whether our so-called positive knowledge is really perfectly neutral. Fear of value judgements has severely restricted the discussion of distribution in economics; economists try hard to avoid value judgements, or reduce those that have to be made to a few about which it can be claimed there is a broad consensus. Dunn (1971, 161) has described this as "a hangover from the uneasy days when science worked out an unwritten truce with the political and religious establishment", within those territory all ethical matters lay. Yet neglect of who gets what is itself a serious value bias. In a society with considerable inequalities in wealth it is to the advantage of the elite to have academics who do not ask embarrassing questions about the justice of the distribution. The Pareto criterion of optimality in which so much traditional welfare theory has its roots is a very convenient assumption in a non-egalitarian society, for it takes the existing distribution as given and requires approval of policies which benefit only the rich while leaving the poor with the same as before. The assumption of consumer sovereignty is also convenient in a capitalist society with democratic aspirations, for it follows from this that what consumers choose is necessarily right and the unfortunate side-effects are then their responsibility and not that of the businessman, who is simply satisfying the people's revealed preferences.

The most obvious example of the perpetuation of supposedly positive knowledge in support of sectional or class interest is probably the association of social welfare maximization with free competition. If all markets are operating perfectly the price system ensures that resources are allocated in a manner apparently sanctioned by the public, because it can be traced from consumer preferences. The distribution of real income can thus be portrayed as the outcome of some democratic process, each individual or group being rewarded in accordance with contribution to a system in which the people, as consumers, are the final arbitrators. But we live in a world of imperfect markets, in which external diseconomies may be assuming steadily greater magnitude in the eyes of the general populace. The attractions of the theory of perfect competition arise in part from attributes other than its capacity to account for the operation of real-world economic systems. Graaff (1957, 170) claims that, "Much of the appeal of what we might call *laissez-faire* welfare theory, which is largely concerned with demonstrating the optimal properties of free competition and the unfettered price system, is undoubtedly due to its elegance and simplicity. Admit the existence of external effects, and both disappear." Dobb (1969, vii) suggests that the extent to which formal sophistication has served as "a cloak for deficient logic and plain confusion" in welfare economics is "nowhere more evident than in the theorems about the welfare-yielding attributes of perfect competition". The notion that free competition inevitably leads us along a welfare-maximizing path is now firmly rejected in favour of some measure of planning, except by the most conservative economists.

The persistence of free-market thinking for so long has undoubtedly been encouraged by the capitalist interests who gain from a *laissez-faire* society. Business can influence what is thought and taught, as well as what is bought. For example, Mishan (1969a, 78) suggests that the lack of interest in external disutilities of economic growth is partly because "the public has allowed itself so far to be duped by business spokesmen into accepting GNP as index of its welfare and progress". Dobb (1969, 121) complains that "some traditional habits of thought, slow to be supplanted, have especially handicapped economists' thinking about a socialist economy". He cites as examples the notion that national income can be measured independently of its distribution, and the concentration on stationary equilibrium and the consequent lack of attention to the function of planning in the maintenance of long-term economic progress. Attitudes to social policy have been slow to change. The welfare state, in which there is a protected minimum standard of income, nutrition, health, housing and education for every citizen *as a political right*, may still smack of charity and paternalism (Romanyshyn, 1971, ch. 1). It may also be regressive in its actual operation, helping the middle class more than the poor. In the USA the value emphasis on individual initiative and the Protestant work ethic in a climate of social Darwinism have helped to hold back legislation on welfare-state provisions which the country could well afford. All this works out to the advantage of those sections of society who gain from existing inequalities and from a policy of government non-intervention. And much of it is supported by what is claimed to be positive knowledge, as Galbraith (1975) has stressed.

The deficiency of the kind of economic theory that pervades so much of human geography is thus ideological as well as technical. This has been stressed in earlier chapters. While neo-classical economics provides helpful analytical devices, the theory itself rests, to an important degree, on ideas about man's economic world that reflect specific class interests. The same criticism is levelled at orthodox (i.e. "bourgeois") social science in general, a position summarized by Radice (1975, 10) as follows:

> The response of Marxism *and* of radical social science is that the orthodoxy is itself ideological: it implicitly treats fundamental aspects of the *status quo* as eternal and natural, and falsely claims neutrality and objectivity for its views in consequence. The historical materialist method of Marx goes further than this, arguing that the social sciences as ideological formations are part of the development of society along with the economic and social formations to which they correspond, and that a truly scientific social science, equally product and agent of the transformation of society, must be critical, must seek to transcend these formations. Neutrality and objectivity as eternal criteria do not exist: the only real human knowledge or science is gained through *praxis*, the unity of theory and practice in social action, not by detached observation, and the theoretical component of praxis is inseparable in the final analysis from "political" practical activity.

Such a view has not yet had much impact on geographical inquiry. But it does help us to understand that theory detached from actual economic or social situations may be merely formal abstraction without empirical relevance. As Dobb (1973, 11) says of this kind of knowledge, "Its apparent neutrality is because it contains very little in the way of factual statements about economic situations or processes and their behaviour—so little, perhaps, as to evoke serious doubt as to whether it is entitled to rank as an economic theory at all in the sense of a theory that *explains* social action and behaviour." The lesson for geography is that *useful* knowledge is unlikely to be neutral, unless it comprises simply a solution to a mathematical problem. It behoves us to look critically at models that might be mistaken for neutral analysis. What are accepted as constraints "exogenously given" may be the key variables, as with the budget constraint and given prices in the neo-classical theory of consumer "choice". Perhaps the most important academic contribution of what is now almost a decade of emphasis on relevance in geography is the growing awareness of the deeper significance of concepts, categories and assumptions hitherto accepted almost without question as being both empirically relevant and ideologically neutral.

The radical critique of neo-classical economics has helped to reveal much of the hidden ideological stance in supposedly value-free theory. Marxian economics is experiencing a revival, while in geography familiarity with Marx is growing almost to the extent of the fashion effect that aided the quantitative revolution. But, as before, there is a tendency to apply new paradigms uncritically. Marx may have been able to dissect the operation of a capitalist economy with particular clarity, and see the essential unity of economy, polity and society that we so often miss today. But Marx does not hold the key to every modern problem in complex, pluralistic societies. A particularly disturbing aspect of the contemporary academic scene is the tendency to accept or reject things largely as a matter of faith—whether it be Marxian analysis, Samuelson's *Economics*, or the need for geography in a university curriculum.

The status of geography as an academic discipline is itself illustrative of the problem. Few if any of its professional practitioners would question the discipline's right to an independent existence. Yet the spatial or areal perspective imbued by geographical training may itself impose blinkers that obscure the operation of "non-geographical" variables—a theme that will be familiar from earlier chapters. Any such narrow view of societal problems risks unconsciously supporting the *status quo*, by failing to identify root causes. Geography must stand or fall by its demonstrated capacity to enhance human well-being, and not by virtue of its convenience to the existing organization of society or academia.

So, to those who argue for strict neutrality in geography we may respond that academics and universities are never entirely detached politically. Educational institutions perform a function as preservers of social stability, through the passing on of "accepted" attitudes and values, as well as serving as centres for innovating thought. Generating the knowledge and skills required by society as presently structured is indeed the prime function of many universities today, as vocational training has become more important. But this can be selective; many American universities see their major role as providing for the manpower needs of business and related professions—putting programmes in law, management and mortuary science before the training of social workers or city planners. In South Africa, the Afrikaans universities and carefully controlled black institutions are supportive of the existing social order while the role of the English universities as custodians of liberal values is increasingly threatened. In 1939 Jan Hofmeyr stated that in the conflict between democracy and authoritarianism, "no University worthy of its great tradition can fail to range itself on the side of democracy" (quoted in Paton, 1971, 249), yet to do this in contemporary South Africa is to oppose the existing government. Either position is a commitment, for it is as much a political act to accept the *status quo* without complaint as it is to criticize and challenge it.

If we choose to abandon what we suppose to be strict ethical neutrality, we do no more than recognize reality. And we may be able to find some quite respectable precedents. McBeath (1955) attributes the habit in the social sciences of taking the political situation and social values as given to topical specialization and reminds us that the great social and political thinkers of antiquity operated on different assumptions. Plato's *The Republic* begins with the moral problem of justice or righteousness in the individual and finds that it cannot be solved without considering the nature of society and its economic, educational and political arrangement. Aristotle's work in ethics introduces his work on politics. These scholars, like Marx, could see the unity of economics, ethics, politics and so on; it is the modern social scientists who have made such distinct compartments of knowledge. The contemporary world is much more complex than the city-states of ancient Greece, or the sharply divided capitalist societies of the nineteenth century, and specialization is required to understand it. But in the process we have lost something of the overall synoptic view. When we do look beyond our own discipline and see its dependence on others, we usually stop well short of ethics, philosophy, and other subjects dealing with the non-factual.

A quarter of a century ago Hla Myint (1948, 235) concluded a classic review of welfare economics with the advice to "step boldly and consciously into the Ethical level'. He gave as reasons that, "One of the best ways of maintaining scientific impartiality is to make deliberate and uninhibited value judgements and to use them as a base of self-criticism in our purely scientific analysis", and (more important) that ultimately "economic theory can only justify its existence by practical application, and in the sphere of practical social policy the economist, like any other citizen, must make his own value judgements or else share the moral responsibility for the standards of values prevailing in the society in which he lives". Both seem sufficient reason for geography to follow his advice. But in doing so we must also recognize his vital precondition—that we must have carefully disciplined ourselves to the requirements of scientific analysis. And we must keep in mind his warning (Myint, 1948, 230):

> if we wish to pass from scientific welfare analysis to practical social policy we are obliged to enter the ethical level and to make normative judgements concerning whether or not the given ends ought to be pursued. In doing this, however, our arguments have lost the authority and precision of scientific analysis; for it is not possible to demonstrate by logic that a given end is good or bad, or

to apply the quantitative calculus in appraising the ethical quality of the ultimate ends.

This does not, of course, mean that we are absolved from the discipline of analytical thought as soon as we face ethical issues. Discussion of goals relating to equity requires a special discipline, that should be an essential part of training in geography and any other social or policy science.

13.3 On a humanistic paradigm

All this leads inevitably to a new paradigm for geography. Its essential nature is humanistic—the development of a humane human geography, or putting the "human" back into the subject. It is a "people geography" about real people, and *for* the people in the sense of contributing to the enlargement of human being for all—especially for the most deprived. It is devoted to human freedom as something that cannot be exercised within the constraints imposed by the difficulty of satisfying basic needs—freedom as "a self-realisation of man which is an eternal becoming and an eternal surpassing, a continual enrichment of everything human, an all-round development of all facets of humanity" (Mandel, 1962, 686). It is committed to the creation of a society and a world in which impediments to human realization and happiness are removed. It is necessarily a policy-oriented paradigm, which would recognize, with Nath (1969, 227), that policies in any country "should be judged according to their effects on general welfare, because any other aim for social policy is bound to be ethically less attractive".

In promoting the new paradigm, powerful entrenched professional interests must be overcome. As well as political conservatives who see their preferred academic and social order threatened, there is the more serious and respectable obstacle of the "knowledge-for-its-own-sake" argument. That the individual scholar should be completely free to pursue his or her own curiosity wherever it leads is generally considered basic to academic freedom. But it is no more than a value judgement, however widely held. It implies that whatever we choose to do—whatever our topic for research—it is right by virtue of it being our choice. This is the academic equivalent of consumer sovereignty. Faced with a choice between expending scarce intellectual resources on different lines of inquiry (e.g. the location of nineteenth-century industry or the geography of *apartheid*), the scholar maximizes his personal utility by doing as he pleases. But what about the collective position of an academic profession like geography? How do we decide what is a preferable state, or when "progress" has been made? Just as in welfare analysis, values enter the picture, for professional geography might be thought of as having some collective welfare function in which different fields or contributions to knowledge are weighted differently. Thus, by broad if not universal consent, a contribution to quantitative methodology is today judged more important than empirical findings concerning nineteenth-century industrial location or the environmental adaptation of Mexican Indians. Rigorous theory is given higher value than subjective social reporting. The more knowledge is extended in the highly valued fields by comparison with others, the more "progress" is being made. So, however much we may stand by the maxim of knowledge for its own sake and freedom of individual inquiry, some contributions and hence contributors are "more equal than others" in geography, just as in any implicit SWF. If this were not so there could be no way of claiming academic progress, except perhaps by numbers in the profession or pages of research published.

This leads to the origin of the criteria on which the significance or relevance of different contributions to knowledge are judged. If there is some consensus, how does it arise? Presumably, particular lines of inquiry will gain high value by virtue of their demonstrated capacity to make sense of the segment of reality that interests us. Other factors include the status and persuasive power of individuals committed to particular approaches, and the force of the "bandwagon" effect. A discipline reacts to external influences: thus if quantification and scientific rigour are the watchwords in the social sciences at large, geography will tend to emulate and place high value on these attributes in judging its own research. In an era where society attaches high prestige to technological gymnastics, social scientists may be predisposed to a mechanistic or engineering view of the human state. It is no coincidence that the decade during which geography became carried away by computers saw man land on the moon; it was the decade of what Hurst (1972c) has termed "the geographer as *mechanic*". Just as in an earlier age Carl Ritter reflected in his geography some of the teleological philosophy of a time when Wordsworth saw "God and nature communing", just as the determinists reflected the aftermath of Darwinism, so the new geography of the 1960s reflected the contemporary reverence for technology, functionalism and scientific or managerial rationality.

The danger, of course, is that a particular set of values becomes self-perpetuating. It is then that an academic discipline becomes supportive of the *status quo*, instead of open to new thinking and the exploration of new values. This can happen quite easily. The intellectual innovators of one generation can become entrenched behind their own ideas, unduly defensive in the face of the assaults of a new generation. Journal editors, conference chairmen, staff selection boards and grant committees, by imposing currently accepted criteria of relevance and methodological propriety, help to perpetuate them. Courses of instruction are slow to change, and the innovations of research and curriculum development within the universities may take a decade to reach the schools. Textbooks are major stabilizers of value positions, particularly in regional geography where many of those in common use today are as untouched by the new geography of the 1960s as by the relevance theme. Thus we may be slow to detect and respond to new societal values that in the future may form the basis on which our contribution is judged.

Can we perhaps detect a shift in values, consistent with our view of the geographer as humanist? In the contemporary social sciences, there are signs of a new humanism emerging from the crises and chaos of the age of materialism and massive technology. As John Romanyshyn (1971, 408) points out:

> All around us there are signs that human beings are coming alive to new and exciting potentialities in the nature of man and the possibilities for social life. The Protestant ethic has outlived its usefulness. Man was made for joy, for the creation of meaning, for ritual and drama, for love, for poetry and mystery, for self-transcendence, and for union with all mankind. There is more, much more, to man than the narrow image of him that we have incorporated into our economic and political life. Here lies the hope for human welfare.

Similarly, Mishan (1969a, 78) feels that:

> The major weakness of any criterion designed to rank social welfare by comparing alternative sets of goods is that of irrelevance. Once subsistence levels are exceeded, the possession of more goods is neither the sole nor the chief source of men's satisfaction; indeed the technical means designed to pursue further material ends may produce a civilization uncongenial to the psychic needs of ordinary men. A civilization offering increasing opportunities for rapid movement, titillation, research, effortless living and push-button entertainment does not compensate for a deepening sense of something lost: of the myths, perhaps, on which men's self esteem depends; of a sense of belonging; of the easy flow of sympathy and feeling between members of a group; of the enduring loyalty that comes only from hardships borne together; of a sense of space and unpreempted leisure, and of the solidarity of the here and now....

And Richard Turner (1972, 85–6), in a critique of the society chosen for our case study in Chapter 9, says:

> A grossly unequal society is immoral at any time. In our time it is also stupid. We can no longer afford the waste of resources involved. We can no longer afford to stifle creativity, inhibit cooperation and foster fierce and destructive competition for scarce goods.
>
> We have no choice but to look for happiness not in things but in relationships with other people.
>
> Meanwhile in South Africa, the whites are preparing to fight to the death for the right to own a second car. They are arming themselves to kill people for more things. How practical is it to want a second car when the world is running out of petrol? How practical is it to try to pass a camel through the eye of a needle?

It is not necessary to accept all these sentiments to feel a similar anxiety about the present and future of society. It is easy to exaggerate the ills of the age in which we live, for in historical perspective it may appear one of relative comfort and calm. But it is our age, and we are faced with great practical and moral problems if we are to extricate ourselves from the dehumanizing existence of a competitive, materialistic society. And we get nowhere by sitting on the fence as detached and objective observers of the steady debasement of human life.

Why should we not *begin* with some of these problems, rather than deal with them as an afterthought if at all? For example, why should not geography in South Africa begin with the morality of *apartheid*, and study the spatial organization of the economy and society from this perspective? The government is attempting a basic redesign of the national geography in pursuit of narrow sectional interests, yet the moral issues seem to attract little overt attention in geographical circles. This is, after all, *the* major national problem—the real issue in a sea of red herrings. To work within the framework of national policy, worrying about whether the so-called Homelands can attract more industry or where the next segregated township should be, important though these matters are in a certain context, is to risk avoiding the more fundamental problem of whether the context is *right*. Similar if less obvious moral dilemmas face any social scientist in any society. To deny them is to lose touch with the nature of society itself.

Returning to the quotations above, there is a unity of view within them that has something to do with the contemporary catchword of liberation. One part of mankind appears to have become captive of its own achievements in technology, economic growth, and the creation of an affluent society in which interpersonal relationships and some of the more intangible pleasures of life are becoming increasingly lost. Another part is still captive of the ills of an earlier age—poverty, ignorance, disease, economic exploitation, racial discrimination, and so on. We all have a personal interest in the process of liberation, for we are ourselves among the captives. As geographers we have a special role—a truly creative and revolutionary one—that of helping to reveal the *spatial* malfunctionings and injustices, and contributing to the design of a spatial form of society in which people can be really free to fulfil themselves. This, surely, would be progress in geography.

Further Reading

This book has been heavily documented with citations to the supporting literature, so as to assist the reader wishing to trace the origin of the ideas presented or to take matters of detail further. As a student text, the book is fairly self-contained, and reference to a few works would be sufficient for amplification of the basic content. The following are suggestions as to the most useful supplementary reading for a university course offering a welfare view of human geography.

For broader background on the development of human geography, Chisholm (1975) is the obvious first source. In Part One, readers unfamiliar with elementary (neo-classical) economic theory will find selective reading of a standard text such as Samuelson (1973) helpful, but especially useful is Hunt and Sherman (1972), where conventional and radical views are juxtaposed. For a brief grounding in welfare economics, Mishan (1969) and Nath (1973) are strongly recommended. A fairly rapid reading of Mandel (1962) on Marxist economics would be well worth the effort, but the abbreviated version (Mandel, 1973) will suffice for most readers. Broad critiques of the conventional wisdom in economics are offered by Mishan (1967) and Galbraith (1975), both of which have much of value to say about contemporary society. The conventional spatial perspective is set out in such texts as Adams, Abler and Gould (1971), Morrill (1971), Cox (1972) and Haggett (1972), while treatments more relevant to the welfare theme include those of Cox (1973) and Harvey (1973).

Part Two has been deliberately written to provide treatments of social justice and planning strategy comprehensive enough that supplementary reading for course purposes should be largely unnecessary. On social justice, Ginsberg (1966) provides a useful summary for those who want to go one step further. On the planning of change, there is a vast choice of specialist texts (e.g. Chadwick, 1971; Wilson, 1974), but more in line with the orientation of this book is the discussion of measuring and planning the quality of life by Drewnowski (1974).

In Part Three, the outline of world development problems can be followed up most profitably by reading Brookfield (1975). Spatial aspects of the South African case are further elaborated in Smith (1976) while Thompson and Butler (1975) provide the latest collection of papers from a political-sociology perspective. Davidson (1975) takes a perceptive view of African development with broader implications. The case of the USA is considered in more detail in Smith (1973). The location/allocation problems can best be followed up by going to the original sources of the cases presented, as cited in the text.

Discussion of welfare issues along with relevant cases are also appearing now in the professional journals, such as those of the Institute of British Geographers (*Transactions* and *Area*) and the Association of American Geographers (*Annals* and *Professional Geographer*). *Antipode* offers a forum for radical views. Much of value appears outside the geographical literature, however, as the bibliography that follows will show—cross-disciplinary reading is now essential for the student of geography.

Finally, there are a number of publications of the Open University that are directly relevant to a welfare view of geography. These include the course units for Selection III of D 204 *Fundamentals of Human Geography* and parts of D 302 *Patterns of Inequality*.

Bibliography

The following abbreviations are used:

AAG   Association of American Geographers
HMSO   Her Majesty's Stationery Office
IBG   Institute of British Geographers
RSA   Regional Science Association
SAIRR   South African Institute of Race Relations
USGPO United States Government Printing Office

ABLER, R., ADAMS, J. S. and GOULD, P. 1971: *Spatial Organization: The Geographer's View of the World.* Prentice-Hall, Englewood Cliffs, NJ.

ABRAMS, M. 1973: Subjective Social Indicators. *Social Trends* 4, HMSO, London, 35–50.

ADAM, H. 1971a: *Modernizing Racial Domination: The Dynamics of South African Politics.* University of California Press, Berkeley.

    editor, 1971b: *South Africa: Sociological Perspectives.* Oxford University Press, London.

ADELMAN, I. and MORRIS, C. T. 1965: Factor Analysis of the Inter-relationship between Social and Political Variables and Per Capita Gross National Products. *Quarterly Journal of Economics* 79, 555–78.

    1967: *Society, Politics and Economic Development.* Johns Hopkins Press, Baltimore.

    1973: *Economic Growth and Social Equity in Developing Countries.* Stanford University Press, Stanford, Calif.

AGEE, P. 1975: *Inside the Company: CIA Diary.* Penguin, Harmondsworth.

AGGER, R. E., GOLDRICH, D. and SWANSON, B. E. 1964: *The Rulers and the Ruled.* John Wiley, New York.

AHLUWALIA, M. S. 1974: Income Inequality: Some Dimensions of the Problem. H. Chenery *et al.*, *Redistribution with Growth.* Oxford University Press, Oxford, 3–37.

ALBAUM, M., editor, 1972: *Geography and Contemporary Issues.* Wiley, New York.

ALKER, H. R. 1970: Measuring Inequality. E. R. Tufte, editor, *The Quantitative Analysis of Social Problems.* Addison-Wesley, Reading, Mass., 191–211.

ALKER, H. R. and RUSSETT, B. M. 1964: On Measuring Inequality. *Behavioral Science* 9, 207–18.

ALLARDT, E. 1973: *About Dimensions of Welfare: An Exploratory Analysis of a Comparative Scandinavian Survey.* Research Group for Comparative Sociology, University of Helsinki.

    1975: *Dimensions of Welfare in a Comparative Scandinavian Study.* Research Group for Comparative Sociology, University of Helsinki, Research Report No. 9.

ALLEN, D. E. 1968: *British Tastes*. Hutchinson, London.

ALONSO, W. 1967: A Reformulation of Classical Location Theory and its Relation to Rent Theory. *Papers RSA* **19**, 23–44.

ALPEROVICH, A. 1972: *Welfare Criteria and Models for Locating Public Facilities*. Discussion Paper 19, Research on Conflict in Locational Decisions, Regional Science Department, University of Pennsylvania.

AMBROSE, P. and COLENUTT, B. 1975: *The Property Machine*. Penguin, Harmondsworth.

AMOS, J. C. 1970: *Social Malaise in Liverpool: Interim Report on Social Problems and their Distribution*. City of Liverpool.

ATKINSON, A. B. 1970: On the Measurement of Inequality. *Journal of Economic Theory* **2**, 244–63.

1975: *The Economics of Inequality*. Clarendon Press, Oxford.

AXELROD, M. 1956: Urban Structure and Social Participation. *American Sociological Review* **21**, 13–18.

BANDMAN, M. K., editor, 1976: *Modelling of Territorial Production Complexes* (three volumes). Institute of Economics and Organization of Industrial Production, USSR Academy of Sciences—Siberian Branch, Novosibirsk.

BANNOCK, G., BAXTER, R. E. and REES, R. 1972: *A Dictionary of Economics*. Penguin, Harmondsworth.

BARKER, E. A. 1971: Distress in the Reserves. P. Randall, editor, *Some Implications of Inequality*, Spro-cas, Johannesburg, 13–16.

BARRETT, J., BRAND, S., COLLIER, D. S. and GLASER, K. 1974: *Accelerated Development in Southern Africa*. Macmillan, London.

BASTER, N., editor, 1972: *Measuring Development*. Cass, London.

BEDERMAN, S. H. 1974: The Stratification of "Quality of Life" in the Black Community of Atlanta, Georgia. *Southeastern Geographer* **14**, 26–37.

BEDERMAN, S. H. and ADAMS, J. S. 1974: Job Accessibility and Underemployment. *Annals, AAG* **64**, 378–86.

BELL, C. L. G. 1974: The Political Framework. H. Chenery *et al.*, *Redistribution with Growth*, Oxford University Press, Oxford, 52–72.

BELL, R. T. 1973a: *Industrial Decentralisation in South Africa*, Oxford University Press, Cape Town.

1973b: Some Aspects of Industrial Decentralisation in South Africa. *South African Journal of Economics* **41**, 401–37.

BERGHE, P. VAN DEN 1967: *South Africa: A Study in Conflict*. University of California Press, Berkeley and Los Angeles.

BERRY, B. J. L. 1960: An Inductive Approach to the Regionalization of Economic Development. N. Ginsburg, editor, *Essays on Geography and Economic Development*, Research Paper 62, Dept. of Geography, University of Chicago.

1961: Basic Patterns of Economic Development. N. Ginsburg, editor, *Atlas of Economic Development*, Chicago University Press, Chicago, 110–19.

1964: Approaches to Regional Analysis: A Synthesis. *Annals, AAG* **5**, 2–11.

1968: *Metropolitan Area Definition: A Re-Evaluation of Concept and Statistical Practice*. Working Paper 28, US Dept. of Commerce, Bureau of the Census, Washington, DC.

1970: The Geography of the United States in the Year 2000. *Transactions, IBG* **51**, 21–53.

1972: More on Relevance and Policy Analysis. *Area* **4**, 77–80.

1973: *The Human Consequences of Urbanisation*. Macmillan, London.

BERRY, B. J. L. and HORTON, F. E. 1970: *Geographic Perspectives on Urban Systems*. Prentice-Hall, Englewood Cliffs, NJ.

BERRY, B. J. L. and MARBLE, D. F., editors, 1968: *Spatial Analysis: A Reader in Statistical Geography*. Prentice-Hall, Englewood Cliffs, NJ.

BERRY, B. J. L. and NEILS, E. 1969: Location, Size and Shape of Cities as Influenced by Environmental Factors: The Urban Environment Writ Large. H. S. Perloff, editor, *The Quality of the Urban Environment*, The Johns Hopkins Press, Baltimore, 257–302.

BEST, A. G. C. and YOUNG, B. S. 1972: Homeland Consolidation: The Case of Kwazulu. *South African Geographer* **4**, 63–74.

BIESHEUVEL, S. 1972: *The Black–White Wage Gap*. SAIRR, Johannesburg.

BISH, R. L. 1971: *The Public Economy of Metropolitan Areas*. Markham, Chicago.

BLOCH, P. B. 1974: *Equality of Distribution of Police Services—A Case Study of Washington, DC*. The Urban Institute, Washington, DC.

BLOWERS, A. T. 1972: Relevance: Bleeding Hearts and Open Values. *Area* **4**, 290–2.

1974: Relevance, Research and the Political Process. *Area* **6**, 33–6.

BOAL, F. W., DOHERTY, P. and PRINGLE, D. G. 1974: *The Spatial Distribution of Some Social Problems in the Belfast Urban Area*. Research Paper, Northern Ireland Community Relations Commision, Belfast.

BOARD, C. 1976: Migrant Labour. D. M. Smith, editor, *Separation in South Africa: People and Policies*, Occasional Paper No. 6, Dept. of Geography, Queen Mary College, 63–76.

BOARD, C., DAVIES, R. J. and FAIR, T. J. D. 1970: The Structure of the South African Space Economy: An Integrated Approach. *Regional Studies* **4**, 367–92.

BODDY, M. J. 1976: The Structure of Mortgage Finance: Building Societies and the British Social Formation. *Transactions, IBG*, New Series **1**, 58–71.

BOUDEVILLE, J-R. 1966: *Problems of Regional Economic Planning*. University Press, Edinburgh.

BOOMS, B. H. and HALLDORSON, J. R. 1973: The Politics of Redistribution: A Reformulation. *American Political Science Review* **67**, 924–33.

BRAMHALL, D. F. 1969: An Introduction to Spatial General Equilibrium. G. J. Karaska and D. F. Bramhall, editors, *Locational Analysis for Manufacturing*, MIT Press, Cambridge, Mass., 467–76.

BRAZER, H. E. 1964: Some Fiscal Implications of Metropolitanism. B. Chinitz, editor, *City and Suburb: The Economics of Metropolitan Growth*, Prentice-Hall, Englewood Cliffs, NJ, 127–50.

BREHENY, M. J. 1974: Towards Measures of Spatial Opportunity. *Progress in Planning* **2**, 85–142.

BROOKFIELD, H. C. 1973: On One Geography and a Third World. *Transactions, IBG* **53**, 1–20.

1975: *Interdependent Development*. Methuen, London.

BROWN, L. A. 1968: *Diffusion Processes and Location: A Conceptual Framework and Bibliography*. Regional Science Research Institute, Philadelphia.

BROWN, L. A. and LANGBRAKE, D. B. 1969: On the Implementation of Place Utility and Related Concepts: The Intra-Urban Migration Case. K. R. Cox and R. G. Golledge, editors, *Behavioral Problems in Geography: a Symposium*, Dept. of Geography, Northwestern University, Evanston, 169–96.

BROWN, L. A. and MOORE, E. G. 1970: The Intra-Urban Migration Process: A Perspective. *General Systems* **15**, 109–22.

BRUS, W. and LASKI, K. 1965: Problems in the Theory of Growth under Socialism. E. A. G. Robinson, editor, *Problems of Economic Development*, Macmillan, London, 21–54; reprinted in Nove, A. and Nuti, D. M., editors, *Socialist Economics*, Penguin, Harmondsworth, 173–209 (page references are to this edition).

BUCHANAN, J. M. 1968: *The Demand and Supply of Public Goods*. Rand McNally, Chicago.

BUCHANAN, K. 1967: Hunger: causes, extent and implications. *Outlook* October 1967, 14–17; reprinted in J. L. Roach and J. K. Roach, editors, *Poverty: Selected Readings*, Penguin, Harmondsworth, 215–26.

1972: Contours of the Future. J. L. Roach and J. K. Roach, editors, *Poverty: Selected Readings*, Penguin, Harmondsworth, 324–30.

BUNGE, W. 1962: *Theoretical Geography*. Lund Studies in Geography, Series C, 1. Gleerup, Lund.

1974: The Human Geography of Detroit. R. A. Roberge, editor, *La Crise Urbaine: A Challenge to Geographers*, University of Ottawa Press, Ottawa, 49–69.

BUTLER, J. and THOMPSON, L., editors, 1975: *Change in Contemporary South Africa*. University of California Press, Berkeley and Los Angeles.

BUTTIMER, A. 1972: "Inequality", "Inefficiency", and "Spatial Injustice". Paper read at the Annual Meeting, AAG, Kansas City (mimeo).

1974: *Values in Geography*. Commission on College Geography, Resource Paper 24, AAG, Washington, DC.

CAMPBELL, A. 1972: Aspiration, Satisfaction, and Fulfilment. A. Campbell and P. E. Converse, editors, *The Human Meaning of Social Change*, Russell Sage, New York, 441–66.

CAMPBELL, R. W. 1974: *Soviet-type Economies*. Macmillan, London.

CATANESE, A. J. 1972: *Scientific Methods of Urban Analysis*. University of Illinois Press, Urbana, and Leonard Hill, Aylesbury.

CHADWICK, G. 1971: *A Systems View of Planning*. Pergamon Press, Oxford.

CHENERY, H., AHLUWALIA, M. S., BELL, C. L. G., DULAY, J. H. and JOLLY, R. 1974: *Redistribution with Growth*. Oxford University Press, Oxford.

CHISHOLM, M. 1970: *Geography and Economics*. G. Bell & Sons, London.

1971a: In Search of a Basis for Location Theory: Microeconomics or Welfare Economics. C. Board *et al.*, editors, *Progress in Geography* **3**, 111–33.

1971b: Geography and the Question of Relevance. *Area* **3**, 65–8.

1975: *Human Geography: Evolution or Revolution?* Penguin, Harmondsworth.

CHISHOLM, M. and OEPPEN, J. 1973: *The Changing Pattern of Employment*. Croom Helm, London.

CHORLEY, R. J. and HAGGETT, P., editors, 1967a: *Models in Geography*. Methuen, London. 1967b: Models, Paradigms and the New Geography. R. J. Chorley and P. Haggett, editors, *Models in Geography*, Methuen, London, 19–41.

CHRISTALLER, W. 1933: *Die zentralen Orte in Suddeutschland*. Translated by C. W. Baskin (1966) as *Central Places in Southern Germany*, Prentice-Hall, Englewood Cliffs, NJ.

CHURCH, R. and REVELLE, C. 1974: The Maximal Covering Location Problem. *Papers, RSA* **32**, 101–18.

CLARK, C. 1951: *The Conditions of Economic Progress*. Macmillan, London.

CLAWSON, M. 1959: *Methods of Measuring the Demand for and Value of Outdoor Recreation*. Reprint 10, Resources for the Future, Washington, DC.

COATES, B. E. and RAWSTRON, E. M. 1971: *Regional Variations in Britain: Studies in Economic and Social Geography*. Batsford, London.

COLE, J. P. and KING, C. A. M. 1968: *Quantitative Geography*. John Wiley, London.

COLEMAN, J. S. 1974: Review Essay: Inequality, Sociology and Moral Philosophy. *American Journal of Sociology* **80**, 739–64.

CONZEN, M. P. 1975: Capital Flows and the Developing Urban Hierarchy: State Bank Capital in Wisconsin, 1854–1895. *Economic Geography* **51**, 321–38.

COPPOCK, J. T. and WILSON, C. B., editors, 1974: *Environmental Quality*. Scottish Academic Press, Edinburgh.

COUGHLIN, R. E. 1970: *Goal Attainment Levels in 101 Metropolitan Areas*. Regional Science Research Institute, Discussion Paper 41, Philadelphia, Pa.

COX, K. R. 1972: *Man, Location and Behaviour: An Introduction to Human Geography*. John Wiley, New York.

  1973: *Conflict, Power and Politics in the City: A Geographic View*. McGraw-Hill, New York.

COX, K., REYNOLDS, D. R. and ROKKAN, S. 1974: *Locational Approaches to Power and Conflict*. Sage Publications, Beverly Hills, Calif.

CRAVEN, E., editor, 1975: *Regional Devolution and Social Policy*. Macmillan, London.

CULYER, A. J. 1973: *The Economics of Social Policy*. Martin Robertson, London.

CULYER, A. J., LAVERS, R. J. and WILLIAMS, A. 1972: Health Indicators. A. Shonfield and S. Shaw, editors, *Social Indicators and Social Policy*, Heinemann, London.

CURTRIGHT, P. 1967a: Inequality: A Cross-National Analysis. *American Sociological Review* **32**, 562–78.

  1967b: Income Redistribution: A Cross-National Analysis. *Social Forces* **46**, 180–90.

  1968: The Distribution and Redistribution of Income: Political and Non-political Factors. W. Bloomberg and H. J. Schmandt, editors, *Power, Poverty, and Urban Policy*, Sage Publications, Beverly Hills, Calif., 531–64.

DAHL, R. A. 1957: The Concept of Power. *Behavioural Science* **2**, 201–15.

DAHL, R. A. and LINDBLOM, C. E. 1963: *Politics, Economics and Welfare*. Harper, New York.

DALKEY, N. C. and ROURKE, D. L. 1973: The Delphi Procedure and Rating Quality of Life Factors. Environmental Protection Agency, *The Quality of Life Concept*, Washington, DC, II—209–21.

DAVIDSON, B. 1975: *Can Africa Survive?* Heinemann, London.

DAVIES, B. 1968: *Social Needs and Resources in Local Services*. Michael Joseph, London.

DEAR, M. J. 1974: A Paradigm for Public Facility Location Theory. *Antipode* **6**, (1), 46–50.

DE NEUFVILLE, J. I. 1975: *Social Indicators and Public Policy*. Elsevier, Amsterdam.

DENIKE, K. G. and PARR, J. B. 1970: Production in Space, Spatial Competition, and Restricted Entry. *Journal of Regional Science* **10**, 49–64.

DEPARTMENT OF CITY PLANNING—LOS ANGELES, 1973: *A Model for Subsidized Housing Location*. Los Angeles, Calif.

DEPARTMENT OF OVERSEAS DEVELOPMENT, 1975: *The Changing Emphasis in British Aid Policies: More Help for the Poorest*. HMSO, London.

DESAI, M. 1974: *Marxian Economic Theory*. Gray-Mills, London.

DESMOND, C. 1971: *The Discarded People*. Penguin, Harmondsworth.

DE SOUZA, A. R. and PORTER, P. W. 1974: *The Underdevelopment and Modernization of the Third World*. Commission on College Geography, Resource Paper 28, AAG, Washington, DC.

DICKINSON, J. C., GRAY, R. J. and SMITH, D. M. 1972: The "Quality of Life" in Gainesville, Florida: An Application of Territorial Social Indicators. *Southeastern Geographer* **12**, 121–32.

DICKINSON, J. P. and CLARKE, C. G. 1972: Relevance and the "Newest Geography". *Area* **4**, 25–7.

DIENES, L. 1974: Environmental Disruption and its Mechanism in East-Central Europe. *Professional Geographer* **26**, 375–81.

DOBB, M. 1969: *Welfare Economics and the Economics of Socialism*. University Press, Cambridge.

1973: *Theories of Value and Distribution since Adam Smith: Ideology and Economic Theory*. University Press, Cambridge.

DONABEDIAN, M. 1973: *Research and Development of a Relative Community Health Index*. Bureau of Records and Statistics, Community Health Services, Los Angeles County Dept. of Health Services.

DONALDSON, P. 1973: *Worlds Apart: The Economic Gulf between Nations*. Penguin, Harmondsworth.

DONNISON, D. 1975: Equality. *New Society*, 20 Nov., 422–4.

DOSSER, D. 1964: Notes on Carl S. Shoup's "Standard for Distributing a Free Governmental Service". *Public Finance* **19**, 395–401.

DREWNOWSKI, J. 1970: *Studies in the Measurement of Levels of Living and Welfare*. UN Research Institute for Social Development, Geneva.

1972: Social Indicators and Welfare Measurement: Remarks on Methodology. N. Baster, editor, *Measuring Development*, Cass, London, 77–90.

1974: *On Measuring and Planning the Quality of Life*. Mouton, The Hague.

DREWNOWSKI, J. and SCOTT, W. 1968: The Level of Living Index. *Ekistics* **25**, 266–75.

DUNCAN, S. 1970: The Plight of the Urban African. *Topical Talks* **23**, SAIRR, Johannesburg.

DUNCAN, S. S. 1976: Research Directions in Social Geography: Housing Opportunities and Constraints. *Transactions, IBG*, New Series **1**, 10–19.

DUNN, E. S. 1971: *Economic and Social Development*. Johns Hopkins Press, Baltimore and London, for Resources for the Future, Inc.

ELKIN, R. and CORNICK, D. L. 1970: Utilizing Cost and Efficiency Studies in Decision-Making Progress in Health and Welfare. H. A. Schatz, editor, *Social Work Administration: A Resource Book*, Council on Social Work Education, New York, 364–71.

ELLIOTT, C. 1972: Income Distribution and Social Stratification: Some Notes on Theory and Practice. N. Baster, editor, *Measuring Development*, Cass, London, 37–56.

ENVIRONMENTAL PROTECTION AGENCY, 1972: *The Quality of Life Concept: A Potential New Tool for Decision-Makers*. Office of Research and Monitoring, Environmental Studies Division, Washington, DC.

EVERSLEY, D. 1975: Regional Devolution and Environmental Planning. E. Craven, editor, *Regional Devolution and Social Policy*, Macmillan, London.

EYLES, J. 1971: Pouring New Sentiments into Old Theories: How Else can we Look at Behavioural Patterns? *Area* **3**, 242–50.

1974: Social Theory and Social Geography. C. Board *et al.*, editors, *Progress in Geography* **6**, 27–87.

FAIR, T. J. D. 1965: The Core–Periphery Concept and Population Growth in South Africa, 1911–1960. *South African Geographical Journal* **47**, 59–71.

1970: Population Indicators and Regional Economic Development. *South African Geographical Journal* **52**, 124–8.

1971: Southern Africa: Bonds and Barriers in a Multi-Racial Region. R. Mansell Prothero, editor, *A Geography of Africa*, Routledge & Kegan Paul, London, 325–79.

1972: *The Metropolitan Imperative*. Inaugural Lecture, Witwatersrand University Press, Johannesburg.

FAIR, T. J. D. and SCHMIDT, C. F. 1974: Contained Urbanisation: A Case Study. *South African Geographical Journal* **56**, 155–66.

FAIR, T. J. D. and SHAFFER, N. M. 1964: Population Patterns and Policies in South Africa, 1951–1960. *Economic Geography* **40**, 261–74.

FANTUS COMPANY, 1962: *Cost Comparison Study*. Manitoba Department of Industry and Commerce, Winnipeg.

FARIS, E. L. R. and DUNHAM, H. W. 1939: *Mental Disorders in Urban Areas*. University of Chicago Press, Chicago.

FLETCHER, R. 1965: *Human Needs and Social Order*. Michael Joseph, London.

FOSTER, C. D. 1966: Social Welfare Function in Cost–Benefit Analysis. J. Lawrence, editor, *Operational Research and the Social Sciences*, Tavistock, London.

FOX, K. A. 1974: *Social Indicators and Social Theory*. John Wiley, New York.

FRANK, A. G. 1969: *Capitalism and Underdevelopment in Latin America*. Penguin, Harmondsworth.

FRANKENA, W. K. 1962: The Concept of Social Justice. R. B. Brandt, editor, *Social Justice*. Prentice-Hall, Englewood Cliffs, NJ, 1–29.

FRIED, R. C. 1973: *Comparative Urban Performance*. Working Paper 1, European Urban Research, University of California, Los Angeles.

FRIED, R. C. and RABINOVITZ, F. 1975: *Comparative Urban Politics: A Performance Approach*. Prentice-Hall, Englewood Cliffs, NJ.

FRIEDMAN, M. 1962: *Capitalism and Freedom*. University Press, Chicago.

FRIEDMANN, J. 1966: *Regional Development Policy*. MIT Press, Cambridge, Mass.
   1972: A General Theory of Polarized Development. M. Hansen, editor, *Growth Centres in Regional Economic Development*, The Free Press, New York.
   1972–3: The Spatial Organization of Power in the Development of Urban Systems. *Development and Change* **4** (3), 12–50.
   1973: *Urbanization, Planning and National Development*. Sage Publications, Beverly Hills, Calif.

FRIEDMANN, J. and WULFF, R. 1976: *The Urban Transition: Comparative Studies of Newly Industrializing Societies*. Edward Arnold, London.

GALBRAITH, J. K. 1975: *Economics and the Public Purpose*. Penguin, Harmondsworth.

GARRISON, W. L. and MARBLE, D. F., editors, 1967: *Quantitative Geography. Part I: Economic and Cultural Topics*. Studies in Geography **13**, Department of Geography, Northwestern University, Evanston, Ill.

GILBERT, A. 1974: *Latin American Development: A Geographical Perspective*. Penguin, Harmondsworth.

GILLIN, E. F. 1974: Measuring Economic Welfare. *Trends*, Rural Bank of New South Wales, Sydney, **9** (7), 6–15.

GINSBERG, M. 1965: *On Justice in Society*. Penguin, Harmondsworth.

GINSBURG, N., editor, 1961: *Atlas of Economic Development*. University of Chicago Press, Chicago and London.

GODLUND, S. 1961: *Population, Regional Hospitals, Transport Facilities and Regions: Planning the Location of Regional Hospitals in Sweden*. Lund Studies in Geography, Series B—Human Geography. Gleerup, Lund.

GOLDMAN, M. I. 1971: Environmental Disruption in the Soviet Union. T. R. Detwyler, editor, *Man's Impact on Environment*, McGraw-Hill, New York.

GOLLEDGE, R. G. and RUSHTON, G. 1972: *Multidimensional Scaling: Review and Geographical Applications*. AAG, Washington, DC.

GOULD, P. 1969: Problems of Space Preference Measures and Relationships. *Geographical Analysis* **1**, 31–44.
   1973: The Open Geographic Curriculum. R. J. Chorley, editor, *Directions in Geography*, Methuen, London, 253–84.

GOULD, P. and LEINBACH, T. R. 1966: An Approach to the Geographic Assignment of Hospital Services. *Tijdschrift voor Economische en Sociale Geografie* **57**, 203–6.

GOULD, P. and WHITE, R. 1974: *Mental Maps*. Penguin, Harmondsworth.

GOULET, D. A. 1968: On the Goals of Development. *Cross Currents* **18**, 387–405.
1971: *The Cruel Choice*. Atheneum, New York.

GRAAFF, J. DE V. 1957: *Theoretical Welfare Economics*. University Press, Cambridge.

GRANBERG, A. G., editor, 1976: *Spatial National Economic Models*. Institute of Economics and Industrial Engineering, USSR Academy of Sciences—Siberian Branch, Novosibirsk.

GRAY, F. 1975: Non-explanation in Urban Geography. *Area* **7**, 228–35.
1976: Selection and Allocation in Council Housing. *Transactions, IBG*, New Series **1**, 34–46.

GREEN, L. P. and FAIR, T. J. D. 1962: *Development in Africa*. Witwatersrand University Press, Johannesburg.

GREENHUT, M. L. 1956: *Plant Location in Theory and in Practice*. University of North Carolina Press, Chapel Hill.
1963: *Microeconomics and the Space Economy*. Scott Foresman, Chicago.

GREGORY, S. 1963: *Statistical Methods and the Geographer*. Longmans, London.

GRIGG, D. 1973: Geographical Studies of Economic Development with Special Reference to Agriculture. M. Chisholm and B. Rodgers, editors, *Studies in Human Geography*, Heinemann, London, 18–84.

GROSS, P. F. 1972: Urban Health Disorders, Spatial Analysis, and the Economics of Health Facility Location. *International Journal of Health Services* **2**, 64–83.

HADDAD, P. R. and SCHWARTZMAN, J. 1974: A Space Cost Curve of Industrial Location. *Economic Geography* **50**, 141–3.

HÄGERSTRAND, T. 1967: *Innovation Diffusion as a Spatial Process*. Chicago University Press, Chicago (translation of *Innovationsförloppet ur korologisk synpunkt*, C. W. K. Gleerup, Lund, Sweden, 1953).
1974: The Impact of Transport on the Quality of Life. Paper presented at the Fifth International Symposium on Theory and Practice in Transport Economics, Athens, Oct. 1973.

HAGGETT, P. 1965: *Locational Analysis in Human Geography*. Arnold, London.
1972: *Geography: A Modern Synthesis*. Harper & Row, New York.

HALL, P. 1974a: The New Geography: Games of Space Chess. *New Society*, 20 June, 693–5.
1974b: The New Political Geography. *Transactions, IBG* **63**, 48–52.

HAMMOND, R. and McCULLOGH, P. S. 1974: *Quantitative Techniques in Geography: An Introduction*. Clarendon Press, Oxford.

HARRIES, K. D. 1974: *The Geography of Crime and Justice*. McGraw-Hill, New York.

HARRISON, P. 1975: An Unequal World. *New Society*, 13 March, 647–9.

HARROP, K. J. 1973: *Nuisances and their Externallity Fields*. Seminar Paper No. 23, Dept. of Geography, University of Newcastle upon Tyne.

HARTSHORNE, R. 1939: *The Nature of Geography*. AAG, Lancaster, Penn.
1959: *Perspective on the Nature of Geography*. Rand McNally, Chicago.
1960: Geography and Economic Growth. N. Ginsburg, editor, *Essays on Geography and Economic Development*, Chicago University Press, Chicago, 3–25.

HARVEY, D. 1967: The Problem of Theory Construction in Geography. *Journal of Regional Science* **7**, 211–16.
1969: *Explanation in Geography*. Edward Arnold, London; St Martin's Press, New York.

1971: Social Processes, Spatial Form and the Redistribution of Real Income in an Urban System. M. Chisholm *et al.*, editors, *Regional Forecasting*, Butterworth, London, 270–300.

1972a: Social Justice in Spatial Systems. R. Peet, editor, *Geographical Perspectives on American Poverty*, Antipode Monographs in Social Geography 1, Worcester, Mass., 87–106.

1972b: Revolutionary and Counter-Revolutionary Theory in Geography and the Problem of Ghetto Formation. *Antipode* 4 (2), 1–18; and *Perspectives in Geography* 2, Northern Illinois University Press.

1973: *Social Justice and the City*. Edward Arnold, London; Johns Hopkins University Press, New York.

1975: The Geography of Capital Accumulation: A Reconstruction of the Marxian Theory. *Antipode* 7 (2), 9–21.

HAWLEY, W. D. and WIRT, F. M. 1968: *The Search for Community Power*. Prentice-Hall, Englewood Cliffs, NJ.

HAWORTH, L. 1968: Deprivation and the Good City. W. Bloomberg and H. J. Schmandt, editors, *Power, Poverty and Urban Policy*, Urban Affairs Annual Reviews 2, Sage Publications, Beverly Hills, Calif., 27–47.

HEERDEN, W. VAN 1960: The Road to Separate Racial Development in South Africa. *Optima* 10, 184–93.

HENDERSON, J. M. and QUANDT, R. E. 1958: *Microeconomic Theory: A Mathematical Approach*. McGraw-Hill, New York.

HIGBEE, E. 1970: *A Question of Priorities*. William Morrow, New York.

HILL, M. 1968: A Goal Achievement Matrix for Evaluating Alternative Plans. *Journal of the American Institute of Planners* 34, 19–29.

1973: *Planning for Multiple Objectives: An Approach to the Evaluation of Transportation Plans*. Monograph No. 5, Regional Science Research Institute, Philadelphia.

HIRSCH, W. Z. 1968: The Supply of Urban Public Services. H. S. Perloff and L. Wingo, editors, *Issues in Urban Economics*, Johns Hopkins Press, Baltimore, 477–525.

HIRSCHMAN, A. O. 1958: *The Strategy of Economic Development*. Yale University Press, New Haven, Conn.

HODDER, B. W. and LEE, R. 1974: *Economic Geography*. Methuen, London.

HOFFENBURG, M. 1970: Comments on "Measuring Progress Towards Social Goals: Some Possibilities at National and Local Levels" [Terleckyj, 1970]. *Management Science* 16, B-779–83.

HOOVER, E. M. 1937: *Location Theory and the Shoe and Leather Industries*. Harvard University Press, Cambridge, Mass.

1948: *The Location of Economic Activity*. McGraw-Hill, New York.

HORNER, J. A. 1972: *Black Pay and Productivity in South Africa*. SAIRR, Johannesburg.

HORRELL, M., HORNER, D., KANE-BERMAN, J. and MARGO, R. 1973: *A Survey of Race Relations in South Africa 1972*. SAIRR, Johannesburg.

HORRELL, M., HORNER, D. and HUDSON, J. 1975: *A Survey of Race Relations in South Africa 1974*. SAIRR, Johannesburg.

HORRELL, M. and HODGSON, T. 1976: *A Survey of Race Relations in South Africa 1975*. SAIRR, Johannesburg.

HOSELITZ, B. F. 1960: *Sociological Aspects of Economic Growth*. The Free Press, Glencoe, Ill.

HOWE, G. M. 1972: *Man, Environment and Disease in Britain*. David & Charles, Newton Abbot; Barnes & Noble, New York.

HUNT, E. K. and SCHWARTZ, J. 1972: *A Critique of Economic Theory*. Penguin, Harmondsworth.

HUNT, E. K. and SHERMAN, H. J. 1972: *Economics: An Introduction to Traditional and Radical Views*. Harper & Row, New York.

HURST, M. E. E. 1972a: Metropolitan Spatial Injustice: An Alternative Approach to Instruction in Urban Geography. Paper read at the Annual Conference, AAG, Kansas City, 1972 (mimeo).

1972b: Establishment Geography: or how to be irrelevant in three easy lessons. Geography Department, Simon Fraser University (mimeo).

1972c: Whither Economic Geography? Paper read at the International Geographical Union Conference. Section VIII, August 1972 (mimeo).

HYMER, S. 1975: The Multinational Corporation and the Law of Uneven Development. H. Radice, editor, *International Firms and Modern Imperialism*, Penguin, Harmondsworth, 37–62.

INGRAM, J. C. 1970: *International Economic Problems*. 2nd edn, John Wiley, New York.

INKELES, A. and SMITH, D. H. 1975: *Becoming Modern*. Heinemann, London.

ISARD, W. 1956: *Location and Space-Economy*. MIT Press, Cambridge, Mass.

et al. 1960: *Methods of Regional Analysis*. MIT Press, Cambridge, Mass.

et al. 1969: *General Theory: Social, Political, Economic and Regional*. MIT Press, Cambridge, Mass.

JACKMAN, R. A. 1975: The Problem of Externalities in a Spatial Economy. E. L. Cripps, editor, *Regional Science—New Concepts and Old Problems*, Pion, London, 18–30.

JACKSON, D. 1972: *Poverty*. Macmillan, London.

JEFFERSON, T. 1820: Letter to W. C. Jarvis. Cited in B. Stevenson, *The Homebook of Quotations, Classical and Modern*. 10th edn, Dodd, Mead & Co., New York, 1967, 432.

JOHANSEN, L. 1963: Labour Theory of Value and Marginal Utilities. *Economics of Planning* **3**, 89–103. Reprinted in Hunt and Schwartz, editors, *A Critique of Economic Theory*, Penguin, Harmondsworth, 1972, 295–311.

JOLLY, R., KAMUNVI, F., KING, M. and SABULIBA, P. 1966: The Economy of District Hospital. M. King, editor, *Medical Care in Developing Countries*, Oxford University Press, Nairobi, ch. 12.

JOLLY, R. and KING, M. 1966: The Organization of Health Services. M. King, editor, *Medical Care in Developing Countries*, Oxford University Press, Nairobi, ch. 2.

KAHN, E. 1970: Apartheid or Separate Development. *Standard Encyclopaedia of Southern Africa*. Nasau, Cape Town, Vol. I, 472–86.

KANSKY, K. J. 1963: *Structure of Transportation Networks*. Research Paper No. 84, Dept. of Geography, University of Chicago.

KARASKA, G. J. and BRAMHALL, D. F., editors, 1969: *Locational Analysis for Manufacturing*. MIT Press, Cambridge, Mass.

KATZMAN, M. T. 1968: Distribution and Production in a Big City Elementary School System. *Yale Economic Essays* **8**, 201–56.

KEEBLE, D. E. 1967: Models of Economic Development. R. J. Chorley and P. Haggett, editors, *Models in Geography*, Methuen, London, 243–302.

KELLING, G. L., PEKE, T., DIECKMAN, D. and BROWN, C. E. 1974: *The Kansas City Preventive Patrol Experiment*. Police Foundation, Washington, DC.

KIESLING, H. J. 1967: Measuring a Local Government Service: A Study of School Districts in New York State. *The Review of Economics and Statistics* **47**, 356–67.

KING, L. J. 1969: *Statistical Analysis in Geography*. Prentice-Hall, Englewood Cliffs, NJ.

KING, M. A. 1974: Economic Growth and Social Development—A Statistical Investigation. *Review of Income and Wealth*, Series 20, (3), 251–72.

KNETSCH, J. L. 1963: Outdoor Recreation Demands and Benefits. *Land Economics* **39**, 387–96.

KNOX, P. L. 1974a: Level of Living: A Conceptual Framework for Monitoring Regional Variations in Well-Being. *Regional Studies* **8**, 11–19.

   1974b: Spatial Variations in Level of Living in England and Wales in 1961. *Transactions, IBG* **62**, 1–24.

   1975: *Social Well-being: A Spatial Perspective*. University Press, Oxford.

KOELLE, H. H. 1974: An Experimental Study on the Determination of a Definition for the "Quality of Life". *Regional Studies* **8**, 1–10.

KOLARS, J. F. and NYSTUEN, J. D. 1974: *Geography: The Study of Location, Culture, and Environment*. McGraw-Hill, New York.

KRIEGER, M. H. 1969: *Social Indicators for the Quality of Individual Life*. Working Paper No. 104. Institute of Urban and Regional Development, University of California, Berkeley.

KRUECKEBERG, D. A. and SILVERS, A. L. 1974: *Urban Planning Analysis: Methods and Models*. John Wiley, New York.

KUHN, H. W. and KUENNE, R. E. 1962: An Efficient Algorithm for the Numerical Solution of the Generalized Weber Problem in Space Economics. *Journal of Regional Science* **4**, 21–33.

KUPER, L. 1974: *Race, Class and Power: Ideology and Revolutionary Change in Plural Societies*. Duckworth, London.

KUZNETS, S. 1957: Quantitative Aspects of the Economic Growth of Nations: II. Industrial Distribution of National Product and Labor Force. *Economic Development and Cultural Change* **5**, Part II.

   1959: Quantitative Aspects of the Economic Growth of Nations: IV. Distribution of National Income by Factor Shares. *Economic Development and Cultural Change* **7**, Part II.

   1963: Quantitative Aspects of the Economic Growth of Nations: VIII. Distribution of Income by Size. *Economic Development and Cultural Change* **11**, Part II.

   1966: *Modern Economic Growth: Rate, Structure and Spread*. Yale University Press, New Haven, Conn.

LASSWELL, H. D. 1958: *Politics: Who Gets What, When, How*. World Publishing Co., Cleveland, Ohio.

LASSWELL, H. D. and KAPLAN, A. 1950: *Power and Society: A Framework for Political Inquiry*. Yale University Press, New Haven, Conn.

LASUÉN, J. R. 1971: Multi-Regional Economic Development: An Open System Approach. T. Hägerstrand and A. Kuklinski, editors, *Information Systems for Regional Development*, Lund Studies in Geography, Series B, **37**, 169–211.

LAWRENCE, R. J. 1972: Social Welfare and Urban Growth. R. S. Parker and P. N. Troy, editors, *The Politics of Urban Growth*. Australian National University Press, Canberra, 110–28.

LEA, A. C. 1973: *Location–Allocation Systems: An Annotated Bibliography*. Discussion Paper 13. Dept. of Geography, University of Toronto.

LEE, C. 1973: *Models in Planning*. Pergamon Press, Oxford.

LEE, R. 1976: Public Finance and Urban Economy: Some Comments on Spatial Reformism. *Antipode* **8** (1), 44–50.

LEGASSICK, M. 1974: South Africa: Capital Accumulation and Violence. *Economy and Society* **3**, 253–91.

LENSKI, G. 1966: *Power and Privilege: A Theory of Stratification*. McGraw-Hill, New York.

LEVY, F. S., MELTSNER, A. J. and WILDAVSKY, A. 1974: *Urban Outcomes: Schools, Streets, and Libraries.* University of California Press, Berkeley.

LEWIS, G. M. 1968: Levels of Living in the Northeastern United States c. 1960: A New Approach to Regional Geography. *Transactions, IBG* **45**, 11–37.

LEY, D. 1974: The City and Good and Evil: Reflections on Christian and Marxist Interpretations. *Antipode* **6** (1), 66–74.

LICHFIELD, N. 1970: Evaluation Methodology of Urban and Regional Plans: A Review. *Regional Studies* **4**, 151–65.

1971: Cost–Benefit Analysis in Planning: A Critique of the Roskill Commission. *Regional Studies* **5**, 157–83.

LINEBERRY, R. L. 1974: Mandating Urban Equality: The Distribution of Municipal Public Services. *Texas Law Review* **53**, 26–59.

LINEBERRY, R. L. and WELCH, R. E. 1974: Who Gets What: Measuring the Distribution of Urban Public Services. *Social Science Quarterly* **54**, 700–12.

LITTLE, A. and MABEY, C. 1972: An Index for Designation of Educational Priority Areas. A. Shonfield and S. Shaw, editors, *Social Indicators and Social Policy*, Heinemann, London, 67–93.

LIU, B-C. 1973: *The Quality of Life in the United States 1970: Index, Rating and Statistics.* Midwest Research Institute, Kansas City, Mo.

LLOYD, P. E. and DICKEN, P. 1972: *Location in Space: A Theoretical Approach to Economic Geography.* Harper & Row, New York.

LÖSCH, A. 1954: *The Economics of Location.* Yale University Press, New Haven, Conn.

MAASDORP, G. G. 1974: *Economic Development Strategy in the African Homelands.* SAIRR, Johannesburg.

1976: The Development of the African Homelands, with Special Reference to KwaZulu. D. M. Smith, editor, *Separation in South Africa: People and Policies.* Occasional Paper No. 7, Dept. of Geography, Queen Mary College, London.

MacBEATH, A. 1955: The Need for a Social Philosophy. *Philosophy* **30**, 99–111. Reprinted in W. D. Birrel *et al.*, editors, *Social Administration.* Penguin, Harmondsworth, 1973, 283–95.

McCARTY, H. H., HOOK, J. C. and KNOS, D. S. 1956: *The Measurement of Association in Industrial Geography.* Dept. of Geography, University of Iowa, Iowa City.

McDERMOTT, P. J. 1973: Spatial Margins and Industrial Location in New Zealand. *New Zealand Geographer* **29**, 64–74.

McGEE, T. C. 1971. *The Urbanization Process in the Third World.* G. Bell & Sons, London.

McGLASHAN, N. D., editor, 1972: *Medical Geography.* Methuen, London.

McGRANAHAN, D. V. *et al.* 1970: *Content and Measurement of Socio-Economic Development: An Empirical Enquiry.* UN Research Institute for Social Development, Geneva.

MACK, R. W. 1970: Is the White Southerner Ready for Equality? R. W. Mack, editor, *The Changing South*, Aldine, Chicago, 9–20.

McLOUGHLIN, J. B. 1969: *Urban and Regional Planning: A Systems Approach.* Faber & Faber, London.

MANDEL, E. 1962: *Marxist Economic Theory.* Merlin Press, London.

1973: *An Introduction to Marxist Economic Theory.* 2nd edn, Pathfinder Press, New York.

MANSFIELD, N. W. 1971: The Estimation of Benefits from Recreation Sites and the Provision of a New Recreation Facility. *Regional Studies* **5**, 55–69.

MARGOLIS, J. 1968: The Demand for Urban Public Services. H. S. Perloff and L. Wingo, editors, *Issues in Urban Economics*, Johns Hopkins Press, Baltimore, 527–65.

MARX, K. 1859: A Contribution to the Critique of Political Economy. R. C. Tucker, editor, *The Marx–Engels Reader*, W. W. Norton, New York, 1972.

1867: *Capital*. Vol. 1, Lawrence & Wishart, London, 1974.

1875: Critique of the Gotha Program. R. C. Tucker, editor, *The Marx–Engels Reader*, W. W. Norton, New York, 1972.

MASLOW, A. H. 1954: *Motivation and Personality*. Harper, New York.

MASSAM, B. H. 1972: *The Spatial Structure of Administrative Systems*. Resource Paper 12, AAG, Washington, DC.

1974: Political Geography and the Provision of Public Services. C. Board *et al.*, editors, *Progress in Geography* **6**, 179–210.

1975: *Location and Space in Social Administration*. Edward Arnold, London.

MASSER, I. 1972: *Analytical Models for Urban and Regional Planning*. David & Charles, Newton Abbot.

MEADOWS, D. H., MEADOWS, D. L., RANDERS, J. and BEHRENS, W. W. 1972: *The Limits to Growth*. Potomac Associates, London.

MEDIO, A. 1972: Profits and Surplus-Value: Appearance and Reality in Capitalist Production. E. K. Hunt and J. G. Schwartz, editors, *A Critique of Economic Theory*, Penguin, Harmondsworth, 312–46.

MEER, F. 1976: The Group Areas Act and its Operation. *The Ghetto People*. Africa Publications Trust (in press).

MERRITT, R. L. and ROKKAN, S., editors, 1966: *Comparing Nations: The Use of Quantitative Data in Cross-National Research*. Yale University Press, New Haven, Conn.

MICHELSON, W. H. 1970: *Man and His Urban Environment: A Sociological Approach*. Addison-Wesley, Reading, Mass.

MISES, L. VON, 1935: Economic Calculation in the Socialist Commonwealth. A. Nove and D. M. Nuti, editors, *Socialist Economics*, Penguin, Harmondsworth, 1972, 75–91.

MISHAN, E. J. 1964: *Welfare Economics: Five Introductory Essays*. Random House, New York.

1967: *The Costs of Economic Growth*. Staples Press; Penguin, Harmondsworth, 1969.

1969: *Welfare Economics: An Assessment*. North Holland Publishing Co., Amsterdam.

1972: *Cost–Benefit Analysis*. George Allen & Unwin, London.

MISHRA, R. 1975: Marx and Welfare. *The Sociological Review* **23**, 287–313.

MOORE, E. G. and BROWN, L. A. 1970: Urban Acquaintance Fields: An Evaluation of a Spatial Model. *Environment and Planning* **2**, 443–54.

MORRILL, R. L. 1967: The Movement of Persons and the Transportation Problem. W. L. Garrison and D. F. Marble, editors, *Quantitative Geography. Part I: Economic and Cultural Topics*. Studies in Geography, 13, Dept. of Geography, Northwestern University, Evanston, Ill.

1970: *The Spatial Organization of Society*. Wadsworth, Belmont, Calif.

1974: Efficiency and Equity of Optimum Location Models. *Antipode* **6** (1), 41–6.

MORRILL, R. L., EARICKSON, R. J. and REES, P. 1970: Factors Influencing Distances Travelled to Hospitals. *Economic Geography* **46**, 161–71.

MORRILL, R. L. and WOHLENBERG, E. H. 1971: *The Geography of Poverty in the United States*. McGraw-Hill, New York.

MOSES, L. N. 1968: The General Equilibrium Approach. D. L. Sills, editor, *International Encyclopedia of the Social Sciences*, 15, Crowell Collier, New York, 100–108.

MUMPHREY, A. and WOLPERT, J. 1973: Equity Considerations and Concessions in the Siting of Public Facilities. *Economic Geography* **49**, 109–21.

MUSGRAVE, R. A. 1959: *The Theory of Public Finance.* McGraw-Hill, New York.
  1968: Discussion of Part III. H. S. Perloff and L. Wingo, editors, *Issues in Urban Economics.* Johns Hopkins Press, Baltimore, 567–74.
MYINT, H. 1948: *Theories of Welfare Economics.* Augustus Kelley, New York (1962 Reprint).
  1963: *The Economics of the Developing Countries.* Hutchinson, London.
MYRDAL, G. M. 1957: *Economic Theory and Underdevelopment.* Duckworth, London.
MYRDAL, G. M. 1968: *The Asian Drama: An Enquiry into the Poverty of Nations.* Pantheon, New York.
NATH, S. K. 1969: *A Reappraisal of Welfare Economics.* Routledge & Kegan Paul, London.
  1973: *A Perspective of Welfare Economics.* Macmillan, London.
NEL, P. A. 1974: The Non-White Worker in South Africa. *South African Progress,* 164–7.
NETZER, D. 1968: Federal State and Local Finance in a Metropolitan Context. H. S. Perloff and L. Wingo, editors, *Issues in Urban Economics,* Johns Hopkins Press, Baltimore, 435–76.
  1970: Financing Urban Government. J. Q. Wilson, editor, *The Metropolitan Enigma,* Anchor Books, New York, 76–95.
NIDDRIE, D. L. 1968: *South Africa: Nation or Nations?* Van Nostrand, Princeton, NJ.
NORDHAUS, W. and TOBIN, J. 1972: Is Growth Obsolete? National Bureau of Economic Research, *Economic Growth,* Columbia University Press, New York.
NOURSE, H. O. 1968: *Regional Economics.* McGraw-Hill, New York.
NOVE, A. and NUTI, D. M. 1972: *Socialist Economics.* Penguin, Harmondsworth.
OECD, 1973: *List of Social Concerns Common to Most OECD Countries.* The OECD Social Indicator Development Programme, Manpower and Social Affairs Directorate, OECD, Paris.
ONTELL, R. 1973: *The Quality of Life in San Diego.* The Urban Observatory, San Diego, Calif.
PACKARD, V. 1972: *A Nation of Strangers.* David McKay, New York.
PAHL, R. E. 1970: *Patterns of Urban Life.* Longmans, London.
PARR, J. B. 1974: Welfare Differences within a Nation: A Comment. *Papers, RSA* **32,** 83–91.
PATEL, J. S. 1964: The Economic Distance between Nations: Its Origin, Measurement and Outlook. *Economic Journal* **74,** 119–31.
PATON, A. 1971: *Hofmeyr.* Oxford University Press, Cape Town (abridged version).
PATTANIAK, P. K. 1968: Risk, Impersonality and the Social Welfare Function. *Journal of Political Economy* **76,** 1152–69. Reprinted in E. S. Phelps, editor, *Economic Justice,* Penguin, Harmondsworth, 1973, 298–318.
PATTEN, J. W. 1963: Separate Development: A Look at the Facts. *Optima* **13,** 17–23.
PEARCE, D. W. 1971: *Cost–Benefit Analysis.* Macmillan, London.
PEET, R., editor, 1970: *Geography of American Poverty.* Special Issue of *Antipode* **2,** (2), Worcester, Mass.
  editor, 1972: *Geographical Perspectives on American Poverty.* Antipode Monographs in Social Geography, Worcester, Mass.
  1975: The Geography of Crime: A Political Critique. *Professional Geographer* **27,** 277–80.
PERLOFF, H. S. 1969: A Framework for Dealing with the Urban Environment: Introductory Statement. H. Perloff, editor, *The Quality of the Urban Environment.* Resources for the Future, Washington, DC, 3–25.

PERLOFF, H. S., DUNN, E. S., LAMPARD, E. E. and MUTH, R. F. 1960: *Regions, Resources and Economic Growth*. Johns Hopkins Press, Baltimore.

PHELPS, E. S. 1973: *Economic Justice*. Penguin, Harmondsworth.

PIGOU, A. C. 1920: *The Economics of Welfare*. 4th edn (1932), Macmillan, London.

PRED, A. R. 1969: *Behaviour and Location: Foundations for a Geographic and Dynamic Location Theory*. Part 2. Lund Studies in Geography, Series B—Human Geography, 28.

— 1971: Large-City Interdependence and the Preelectronic Diffusion of Innovations in the US. *Geographical Analysis* **3**, 165–81.

— 1975: On the Spatial Structure of Organizations and the Complexity of Metropolitan Interdependence. *Papers, RSA* **35**, 115–42.

PRESS, S. J. 1971: *Some Effects of an Increase in Police Manpower in the 20th Precinct of New York City*. Rand Institute, New York.

PREST, A. R. and TURVEY, R. 1965: Cost–Benefit Analysis: A Survey. *Economic Journal* **75**, 683–735.

PRINCE, H. 1971: Questions of Social Relevance. *Area* **3**, 150–3.

RADICE, H. 1975: *International Firms and Modern Imperialism*. Penguin, Harmondsworth.

RANDALL, P., editor, 1971a: *Education Beyond Apartheid*. Spro-cas, Johannesburg.

— 1971b: *Towards Social Change*. Spro-cas, Johannesburg.

— 1972a: *Power, Privilege and Poverty*. Spro-cas, Johannesburg.

— 1972b: *Law, Justice and Society*. Spro-cas, Johannesburg.

RAWLS, J. 1958: Justice as Fairness. *Philosophical Review* **67**, 164–94.

— 1962: Justice as Fairness. P. Laslett and W. G. Runciman, editors, *Philosophy, Politics and Society*. Second Series, Blackwell, Oxford.

— 1967: Distributive Justice. P. Laslett and W. G. Runciman, editors, *Philosophy, Politics and Society*, Third Series, Blackwell, Oxford, 58–82.

— 1971: *A Theory of Justice*. Harvard University Press, Cambridge, Mass.

RAWSTRON, E. M. 1958: Three Principles of Industrial Location. *Transactions, IBG* **25**, 132–42.

REIF, B. 1973: *Models in Urban and Regional Planning*. Leonard Hill, Aylesbury.

REINER, T. A. 1971: A Multiple Goals Framework for Regional Planning. *Papers, RSA* **26**, 207–39.

— 1974: Welfare Differences within a Nation. *Papers, RSA* **32**, 65–82.

REVELLE, C., MARKS, D. and LIEBMANN, J. C. 1970: An Analysis of Private and Public Sector Location Models. *Management Science* **16** (II), 692–707.

RHOODIE, N. 1972: *South African Dialogue*. McGraw-Hill, Johannesburg.

RICHARDSON, H. W. 1969a: *Regional Economics: Location Theory, Urban Structure and Regional Change*. Weidenfeld & Nicolson, London.

— 1969b: *Elements of Regional Economics*. Penguin, Harmondsworth.

— 1973: *The Economics of City Size*. Saxon House, Farnworth; Lexington Books, Lexington, Mass.

RIVLIN, A. M. 1971: *Systematic Thinking for Social Action*. The Brookings Institution, Washington, DC.

ROBINSON, E. A. G., editor, 1970: *The Gap Between the Rich and the Poor Countries*. Macmillan, London.

ROBINSON, J. 1972: Consumer's Sovereignty in a Planned Economy. A. Nove and D. M. Nuti, editors, *Socialist Economics*, Penguin, Harmondsworth, 263–74.

ROBINSON, J. P. and CONVERSE, P. E. 1972: Social Change Reflected in the Use of Time. A. Campbell and P. E. Converse, editors, *The Human Meaning of Social Change*, Russell Sage Foundation, New York, 17–86.

ROMANYSHYN, J. M. 1971: *Social Welfare: Charity to Justice*. Random House, New York.

ROSE, H. M. 1971: *The Black Ghetto: A Spatial Behavioural Perspective*. McGraw-Hill, New York.

ROTHENBURG, J. 1961: *The Measurement of Social Welfare*. Prentice-Hall, Englewood Cliffs, NJ.

RUMMEL, R. J. 1969: Indicators of Cross-National and International Patterns. *The American Political Science Review* **63**, 127–47.

1972: US Foreign Relations: Conflict, Cooperation and Attribute Distances. B. M. Russett, editor, *Peace, War, and Numbers*. Sage Publications, Beverly Hills and London, 71–113.

RUNCIMAN, W. G. 1966: *Relative Deprivation and Social Justice*. Routledge & Kegan Paul, London; Penguin, Harmondsworth, 1972.

RUSHTON, G., GOODCHILD, M. and OSTRESH, S. 1973: *Computer Programs for Location–Allocation Problems*. Monograph 6, Dept. of Geography, University of Iowa.

RUSSETT, B. M., DEUTSCH, K. W., ALKER, H. R. and LASSWELL, H. D. 1964: *World Handbook of Political and Social Indicators*. Yale University Press, New Haven, Conn.

SALIH, K. 1972: *Judicial Relief and Differential Provision of Public Goods: A Case Analysis and Certain Prescriptions*. Discussion Paper 20, Research on Conflict in Location Decisions, Regional Science Department, University of Pennsylvania.

SAMUELSON, P. A. 1973: *Economics*. 9th edn, McGraw-Hill, New York.

SCHLEMMER, L. 1972: *Social Change and Political Policy in South Africa*. SAIRR, Johannesburg.

SCHMIDT, C. F. 1975: A Spatial Model of Authority–Dependency Relations in South Africa. *Journal of Modern African Studies* **13** (3), 483–90.

SCHNEIDER, J. B. 1967: Measuring the Locational Efficiency of the Urban Hospital. *Health Services Research* **2**, 154–69.

SCHNEIDER, J. B. and SYMONS, J. G. 1971: *Regional Health Facility System Planning: An Access Opportunity Approach*. Discussion Paper No. 48, Regional Science Research Institute, Philadelphia.

SCITOVSKY, T. 1964: *Papers on Welfare and Growth*. Stanford University Press, Stanford, Calif.

1971: *Welfare and Competition*. Revised edition. Allen & Unwin, London.

SCOTT, A. 1970: Location–Allocation Systems: A Review. *Geographical Analysis* **2**, 95–119.

SCOTT, W. 1973: *The Measurement of Real Progress at the Local Level*. UN Research Institute for Social Development, Geneva.

SEERS, D. 1972: What are we Trying to Measure? N. Baster, editor, *Measuring Development*, Cass, London, 21–36.

SEMPLE, R. K. and GAUTHIER, H. L. 1972: Spatial–Temporal Trends in Income Inequalities in Brazil. *Geographical Analysis* **4**, 169–79.

SEN, A. K. 1970: *Collective Choice and Social Welfare*. Oliver & Boyd, Edinburgh and London.

1973: *On Economic Inequality*. Clarendon Press, Oxford.

SHANNON, G. W., BASHSHUR, R. L. and METZNER, C. A. 1969: The Concept of Distance as a Factor in Accessibility and Utilization of Health Care. *Medical Care Review* **26**, 143–61.

SHANNON, G. W. and DEVER, G. E. A. 1974: *The Geography of Health Care*. McGraw-Hill, New York.

SHANNON, G. W., SPURLOCK, C. W. and SKINNER, J. L. 1975: A Method for Evaluating the Geographic Accessibility of Health Services. *Professional Geographer* **27**, 30–36.

SHAW, C. R. and MCKAY, H. D. 1942: *Juvenile Delinquency and Urban Areas*. University of Chicago Press, Chicago.

SHERMAN, H. J. 1972: Value and Market Allocation. E. K. Hunt and J. Schwartz, editors, *A Critique of Economic Theory*, Penguin, Harmondsworth, 347–64.

SHOUP, C. S. 1964: Standards for Distributing a Free Governmental Service: Crime Prevention. *Public Finance* 19, 383–92.

SIMMIE, J. M. 1974: *Citizens in Conflict: The Sociology of Town Planning*. Hutchinson, London.

SIMONS, H. J. and SIMONS, R. E. 1969: *Class and Colour in South Africa—1850–1950*. Penguin, Harmondsworth.

SLATER, D. 1973: Geography and Underdevelopment. *Antipode* 5 (3), 21–32.

   1975: Underdevelopment and Spatial Inequality: Approaches to the Problems of Regional Planning in the Third World. *Progress in Planning* 4, Part 2, 97–167.

SMITH, D. M. 1966: A Theoretical Framework for Geographical Studies of Industrial Location. *Economic Geography* 42, 95–113.

   1971a: *Industrial Location: An Economic Geographical Analysis*. John Wiley, New York.

   1971b: Radical Geography: The Next Revolution? *Area* 3, 153–7.

   1972a: Towards a Geography of Social Well-being: Interstate Variations in the United States. R. Peet, editor, *Geographical Perspectives on American Poverty*, *Antipode* Monographs in Social Geography, 1, Worcester, Mass., 17–46.

   1972b: Geography and Social Indicators. *South African Geographical Journal* 54, 43–57.

   1973a: *The Geography of Social Well-being in the United States*. McGraw-Hill, New York.

   1973b: Alternative "Relevant" Professional Roles. *Area* 5, 1–4.

   1973c: *An Introduction to Welfare Geography*. Occasional Paper 11, Dept. of Geography and Environmental Studies, University of the Witwatersrand.

   1974a: Vers une Géographie du bien-être social: la différenciation des Etats aux Etats-Unis. R. A. Roberge, editor, *La Crise Urbaine: A Challenge to Geographers*, University Press, Ottawa, 120–53.

   1974b: Race-Space Inequality in South Africa: A Study in Welfare Geography. *Antipode* 6 (2), 42–69.

   1974c: *Crime Rates as Territorial Social Indicators*. Occasional Paper No. 1, Dept. of Geography, Queen Mary College, London.

   1974d: Who Gets What *Where* and How: A Welfare Focus for Human Geography. *Geography* 59, 289–97.

   1975a: On the concept of Welfare. *Area* 7 (1), 33–6.

   1975b: Mapping Human Well-being. *International Social Sciences Journal* 27, 364–71.

   1975c: *Patterns in Human Geography: An Introduction to Numerical Methods*. David & Charles, Newton Abbot; Penguin, Harmondsworth, 1976.

   editor, 1976a: *Separation in South Africa: People and Policies*. Occasional Paper No. 6, Dept. of Geography, Queen Mary College, London.

   1976b: *Separation in South Africa: Homelands and Cities*. Occasional Paper No. 7, Dept. of Geography, Queen Mary College, London.

   1977. *Where the Grass is Greener: Geographical Perspectives on Inequality*. Penguin, Harmondsworth.

SMITH, D. M. and GRAY, R. J. 1972: *Social Indicators for Tampa, Florida*. Urban Studies Bureau, University of Florida, Gainesville (mimeo).

SMITH, R. H. T., TAAFFE, E. J. and KING, L. J., editors, 1968: *Readings in Economic Geography: The Location of Economic Activity*. Rand McNally, Chicago.

SOJA, E. W. 1968: *The Geography of Modernization in Kenya*. Syracuse University Press, Syracuse, NY.

SPINDLER, A. 1968: Systems Analysis in Public Welfare. *Public Welfare* **28**, 227–30.

STAGNER, R. 1970: Perceptions, Aspirations, Frustrations and Satisfactions: An Approach to Urban Indicators. *Annals of the American Academy of Political and Social Science* **388**, 59–68.

STAMP, L. D. 1964: *The Geography of Life and Death*. Collins, London.

STEVENSON, G. M. 1972: Noise and the Urban Environment. T. R. Detwyler and M. G. Marcus, editors, *Urbanization and Environment: The Physical Geography of the City*, Duxbury Press, Belmont, Calif., 195–228.

STIGLER, G. J. 1966: *The Theory of Prices*. Macmillan, New York.

STÖHR, W. B. 1974: *Interurban Systems and Regional Economic Development*. Commission on College Geography, Resource Paper 26, AAG, Washington, DC.

SYMONS, J. G. 1971: Some Comments on Equity and Efficiency in Public Facility Location Models. *Antipode* **3** (1), 54–67.

TAAFFE, E. J., MORRILL, R. L. and GOULD, P. R. 1963: Transport Expansion in Underdeveloped Countries: A Comparative Analysis. *Geographical Review* **53**, 502–29.

TAYLOR, C. L., editor, 1968: *Aggregate Data Analysis: Political and Social Indicators in Cross-National Research*. Mouton, The Hague.

TAYLOR, C. L. and HUDSON, M. C. 1972: *World Handbook of Political and Social Indicators*. 2nd edn, Yale University Press, New Haven and London.

TAYLOR, J. 1976: *Problems of Minimum Cost Location: the Kuhn and Kuenne Algorithm*. Occasional Paper No. 4, Dept. of Geography, Queen Mary College, London.

TEITZ, M. 1968: Towards a Theory of Urban Public Facility Location. *Papers, RSA* **21**, 35–51.

TERLECKYJ, N. E. 1970: Measuring Progress Towards Social Goals: Some Possibilities at National and Local Levels. *Management Science* **16**, B-765–778.

—— 1975: *Improvements in the Quality of Life: Estimates of Possibilities in the United States*. National Planning Association, Washington, DC.

THEAKSTONE, W. H. and HARRISON, C. 1970: *The Analysis of Geographical Data*. Heinemann, London.

THOMPSON, J. H., SUFRIN, S. C., GOULD, P. R. and BUCK, M. A. 1962: Towards a Geography of Economic Health: The Case of New York State. *Annals, AAG* **52**, 1–20.

THOMPSON, W. R. 1965. *A Preface to Urban Economics*. The Johns Hopkins Press, Baltimore.

TIDSWELL, W. V. and BARKER, S. M. 1971: *Quantitative Methods: An Approach to Socio-Economic Geography*. University Tutorial Press, London.

TIEBOUT, C. M. 1956: A Pure Theory of Local Expenditures. *Journal of Political Economy* **64**, 416–24.

TINBERGEN, J. 1967: *Development Planning*. Weidenfeld & Nicolson, London.

TOMEH, A. K. 1964: Informal Group Participation and Residential Patterns. *American Journal of Sociology* **70**, 28–35.

TREWARTHA, G. 1973: Comments on Gilbert White's article "Geography and Public Policy". *Professional Geographer* **25**, 78–9.

TUCKER, R. C., editor, 1972: *The Marx–Engels Reader*. Norton, New York.

TURNER, R. 1972: *The Eye of the Needle: An Essay on Participatory Democracy*. Spro-cas, Johannesburg.

ULLMAN, E. L. 1961: Geographic Theory and Underdeveloped Areas. N. Ginsburg, editor, *Essays on Geography and Economic Development*, Chicago University Press, Chicago, 26–32.

UNITED NATIONS, 1961: *Report on the World Social Situation*. UNO, New York.

UNITED NATIONS RESEARCH INSTITUTE FOR SOCIAL DEVELOPMENT, 1969: *Compilation of Development Indicators (for 1960)*. Statistical Unit, UNRISD, Geneva.

US DEPARTMENT OF COMMERCE, Bureau of the Census, 1967: *Poverty Areas in the 100 Largest Metropolitan Areas*. Supplementary Report PC (51)–54. *US Census of Population*, USGPO, Washington, DC.

US DEPARTMENT OF HEALTH, EDUCATION AND WELFARE, 1969: *Toward a Social Report*. USGPO, Washington, DC; University of Michigan Press, Ann Arbor, 1970.

US DEPARTMENT OF HOUSING AND URBAN DEVELOPMENT, 1973: *The Model Cities Program*. Office of Community Development, Evaluation Division, USGPO, Washington, DC.

US OFFICE OF EDUCATION, 1969: *Toward Master Social Indicators*. Educational Policy Research Center, Research Memorandum 6742–2, US Dept. of HEW, Washington, DC (mimeo from Leasco Information Products Inc.).

VISE, P. DE, 1973: *Misused and Misplaced Hospitals and Doctors: A Location Analysis of the Urban Health Care Crisis*. Commission on College Geography, Resource Paper 22, AAG, Washington, DC.

WALMSLEY, D. J. 1973: The Simple Behavioural System: An Appraisal and Elaboration. *Geografiska Annaler* **55b**, 49–56.

WATTS, H. L. 1971: Poverty. P. Randall, editor, *Some Implications of Inequality*, Spro-cas, Johannesburg, 40–57.

WEBER, A. 1929: *Alfred Weber's Theory: the Location of Industries*. Translated by C. J. Friedrich, Chicago University Press, Chicago.

WEBER, M. 1946: Class, Status and Party. W. D. Hawley and F. M. Wirt, editors, *The Search for Community Power*. Prentice-Hall, Englewood Cliffs, NJ, 1968, 5–20; reprinted from H. H. Gerth and C. Wright Mills, editors, *Max Weber: Essays in Sociology*. Oxford University Press, Oxford.

WESTAWAY, J. 1947a: Contact Potential and the Occupational Structure of the British Urban System 1961–1966: An Empirical Study. *Regional Studies* **8**, 57–73.

— 1974b: The Spatial Hierarchy of Business Organizations and its Implications for the British Urban System. *Regional Studies* **8**, 145–55.

WHITE, G. 1972: Geography and Public Policy. *Professional Geographer* **24**, 101–4.

WILCOX, C. 1969: *Toward Social Welfare*. Richard D. Irwin, Homewood, Ill.

WILCOX, L. D., BROOKS, R. M., BEAL, G. M. and KLONGLAN, G. E. 1972: *Social Indicators and Societal Monitoring: An Annotated Bibliography*. Elsevier, Amsterdam.

WILLIAMS, A. 1966: The Optimal Provision of Public Goods in a System of Local Government. *Journal of Political Economy* **74**, 18–33.

WILLIAMS, M. 1975: An Analysis of South African Capitalism—Neo-Ricardianism or Marxism? *Bulletin of the Conference of Socialist Economists* **4** (1), 1–38.

WILLIAMSON, J. G. 1965: Regional Inequality and the Process of National Development: A Description of the Patterns. *Economic Development and Cultural Change* **13**, 3–45; reprinted in L. Needleman, editor, *Regional Analysis*, Penguin, Harmondsworth.

WILSON, A. G. 1974: *Urban and Regional Models in Geography and Planning*. John Wiley, London.

WILSON, A. G. and KIRWAN, R. 1969: *Measures of Benefits in the Evaluation of Urban Transport Improvements*. Working Paper 43, Centre for Environmental Studies, London.

WILSON, D. 1970: *Asia Awakes: A Continent in Transition*. Weidenfeld & Nicolson, London.

WILSON, J. O. 1969: *Quality of Life in the United States: An Excursion into the New Frontier of Socio-Economic Indicators*. Midwest Research Institute, Kansas City, Mo.

WILSON, T. 1972: *Migrant Labour in South Africa*. South African Council of Churches and Spro-cas, Johannesburg.

WINCH, D. M. 1971: *Analytical Welfare Economics*. Penguin, Harmondsworth.

WOLPE, H. 1972: Capitalism and Cheap Labour-power in South Africa: from Segregation to Apartheid. *Economy and Society* 1, 425–56.

1974: The Theory of Internal Colonialism—the South African Case. *Bulletin of the Conference of Socialist Economists* 9, Autumn, 1–12.

WOLPERT, J. 1965: Behavioural Aspects of the Decision to Migrate. *Papers, RSA* 15, 159–69.

WOOD, C. M., LEE, N., LUKER, J. A. and SAUNDERS, P. J. W. 1974: *The Geography of Pollution: A Study of Greater Manchester*. Manchester University Press, Manchester.

YATES, M. H. 1963: Hinterland Delimitation: A Distance Minimizing Approach. *Professional Geographer* 15, 7–10.

1968: *An Introduction to Quantitative Analysis in Economic Geography*. McGraw-Hill, New York.

1974: *An Introduction to Quantitative Analysis in Human Geography*. McGraw-Hill, New York.

Index